Invisible Wounds

Invisible Wounds

THE MEMOIRS OF A BROKEN MAN

Anonymous

Front Cover Design by Miray Scheidel

Anonymous

CONTENTS

Disclaimer	2
The Fair Warning	3
Chapter 7	5
Chapter 8	32
Chapter 9	52
Chapter 10	84
Chapter 11	96
Chapter 12	141
Chapter 13	207
Chapter 14	236
Chapter 15	313
Chapter 16	357
Chapter 17	386
The Farewell	409
Poetry & Thoughts	413
Discussion Board	463

Copyright © 2021 by Anonymous

All rights reserved. No part of this book may be reproduced in any manner whatsoever without written permission except in the case of brief quotations embodied in critical articles and reviews.

Explicit content, not suitable for audience under the age of 18.

Print Book ISBN 978-0-578-89363-1

E-Book ISBN 978-0-578-89364-8

Front Cover Design by Miray Scheidel

Printed by, Ingram Spark

First Printing, 2021

Dedication

Dedication

This book is dedicated to you the reader, whether you are lost and trying to find yourself, whether you are hurt and trying to heal, whether you are married going through a divorce, whether you are in love and going through a heartache, whether you are happy and flourishing, whether you are established and successful, this story is for all of you, and for everyone I have not named, because we all have a past, because we have all experienced pain we are still trying to heal from and this story is here to help everyone. We have been purely focused on providing for us and our families, that we have forgotten about an entire world out there that also needs pieces of our intelligence, experience, and love. We will all learn to heal together.

It Is Always Love

Disclaimer

Disclaimer

I have recreated events, locales and conversations from my memories and journal entries of them. In order to maintain their anonymity and privacy, I have changed the names of individuals and places, I have also changed identifying characteristics and details such as physical properties, occupations, and places of residence.

Thank You for being You

The Fair Warning

The Fair Warning

At this point I would like issue a warning to anyone that is about to read this story. This story is not written in a formal manner, the language is explicit, I can honestly care less about being politically correct, or hurting anyone's feelings. With that being said if you are an individual who is easily offended, or always has a negative opinion about everything this is not for you. Also there are situations in this story that may very well trigger peoples past trauma so I urge you to be careful while reading this story and when you feel any past thoughts or emotions coming to light please place the book down and take a breather, it is a difficult story to read and if you choose to not continue reading then, there are no hard feelings and I understand and I wish you well.

This story will cover pretty much every perspective about life as a whole. Many people will be able to relate, and others will not. It is what it is, as long as you understand the meaning and the point of this story, we all will be able to grow and become better individuals. Everything is explained as straight forward and frank as possible. If you try to interpret anything from this story, then I don't know what to tell you, unless you are confused about a situation then ask. I do not beat around the bush and I tell you exactly how it is, so for you to choose to interpret something that is already explained yes by all means you're an idiot.

Before we begin, I would like to articulate something to you my fellow readers. I do not want anyone jumping to conclusions or making accusations or whatever craziness your mind tells you to do, keep that shit to yourself.

This is not a war story, and this is not a story of love, well somewhat love but that is not what this is about. I am writing this because I honestly have no one to talk to and vent to. I have this horrible void and emptiness that fucking encompasses every part of my soul on a daily basis and I just don't have anyone I can be open with, and honestly if I did, I wouldn't allow for them to carry this weight for me. So there are many things I just need to get off my chest whether it helps fill this void or not, I will not honestly be able to say but, all I can say is that it needs to be heard and by everyone if possible.

So for those that stick through, all I ask is that you read this tale throughout its entirety and I promise you all your questions will be answered, and if by some chance they are not, I will be happy to answer them via e-mail.

So, I guess we will begin.

Chapter 7

Seventh Grade, The Change

I will begin this with a commiseration due to the fact that in the 6th grade there was a tragic event we all know as 9/11. May everyone's soul rest easy.

So, the big day finally comes. The first day at St. Vincenzo's School, I thought I wasn't going to know anyone, but to my surprise a fellow student from Valentine Crescent also transferred to St. Vincenzo. His name is Eduardo and to be fair we got along, was he annoying at times yes, but I knew his family and we were cool didn't really bump heads often. The school had this weird way of setting up and dividing classes. It was weird honestly, I guess because I wasn't used to it, but I wasn't stuck with Eduardo lol we had different homerooms and a few classes together, so it wasn't that bad honestly.

Always good to see a familiar face every now and then. Once the principle was done talking all the classes start heading to their homerooms. At this point I am already trying to analyze who is who in the school and the class. Of course, we have the obvious tough guy, the jokester, the one that gets all the girls, the one that knows all the gossip, and who is labeled the best-looking girl in the school you know that's important lol. It is not to judge people, but school is school, and these people are roaming so it is always best to identify them early. Eventually after hallway traffic, we finally get to class annnddddd, I get stuck with the tough guy and asshole but of course who would have thought. Any way that's just my luck, this just means I have to prove myself so people don't get this viewpoint that they can just walk over me, and things will be ok. At this point in my life I am a very outspoken and outgoing guy I get along with everyone. I begin talking to the people in the class and meet Dennis, Dennis, Dennis, lol yes it was for some reason a very common name in that school, Fabien, Justin, Amber, Josephine, Lucy, and Valerie. As the day progressed, I met more people which were Marcel, a few other people I forgot their names I can't lie to you and Roland. Roland furthermore becomes a very close friend of mine but that is a bit later, but a great dude just wanted to mention. These kid's mentalities are well above and beyond mine. It turned into a mystery I had to solve. It gravitated me to them, like what happened by the age of 13 that you have such a high level of perspective about life, but that's not for me to say everyone has their story and I wish I could tell you all of theirs but it wouldn't be fair to them. Their story is theirs to tell if they choose to but just great people all in all. Back to the story.

Clearly as the new guy I am awaiting my initiation into their school. A few days go by and it is initiation day lol. It was nothing serious just Fabien and Little Dennis wrote a 16-bar freestyle for me. It was pretty funny I can't even lie. Honestly, I don't remember much of it except the end when they spit the last bar which went "go back to Valentine Crescent and take a seatin." The actual school name rhymed with seatin so it was pretty funny but, the whole class just broke out in laughter, it was pretty funny I am telling you, you had to be there they had this whole presentation and called me out in front of the entire class. They waited for the teacher to step out for a moment and they looked at each other and looked at me, stood up and Fabien took this paper out of his pocket flipped it open and just started rapping it was hilarious.

The class was as follows, I had class with Fabien, Roland, Natalia, Dennis, Little Dennis, Lucy, Justin, and a couple with Eduardo. A few other classes I had with were Josephine, Valerie, Dennis and others I honestly do not remember. Josephine was mad cool and cute but, Justin had a huge crush on her it was pretty obvious. Every day he would try and ask her out and every day it wouldn't work lol. It was great seeing him try though I couldn't blame him for trying though. I want to talk about Valerie even though I really shouldn't, I mean at first she was cool and quiet, but I felt bad for her because well most teachers already had a negative view point of me because I hung out with the fuck ups of the school or the class clowns or whatever you would like to call them. Some of the fuck ups I hung around used to tease her and at the time I didn't know they did, you know I just met everyone and one day they had called her Anne Frank, so at the time I could see how they would say that she had some facial similarities, and I laughed and felt so bad afterward like they were just teasing it was harmless but you would see it in her face she felt hurt about it but these kids were harmless, but the way I understand people is not the way everyone understands people especially someone who was clowned and considered anti-social so I did really feel bad but, that day when she caught me laughing at their joke was the day she labeled me. From there on I had absolutely no chance at getting to know her or understanding her mentality, so I honestly just stayed away from her. She was cute I tell ya she just didn't talk much and that's what intrigues me about people a lot is why don't they talk why are they to themselves when there's just so much to learn from people.

Dennis he was a very intelligent kid, very book smart real cool kid. He was funny too and the initials of his full name spelled out DAD lol I told him that wasn't a coincidence his parents planned that lol. He was a good kid great sense of humor, and made me some mixtapes I still have to this day lol I would ask him "yo Dennis make me a Tupac mix cd" he would be like sure no problem Mikey I'll bring it in tomorrow. He was so down to Earth nothing ever bothered him or annoyed him. The other Dennis was a quiet cool kid. His parents owned a restaurant across the street from the school. I don't ever recall eating there but people spoke very highly of the restaurant. Little Dennis was Fabien's apprentice. They were the best of friends it was great to have them both in class lol. Class was always stopped due to their shenanigans lol. Every time Fabien would get in trouble in class and try to explain himself to the teacher, he digs himself in to a worse situation. Little Dennis starts calling him and laughing like yelling at him telling him to shut up before he gets sent to Sister Rose's office. It would be vice versa as well when Dennis would get in trouble. I loved being in class with them, class wasn't just exciting or entertaining but simply being around a great group of individuals felt like home it felt like Valentine Crescent.

Interestingly enough Fabien and Natalia were extremely close friends, sort of like me and Lydia. Every time someone would say something like a joke or similar to Fabien, Natalia would step in and defend him or quickly make jokes back at the other person for trying to make fun of Fabien and Fabien would do the same instantaneously. But, (yes, I am starting a sentence with but so calm down) there was a little something there between them. I'm not talking tension, well yea there was but that's beside the point, there were feelings in that little friendship of theirs. I kind of felt like I was the only one who noticed too. I asked Roland about it he said they never went out but that doesn't mean they never creeped. Anyway I asked Fabien about it and he said "I don't like her like that we just friends," and I said "yeah ok you two are going to end up together sooner or later" lol, and he just laughed and told me to shut up and we went on our way to the next class.

So, Roland, Roland, Roland that is my main man lol. Everyone called him Taz, why well till this day I still don't know lol. He was the "player" this man knew everyone and their families from Bayer County to Concord to Long Island I mean everything, and everyone in between knew him. Honestly just a great genuine dude man, can't speak highly of him enough in this book, just likes to laugh, get girls, achieve his goals, and see everyone happy, when I say that I don't mean just the immediate people around him happy I mean just everyone in general. He was like the brother I never had. He was always talking to me about girls and not to smoke weed and to be mindful of people who just want to use you so they can benefit from you. I always listened to him due to the fact that not only that he sounds like he knows what he is talking about, but he has been through a lot so his viewpoint of life and people has a lot of weight. He wasn't just some 13-14-year-old kid going to school studying and taking exams, well actually none of these kids from St Vincenzo were like that at all, they just lived in the streets honestly. They had a wealth of life experience before they even hit high school. Yes, for those of you who are reading and are thinking well you were in 7th grade what could you have possibly gone through, well life that's what you ignorant fuck. As much as I would like to tell you their stories I simply can't because it's not mine to tell.

He was pretty much my best friend in St Vincenzo. He was always telling me who he slept with, his experiences getting drunk and high, pretty much everything. Let me tell you that he has some funny stories lol. So, if my memory serves me correctly it was October and Fabien's birthday was coming up. Roland told me I should go to his birthday party. I said me and Fabien are cool and all but, I doubt he would even invite me because I have only known him barely a month and I became close friends with Roland more so than anyone else. He told me not to worry Fabien is cool as hell he will invite me. Sure, enough so he did and Fabien told me "to make sure I made it because there was going to be mad girls and liquor there," so I was like "word

I'm in," he said "alright see you there." But there was one thing I overlooked lol, good ol momma dukes lmfao. Man listen lol you already know the answer lol. She doesn't know these kids from a dime in a dozen, well I honestly don't even know what that phrase means but it felt like it fit good there, so we are sticking with it lol. Anyway, she clearly said no. Now how do I go back and tell this man I can't go, see these kids didn't have curfew, and they all live in broken homes and they are the men of the house. I don't recall what I told them lol I think it was something along the lines of I was hanging out with friends from my old school and got caught coming home at like 1 in morning and got grounded. I apologized and said I will definitely make it next time, he said cool no worries man, but you missed a hell of a party lol. Man, everyone came up to me and told me how crazy the party was and in my head I'm like damn ma why just whyyyyy. Roland comes and makes it worse lol he said "yo you missed it, there were hella girls there man I racked up all them digits lol."

So, from being around Fabien and Roland so much I ended up meeting the 8th graders. Whom were clearly the popular ones, but it was Alexander, Jaxson, and Jayla. Let us take a pause rite now so I can clearly state that Jayla was by far thee best looking girl not only in that school but probably in that area as a whole.

Anyways moving on lol, Alexander was a big dude not like fat, but he had weight on him, and he was funny well all in all that whole school had a lot of comedians in it; never a dull day at that school. Jaxson was pretty much the school athlete; he would leave basketball practice early to go play baseball for the city kid was talented. They were all good kids honestly. They all just wanted to laugh and have fun and have a good time.

There were no problems in the school or anyone. Except for this one minor incident. It stemmed from nothing honestly. So, one day after going back to homeroom from one of our classes, our teacher says she has to step out for a meeting and no other teacher can cover her because they are all teaching their said classes. So, she says be good and don't cause no trouble lol. We have Dennis, Fabien, and Justin in the class why she would say such a thing is unknown lmfao. So, everyone begins chit chatting talking laughing. I reach for a pen under my desk because I usually bring packs, so it seems to be that all my pens are gone again. I think to myself "dam I lost all those pens again that's crazy I don't know how I keep losing them." Boy was I wrong lol. I then turn around to Justin he is drawing or writing or something (his seat is behind mine in our homeroom), and this kid is using my pen like what thee fuck. So, I ask him straight forward "Justin is that my pen?" He replies, "yea so what" I said, "wait so you been the one robbing my pens?" He said, "yea you aint going to do nothing about it anyway?" I said "yo you owe me like 2 packs of pens" he replied, "I don't owe you shit." Whoa, whoa, whoa lol hold up now, at this point the class got quiet and Dennis and Fabien of course instigating. So, Fabien got this all played out in his head already, so he starts walking towards the front of the class lol. I told Justin "shut up you robbed my pens now you have to buy me the two packs back you robbed and how the fuck you use two packs of pens in like 2 weeks" he stood up and said "I aint buying you shit, you aint going to do nothing about it anyway." I get rite the fuck up, and Fabien yells from the door "yo fight go ahead you in the clear no teachers around I'll tell you when they come." So, what thee actual fuck? I'm supposed to be scared of you because you're 6 inches taller than me and weigh 70 more pounds than me? That didn't make sense to me, so I punched him then he punched me then I punched him back and now we were going at it and the class was loud as hell. Fabien yells while running to his chair teacher, teacher, teacher! Lol so we all sat down real fast and acted like we were talking and laughing. So, Mrs. Dayanna was like "what is all the commotion I'm trying to teach my class down the hall, and I can hear you guys." So, we apologize and tell her our homeroom teacher said she had to go to a quick meeting with Sister Rose and she would be back. Mrs. Dayanna said, "ok just keep it down so we apologized again."

She walks off to go teach her class and listen we as a class already knew, Fabien go rite up with me and Justin and ran to the door and once we were in the clear he said "ya clear ya clear ya clear!" Justin swung and missed I saw an opportunity and hit em again and everyone was like ohhhhh! Then he hit me good if I remember correctly, he caught me rite over my left eye and that shit hurt, then I got upset he caught me good. So, I cocked back rite after and hit him as hard as I could at the time and boy was it a game winner lol. So, in the back of the class we have those sliding wood closet doors where the kids put their coats and umbrellas, before that is a long tall table to the right and to the left is our homeroom computer. So, me and Justin are the last 2 chairs in the third row, so when I hit him as hard as I could the kid flew back broke the closet door and fell inside lol. The whole class was in an uproar and Dennis and Fabien were like OH SHITTTTT! Fabien turned around and said while running to his chair "teacher, teacher, teacher!" Lmfao So Mrs. Dayanna came in angry as all, saw Justin in the back trying to fix the door and said, "what in heavens name is going on in here." As a class we were all in sync we all said "we don't known Justin was getting something in the back and fell and broke the door and now he is trying to fix it but it was funny you should have seen it lol." Clearly, she didn't believe us, and boy was she mad we interrupted her class lmfao. When Justin fell back and hit that closet that shit was loud. Since she didn't believe us, she said "I am going to stay here and wait till your teacher comes back." Clearly, we were still loud and laughing and Justin finally got the door fixed and sat back down. Another few moments she turns around and yells "Roland get back to class rite now!" Lmfao Just a situation that didn't need to happen but there was tension it was going to happen sooner or later.

Our homeroom teacher comes back and she asks Mrs. Dayanna if everything was ok, she replied "yes but they were very loud" but she let us off the hook because she couldn't prove anything other than Justin fixing the door lol. We finish class and start walking to our next class down the hall and up the stairs and I don't recall who I saw first Roland or Jaxson but when I saw Jaxson he gave me daps and was like "yo I heard you fucked up Justin good shit!" Lol I was so confused, like how did everyone know because after that everyone gave me daps which confused me because at this day and age no one was carrying cell phones in 7th grade and this was literally rite after we left homeroom like who told everyone and how? Clearly either Dennis or Fabien but they never left homeroom. Anyways moving forward lol Justin never fucked with me again and there was still tension because the whole school knows he got fucked up by a kid way smaller than him. I am well past that though I didn't care enough about it we literally fought over pens like it wasn't that serious just off the principle of him believing just because he was bigger than me I am somehow supposed to fear him or allow for him to rob me, ehhh I don't play that bullshit I don't care about your size, if you about it then we about it we can throw hands.

    As months progress we get a new kid named Jeremiah from Finnegan School. Let me tell you this school is completely hidden from the rest of the universe. It's on 51st in Tunica Avenue and if you don't know where the school is, you my friend will never find it lol. He was a cool dude, he was a comedian as well, so obviously he was going to fit in well. Fabien and Roland were both like "hey Mikey" I said, "what's up" they said, "at least you aint the new guy anymore" so I asked "is that a good thing?" They said "yes" lol I said, "ok good." So, Jeremiah just added onto our group and all the teachers were upset. We were all loud and reckless in class everyday constantly getting in trouble, I mean it was fun we were getting along perfectly fine. Basketball season approaches and we all try out, me, little Dennis, Fabien, Roland, Justin, Jaxson, Javier, Alexander, and Jeremiah. The coach, whose ironic name was Javier as well was cool he said we all made it but really we were all pretty good all we did was play basketball I mean we aren't organized basketball players we all just try and score but that's the point isn't it lol.

While playing basketball me and Justin became cool, I mean we weren't the best of friends, but all the problems were settled and there wasn't tension anymore we shook hands. So, one week after tryouts we get a new transfer. He is Jo Han, Mrs. Dayanna's son. This kid is tall and strong he joined the basketball team and he was good but, oh boy did he have an ugly jump shot, this kid would bring the ball up over his head and have a late release, but it worked for him. He was a funny guy. The thing about the school was that the people, they didn't really like problems everyone just got along well we all meshed together. There was one exception, his name was Marcel. Just nothing serious he would just say little smart remarks that were extremely annoying, we were going to fight in one gym class session but Roland grabbed me and took me from the locker room and brought me out to the gym and told me to drop it. So, nothing ever progressed from it.

Weeks progress we play a few basketball games win some lose some as always. In school we had a basketball meeting and we had to go to the girl's coach's room why I don't remember but anyways, as we are walking over to the other side of the school the 6th graders are walking out towards us the opposite way as if they were going to our classroom. We see Javier and say what's up I mean you can't miss the kid he's almost 6ft tall and a 6th grader lol so he is towering everyone and a couple students behind him, she was there, this girl was so short and adorable she was beautiful, man listen. Her eyes caught my attention, just an intense, deep, mystical look in her eyes. I wouldn't say like seeking for help but there was definitely sorrow in her eyes, and they just grabbed a hold of me and took me as prisoner for those seconds that seemed like a life time in that hallway it was weird like I felt like I took a glimpse at her soul. So, as she walks by, I turn and gaze at her like not break my neck, it was much worse. It was like she paralyzed me, like I wanted to say something to her but couldn't, like I tried but we continued walking past each other and I kept trying to see where she was gong but I couldn't she was too short I lost her. Then I felt these two hands on my shoulders and heard a laugh and Roland was behind me, he was laughing the entire time and spun me around. He said, "dam Mikey that girl broke ya neck and made you do a 360 that's embarrassing." So, I said "hey bro you know everyone in the school who is she?" He replied, "yea I know her, but you have no chance so forget about her and move on there are other girls in the school." That definitely broke my spirit especially hearing it from him but, from him you know it's true, so I dropped it, I mean I definitely thought about her for a while but left it alone and eventually forgot about it.

So, a few weeks go by and guess what? Fabien is going out with Jayla lmfao of course I mean of course. It was just a matter of time; we knew he liked her and the thing about it is we never seen him talking to her then all of a sudden, he's making out with her in the hallway out of the blue lol. Then we went to homeroom and our teacher left for a few minutes and Jayla popped rite up out of the blue like in the movies and they start making out and you could feel the school rumble lol all you heard was Sister Rose's voice with an angry tone in it yelling "Fabien get in my office rite now I will not say it again." Man was that hilarious this kid just stayed getting in trouble. Fabien looks at us in the class and he says, "oh shit, oh shit, oh shit she is going to expel me I'll see you guys next year." I mean like really though in the hallway they couldn't just come into class like they had one foot out the door and one foot in the door just come in, so no one sees you lol. Anyways lol that shit was funny the whole entire class hit the floor laughing. Well we are in class and time is going by 20 minutes, 30 minutes, an hour lol and this kid is nowhere to be seen and we all have the same thought, that he is a goner lmfao. The class is just laughing and of course Dennis is about to lose his best friend he's telling jokes and a bit sad at the same time. Then the floor begins to rumble the door opened all you hear is "now get back to class." So, he walks back into class and we are just dying of laughter. He tells us how she lectured him I don't remember if it was about kiddy love or just doing anything sexual in the school or both honestly, but he said if she catches him again no remorse, he's a goner lol. Obviously, they still do, they just are very cautious where and when they have their little fun. The day continues and we go out until lunch and Fabien and Roland are always talking to the eighth graders, Lucas, Alexander, Jaxson, Jayla, Demi and some other eight graders they introduced me to all of them, but I don't remember half of them. Then you have Roland who walks around to the back fence and starts talking to all the Richmond Hillers from the high school he just makes rounds saying what's up to all his friends that's pretty much a lot of his day lol. Kids like a mini politician I swear.

The day comes to an end, and I am thinking I really don't want to go to school tomorrow because I have catechism class every Thursday. Which I usually pick up Elian at his house and we go together. We have different teachers he has Father Ricardo, and I have Joshua and an assistant I always forget her name and guess what, I forgot her name now too so I don't mean any disrespect so we will call her Agnes is that ok? Ok we'll go with Agnes. So, Elian has class with Lydia, and Charlotte, I have class with Camren, Raymond, and Nate we sat in the back of the class always getting in trouble. So, on this day Joshua and Agnes were not there, heyyyyyy that means substitute teacher which means easy night. Well, oh boy was that the furthest from the truth, boy were we so wrong. So, the sub walks into class and starts to gather her things and settle in me, Cam, Raymond, Nate, were all just laughing and joking. The sub starts talking and I am in my chair by my self-minding my own got damn business and Raymond, Nate, and Cam just keep making me laugh while the sub was talking, and

I felt bad, but these guys are funny. The sub was trying to tell us her name and Raymond made me laugh so she told me to move up, I said "I wasn't even talking I was just laughin." Nope she was wasn't having it and then Raymond said something funny as hell and I just busted out laughing and she gave me thee meanest look and she gave me a last warning. So the thing was Raymond is like a mini Vin Diesel and he transferred out of Valentine Crescent too and went to Lincoln School rite across the street from Valentine Crescent and he was telling us stories about there and they were funny then the sub caught me laughing again and ok at this point I felt bad so I just moved up. Then Cam, Raymond, Natalia, and Nate were all laughing at me and said "yea that's what you get" I told the sub "see I wasn't even talking I was just laughing now everyone's laughing at me." She replied, "well you shouldn't have said nothing in the first place." Ohhhhh so the sub got a mouth ok, ok that's cool that's cool because now I can play the game too so well see how far it goes before, I get kicked out of class. She asked if I knew her name because she told the class her name, and I had no response then I felt really bad just because she's just trying to do her job, but what kind of elementary school kids would we be if we let the sub get one on us you know. So, since she was right, I just stopped in my head I was like fuck it I'll talk to everyone after class but damn this class going to drag out now.

So, I apologized for my actions and said it won't happen again, she said "ok it better not my name is Melina." The crew is in the back and you can hear them whispering and laughing and shit, man fuck them lol they all are talking and I'm the one in trouble lol. Natalia, I met there at catechism class, she was cute, cool, and down to Earth. So the class finally begun, Melina was talking she made the class interesting to say the least but I was still bored up front, so what did I do I just started playing with a pen or pencil I don't remember honestly but one of them. I would just twist in with my fingers or flicking it, but it kept falling, and every time it fell Melina gave me this look like if you keep dropping that damn pen, I'm going to hurt you. I couldn't help it I was bored. So, it dropped again lol and she got mad and said, "if that pen drops one more time, I'm going to kick you." Well I didn't believe her but I know I was getting annoying so I stopped but kept playing with it just not flicking it so it wasn't like it can fall again rite? Ok well wrong lol it fell and I was actually listening to her lecture and when I went to go write notes it actually flew out of my hand I don't know how lol and I was about to go pick it up and Melina picked it up before me walked to my desk and kicked thee shit out of me with her pointed heels man, that was one of thee worst shin kicks, Jesus Mary and Joseph, I was like damn that hurt, it was funny though because I didn't believe she was actually going to do it. She said "that's what you get for testing me." I replied "it was an accident that time it really was" but since I was laughing while I said it, she didn't believe me. So, I was like I'm not going to even chance it this time, so I put the pen in the groove on the desk, so I don't play with it anymore or take notes. As I was putting it back in the groove it fell, and everyone started laughing and Raymond was like she is going to kick your ass then kick you out the class lol. She walked to my desk and I explained I was going to put it in the groove and not use it and I guess she believed me because she didn't kick me. Anyways the class finished, and she apologized to me and I was like its ok I know I deserved it I was getting annoying. Then we all met up downstairs me, Elian, Lydia, Cam, Charlotte Adelyn, Raymond, Bruce, Angelina, Nate and Ms. Emma. We were all talking like always and Elian and Ms. Emma told me that the community was having a meeting again every Thursday.

So, you know this isn't a continuous story. It pains me to write this out honestly and I cry a lot, more than any man ever should. It has been months since I actually opened this and wrote out a few pages. I have so much to say and I hope that I may be able to finish this and let this story get into the hands of a person who needs to hear this story and advice I provide. People need to know they are not alone, and I am here for you and I care about you.

Hopefully this story may help you in any way to uplift you from your regression and depression. I guess we will get back to the story, please bear with me. So, I told Ms. Emma and Elian I will go to a meeting and see how it is. So next week comes and it is Thursday and Elian called and asked me to pass by and check out the community. So, Elian's my brother and I told him I would go, and I am a man of my word so I went, and let us just say my thoughts were in the premise of what the fuck did I get myself into. First off it was all in Spanish lol if you haven't figured out, I don't know Spanish very well, second, I didn't know anyone in there except Elian and Ms. Emma and Father Ricardo. So, they helped me and told me that they have a nice lady who is willing to translate for me. So, to my surprise guess who showed up to translate for me? Go ahead guess shits crazy I tell ya. If you haven't guessed the very nice woman who came and translated for me was no one other than Melina. Yes, the substitute teacher who kicked the shit out of me. Amazing rite lol she actually was really nice. She was my translator for the whole time I went to the meetings on Thursday nights. I apologized to her again for the whole ideal that happened in class and with me disrupting the class I felt really bad. She was cool about it. So, these meetings were pretty serious though, this wasn't like your regular church settings and people talking about their sins. They were talking about everything, all life experiences good and bad. Women talking about being raped and prostituting or the not understanding why their parents hated them and they were alcoholics both child and parent, people who abused drugs on an everyday basis, homeless people finding success, it was more of I guess we can say group therapy but this group wasn't simply people from church it was a family in which we all helped each other with our problems and depressions and suicidal ideation and manifestations.

Listen, people don't really understand that many times the

thoughts we have that weigh us down, is pressure that must be relieved. At times I am telling you that you need to open up and talk about it. Sometimes the best person to talk to about these stressors is someone you don't even know. Allow me to elaborate. You speaking about issues stressing you out and holding you down, to an individual you don't know may be more comforting in the sense that you may feel that this person does not hold the ability to judge you because they do not know you. Now if you trust someone and you want to openly express a concern and or thoughts that bother you and you hold yourself back and don't allow yourself to fully express these stressors, thoughts, concerns then you have an issue with the person you are confiding in. This may be a biased subjective concern because you know the person. So, you may believe that you are able to predict the outcome of the conversation and you already know the advice they will give you and if you do that you are doing yourself a disservice. You are basically giving yourself your own advice.

Christmas of 2017 just passed, and it was definitely a depressing one I really would like to tell you all about it but I can't just jump 13, 14, 15 years after everything I have to explain as much as I would like to but I guess we will just continue and we will cross that bridge when we get to it.

So, the meeting ended, and Elian and Melina asked if I would come next week and I said yea sure. I don't know why but I said yes already so I am a man of my word and I had to go. So back to school, we got a new girl in our class and man was she Beautiful. Her name was Gracelynn but, there was something familiar about her but whatever I just dismissed it as fast as the thought came. She came from Nixon school right across the street from us, literally like 10 feet away lmfao. So, she was real nice, down to earth funny too. We all got along from the start the girls accepted her in really easy like she was always with us. In the morning I would always get bread and butter you know hood breakfast lol, before class begins usually with whoever wants to go. Jeremiah went with me and Gracelynn was there so we all started talking and what not then headed back to school, when we got there I kept talking to her so I asked her was she always in Nixon or did she ever go to school somewhere else and you know what man, she did lol. Man listen she told me she went to Valentine Crescent for preschool and part of kindergarten and there it was that's why she looked so familiar to me lol. I know like I'm capable of remembering what someone looked like 10 years ago as a child and are able to detect facial definitions and characteristics as they grow and develop. No, lol she just seemed familiar and she was lol. I had told her previously that she looked familiar and she remembered when I told her so when we were talking, she started laughing like see I knew it lol. We got real cool after that, that was home girl. Our lunch table was huge at this time people kept coming in and adding to our table it was great we had Roland, Fabien, Dennis, Dennis, Dennis, lol Jo Han, Eduardo, Justin, Marcel, Gracelynn, Lara, Josephine, and actually I think if I remember correctly Lucas, Jerome, and Demi were there also but I would have to ask Roland that but either way there were plenty of 6th and 8th graders. So many laughs at that table and weird ass conversations I won't discuss here lol, but I really do miss those days, people and school they treated me well.

We had basketball practice and it was a funny one. We played a scrimmage and 5 on 5. With each other after running up and down them damned stairwells, Jesus Christ I hated running laps incorporated with steps. It was like the basketball court but the entrance was a hallway and stairs on both sides so you run laps and when you pass buy the entrance you had to go up the steps to the other side of the hallway and back down the other steps and go finish the laps. Roughly 35 laps before practice then the scrimmage. So me and Jeremiah were on the same team and this one time during the scrimmage it was mad random but funny for some reason I was in the paint and Jeremiah threw me the ball and said skittles and I shot the ball up and said taste the rainbow and made it. Ok so first off you ever say some weird shit and don't know where it came from yea that is what happened to Jeremiah and instead of me saying "yo what the fuck" lol taste the rainbow came out it was the weirdest thing but everyone was laughing like me and him had some type of inside joke or something lol and we didn't. So, at this time I was very fast and pretty athletic, I was decent in organized basketball, but street ball was were my skills were at, never could explain it. But hey listen we went on a like an 18-2 run and I was always in the paint after the fast break and Jeremiah was throwing that basketball across the court to me yelling skittles lmfao. We won 2-3 scrimmages though it was a good practice. After practice I went to Jeremiah's house and hung out for a while. Jeremiah was a funny guy, great sense of humor, he didn't live too far from the school and there was a basketball court by his house. We played some video games and listened to the new 50 cent album. He called a few of his friends over and were went to the court and played a couple 2 on 2 games, shit I was exhausted and on top of that I still had to walk like 34 blocks home.

So Thursday comes and Elian is asking me if I'm going to the community, so I said yea I had already told him I'd go, I just don't know why I kept going back, but I did, I guess it was just nice seeing all those people being comfortable around each other and trusting each other to the point they have no problem talking about personal issues around one another. I think the best part also was the priest, he wasn't the only one giving advice, and it wasn't what you would call bible advice or typical priest advice you know. Everyone had their own input on it and if someone had experienced it everyone would quiet down and let that person share their experience and how they got through the situation. Which I thought was pretty interesting. Also, if someone needed a place to stay or food for their family or help paying bills everyone would chip in and help or state where they may find government assistance or aid or open their doors to said individual. Hearing everyone's problems and seeing how many people had it worse than me I guess it helped me mature. I mean yea I was only 13 at the time had no bills or real problems but, all my problem were there waiting for me to run into them on this road called life and having and hearing these people's experience and how they ventured through their issues definitely helped. So, we left and the night ended and me and Elian, Melina and a few others stayed and talked and then we all went home. Back at it again in school laughing being mischievous little delinquents that we are getting detention and just having fun. After school me, Lucy, Dennis, and Gracelynn were going out and Gracelynn and Dennis went to the store, I didn't go in at first but then I was like eh the hell with it I'm hungry and if were walking why not grab a bite for it. Well lol so I'm looking around to get a drink and I walk to the back and sure enough Dennis and Gracelynn just back there making out, in my head I was like Gracelynn noooooo lol, but then rooting for my boy Dennis lol. Well I stopped having a crush on her and stopped flirting after that lol.

So, the big basketball game is coming up, you know St Vincenzo vs Valentine Crescent me vs my old school lol. Guess what the game we're all supposed to go all out Jaxson can't make it because he has a playoff baseball game. Anyway, game day is here their team had Nate, Elian, Rome, Cam and I can't recall who else, we had Roland, Fabien, Dennis, Jo Han, Justin, Jeremiah, Javier and me. I don't remember much of the game honestly but, I do remember Nate knocking down threes, Elian was getting all his fast break layup points and Rome made a couple buckets. Roland was dropping his left- handed threes; I say that because he is right-handed but does pretty much everything lefty it was weird I don't know how he did that. Jo Han dropped a few threes and Jeremiah was dropping buckets Fabien had several points and I think I made a layup. Either way we won the game. Hung out for a bit with them and then had to head back to school for God only knows the reason why they didn't let me walk 2 blocks home, but my father came to pick me up. We went home and I went to hang out with Elian at his house across the street ate then I went home. Me and Elian hung out a lot, usually when we hang out for some reason, we always find money like this kids a magnet I swear. Seriously if you hang out with this guy you are almost guaranteed to find money on the street. I think the most interesting currency we found was a blank check, yea it's not currency but it could have been lol. No, seriously who finds a blank check laying on the street and yea we contemplated on putting a number and finding someone to cash it because it was all signed and everything, we just needed a dollar amount and the write out of it. We were on the way to his house and we cut it up , it would have been wrong to fill it out I would have felt bad if we went through with it but Elian isn't like that either so I guess the decision was already made when we found it, just the thought of cashing it out was entertaining.

If it wasn't the next day or some time that same month we found a check for like 600 and some odd dollars, that was a simple 300 split we found it on 16th street and Bristol Ave and it had some lady's name on it and her address. When we looked at the address it was the building next door to where we found it at, so we thought damn how we are going to know which apartment she is in. So we walked like 50ft to the apartment and you know these apartments you need a key to get in the front door before the hallway so someone can buzz you in, luckily for us some lady was walking out as we were coming upon the door and she let us in and she held the door for us. And simultaneously me and Elian looked at each other like what if, then paused and shook our heads like nah lol. So, we looked at the check for her name again and by this time the lady was at the end of the block and Elian was like I'll go ask her just in case. Whelp sure enough she gave Elian a huge hug lol I was like wait what just happened was he hitting on her lol, so I started rooting for my boy quietly lol. Turns out it was her lol she showed Elian her license and names matched on the check and her license she said she was going to the bank to cancel the check but now she doesn't have to.

Anyway back to the story lol we found like 20 dollars on the floor while heading back to his house so at this point we were on 15th street and New Post Ave rite in front of the school literally across the street from his house, I was about to cross but a huge Ford van was parked on the corner I couldn't see but I made a judgment call because the street phone I passed 20 feet away I looked to see if any cars were coming and the light was green and no cars were around, I continue to cross and as I pass the White Ford van I feel a strong tug on the back of my shirt and all I hear is NOOOOOOO MIKEY!!!!!

And I just fly backwards and all I see is this massive 18- wheeler speeding up the road, now I'm talking this truck was literally inches in front of me if Elian didn't pull me back, I would have been splattered. It just didn't make any sense how in those few seconds did a heavy ass 18- wheeler gain enough momentum and speed from 15th and Bristol Ave to 15th and New Post Ave maybe like 200- 300 feet maximum is the length of that block Lincoln school is on. I got up and we both laughed I said thanks bro and asked any crazier drivers heading up the street, he laughed and said no man we good to cross lol. I miss my boy Elian man if you are reading this, I love you man thanks again lol. We went to his house picked up his skateboard and he lent me his bike and some candles we use to wax surfaces for board slides and grinds and went to 1st Street Park.

It has been a while since I have written in this book, me and Amelia are going through it man, you will meet her towards the end of the story, an amazing woman but I am a bit depressed at the moment I will try and pick up and continue tomorrow. Have a good night.

Well good morning ladies and gentlemen, back to the story, my birthday is coming up, so I decided to do something small it was a small bowling party at Bowlers Den something to get everyone out and just relax and converse, something different. Well lol let me tell you that it did not turn out as planned lmfao. So, no one came like no one showed up just me my mom, my sister, and her friend Yalena, but an hour later rite after Adina the owner of Bowlers Den said "hey Mikey don't worry if no one comes I will only charge you for who is here." Adina was great hands down one of the nicest women I have ever met. I was always in a bowling league she knew me and my mom very well, so she charges per person no matter if they show or don't for parities because you're taking up lanes but since I been going there for so many years she comped it, I loved that woman. Any who a bit after she said that Roland showed up, my boy. He was ready to bowl and relax and we just had fun ate pizza he hit on my sisters' friend lol it was a good time. So, I write lol a lot at the moment because recalling these events and remembering the situations and conversations they were pretty funny so I apologize if you don't understand the lol or if it's annoying but it will stop soon just for your information. Any who, talking to Roland I really wasn't that upset to be honest. These kids just want to drink, smoke bud, and have sex and none of those variables or coefficients are involved in a bowling party. Roland just doesn't care about anything if you invite him, he will be there no matter the event no matter how far the event he just enjoys being around people it's just that simple for him. Going back to school Monday nothing changed there was no animosity no hate we all hung out at lunch laughed we were all still cool, you know I understood why they didn't come I wasn't bothered by it. So, it was coming close to the end of the school year and my mom was asking me if I wanted to stay at St Vincenzo or transfer back to Valentine Crescent. This killed me because I got real cool with so many people in that school I felt like I grew up there you know the girls were beautiful the teachers were mean we all got in trouble and got detention together grew bonds and connections with them, they welcomed me like their own and I appreciated that. On the other hand, I had Elian, Lydia and the whole class in Valentine Crescent and I didn't have to take a bus or walk 30 blocks back home lol. So, Valentine Crescent it was lol.

So I told the people in the class and they were cool like the class was just mellow you know they knew I liked them they were liked don't worry about it we will still hang out and you know back in elementary school signing the back of pictures K.I.C, we will keep in contact or keep in touch. We were so corny back then lol.

During the summertime my mom had me in a recreational program housed in Warwick School back on 17th street by The Towers. Pretty much all we did was eat breakfast, play basketball or baseball and certain days we would have movie day or pool day I believe if my memory serves me correctly movie day was every Friday and pool day was Thursdays. So, my mom enlisted me and my sister, but my sister now finished Freshman year of high school from Saint something or St Colide High I don't know I don't remember honestly it wasn't far from the viaduct on Washington street in Fairfield. Any which way, I met a lot of people there I think Galvin and Fabien were the names of people I spent the most times with.

Galvin was a tall black kid sense of humor was great and he was into all the anime and card games so I picked up Yu-Gi-Oh from him which may be a foreign language to many people but it's a television cartoon that was about monsters and had a card game developed from it. And Fabien was the popular kid that knew pretty much everyone, and he got all the girls. Hmmm you know looking back a bit I did have a pretty good history of hanging out with a huge diversity of kids from the geeks to the popular kids to the athletes huh dam good thing to notice. So, Fabien lived across the street from Warwick School so when his parents would not be home, we would go to his house and hang out after recreation. So, this whole recreation thing was pretty much from what I tended to gather is to keep us all delinquents out of trouble until our parents came home from work.

Well ok that kind of made sense but not. We have to be there at

8am and it finishes at 12-1pm. Let me explain something, all that accomplished was waking us up early, recreation was not a deterrent to keep us from roaming the streets unsupervised and getting into trouble I would like to just clarify that. If us kids were not in recreation trust me we would be getting up at 11am 12pm to go hang out and wait for all our other friends to wake up so we wouldn't even be leaving the house till 2-3pm just about when some parents are coming home and catch us at the time we are leaving to hang out then ask us to go to the grocery store or run errands then we wouldn't even be able to meet up with our friends till almost 4-5pm. Day to day I hung out with everyone unless someone didn't show up one day then I just spent time with the geeks or the popular kids it all depended. Mainly the day consisted of breakfast then play dodgeball or baseball majority vote because it was the same basketball court so we couldn't play all three sports simultaneously but around 11am they kicked everyone off the court so we can play basketball. Then when it was time to go home everyone walked home and back at it again tomorrow.

One day after recreation I saw Galvin walking home towards 18th street in Bristol so I told my sister I was going to hang out with him just in case my mom asked where I was, she would just tell her I was on 18th street. So, I caught up with him and asked him where he was going and asked if I could hang out with him for a while. So, we went to 19th-20th street in Altoona Ave and he bought a deck of Yu-Gi-Oh cards. Then all of sudden we are walking back to New Post Ave and passing The Palm pizzeria and I ask, "you live on this block?" He said "no my friend Bruce lives here," I said "oh shit you know Bruce" he said "yea you know em too," "yea of course we been going to school together since we were kids." Then we get to Bruce's house and he greets us at the door has like "yo you guys know each other" we were like "yea we met in recreation," "cool man come in." So we walk into the house and turn right in to the living room and the couches are to the back right by the windows and in front of them is a table and a television with the Nintendo Gamecube on and you guessed what game was on, Super Samsh Bros Melee heyyyyyyyy. What a phenomenal game, it was great I learned to play from Bruce and Galvin. Bruce was a gamer all the Resident Evil's, Silent Hill's, Metroid Primes, Castelvanias this kid knew them and beat them all record timing. If I remember correctly his favorite game was Metal Gear Solid, and nope I tried to play that game way too hard for me lmfaoooooooo.

Anyway we all got along well and time flew by so it was time for me to go home so I left and while I was leaving I closed and shut the door behind me walked down the 3-4 steps of his house and look up and bam who was there across the street, pretty girl on the block with a crazy booty Yulianna and I really shouldn't be saying that lol anywayssss. I said what's up from a distance and went home lol. Weeks pass by we are in the middle of July recreation is almost over and we are playing baseball actually we all got caught up in the game today no one cared about basketball. So I am up to bat and we are down 2 I hit a solo dolo home run and then the pitcher knocked out the next 2 batters so we lost its all good though. Me my sister and a friend of hers are walking home and all I hear is "yo hold up yo yo." So I turn around and when I say I saw 4-6 kids running at me I was like what the fuck I was so confused like fuck did I do so listen I'm not getting jumped by 6 kids fuck I look like so I start running. I'm ok fighting 1 on 1 doesn't matter how big the kid is but no training at this time with my conditioning maybe, maybe handle 2 kids my age but you would be a fool to think I'ma stand around and get surrounded and jumped by 6 kids. Then they caught me lol well 2 of them caught me that boy was fast as lightning shit and I didn't see him catch up to me and when he did, he pushed me up to a fence near Bristol Ave. Then all the kids caught up and I'm like "fuck is this about" and one kid was like "when you were at bat when you hit the homerun you threw the bat and hit my boy," I was like "what the fuck I didn't even know that happened my bad, and ya want to bang about this now a whole hour after the shit happens and on that ya want to jump me chump shit." So, pissing them off didn't help they roughed me up lol and my sister just walked by and walked her happy ass back home.

Didn't ask if I was ok didn't call the cops, she aint do shit lmfao but it wasn't that bad when they realized I really didn't know what I did they pulled punches lol it's all gravy. Minor aches and pains a couple black and blues nothing visible. A couple weeks later rite before recreation is over its pool day and I was hanging out with Fabien the whole day. We were in the pool with Janessa if I remember her name correctly and Janessa was beautiful, but Fabien was trying to get at her, so I never made a move. She flirted a lot though so I didn't mind lol we hung out all together in the pool and when we got back to Lincoln, recreation was over for the day a few of us went to Fabien's house because his parents didn't really come home till late like 5-6pm so we would just drink and have a few shots of liquor from his parents cabinet and he just refilled it with whatever he had in the fridge whether it was apple juice or plain water lol I always wanted to know if his parents ever noticed honestly lol. Either way he gave me the notice that he wanted me to leave and kick everyone else out because he didn't have much time to be alone with Janessa. So of course, being the amazing friend that I am I started the rollout lol "yo my bad bro I would love to hang out more, but I have to get going home." I asked if anyone else was coming and they said "we aint going to drink at your house" I'm like "no stupid I'm going home" while clearing my throat I'm eyeballing them and pointing at Janessa and Fabien and the kids finally get it, stoopid asses lol and then we all leave together and Fabien and Janessa got the house to themselves.

Next day vibe was weird, so I asked Fabien if they slept together and he said yea I fucked her, I said oh ok because both of ya acting a bit funny lol he said nah we good and Janessa never confirmed this but okies lol. The Summer Recreation Program comes to a defining end and I'm finally back at it running the streets with Elian or alone some if I'm just out visiting Roland or Fabien from St Vincenzo. Great experiences honestly and great people man just great people.

Chapter 8

Eighth Grade, My New Brother

Summer had finally come to an end, and it was time to go back to school. I wasn't the cool guy that would do the late entrances and all that attention stuff that shit is corny lol. I went back to Valentine Crescent just like a usual day 15 minutes early before they opened the gym door. The first person I saw was Nate and he was like "oh you back" and I said, "hell yea I'm back." The doors opened and everyone came and met up at formation in the gym. Some of the new kids were Evander, Mabel, Daziel and Shayne. As a class we always got along with transfer students never had a problem other than Dennis he just had anger issues and his release was grabbing things and throwing it across the room, which was his temper tantrum it's not really funny, but it was. We all had our issues it was just his way of releasing it he didn't know any better at the time can't blame the kid for it.

Anyways break came and Ms. Emma wanted to talk so I stepped outside and she said she saw me on the roster for her class and asked, "why did I come back?" I explained to her that I liked the other school the kids were great, real nice, treated me well but it just wasn't my place, I want to graduate with the friends I grew up with and I didn't grow up with them. She said ok "I never told any of the kids you were coming back but I'm glad you're back."

Ms. Emma loved me she was a great person and she has a great heart, I miss her. Moving forward, as we were finishing our conversation all I hear is "ah fuck dude." I couldn't help to laugh because me and her already knew and she just yellllllllled Elian's name lmfao. Listen if you want to get her irritated, upset, or mad simply just swear she hates it and Elian means no harm to anyone but his skater persona heavy metal music listening self just can't stop swearing lmfaoooo. I had completely forgot he can't hold his tongue for the life of him. If I be damned this was going to be a long funny year with Elian, Nate, Bruce, Cam, Shayne, Damien and that's not even counting the girls but boy, was I happy I returned. As lunch came and we sat at the table we all got introduced to the new kids. Mabel was nice sweet but quiet, Evander was the rapper, and Daziel shit well he barely knew English we had minor communication barriers. Shayne we pretty much knew from out in the street skateboarding with Elian and hanging out by Bruce's house.

So weeks pass by Elian is getting kicked out of class because he just swears too much, Damien got suspended for a bad tantrum he threw, I don't recall how it was sparked but pretty much when he gets like that we all just get up and get out of class and let him wreak havoc turn tables and what not till he gets tired, not really much else you can do honestly. Now basketball tryouts come, and we all got in the team, the school was small, so we needed everyone honestly. The team is me, Evander, Nate, Elian, Rome, Cam, and a few others. During this time, it's pretty much class and basketball, the day usually ends around 7-8pm unless the girls basketball team needs to practice or has a game, or they practice with us sometimes. We had spent a lot of time with each other, and we all got close. At this time in particular I got close with Evander and Cam. Cam was a good kid but when I first went to his house some things kind of clicked. I realized he was adopted; he was black, and his parents were white. Being adopted alone comes with underlying problems and everyone handles their issues differently but mainly they have this persona this front they put to hide their problems, which is reasonable and understandable in certain circumstances but not ideal for everyday life. His parents were pretty well off they had apple computers everywhere in the house. I'm unsure if anyone remembers the old apple computers the big round ones with the see through color logos whether it was red or blue and the thin back computers well anyways his parents didn't bother very much when he had company the basement / garage was like a lounge with a decent sized television video games it was cool. We hung out there a lot after practice unless I was with Evander, Elian, or Daziel.

During school it was just a down to earth environment, it was comfortable we all just loved to laugh, and we all clicked. I started to see how close everyone grew together without me there last year I can't lie it did bother me a bit, but people grow people change maybe it's for the best or at least you hope. Then seeing everyone talk to Evander and Elian like they have known each other for centuries was nice well most people in class knew Elian through me and church so he fit in the puzzle always he was just never in our school. I started to talk to Daziel a lot more now and we became really cool. It definitely took some time to say the least because I barely knew Spanish and he barely knew English, but we helped each other, and it worked well lol. The class was close and now it was great the whole class had inside jokes and there weren't really any cliques other than a couple anomalies we never rejected any one that I can recall it was just a couple people that didn't like to be bothered so we didn't bother them. Being the 8th graders we knew all the 5th, 6th, and 7th graders. When switching classes it got real loud in that hallway but like I keep saying we were cool, but never disrespected the teachers or ever been rude if they kick us out, they kick us out and we kept it moving no animosity tomorrow was a new day. Ms. Rohana our math teacher, I believe hated swearing more than Ms. Emma lol. When Elian would curse it came to a point, she wouldn't say anything he would be like sorry I'm going to Ms. Madeiras office rite now lmfao she was our principle. Ms. Mabelle our reading teacher didn't really care as long as we didn't get too loud and disrupt class, she would let us swear and curse she was cool real lenient.

Ok so that was that lol, the basketball games started we concentrated on that. It was crazy though because the league we had joined made us drive to West Bubble Fuck somewhere in Greenville to a gym called Boys Town lmfao. We never ever actually figured out how all this came to be and who authorized a gym to be called Boys Town like that was a great idea lmfao idiots. Anyways a majority of the games were played there and to say the least we were not a good team lmfao. But that was life, basketball, hangout, study wasn't in the vocabulary, I had good memory back then my grades were As, and Bs. Usually when I would hang out with Elian, Daziel would be with me so we would just go visit Bruce on 19th Street and if Nate was there we would all just hang out outside talking bullshitting with Pierre, Abel them kids were funny and they knew about bikes. So sometimes usually in the Summer we would have a circuit up to the Monastery and around then to back to Bristol Ave then back up to Bruce's. Sometimes Yulianna was outside her crib doing whatever I don't remember but she usually just sat outside, and Daziel didn't know her so I just introduced them I can't have Daziel being the only one in the group that didn't know her it would have been awkward and Bruce is the one that introduced me to all the kids on his block unless I met them prior in recreation.

Back to school, we had a game coming up against St. Vincenzo at home, so we didn't have to drive to Boys Town. During our practice we were learning new plays and running drills, we had taken a break and let the girl's team have a full court scrimmage because they had a game the next day and our next game was a couple weeks away. Most of the time we practiced with the girl's team because we only had one small court the school was small lol. Any way after the scrimmage they cut the practice short so we the guy's team were sitting close to the exit just dressing up getting ready to leave and talking shit and laughing and pretty much we we're all getting ready to go home. Charlotte was sitting one bleacher away from us we were by the boy's bathroom by the exit I believe it was me Elian, and Evander, and I told them "damn she looks tired." Someone had called my name and I turned around and literally like a minute or two later all I hear is "get away from me." So as usual I turn around to check and see what was going on and Cam all up in Charlotte's face annoying her. Clearly my thought is damn this kid can be annoying at times. She was just sitting there with her head down like if she had a headache or something, then she sat up and sighed and Cam pushed himself up on her, but it was crazy because she was sitting and he was standing so pretty much his dick was all up in her face and she said "yo what the fuck get off me," man I lost it I ran over there and pushed him of her and said "yo what the fuck is the matter with you my guy she said back off now relax." Clearly, I had thought we were going to drop it right then and there after he realized how serious I was. Annnnnnnnndddd nope I was wrong instead of dropping it he tried to drop me. He swung at me, like me thinking we were cool and I was going to drop the issue and forget it happened because people get annoying and cross the line sometimes, but even at that for being Charlotte and how cool she was not even out for respect for her to drop it because clearly when a girl says no its no, nope he swung at me. This immature ass small minded fuckhead punched me in the face like I was wrong for pushing him off her and I don't take that shit lightly my g. But my glasses fell off like every time I get into a fight, but I was used to it so my immediate response I punched him right back without hesitation and we stood toe to toe swinging at each other continuously. His father was the coach with Aaron's dad and they realized what was happening they yelled at us to stop and we didn't we kept going and then I just cocked back and hit him as hard as I could and I didn't knock him out but boy he felt that shit, he ran out of the gym and ran outside and yelled at me and said fight me outside I'm not going to fight you in front of my father. Out of respect for his dad and Aaron's dad they called me over and said, "what the fuck is going on?" I explain to them what happened, and he tells me I'm suspended for 2 practices and 2 games, but I still have to show up to them. Isn't that some bullshit, his son sexually harasses my friend and when I stop it, I get suspended, listen I lost all respect for that man at that instance.

Aaron's dad couldn't do anything because he wasn't really the head coach, he pretty much volunteered time when he could. Some bullshit right? Anyways we all meet outside and Cam still wants to fight, so Evander tells me just fight him if he does anything dirty or shady he will jump in, I'm already mad and not in the mood to fight anymore so I told him to fuck off and just started walking home. All I hear is "you a bitch, you don't want to fight me you a sucker," and all that bullshit so whatever. I hate when ignorant people open their mouth, like he didn't want to stay and finish the fight because his father caught wind of what was happening, so he ran out the gym to fight me "outside" oh shut the fuck up. One thing about me is if you are wrong and I catch you in the act I don't care where we are or who is watching I don't like fighting in front of women but if the situation calls for it we banging it's as simple as that, place, time, and presence of people are irrelevant if the matter is extreme everyone catches hands.

I love women and I have a very big soft spot for women and people tell me that I'll never get married because I'm too nice, hah imagine that well aside from that my entire house hold were women, I lived with all women but the fact of the matter is I knew what I did was right no if ands or buts, unless they're big I like big butts lol. So any who, I get home and tell my mom what happened and now she all mad because I got into a fight now I'm like what thee actual fuck I don't care who is all mad and shit, fuck that why is no one happy that I did what was right. So, I am going to take a break for a second and explain something.

I am going to bring up many issues that need to be addressed in today's world, one issue being men. This does not directly relate to me simply because I am weird, and I simply don't care because I adapt to any change in life extremely well and extremely fast. So, upon the topic I had no men around me. The way the family was, there was my cousin Zade, and his brother Kyle. We are all evenly separated well by age meaning that when I graduate 8th grade this year, Zade is graduating high school, and Kyle would be graduating college. So, if anyone is understanding this there were no men in the house except for me. My grandfather was home most days of the week but with a strong communication barrier because I didn't know Spanish, I was unable to establish a clear relationship with him to be able to express the situations brought to me by life and the decisions I have made. As for my father well, I don't know you can ask him because one day I came home from school and he never came back home from work and my mom never did say anything to me about it and we went our separate ways. No care in the world you don't come home you're a grown ass man no one wants to explain what happened I'm not sitting around waiting for an explanation I grabbed my balls and moved the fuck on. There is more to the story that will develop next year but we leave that there. The elephant in the room is that We are not teaching our children moral obligations. We are not ensuring and establishing that a man is supposed to in any situation he is in See all available options, analyze the situation, make a decision, whether it was right or wrong, commit to the decision, and take accountability for your actions and whatever consequences come you stand up head high and accept it. If the decision was the wrong one these young men need a mentor to assess their decision- making process and thought process and come to an understanding of why that decision was believed to be the best decision under the circumstances of the situation.

They need to be taught that it's ok to make errors because in life you will make mistakes and sometimes the consequences are unimaginable but in order to avoid that they need to be taught what is right and what is wrong they need a clear cut understanding of what is moral and immoral. Please seriously don't talk to me about gender roles and other bullshit because I am the wrong one to throw any of that bullshit to because I will toss that shit out the fucking window I don't care about gender roles and I don't care about politics. Men are supposed to take care of their women period.

Back to the story I go to school the next day and everyone knows about the fight and me and Cam clearly aren't friends anymore and the day goes on. Two games later we are facing St. Vincenzo so everything is all past and over with the game starts and I forgot who the starters were but St. Vincenzo takes the lead Roland, Fabien are dropping 3s even though they had a stacked team with everyone, but Nate and Elian are dropping 3s as well. The second quarter comes they outscored us and 3rd quarter as well but I'm irritated because it's the 4th quarter now and I still haven't played so in my head I'm thinking this dickhead still mad that I beat his son up. Well to me I lost the fight because I didn't fight him the second time but ehh whatever you can decide that I don't really care. His dad for a grown ass man is being childish, he let me play the last half of the 4th quarter. It's alright we lost I knew we were going to, after the game we hung out a bit and they had asked what happened why I didn't play much, laughing and joking I told them be glad I didn't we would have won if I played lol. So, I told them what happened and Roland being who he is he knew what was up, he was like "don't worry about it you did good and you won the fight so that's a plus in my book" lol. I told em "well I lost, he wanted to fight again but I just walked away" and he said, "don't worry there was no need to fight again it was over."

January is coming to an end and my grandmother was put in the hospital, if I remember correctly, they found a tumor in her brain and late or she had a stroke I can't remember correctly. She was constantly sick throughout the last few months of her life, she was the one that kept the family together. Whenever my uncle was acting crazy and throwing tantrums, like I understand really he wasn't left out but we had big storage she behind the house and it had a room, bed, tv all necessities really other than the bathroom but he'd shower in the house, I'm unsure if he ever felt left out or anything like that but it'd make sense. Abuela was just a great hearted person, it just sucks because I think about her, then I just get like flashbacks of all the women I have lost in my life and you will meet most of them later but the day comes and she passes. My mom came in and I was laying on the couch and my sister was sitting on the couch next to me on the right and I honestly didn't really cry at first and my mom realized it and she was balling and said why aren't you crying don't you feel sad, and I did I felt sad I just wasn't crying it was weird. I cried a bit you know but it didn't really hit me until the funeral.

The funeral was I think Colonia Funeral Home on 40th and Covington Blvd, the wake was bad, it was just different more than sad, worse than depressed it was overwhelming. At the burial when we got to the Cemetery by 90th street, just being there the casket is finally closed and they begin to lower her that's when reality struck, that was it there was no coming back from that. Now it comes to the understanding that my mom, my aunts, my uncles, lost their mother us the grandkids lost our grandmother the woman of the house, and worst my grandfather lost his wife. Then it gets worse, they start throwing dirt over the casket and at a point I felt anger like sort of the disrespect of throwing dirt on a beloved family member but it is just tradition I guess the final goodbye or what not but it hurt and that's when I broke down. This point in your life or depending where you are in school or how into your religion you are and how you practice, no one really tells you about grief and loss of a loved one, everyone just says sorry, and my condolences to your family and all these generic ass responses like shut the fuck up don't try to make it better you're just literally making everything worse so spare the bullshit politics.

The big underlying issue about this is that there are 5 stages they say, which I don't know very well I have never researched it in depth but from what I gathered it is Denial / Isolation, Anger, Bargaining, Depression, and finally Acceptance. The Elephant in the room says not everyone goes through all these stages nor do they go in order and also some people never get over or past a certain stage. From personal experience I can tell you about the over workers, the people that work so much to cover their emotions, this person lost someone they were extremely close to and all you see them do is work extreme hours so they don't have to acknowledge their grief sadness and depression I believe it's called displacing, don't quote me I'm unsure, but I have seen it plenty of times and helped many get through it. Then there people like me that are used to seeing people leave, that it does not bother them or phase them. I guess in saying that it sounds extremely harsh, but my phase of getting used to people leave had begun and at this point in my life after my grandmother passed, I didn't fully understand how she passed and I honestly wasn't that close to her. I didn't speak Spanish much and she didn't speak English, so the communication barrier was severe. As in being who I am I have seen her be the head of the household for the family and watch the way her and my grandfather helped people, I loved them so much for that. The way they stopped arguments in the house and solved problems this genuine love to want everything to be ok and to want everyone to do well didn't need communication it didn't need an understanding it didn't need to be vocalized, seeing and feeling the day to day interactions between all family members and my grandparents as well as myself-allowed me to understand them alone. I had realized that 10 years too late.

When a loved one passes away people please do yourself a favor take the time out to grieve properly, make sure you have a support system which will help you along the way. Whether it be family, friends, your child, trust in me when I say you are not alone and should not be left to grieve alone, and if you truly believe you are alone I am always available and I will help you through it. What I believe to be the two most stressful events in a person's life I would have to say the loss of a child and the loss of a spouse / significant other. These are difficult situations nearly impossible to get through alone. As any person would my grandfather fell into a depression, though it was hard to tell because he was a strong man he never allowed any one to see him with his head down he was always out spoken and the only time he would get angry was when we were running late to the airport to go to Dominican Republic, he would start yelling "Maleta go" in my head I would be like "dam Welo it's like 2:30 in the morning the flight don't leave till 9am why we have to be up at 2:30am to be ready for a flight at 9 in the morning lol." Honestly speaking the wake and the funeral were thee only times I have ever seen him cry. Every day after school I would get home and the house would be empty, my grandfather would be out running errands or out speaking to our neighbors, or at the office going to his doctor's appointments. Which was completely understandable no one would want to go home and be by themselves after losing the person they loved most. Then being alone and depressed thoughts begin to run around, what ifs, the how's, the whys, you know its sad man.

This is when the family begun to split, Mattias disappeared like vanished off the face of the Earth, both my aunts were never home, my cousins were never home my sister was never home everyone was just gone. For the people that are lost to the point I am trying to make is when you lose a loved one whether it be that person is a spouse, friend, family member, child whatever the case may be you will indefinitely need to open up about it. It is just human behavior we all in turn need someone close to us that we trust enough to vent to. If you do not vent to someone about your issues and problems and things that bother you, you will be engulfed in rage, sadness, depression, anger and will use it and channel those emotions wrongfully and end up losing even more loved ones close to you because you will not realize that you will be pushing them away. At this point you will be alone and no one will forgive you for being rude and disrespectful because they were only trying to help and all you had to do was communicate, drop your pride and allow that person to help you get past certain situations and events in your life. To walk around with so much pain and guilt inside of you, it is too much for one person to bare, trust me I still walk around with much of it and I talk about a lot of my issues. Problem being my situations and issues are a bit extreme and so people just simply don't or won't understand. When I say open up to someone it will save you, your relationships, your career and it will allow you to grow more in the form of personal development.

Invisible Wounds the title, we all have been hurt but in order to grow as an individual we must open up and express and communicate what is bothering us more effectively to one another or you will succumb to the pain, and anger, and rage, and depression, and it will destroy you from the inside and it will destroy all you have accomplished in your life. Even the people who we see to be the strongest in our lives that support us and are our strength have been through the rough and bottle it in and we need to take care of them as well. I would like to apologize for all the jumping around as well I try to keep the timeline leveled with the topics we are discussing and the part of life I am walking.

Back to school, the end of the year is coming and everyone knows what high school they are going to, Evander is going to Somersworth, I believe so did Angelina, Lydia went to Salem High, I believe Charlotte went to St Colide High or something in Fairfield, Adelyn, Mabel, and Pamela I don't recall, Elian went to Dickerson with Shayne,

Garret got lost in space somewhere lol, me and Daziel went to St. Bernard in West Dover, Nate I don't remember, Bruce I think left to Williamson, Seth went and moved on out to Pennsylvania. Also, I don't recall introducing you to Shayne but whatever, his mom owned Columbia Bakery around the block from the school just great place for desserts if you ever want to get diabetes lol. We loved sugar, garlic bread, and churros.

He actually went out with Lydia they were an alright couple; I would always help her out with her exxes and boyfriend problems, she always supported me and had my back she was a great friend I miss her funny ass. At this point everyone was getting ready for prom and graduation. We are having it at The Banquette on Route 19 like it never changes lol I guess the school had a contract with them or something every year it's at The Banquette lmfao. Then they tell us its chaperoned, which obviously they aren't going to let a bunch of 14-year-old kids party it out alone, but we didn't need 12 chaperones either lol. We all went and honestly no one really brought dates it was pretty much a class thing like the last time we would all be together just a cool vibe. So, Evander came and gathered us all up, all the guys so we leave and go downstairs to the parking lot and find a room. We walk into this room and somehow Evander pulls out this nice Cuban cigar. Evander pulls out matches and lights it and we are all talking and smoking and reminiscing about how fun the year has been. Someone I forgot who walked around the small ass room and finds a boiler, lol out of this big ass Banquette parking lot we manage to light a cigar in the worst place the boiler room lmfao. It made more memories we all thought "Fuck it if we die, we die" lol. After smoking maybe half the cigar then we went back upstairs we were gone for a bit and everyone was looking for us. The night was coming to an end, we ate and had a toast to the class it was a good night. It was a bit depressing when you realize you and all the people you grew with matured with are all taking separate paths now, not all of us were going to be in each other's lives but it was great being on the same path with these people.

Graduation came and went; I don't remember taking a picture with the class or anyone for that matter. We didn't really hangout that day everyone was with their family. Elian, Daziel, and me ended up hanging out later that night. So, let me explain and blueprint my house for the moment. The house I lived in on 13th street the front door had a small hallway where you would dry yourself off or put your umbrella so you wouldn't get the floor wet if it rained or snowed. Then it led to another door directly in front of it, and it lead to the main hallway, so 2 feet to the left there was a door which was Wela and Welo's living room, about 20 feet directly in front of you there was a door to Wela and Welo's kitchen, and adjacent to that door on the right was the basement. So standing in front of the door to the right at the 1 o clock was stairs leading to where I lived, so step, step, step, come on imagine it we are walking up the steps lol at the top of the steps to your immediate right there's a door to the kitchen, 10 feet to the left dun, dun, dun is my room, and adjacent to the right of my door is the door to the living room. So, if I explained that horribly you're welcome lol if you're piecing this together, you're beginning to see why I loved my room. My room was closed off from the rest of the house so I can come and go and sneak out as pleased lol, and I would do just that lol. But if I was hungry, I would just walk straight across the small walkway and get to the kitchen and make something to eat and not bother anyone. Daziel would call me around midnight wanting to go grab an iced tea from the Chinese restaurant at the corner of my block, or Elian would want to go hang out late at Bruce's or go skate at Fairfield Skate Park.

My room was small though lol little twin sized bed and a 5-drawer bureau and a 13-inch Sylvania television with a built in VCR where I would record my morning cartoons while I was at the bowling league every Saturday. Pretty much lived by myself I tell you; my room had a lock I had my key it was great. If Daziel, Elian, or Seth came to hang out we would never be in my house with just Daziel alone the room barely fit us. So, we would go to Daziel's or go biking by Bruce's house. I loved it I never needed a lot never have never will. Just this past weekend I slept on my friends' floor hardass floor, but I don't mind it's better than sleeping on a broken Cot damn it lol.

So, I kind of went off track and forgot what I was going to say. Any way one day during the summer me, Daziel, and Elian, meet up at Elian's house on 14th street to head out to Bruce's house, so Daziel had a bike Elian lent me his Pacific bike and Elian had his skateboard. So we decided to go through Bristol Ave up to Bruce's, so we head out we make a right at the end of Elian's block and come to Bristol Ave we were going to make a left but I saw the red light which was for us and that meant it was green for the cars on Bristol and there were cars coming so I decided to make the left on to the side walk while Elian and Daziel went on the street and let me tell you that was thee worsssssstttttt decision I have made on a bike lol I went left on to the side walk and bam what happened I don't even know lol. I woke up with the bike on top of me I was sitting on the parking, sign blood everywhere and I was told I was yelling for Elian and Daziel just calling their name. They came and picked me up and took me inside some random guys house and getting inside this dude's house all we see is some huge Siberian Husky, dog was massive we were like "oh what the fuck" lol. The guy gave me an ice pack and some type of alcohol for my cuts that shit burned man. Okay so apparently this guy had helped me out because he thought he hit me with his car, but after they went to investigate his car didn't have a scratch on it and I fell at the beginning part of the block this dudes house was 3 houses away but I ended up in front of his house, I don't really know how any of this happened. No one knows how I crashed but let me tell you that shit hurted. As they all walk back into the house apparently Daziel and Elian knew this guy's daughter lol Elian knows everyone as well. Elian was telling me that it was like a scene from in the movies, like one second they look at me then look straight because a car was coming the next, I disappeared lmfao. I wasn't mad but I thought it was pretty funny the way the explained it. The guy let me take the ice pack home because the back part of my head swelled up to the size of a baseball, and Daziel and Elian walked me back the amazing 2 blocks we made it lol.

We told my mom what happened and of course typical Hispanic mom response "see that's what you get for riding the street with cars coming" Elian and Daziel laughing in the background and of course my response "See how much you know I was on the side walk when this happened," she was worried clearly but she was just trying to prove a point that she didn't have lmfao. She asked me if I wanted to go to the hospital, I said fuck no fuck that lol. Everyone tried to convince me to go but, nah nope fuck that and I should have, that big ass knot on the back of my head took a long time to heal. Honestly since that accident I don't recall much of 6th grade or anything prior and sometimes I get headaches and discomfort in the same area where the bulge was, and I know head injuries are unpredictable, but I am still here lol, so I am grateful lol.

After taking some time to heal I got back on that bike and started riding everywhere again, 80th street park, Fairfield, Fredericksberg Heights, everywhere with and without Daziel and Elian. One day I was riding back from 80th street park and I though damn well I haven't seen Roland in a while, so I ride down Broad street, then to Pitsman Ave 67th street and I see he is there cutting hair, Roland's a good dude man, so I flip the bike over and head inside and say hi to his mom then go and greet him. "Yooooooo My Keyyyyyyyy" that's how he pronounces my name lmfaoooooooooo he literally says my then key like separately lmaoo funny ass dude love the kid. The 2 questions come "Do you want a beer?" and "Do you want a cut?" lol No I don't want a beer at 3 in the afternoon and I got a cut last week lol but thanks I appreciate it. I felt bad too because he was always in the middle of cutting hair and he would just stop to catch up with me lol. We just laugh and caught up and he tells me when the next parties are, he is hosting so I can go. Which he usually has 2 big parties, one to end the summer and the other to begin the school year or both in one lmfao. He has get togethers usually and periodically when he has open crib. So, I tell him alright bet I will go to the next one. Usually when I haven't seen him in a few months we hang out all night chill have drinks and support the youths of Salem and the West Dover area. There would be times when no one would come, and we would go eat at Pollo Supremo on Altoona Ave and just make fun of people lol. Or simply just hang out in front of the shop. So, one night the laundromat is across the street and the kid's real young like 10-11 years old are out being their young delinquent ass selves playing loud music and yelling and we head over there to see what the ruckus was about. The kids start break dancing and then me and Roland had to show them badasses off you know we weren't going to let these kids beat us, and someone pulled out a cardboard and Roland was like "watch this I'ma end this right now." So I see where this is going, but it can end pretty bad lol Roland tells all four kids to kneel on the card board while one of them and me watched what was about to unfold, and Roland starts walking back, I am thinking what the fuck where is he going, then he turns around and runs full sprint and completely front flips over all four kids that shit was crazy lmfaooooooooooooo. All the kids get up their like praising him and shit and he's like "yooo My Keyyyyyy" what's our motto and I reply "we do it for the kids" lmfaooooooo and one of their moms comes out starts yelling at us and shit but Roland knew her and he said we just playing with them and having fun but boy if he would have missed that front flip that would have ended bad lmfaooooo but that is his thing he does front flips all the time lmfao.

 Back to it I left from the barber shop and went to Fabien's house on Lock Haven Ave, and if I ever forgot to mention, if you are having a bad day you need a Fabien in your life. I get there and ring the doorbell same thing "Yooooooo my dude Mikey." Dudes were great I loved the St. Vincenzo family we started talking and catching up and he turns his head, and his eyes get huge and kid runs in the house and locks the door in my head I'm thinking what the fuck. So, he opens the door slightly and tells me to tell them he's not there and whoosh, he's gone again. So now after being lost like Waldo and confused like Psyduck lol see the Pokémon reference lol that was funny actually lmfao, anyways these two girls come up the stairs and the light bulb over my head turned on and I completely understood what he was talking about. They ask me is he there I said I am not sure I been here about 15 minutes knocking and ringing the bell and no one has opened yet I'm about to leave honestly, they said "oh ok thank you." They leave and Fabien pokes his baseball head ass out the door and asks what they say, I told him "nothing they said they were just looking for you," he said, "oh ok." Sooooooo clearly, I ask what was that about lol he says he slept with one of the girls and then stopped picking up her phone calls lmfao. I tell him "that's fucked up." He told me "she's crazy bro you don't even understand I had to stop picking up" lmfao. At this point and time was it funny yea, was it fucked up also yea. At that moment if I had known what happened I would have told them yeap he's home actually he's right behind the door lmfao just blow up his spot lmfaoo.

We finish catching up and I head back home. School and September are right around the corner, me and Daziel gather everything we need for class. Thing about it is me and Daziel and most of my friends all saw high school the same. Simply being more homework more essays, more shit we don't want to do. I never experienced that moment that they portray on television like oh my god school is starting this whole new chapter and experience of life I will have like no stop with that cornball shit. We never cared about any of that I don't recall anyone of my friend's male or female explaining that to me.

You know it's not really about depression many times, I am honestly just tired, I'm tired of living down in this basement, I'm tired of the daily routine, I'm tired of it being about everyone, I live my life for people trying to make everyone smile, heal them, make sure they are mentally stable and physically well, assessing their needs and providing for them. People have tried to tell me to be selfish to take care of yourself and I just don't understand why I can't allow that, at this point with this void I just simply don't care about anything anymore. Nothing has worked out for me and as hard and as much as I have tried to force that door of success open it just simply won't budge, but I am here, still pushing and still helping because I love you all so much.

Now comes the point where I hung out with Owen which whom I haven't seen nor heard from in nearly 10 years and I am truly happy how he has grown as a man, learned patience, and tasted success. I am proud of him he was going down a bad path and I was nowhere around to help him step in the right direction since I left for the military. One thing a fear that is my worst, he felt and expressed to me, which was just unusual, because at times we have the same thought process about certain life circumstances, but this was out of the ordinary. He explained my fear of success, which is the question of what comes next? He went from the gutter of Auburn to making six figures and being able to provide heavily for his family. The issue is he felt empty too, and he explained how he made all this money selling cars at a well-known dealership to taking his family on vacation to having no idea as to what is the next step in life, how he felt like he was just surviving.

As young men birthed and raised in poverty and having everything against us, having educators, principals, law enforcement, all telling us that living to or past the age of 18 is highly unlikely and against us, we tend to live in the moment because it forces us to believe there is nothing after 18, they think so low of us that we never learn to see a future past 18 and for those that do make it past the threshold not many become a success story and many come back to the city and get lost in the gang culture, and drugs, and homelessness and all negative aspects about life. Many people use that as a sort of reverse psychology to try and give us something to fight for but it is about the worst type of psychology I have ever experienced, because just like Owen who became successful he does not know what the next move in his life is since he survived and became a success. It is a difficult transition to look into the future and set a plan and try to live it out when all you are taught is to survive.

Now in where here comes my dilemma, depression not yet conquered but almost there, made it past 18 in which I almost damn near died in Elkton Hospital 2 months after I turned 18, I survived war, I made it back and now yet somehow I am still just simply surviving, been in school for 5 years no degree, just working towards nothing it seems to be. Then I have this story to tell, and let us say it becomes a success, let us say I do make it, I have several million dollars in my bank account, so the question becomes, then what? What is next? Where do I go? What am I to do? At the end of the day I have no girlfriend, I have no wife, I have no kids, honestly speaking I am 28 at the moment and I am still a virgin, and let us say I purchase the house I want, I purchase my favorite car, then what; is the question that remains? At the end of the day I go home to this house I open the door to what? Emptiness, another void, another hole that I am supposed to find a way to just simply fill with another form of a false sense of meaning by continuing to help people, it seems the vacancy will always be there and then at that point history has simply come full circle. So, what exactly is the point of it all?

Chapter 9

Freshman Year

Before I begin talking about Freshman Year, which is not really much, but I have been pretty down lately more than the usual because of the situation I am in. I just need people's honest opinion because I'm hurting.

You know, I yearn for the day that I am privileged to see my wife and child grow together. I want to see the day to day interactions between them, the love, and the bond, her thought process on why she would teach our child certain things and what our child can do with the information when they become of age. I would like to see the way she cares, how she teaches emotional support when our child gets hurt in the park and is searching and seeking the answer if they should cry or stand and be strong. That bond that is carried amongst them and how it vibrates throughout the house, I yearn for it and it is always on my mind, to think if I will ever have that pleasure to raise my child with my woman by my side and experience the latter.

I would love one day to wake up next to the love of my life and tell her I love her, kiss her, caress her, simply just to hold her but there is a very big possibility that will never happen and as much as I fight and have fought for it I see it is a losing battle for me. I feel soon enough I am going to have to come to accept the fact that it may never happen and if possible, I would adopt. After speaking to my brother about it he has a point as in we see certain aspects of life very similar even though we come from very different backgrounds and walks of life. He said, "Mikey you can't adopt," and I asked why? He replied, "well the child is going to need a mom" and it hit me hard because as I tried to deny that fact, he in turn is absolutely correct. So, another hopeless question remains, what am I to do?

Me being who I am I see all these guys just take advantage of their women, the situation, their children, I see it on a daily basis. Let me put it into perspective, I meet a girl who is pregnant and as the conversation is moving forward, she states she has to go to an appointment to see her physician because she was feeling ill. The father of the baby doesn't want to take her to the emergency room because he feels like she is constantly complaining during her pregnancy and it always turns up to be nothing. So he would just tell her make an appointment with her doctor and on top of that he would not even take her to the appointment, as sad as this is it's a daily occurrence, and the belittling the verbal abuse just what can I do, I try to help these people as much as I can but it is rough when the woman is dependent on the man and she believes she can't leave and just all the scenarios I can explain, but just seeing people take advantage of what should be a beautiful situation rite? Because life is beautiful I hope we all can agree to that, but it is simple she wants support that is your woman, that is your child, unconditional love and support should be genuine unless the basis of the relationship wasn't but that is a whole different conversation. She also does not just want it she needs your support your child needs your support so stop dismissing everything so quickly and just listen to what she is telling you. It is for a reason it is not to argue she feels something wrong and you must address it as a couple in a working relationship, and just thinking how I would be in the situation would be completely different and excited but people get complacent and people take advantage of situations and that is when you lose it all, so enjoy it no matter how hard it may be, as cliché as it may be you may never have the chance or opportunity again.

We are going back to the story, the first day of school comes and Daziel meets me at my house and we cross the street and grab the bus. We see all these people with the same uniform on and of course the cool kids are in the back, so we migrate to the back lol why you ask because we are fucking dope ass people that's why lol. We start talking and get to know everyone, I forget who we met I don't remember honestly but they were cool people we never really had problems. We finally get to school on the back side of 67th Street and Pitsman Ave.

Listen this school is a big ass box lol it is literally a huge square; the structure was so plain absolutely no thought was put into that architecture lmfao. Well compared to New Castle High school across the street this school looked plain, they had a bridge and everything and we, well we had the most basic layout ever lmfao. So, I get to homeroom because me and Daziel had different homerooms because it went by last names, the people in my homeroom were pretty cool, and Janessa, Kabir, and some others I don't remember. Anyway, class begins and walking through the halls I start seeing all these Valentine Crescent students which was a pretty cool feeling like I don't have to really do anything to meet people since I basically knew most of the juniors there. So transitioning wasn't really a problem for me for those that are going to ask. As these classes are going on you start seeing the cliques, football players, cheerleaders, and tough guys were usually the football players, the basketball players, the followers, pimps, quiet girls, and all that. I know it's literally the first day but when you begin observing and just keep an open ear to all the conversations going on you begin to learn who is who. It's not that it is completely obvious but as long as your ears are open you will hear the conversations.

So, the day continues, and lunch time comes and that is when you see and understand the cliques, and only the cool people played pool. I found Daziel and we sat at a table and just started talking to everyone there mind you this cafeteria food is horrible, I don't think I have ever been to a high school where they let you go out and eat lunch honestly. I have suffered my whole life lol. Bell rings and everyone is walking to their next class and I have to go to Spanish 1 class and I am thinking fuck well I hope what Daziel taught me helps lol because usually people in Spanish class are Spanish speaking kids that want an easy grade but that is not the case with me lol. I am looking for a seat and I find who of all people, my brothers from St. Vincenzo Lucas and Jerome eyyyyyyyyyyyyyyyyyyyyyyyyyyyyyyyyyyyy lol. They are both like "yooooooooooooo my guy Mikeyyyyyyyyyyyyyyyyyyyy" man was I happy lmfaooooooo. Of course, we start catching up, laughing, and bullshitting when all of a sudden, the teacher walks in. The whole class got quiet, she settles in and says good afternoon class my name is Ms. Savannah. Being in class with those two I knew it going to be a great year. First day of class and Jerome gets kicked out because we were in the back of the class disrupting, laughing, talking, and rapping lmfaoo. So, Jerome we already knew had a crush on her so he went up to her desk and started mumbling to her and apologized and she let it slide she let him stay in class just because he apologized and it was day 1. She let me and Lucas off the hook because we eventually stopped. She continued with her lecture and there was this girl that sat in front of Lucas and me. Her name was Kara and boy was she beautiful, and in front of her was this kid named Jeremiah. Me and Jeremiah didn't really get along got a weird vibe from him.

Any which way class ends, and the day is coming to an end, so I meet up with Daziel and we walk to Altoona Ave and catch the bus home. So, Altoona Ave at 3:30 – 4 o'clock is thee absolute worse time ever to grab a bus. There were times where we didn't get home until 5 from all that blasphemous traffic it was ridiculous. So the year starts to take off and I'm in gym class by myself I don't really know anyone there yet and everyone is doing their own thing. I found these kids playing basketball and during high school I was good I had handles had a good 3 point shot and always rebounded well. So, these kids were Alden, Ian, and Amiri. Alden and Ian were football players and Amiri was a part of the three best friends.

While playing basketball I had caught a rebound and went to the 3 point line and shot the ball, right after I shot it someone had called my name so I looked backed, and when I turn around I see the basketball flying at me full speed and it hit me a little lower than center chest around diaphragm and when it bounced off I caught it and was like "yo what the fuck is wrong with ya." All three of them stepped up to me so I stepped right up as well like what the fuck and Ian said "watch were the fuck you shoot that ball it hit my guy on the head," so I told them to relax it wasn't that serious someone had called my name it wasn't my fault they all gave a dirty look and that was that.

Now basketball is coming up and tryouts I couldn't even begin to tell you who was all there I don't even remember lol I tried telling you Freshman year was corny lol. Any way I make the team and from what I remember I had met a couple basketball players that didn't try out for the school and they were amazing ballers and they told me that there was no point in playing for high school and I realized why, way too late. I made the team and we were told when practices were and when the season was going to begin.

Back to class and in Ms. Savannah's room this day we are in class and I went up to the front of the classroom and sharpened my pencil. Then going back to my seat my pencil fell and Jeremiah was going to pick it up and Jeremiah is the jokester of the class had to admit that weird feeling was always there but that kid was funny as hell always made the class laugh and made the class fun. So I had thought he was going to steal my pencil and I saw him reaching down for it so what did I do lol I kicked the shit out of his hand lmfaoo and he got up like "yoooooo what the fuck that shit hurt I was trying to help you out but fuck you," then I felt real bad lol I was like "word really I thought you were trying to punk me and steal it" lol and he said "why the fuck would I do that" lol and we started joking and that was the day he became my best friend lol and damn near 14 years later we are still cool as fuck lol that's my dude though. From that day forward we got in real bad trouble in class because me and Jeremiah clicked like we been best friends forever and with Lucas, Jerome, we started talking to and involving more of the class and we got Kara involved and Ms. Savannah couldn't move us or kick us out enough she got to the point where it was like fuck it she just continued class and eventually we would stop and listen but even she got caught up with the jokes and discussions lol. I tell you one thing I didn't learn shit that year in Spanish 1 lol.

Moving to the next class we had class with let us call him Mr. Monotone lol at this point I have met enough people in all classes to have fun. In Mr. Monotone's class we had Dalton, Jeremiah, Kabir, me, and Cassie. Ok so out of respect and very much love for such an amazing friend of mine I won't say too much but at the time I barely knew her but listen Cassie man, just man, she was / is just a beautiful woman, so well gathered, educated, caring, genuine, she was just in a league of her own honestly and we all knew it, no one had a chance with her. So no one really tried, but she is just one of those amazing women you just never think you have a chance with because you don't think you're good enough for her honestly lol like when they say shoot your shot like nah buddy that's one long shot you not making lmfaooo. She ended up going out with Dalton, Dalton was dope cool as hell.

While in class this one boring lecture day someone had brought in the little pop pellets, the ones that are 25 cents at the store, you know the one you step on and they pop really loud. Mr. Monotone hates talking in class and hates people chewing gum in class, so I think it was either Jeremiah or Kabir had them and when the teacher looked away at the board to write something because this was a boring history class lol they threw it so hard and they threw a handful of them and all you heard was poppop, pop, pop, poppop, lmfaooooooo. He was so upset he turned around and was like "what was that" and Cassie's funny ass said "it was exploding bubble gum" lmfaoooooooooooooo. That shit was so funny the whole class started laughing and boy did he want to kick all of us out for that but couldn't so he made us sit quiet till class was over and he stopped teaching lol Jesus was that thee longest 35 minutes of my life lmfaoooooooooooooo.

So side story, the other night I was at work and we had some down time, Dr. Hammond started talking to us and he was explaining things I have been feeling for a very long time. Other than the chest pain which whatever I shouldn't be talking about this it is his business but, he was explaining that he had issues and didn't feel like himself. More in depth he explained that a couple times in the last week he felt different in the sense when he wrote out scripts for patients and had to sign it was difficult for him. He noticed that he had to think to write his signature, as people know it's such a subconscious act it comes out like a fluid motion without thinking about it. In my head I was like shit doc I been feeling like that for years no two signatures of mine look remotely alike. I can't explain why I always have to think about how I write my name in script and I try to think about my previous signature and it is nowhere close and I have never been able to explain why, but hearing him talk about what he was going through honestly didn't help lol but understanding that I wasn't the only one going through something so weird for such a long time and constantly dismissing it helped a bit. After the chest pain and feeling not like himself he felt he couldn't dismiss it any more honestly you know he has his family and kids and he has an important job that he is very good at so I understand why he let it go on for a short amount of time. It was really only for a week for him, I'm several years into my symptoms and still dismissing it. I am a bit different though a part of me doesn't really care and the other part knows somethings wrong but understands there is nothing I can do about it either way.

Secondly, I spoke with a brother of mine that I haven't seen in a while and he was in a bad place he was involved in a motorcycle accident and was in a coma for about 3 weeks I believe almost a month. Seeing videos of him just trying to get up and walk 10 feet shit just broke me honestly. I have seen this kid run 2 miles in 12 minutes do nearly 100 pushups and sit-ups in 2 minutes and he is an exceptional athlete he was a football player, and to go from that to struggling on a walker to walk 10 feet was rough for me to see. Being in the situation previously I know where his paths leads, people usually just send their best regards and prayers and all that corny ass generic ass shit. I am not like that all that shit tells me is that you don't care. As far as in the future I can see and as much love I got for my brother I needed to reach him. Coming to an understand that recovery will take years if he actually does recover or honestly, he will have residual aches and pains for life and after he explained he recently had his last spinal surgery I knew the path was going to be even harder. Coming to this conclusion and previously being and seeing people in this situation as I said previously, I told him I understand what he is going through and I know he will heal fast and he will be back to himself in a shorter timespan than what the physicians have told him because he is a strong kid and takes very good care of himself. There are some hills that will be harder to climb. I told him listen there are days where he will try to be back to his normal self and won't be able to do the things he once used to and when that time comes it will come with a sadness and depression but don't fall into it. You know being dependent on people because you can't do simple daily tasks you once were able to do will be difficult to overcome but when you feel that way simply give me a call and we'll get through that day together. The day will come the nights will be long and dark you'll feel alone you are going to want to leave because you feel like such a burden on people and you have to understand that you are not. You are surrounded by people who genuinely love you and are trying to help you get back to your old self, some days it may seem they dismiss you because you know they do have a life to live and other priorities to deal with not saying that you're not one of them but one day they will have to put you second and of course that day will be the day you will be at your lowest and you have to rise up over it because it is simply just an odd day out, so always make sure you have someone to talk to.

My point is we have to help each other, we are at a time in life where the word friends is a common word people just throw around. We are in a time where people simply just go after money as if money will take care of you when you're depressed, when you're down, when you're at your lowest, when you need someone there to hug you and to tell you everything will be alright as if some inanimate object will care for you. Money can do a lot of things but one thing it cannot do is love you back.

We have lost several brothers to suicide and can it have been prevented no one will ever know I don't have the answer to that, and we keep losing them a friend of my other brother just took his life recently as well. We just have to do better; I have a lot of friends and I haven't been able to be a good friend to call and check up on everyone. There are just so many and I am going through my own difficulties, but I try and call some every now and then, but it is just difficult to keep up and constantly checkup on them. The way me and my brothers are, if I can't call or checkup I will ask another brother to call and check up on others that I know are not doing well and it is vice versa they tell me who I have to call and talk to, the ones that turned to drugs, the depression, their wives took all and left them with nothing, the PTSD from our time in Afghanistan, we had a friend get shot in the head and was knocked out we though he was dead but the night vision goggle saved him, the brothers I have that are in a difficult situation financially, the ones that are simply lost because they feel they have no purpose in life any more I have a lot of people to help and they are on my mind daily, the alcoholics you know, simply put I have seen alcohol solve several people's problems as much as you guys want to deny it I have seen it but at the end of the day after alcohol has solved all your problems, alcohol then becomes your problem. That downward spiral it leads is just sad man coming back from that is a very difficult task and no one can do that by themselves that's why we have to do better I have to do better. We have been through a lot and we will discuss it here later but it is rough so my people that are going through it, hold on tight there are people that care and we will get to you trust in me we will.

Simply just thinking about this, there was a girl whom I haven't seen or spoken to in years and she has been posting just things that aren't ok. Well to me they are not ok to others it seems ok but I have been helping and studying people for a very long time so something very subtle I know what it means to that person and I can hear that person calling for help. So, she had posted something, and I just knew it was time to contact her and see what was going on. So an explanation of some shortcomings, when someone says they have been busy and haven't had any time to talk or contact people because they have been working a lot and doing an immense amount of overtime to most people that's completely understandable but not for me. I know people and that is the simplest excuse someone can give because it is very believable to the people, they surround themselves with in their little micro world. Me I cannot dismiss that because I know that is a lie, to me that is called isolation, and I know that isolation is one of the beginning stages of suicidal ideation. At that point I had to reach out I cannot afford to lose anyone else no matter if we haven't spoken in years or what not, allowing people to feel as if they are alone is something I cannot allow. It took a couple weeks to meet up and hang out, but we hung out for several hours and she explained the situation she was going through which I understood and gave her advice on but that's not what I was there for. After a few hours she got there and told me she did have thoughts of suicide at one point within the past several months and she broke down and started crying and there it was and I told her that I knew and I saw the signs and that I was there for her, that is all she needed was someone to be there for her I hugged her she cried it out and we continued to talk, and it was a huge relief to her knowing that she wasn't alone and that she had someone to confide in, no matter how difficult life gets we have to be there for each other and this day and age there aren't many people that care but there are people like me around and we see the simplest signs and we reach out. I need people to know that life's inevitabilities are not supposed to be everyday stressors. Things will get better even if it gets worse before it gets better. Trust that, you shouldn't have to worry about things that are out of your control and that life will have its way and there is nothing you can do about it so why stress about it. There is no point, you are killing yourself and compromising your health over things that life will control and you have no say in, so please let it go and go live your life, go accomplish your goals, go travel, start a business, do what makes your heart smile and allow yourself to live the life you know that you deserve. All you people that have problems and think you are alone don't worry I will take care of you and the people like me will find you guys and heal you one way or another, so go do what pleases your soul and makes you happy and forget about the things you cannot control.

Back to school, in English class I had Jeremiah, Dennis, Cassie, Jake and his girl, and Yoel. Jake and Yoel were both football players and Jake was a part of the best friend circle of Alden, Amiri, and Ian, Jake was cool as hell. Our teacher Ms. Gorgianna was this small innocent young woman man was she cool as fuck though. Our class got way out of hand for her to handle because she was so nice lol. She really despised yelling and felt bad about kicking anyone out of class but we had respect for her because she was so down to Earth and nice that we didn't really know when we got out of hand but she would look like she was about to cry and she would call us out like guys come on its too much and when we would realize, we would stop but mainly

Jeremiah was just a funny kid man, I don't know where he got his humor from but he would try and stop but his jokes would be so funny that Ms. Gorgianna herself couldn't stop from laughing and there went the whole period just gone from laughter and learned absolutely nothing lol. So the next day she would move Jeremiah to the back of the class or to the front and turn his table around facing the class and says ok Jeremiah today we have to learn so no talking but she wouldn't notice the faces he would make and just make us laugh more lol. So she started isolating him to the back and it worked for a while until she let him sit with us again and we calmed the joking and stuff. She was great though, great teacher.

Basketball season is moving and like by game 7 I understand what everyone was telling me about hating Basketball. So, what they do Mr. Krystiano and the other coach I forget his name they take all the football players and let them take over the court. It always turns out bad lol everyone wants to be cool and try and dunk and play like its street ball. It is organized basketball this isn't us in the hood playing ball and trying to cross everyone on the court to show off our skills and man were we just loosing every game lol. I was about ready to drop out of the team, and at this time Daziel started in the swim team I believe mid-November early December, and he was convincing me to join but Marcel was on the team and we had bad blood from St. Vincenzo so I avoided the team and stuck it out in Basketball.

The year is moving along, and I jumped a lot in the past 2 paragraphs lol Freshman year was corny but something very sad happened this year and the city changed because of it. So, a week before Christmas just some reason everyone wanted to go to McDonalds on Altoona and get something to eat. I wasn't very hungry at the time and I was tired, and I had a long walk home. So, I left everyone at McDonalds and started making my way home. At this time I am passing Columbia Bakery Shayne's mom's bakery, and I see all the Dickerson kids walking home and I am only a few blocks away from the house now thinking I can get some rest so at the end of 14th and Altoona I turn left to walk down the block to New Post Avenue where I live and I see a whole group of Dickersinians lol huddled at the end of the block. My first thought was, shit a fight now I have to be aware clearly because I have many friends in Dickerson High so just to be on the safe side let me make sure it's no one I know.

That was the wrong idea, there was a car at the corner just blocking traffic, I get to the huddle get through the huddle and come to my knowledge it was a gang fight, no it was a slaying they stabbed this kid multiple times and ran to the car that was blocking traffic and sped off. The amount of blood there, this young kid was bleeding out dying stabbed at 3 in the afternoon broad daylight it was sad man. We were all there and several friends that I have now were there we just didn't know each other at the time and such a sad day no one could do anything for him he was stabbed center chest and just waiting for the ambulance and seeing them take him and all for what? He passed and the assailants were caught and tried. I won't say who passed just for respect, but the city was just never the same. And to live 3 doors down from where it happened it's not about me it didn't affect me and every time now, I pass by I say a prayer and show my respect because they took everything down and it was just sad. No one should ever go through that and recently well yea last month nearly the same situation happened with a young teenager from the Bronx and involved the same gang but the teen wasn't a part of any gang which doesn't justify anything anyway but just being hemmed up like that is incomprehensible man it is just wrong. Lexington City just wasn't the same anymore after that.

Then Daziel got into a fight with Alden which was Daltons friend and that was fucked up, I didn't know what happened and I get to class and the teacher is my basketball coach, Coach Krystiano and he is asking me why I didn't help Daziel in the fight and I said what when was he in a fight and he responded just a few minutes ago before class.

I told him I didn't know and Daziels a man he can handle himself in a fight but what happened if I remember correctly was that Alden had a ring on and hit Daziel and when Daziel went to swing and punch back, I believe Yoel stopped him. So, this situation isn't really important, but the context is because if you know Dalton and the crew, they all live in Fredericksberg Heights.

Which means we all take the bus downtown together, so now how do we take the bus together when there's tension between friends and friends of friends. Back in the day there were rules, street codes there were just things you didn't do. Not saying we are from the street or in gangs or were ever a part of that life style but as men we followed certain code of conducts and had a certain level of respect, because now a days kids don't care if you live next door to them let alone ride the bus down town with them they will just wipe you off the face of the planet simply for likes or to be cool. So, with the level of respect we all had for each other it was just a decision to either keep fighting or end the feud. At the end of the day they put aside their differences and ended the feud, they still didn't like each other which was fine, but they didn't fight or respond back at each other which was the accelerant.

Then on top of all that what happened on Christmas day the news was flooding in that a tectonic plate shifted in the Indian Ocean. There were sirens and signal going on all around the globe rite because the Earth is round lol, I hope we can agree lol, it was a Tsunami siren. They had said that the Tsunami could pretty much reach anywhere and several hours later we got the news that Indonesia was just demolished and day after day after day the death toll just seemed to never stop rising it was pretty devastating and honestly I personally didn't know anyone that was directly affected by it so it didn't really hit me hard and at this point in my life things didn't bother me if it didn't really affect me I put no energy towards it as rude as that sounds but to have that happen on Christmas and that week was pretty shitty and I did feel bad for all the people that died but now 14 years later we hope that the families that survived have recovered and are doing well.

Back to class after break in Science class our teacher she explained how the whole earthquake caused the Tsunami and she was very religious and what not, so we did a project about earthquakes and some other stuff I don't recall. Pretty much now we are in January and things get a bit weird, so I became friends with many people and me and Marcel actually became pretty good friends, Cassie was always cool as fuck, Jeremiah we played a lot of ball since he introduced me to Miller Park, I became cool with Lara through Cassie or I don't remember but they were both cheerleaders and in the homeroom next to mine, Alden and Ian we got pretty cool after they finally broke realized how funny class was when we would make fun of the teacher together and they realized how many people I knew we all got cool. At one point there was a huge fight out in Somersworth between two street gangs which were if I remember correctly. Lucas had told me about it and what not, then all of a sudden at school the classrooms started to get real small. There would go days where some kids just wouldn't show up or weeks go by and you see a few kids there maybe 5- 6 times in a month I don't know what the hell happened but some kids just never showed back up to school at all and that fight in Somersworth couldn't be the cause for it because most kids from St. Bernard were from everywhere not just Warwick County so maybe it was a coincidence but shit just got weird and class got quiet without the funny kids. Daziel at this time had his girl which was Janet and Janet had a friend named Mia and she was cute as fuck but not for me at that time. I just went around hanging out with anyone that didn't have curfew. I met a lot of people it was a good time anytime I went out.

As the year continues in English class with Ms. Gorgianna, we are at the point of Edgar Allen Poe, and Shakespeare and E.A.P was the man great poet weird but great writer and we read the weird Count of Monte Cristo or Cask of Amontillado. Something to that level it was crazy because in the story they guy got bricked alive and I remember thinking what type of shit goes on in peoples head to even write a story or poem like this, where this guy gets buried alive lol. then Shakespeare had a play where everyone in the play died like I don't know man but at this point I wrote a lot of poetry pre high school and I wrote a lot well, not to say a journal of sorts but call it whatever you like, and this notebook did not leave my side by any means. Never did I leave that notebook or ever forget it anywhere, and Cassie used to ask me all the time what was that notebook or what was in it because I never took it out in any class it always stayed on my desk but I never opened it to take notes in so she knew it was different like I tried telling you that girl is something special and her attention to detail and her intuition was just different she was well ahead of her time, and let me tell you now before we get to it that I love that girl and her family, she took care of me during some rough years and her family was very welcoming and genuine and I appreciate it greatly she is just an amazing woman, her and her family will always have a special place in my heart for how amazing they all are and just honest caring people. When Cassie used to ask me what was the book I straight up lied to her every time lol, I felt so bad that I had never let her in but man was she so out of my league I gave myself all the excuses to not approach her lmfao.

She turned into an amazing friend though and I am glad she was around when she was, but that book that she had so questioned me about is this book that I am writing these words right here and at that time I just couldn't let anyone in on this. I started writing this literally in 7th grade and the only person that has seen the words in the book is Ms. Gorgianna because she wanted to see the poetry I wrote and she loved it and she knew how protective I was about this notebook she respected it she took the notebook home one day and literally read all its contents and brought it back and waited for everyone to leave the class to give it to me personally without anyone knowing and I will always respect her for it. Cassie pressed me about it too because she saw me without the notebook that day and was like did you lose it or forgot it because that's weird you always have it on you lol I was like dam Cassie why you notice everything lmfaoooooo I love her so much she was great. You know thinking about this shit now she would have to get the first copy of this book lol probably owe her an apology to lmfaoo because if she knew what this was back then she would have supported me from then, damn I do kind of owe her apology lol my bad Cassie love you always.

So yesterday was a bad day, ok scratch that this weekend is a bad weekend. You have been on my mind and just lately everyone has been annoying me or irritating me and I have been responding back when I shouldn't have it wasn't their fault and I shouldn't have treated them the way I did. Thinking about it, it reminds me how still human I am and how I make these mistakes that I can easily avoid especially being so in tune with my emotions and having been able to learn how to control them and how many years it took me to get here. But just thinking about you and not knowing how you are doing it gets to me from time to time and I slip up when I shouldn't but it is ok I tell myself you know at the end of the day I am still human so it will continue to happen from time to time I just try to control it as much as possible but some days are harder than others and I wish you were still around, I don't have anyone to talk to so it kind of sucks and honestly no one will understand any of this anyway but I can't blame them, one day things will be better, when that day is I am unsure of but I hope it is soon. On the bright side, the really bright side I crossed paths recently with an exceptional young woman. Ok so before everyone asks is she beautiful well yes but I honestly haven't look at her physically all I can say is that she is slim with great facial features but honestly speaking her eyes are captivating to me she is gorgeous but just seeing her and her smile her beauty just radiates through it alone. She is extremely nice, but you know I meet a lot of nice women and my heart and soul do not take to them.

We talked a bit more day and day and nothing hit, it was just nice having someone genuine to talk to that was interested in the conversation I haven't had that in a couple years. Then something happened I don't know what or how she disguised it but her aura leaked and boy let me tell you that is when it hit and it stuck and I absolutely fell for this girl straight up cliché head over heels and it is absolutely embarrassing the feelings I caught for her. I was just confused honestly why I didn't catch it at first because I always do with everyone she is thee first that bypassed me and I just didn't understand how or why she is very easy to focus on and have a conversation with and easy to feel her emotions so how did I miss it. As we continued to talk I found out that she has some misleading beliefs then I realized how innocent she was and her age well she is younger than me by a few years and to add that in with the city she grew up in, but everything started to add up and then I realized she doesn't know who she is. So, it is not that she disguised it, she hasn't developed into this amazing special young woman that she will become, but she is so amazing already I had thought that she knew, and I was completely wrong. Her aura wasn't disguised she honestly just doesn't know how special she is, and she is not conscious about it and that is why I didn't catch it at first, and man does she mean a lot to me. She has put me in a tight spot because there are a few decisions to be made and no matter which decision I make I will be the one getting hurt, and of course it is better me than her always but why does the universe send me these women and at the end of the day she will end up leaving I will never talk to her again nor see her again and I will end up yet again losing such an amazing woman. As long as she moves forward with the right knowledge of who she is and how special she is, and I put her on the path with her beliefs straight than I am happy to have crossed paths with such an exemplary woman any day.

With that being said let me explain this a bit better because in September of 2017 I met a very special young woman named Clarissa. Clarissa when I saw her I already knew how special she was, her aura was leaking out everywhere and with such a big cool aid smile on her face always coming into class with a positive attitude even though some days she has empty look on her face you can feel that she was just not ever down depressed or sad it was just a good feeling being around her. So, I needed to find out who she was, I needed to talk to her. Our teacher wanted us to do homework from the book and I never bought the book so he said find someone in the class and take pics of the book to be able to do the homework, so where did I go I went straight to her and took pics of the book and I had absolutely no intention of doing the home work lmfao, then I asked for her number and I think I told her just if I had any questions if I could hit her up and she said yea of course. So, none of the latter occurred lmfao I did not do the homework and I did not hit her up lmfao. I think a couple weeks went by and either she missed class or I did and I don't remember who hit who up first I am not going into texts it's not that important honestly and yea I have all my texts I don't hide anything and I don't delete anything I never needed to. Any which way we started talking and this girl is exceptional and phenomenal just getting to know her and she is funny great sense of humor so as the semester comes to an end we are sitting outside class waiting for our exam results and I sat next to her and I was tired so I put my head on her shoulder or her lap I don't recall and she started caressing me and playing with my hair and it felt good and I didn't feel anything no pain, no void, no emptiness, I just felt good. Then it came to me she is a true healer. She is extremely special a very rare type of woman, these women can just be in the room, or give you a look, or simply sit next to you and you will feel cured of all your problems. Simply just being in the presence of Clarissa or a healer was an experience of its own, it wasn't about her beauty but she is extremely beautiful let us just establish that right now if I didn't previously, but being around her, a simple smile from her can warm your heart and heal those wounds you're walking around with, talking to her, listening to her speak man do I appreciate those things. So the last day of class I bought her a rose and gave it to her because she is very special so she deserved it and I can also tell she hasn't received a rose or anything nice from someone in a while and she wanted to go out and eat but I know she works and I didn't really want to intrude on her day because we didn't have plans so I felt kind of bad but she reassured me that she didn't have work so she took me to a very nice place to eat I don't remember where it was but that's ok. So I talked to her about what I noticed and how special she was and it felt a bit weird so I apologized for it honestly it did sound weird or crazy because some women don't believe in what I am talking about or think you're simply just crazy for this weird ass shit or can't accept nor don't want to accept it which is all ok in every sense. But she had told me that it wasn't weird and that I wasn't the first to tell her that. She ended up explaining to me how her friend was throwing a party and invited her and she really wasn't in the mood to go, and her friend stated that she didn't have to stay long or something like that but just showing her presence and just being around will make everyone happy and this explains two things. One that there are other people like me even though they don't have in depth knowledge or have studied people women mainly the way I have but when there are special women they let them know in their own way even if they don't understand it, that they are special and that is important, two that they let these woman know they are wanted and needed around and are important to their micro family and friends and society as a whole. Clarissa was very nice to me and I appreciate all she has done for me and the conversations we shared, she is an amazing woman and I wish her the best in her life, she will become an exceptional mother and an amazing wife, she does deserve the best I don't believe there is anything more to say about that, she is just a great person with a warm heart.

These women that I speak of and will continue to talk about are important to us which are the people they cross paths with and society as a whole. We have to take better care of our women because we are not doing a very good job with that but these special women we must tend to differently, we must care for them differently not simply because they are special but they are also more fragile than the rest. So the way we talk to them, the way we approach them, there really is no room for error because when these women get hurt, or feel like there is an agenda behind the socialization they will close themselves out not only to you but to the rest of the world. They are important because their viewpoints, their way of analyzing situations, the way they approach situations and deal with them, the way they learn is all very different from the common woman, and there are various other reasons why and I will explain them all. But we simply must begin taking better care of our women in general. Can we talk about something very quickly since everyone likes theories and all that, we can call this The Theory of Motherhood Compatibility, which states the better we treat our women the better our children will be raised. You guys can take the credit for that if you want, I really don't care, but I hope I am dealing with intelligent people and not people that are thinking what gender role bullshit am I talking about. I say and explain this theory in context to mean that in an inarguable statement, the better we treat our women the happier she will be overall, so your child will be able to see the day to day social interactions between you and your woman, they may not be able to understand it but one thing children understand well is energy. And the energy radiated from a happy and blissful woman and mother will be understood by your child. Instead of the arguing and yelling, the back and forth for senseless reasons, the child will take to that and will be happy and enjoying this life they live. Being able to see their mother and father or father figure diverging into conversation that leads to laughter and positive energy the child will take to that and grow with it and hold that for the rest of their life.

They will be able to say that mom and dad had a pretty good relationship they would be able to explain that dad or mom didn't yell very much because when they had issues they had great communication and talked things through and as we are all humans of course they will yell from time to time but they will also be able to explain that they can't remember very many times they have seen it or if they have they would explain that it was maybe a handful of times that it had happened and from birth to adolescence a handful of yelling arguments is an accomplishment to those that argue and yell back and forth day to day minute to minute. Every time they answer the phone they sigh because they know it is just an argument and that we as adults need to stop. We need to reevaluate ourselves take better care of our women, and in turn we will have a better relationship and path to take better care of our children and raise our children in a more appropriate manner.

I believe in all honesty we have to give women back their power, and I am unsure as to why we are scared as a society to do so. We all know what we ask from our women, we ask that they take our name and we ask for their hand in marriage, we ask that they change their physique and nurse our children for 9 months, we ask for constant support and unconditional love, we ask that they leave their families behind to start a family with us and take care of our kids while we work, we know how strong are our women so why is it that we fear giving them the power they are already holding but unable to use. Without the support of our women the undeniable truth is that we as men would be lost. This fallacy that we live by that our women are solely used for sex because truth be told that is why most relationships these days are ruined because of cheating and having sex with another person which usually is the man that cheats, this we have to change. We tend to make women believe that sex is the way to a man's heart, and it is not. Sexually Desired Love is a feeble love, it is brittle and easily broken; this type of love is a fallacy, one must be careful due to the power of lust which clouds and manipulates the soul into believing it has found another genuine soul but has not. Sex does not lead to love, but love does lead to sex they are by comparison 2 different emotions and paths. To be promiscuous is ok but to use promiscuity to find love or make someone believe they have found love is wrong and we need to stop ruining our women like this. I have met plenty of women who believe they can find love through sex and they have sex as much as they can then they become labeled a hoe or slut but in reality it is not the case you cannot label someone if they are unconscious about what they do many of these women simply want to bond and they use sex because they know that sex pretty much rules men, and after we label these women we ruin them and they feel like they lose their chance in society to find love. I diverted a bit but we just simply need to care better for our women and simply stop using them unless you're both agreed in an open promiscuous relationship then ok go live your life no one cares and no one is judging you but these other women we need to take better care of as men and as a society as a whole.

So, this amazing vivacious beautiful young woman that I recently fell in love with, I am at a crossroads with her. If I tell her who she is it may scare, her for reasons being either she won't understand because it is too early, or it may seem too strong and I am coming from an angle with an agenda. But who am I to deter someone's growth at the expense of how I feel about said person. I am not one to place myself above others ever, but I don't want a chance to compromise someone's growth and development. But if the reward outweighs the risk than the decision is already made and I am just wasting paper, because in the end the probability is very high that I am going to lose her, and she has become very important to me in my life. She has given me peace something I never thought possible post Jaylene. Simply just knowing I will see her and give her a hug and be able to smile because her soul and heart are so gentle and warm and welcoming and innocent is an unfathomable feeling, I haven't felt in almost 10 years. It was weird because she enveloped me in this peace and resolve that I didn't believe was possible because usually when I think about women from my past I tend to cry a lot from the pain and when I spoke to her about a certain ex-girlfriend it felt ok I didn't feel emotional I didn't feel I was going to cry everything just felt ok like it was just peaceful like everything was resolved and to experience it and knowing it is going to be gone again is painful. The situation is, this amazing woman that I would like to devote and dedicate a chapter to because she just simply deserves it I don't know if I can yet and for the moment she will remain Nameless, is I would like to be in a relationship with her but at what expense because the way she makes me feel is worry some to me and it took me many years to control my emotions and with her it is such a struggle, I would like to talk to her every day be around her all day long listen to her talk about her thoughts hold her kiss her caress her simply appreciate her presence but I can't because I am not allowed such privileges because I am not her boyfriend we are not in a relationship and even though it may be possible it still won't be possible because she is striving to achieve her goals and I wouldn't want to get in the way or compromise any of her goals or ambitions because if she does fall for me and realizes how extensively hurt I am and sees how deep my wounds are I fear that she may try to heal them and that is not her job and I feel that I may allow her to do so and thinking about this I can't be that selfish and I can't use people for personal gain, even if it is not defined as so because I do love her I cannot take someone down that path if it will compromise their health and wellbeing and future and then back to square one I go because I will lose her and she will move on with her life rightfully so and all I will have are the few moments we shared these past 6-8 months and that peace and tranquility that she gave me I will have to hold on to and place it near and dear to my heart. I do appreciate all she has done for me and she has no knowledge of what she has done for me and I may tell her but it may be too strong for her to hear so I have yet to decide that but

I believe that she should know how she helps others I believe that it would be beneficial to her growth and development.

It feels like it is over. Just slipped rite through my hands. It felt good to cross paths, I never thought I would ever experience that feeling again she made all the pain go away by just hearing her voice. I guess in all honesty it is what's best because I can't use her to cure my pain but that was never my intention I just realized that is what she was doing to me and I appreciate it so much so I will hold all our conversations and time we spent together very near and dear to my heart. As much as these women come and go in my life they teach me a lot about myself and I learn so much from them so in the end how can I be upset or sad when I appreciate all they do for me and most of them don't know what they have done for me or what they have showed me but learning from them is a privilege I am proud to have every so often when we cross paths and honestly speaking this is about the rite time no one ever stays longer than 8 months 6-8 months is average and I adore and appreciate all the moments we have ever shared.

I have derailed off the story I guess it is time to get back to high school and finish because there is a lot that develops and things to be discussed so I appreciate everyone's patience, I guess we will get back to it.

So continuing Freshman year since the classes got a bit smaller our Freshman class got pretty close with an exception of several people. Not all of us would hang out together but we definitely made class fun. In Spanish class I walked in and the room just look weird and I ask Jeremiah and Lucas "yo we got a test "they said yea dude lol you didn't study" and of course my answer was no.

So, Lucas had his cheat sheet and Jeremiah is mad Spanish, so he was cruising for an easy A in the class Kara sat too far from me during tests and Jerome wasn't there, so I was fucked. So, I made a quick cheat sheet small and simple. Ms. Savannah walks up and down the isles during exams, so my thought was watch when she comes so I just toss the paper out. The test started and mid test she got up and started walking and I was like fuck it's too early and holding on to the sheet was the worst decision lol. I knew it too because she was walking fast and bam, she caught me and kicked me out of class gave me a 0 for the exam. Lucas and Jeremiah of course laughing which I don't blame them it was pretty funny lol they were like "yo you dumb as fuck should of just took the chance and failed it" and I told Lucas "shut the fuck up dude you cheat all the time" lol he said "yea but I don't get caught" lmfaooo well I couldn't argue with that statement lmfao any who, I talked with Ms. Savannah after class and she said she would only give me a 50 for the exam if I did some crazy assignment like 10 chapters doubled by tomorrow and I did, fuck that I couldn't get a 0 and she made me sit in the front of the class for every exam until the year ended lol I was cool with it. The thing is everyone thinks because I'm Hispanic that I am born fluent in Spanish lmfao I try to tell everyone the only people that really spoke to me in Spanish were my grandparents and I barely understood what they were saying so I always had a huge communication barrier as you guys learned in previous chapters I needed a translator while in church that should pretty much define how much Spanish I know.

Any way on an embarrassing note lol for some reason the first 2 years of high school I usually got sick around Easter time I think April May timeframe. This day I was just not having it, I felt weird, so I went to the nurse station and of course she said nothing and gave me nothing and didn't let me go home and shit I was just going to fucking walk out. But walking out of her office and the main office downstairs, I didn't feel good and there were 2 girls down the hall and I just vomited all over the floor and they saw the whole thing that shit was so embarrassing lmfaoo then the nerve of the nurse to be like "oh are you ok you want to go home" like yea and I aint coming back all week the fuck I tried to tell you but me and school nurses don't get along at all I felt like they just didn't know what they were doing because they didn't work at the hospital. So, I called my grandfather and he came and picked me up like the champ he is and watched over me he was a great man I love him so much. The week wasn't very long either I think all that happened on Wednesday, so I went back Monday any who, school is coming to an end and a very unproductive Freshman year lol but met a lot of people.

So, the year comes to an end and Summer comes, I begin hanging out with all the people I met Freshman year Jeremiah, Marcel, always Daziel, Asher, just everybody. Most of the time I would hang out with Marcel and then Daziel and after Daziel I would go to my cousins house up the street from Daziels. My cousins name was Gavin, he and all my other family members are all smart they all went to school together from Warwick, to Lincoln, to Dickerson and all of them were very smart with electronics they all knew computers from inside out but also video games and consoles and anything really and the time they grew up they were very popular. So, Gavin told me he was starting work at a Rec center for the Summer and asked me to apply so his mom got me an application from the Board of Ed, and I got the job. A few weeks into July we started working and he introduced me to the other supervisors or chaperone's, or I don't recall what they called us and one of them was a girl and we will call her Ms. P. She was mad cool we all got along and she had a brother which was a part of the Rec group his name was Gunther he was starting high school next year so we all started talking and come to find out Gunther was coming to St. Bernard. I didn't see him having any issues in the school he was funny and mellow down to Earth. The week passes by at the Rec Center and they pulled me from the Chaperone spot I can't recall why but they were offering me another job at Fairfield Sewerage Authority, but it starts at a later date in the beginning of August. So, I was cool either way I didn't need a job, but they offered me, so I waited.

As I await, I start hanging out again and after playing basketball with Asher in some small park by his house I think to myself, well shit I haven't seen Roland in a while let me pass by since I'm walking home. At the time I walked everywhere no matter how far or how inconvenient the walk was if I wanted to hang out, I was going to be there. So Asher lived by Glendsdale / Somersworth area and the Barber Shop was down in Salem by Broad St lol and if you know the area that's a bit of distance and not on my way home to 13th street lol I just say that simply because it is walking down town. I get there and he was dressed up and cutting someone's hair and seemed sad. I also didn't get any questions about beer or a cut, so I knew something was up, so he was telling me one of his friends had died. So quick before I get to that story, this time in I don't want to say Lexington City really, but the streets were changing and for the worse or worst don't really know which term to use any way I don't care lol. So at this point in the streets it was a time were the one on one fights were becoming obsolete, the shoot outs were on the rise for just outrageous reasons, machetes were becoming more relevant it was just a time you did not want to involve yourself in gangs or fights just was not the time.

So, as he begins to explain the situation about his friend, he says that his friend got into an altercation and when this situation occurred there were a lot of people around. The guy that Roland's friend let us call him Melvin, beat up was in a gang and the gang was there when he lost the fight. So, Melvin was visiting someone in the Fairfield projects and in an unfortunate turn of events that kid was there and so the gang provoked another fight and Melvin fucked him up again and the kid ended up shooting Melvin because many reasons other than losing the fight. Roland being who he is warned me about the Fairfield projects and honestly I didn't know the Fairfield projects got down like that but he warned me and asked me to stay out of there if I had no business being there and even if I did to make it quick. He had to go to the funeral, so we went our separate ways and I knew I had to come back and check up on him after the funeral. The way I grew up with my friends we all had this conscious we didn't take to phone calls very well if something was up if we needed to talk come over my house bro don't call me just show up, you mad, got family or girl issues we never called we just went to each other's house. No one would care either it didn't matter what time the day, nothing just show up and we will talk and take care of what we had to take care of. It was great but now listen man show up to someone's house uninvited lmfaoo.

Any who I start working at the Fairfield Sewerage Authority and you know the first few days are safety videos and this and that. So, the second week comes, and I meet all my supervisors and this kid who also is working there, and his name is Jonas I believe he goes to Fairfield High he was cool. You know this crazy detail they had me on they fucked up their Material Safety Data Sheet and I had to go page by page and reorganize it Jesus Christ that was a long week and a half of just that just massive book so while I was doing it Jonas was laughing at me thought it was funny lol and he was a funny kid well not really a kid he was older than me and he was going to senior or junior year good dude all around he helped me a lot we listened to a lot of Jay-Z while reorganizing that damned book. One of my supervisors I forget his name he started asking me all these questions getting to know me and I told him I go to St. Bernard's High School lol and all of a sudden he gave me a nickname he started calling me Ra- Ra lol because he lived actually across the street and he said all the time he hears all them cheerleaders screaming during the football games at night while he's trying to sleep and has to wake up at the break of dawn lmfaoo so I was like ok what does that have to do with me lol and he said because you're going to a catholic school lmfao I was ok I give it to you lmfao. So the weeks pass by and I'm like you know let me just sign up for bowling this year again its better than playing basketball on the bench so I usually talk to Adina and she hooks me up for the Saturday league in Bowler's Den downtown Lexington City but Adina had left Bowler's Den and new management was there they were all cool we met every one like me, Colton, Bryson and everyone that grew up at Bowler's Den she told new management to take care of us we all been loyal to the alley and they did they took real good care of us because we would always bring people there and we would always make it to Pepsi-and Coca-Cola championships every year so it made the Bowling alley look good well even though I would never get passed round one lmfaooo them dudes at Championship did not play games they would destroy me like 230 to 180 lmfao.

Any ways I lost where I was lol ugh oh ok my supervisor so the job is coming to an end and he tried to get me a job there actually and he couldn't because I didn't have health insurance like myself not under my mother. You know what he did all that he could like we all got really close and cool there they knew me, and Jonas were hard workers just too young to work for the Authority, so it was understandable. Let me tell you I made so much money there lol if I remember correctly I made like 4-4500 dollars in August and I gave it all to my mom I didn't need it I just took 300 dollars to fix up the bike Elian gave me.

End of the Summer is here, and I haven't been able to check up on Roland since his friend passed and I went the week before school started. So I walk in and say hello to his mom and I'm like yoooooooooooooooo and he's cutting his friends hair and we dap up and the corner of my eye there is this girl but like it didn't hit me, like I saw her and then after we dapped he was going to introduce us and of course I knew her, her name was Vivian.

So back story of me and Vivian since I don't believe I have told you. In 6th grade me and her walked to school together every day, she was in 8th grade with my sister. But she was like my sister as well I learned a lot from her. We would either just pick up a snack from the Bodega and walk to school or just walk straight to school and as we awaited for the doors to open we usually got there open it was literally 2 blocks away from our houses we just sat and talked and learning about her and some of her story we became real good friends. Pretty much after she graduated we didn't really communicate at this time cell phones were pretty obsolete and the only people who had them were either extremely popular or had money but they weren't expensive per say it was just there was no need for them and the issue was that she moved a couple times so the house number changed which I never had her house number we always talked and hung out before and after school.

So, I don't know if that was enough back story or not honestly, I don't care lol, but she taught me something interesting. She had taught me and explained about an addiction to lying. Sounds weird right, so what she explained was that what she realized about herself which I don't know if I should be talking but I don't think I am revealing her personal story but forgive me if I am. So she explained that for her lying started as a habit and she wasn't really conscious about it she would lie as we all did when we didn't want our parents finding out what we were doing or who we were with because as all parents have certain people in their mind that they don't want us their kids hanging around. So, she thought it started from there because she was around a lot of guys and you know mothers are exceptionally protective of their daughters.

The guys that we grew up around were all cool yea of course some sold drugs others used drugs and alcohol whatever, but they had this clique and they were protective of her she was a real cool down to Earth girl. So it wasn't like she was just around you know we all grew up together but then she said that the lying just continued even though she would just go to the store or something and her family would call her and ask where she was she would catch herself lying and she couldn't help it. It wasn't like she was a habitual liar it is just what became of her living under the strict overprotective household she was in and after she matured she realized what she was doing but just couldn't avoid it or stop it, she didn't want to keep the bad habit but it followed her and came to a point where she simply couldn't control it. And that was very interesting to me to understand that mentality and to see how after she developed she understood what she was doing because many people after they mature still won't self-evaluate or take accountability of their actions and throw all their mistakes under the generic unaccountable well I was young. She was better than that she was more mature than that and she understood herself and her faults I guess that is why we were so cool at a point and time because she was just very mature at a young age. My whole impression is I am very happy about the people I surrounded myself with and what life has allowed me the privilege to be around and cross paths with because if it wasn't for all these people and me learning from them I don't believe I would be who I was so I am always thankful for everyone I have had the pleasure of meeting and growing with.

Chapter 10

Sophomore Year

Back to the story Vivian tells me that she is going to St. Bernard's and I am happy lol with everyone from Valentine Crescent already there we were going to have more fun in class. So the summer comes to an end and school starts up and me and Daziel take the bus and guess who is on the bus Evander, Dalton, Jake and his girlfriend, and Janessa, Janessa was Lucas' girlfriend I don't think I mentioned her last year she was mad cool I didn't know they were together I knew them separately I knew her from taking the bus and talking to her and Lucas I knew from back in the day lol then I found out they were together lol good people good people. Evander came from nowhere the bus ride this year were going to be great and school.

So we get to school and we go to our homerooms after catching up with everyone and guess who is in my homeroom lol home girl Vivian eyyyyyyy the day just got better and better lol and we had Kabir, Janessa the cheerleader, and a new kid his name was Caesar and we will call him Ceaz because that is his nickname, talking to everyone me and Vivian started talking to Ceaz to find out he came from Claremont Memorial. As a teenager man listen that shit is in bubble fuck territory of New York, but his father lived nearby in Fredericksberg Heights so then it made sense and he was cool as hell great sense of humor, so I knew he was going to get along fine with anyone. He wasn't going to have problems but there really weren't any problems in the school everyone pretty much grew up together and came to the same high school pretty much there were cliques from separate schools, but other than that there were no real issues.

There were actually many new kids this year like Dennis, Jamiel come to know his father was in the FBI or some crazy high government agency, Caesar not Ceaz another kid named Caesar, Janelle just a lot of kids. As walking and finding the new classes I actually have Spanish 2 class with Ms. Gorgianna lol she was my English teacher last year now she is my Spanish teacher and I still have Jeremiah, Cassie, Yoel was in the class this was going to be great and my English teacher I forgot her name but her brother was Herbert I believe his name was he was on the basketball team last year he was pretty cool we hung out several times. So while walking to Math 2 which was Geometry, which I loved probably the only Math class I took serious, well I saw Gunther eyyyyy he looked fine, looked like he was fitting in well and I had class with Vivian in Geometry so everything was going well and I loved the classes and people.

So time passed by and I went to Humanities class and I still couldn't tell you what we did or accomplished in that class I swear it was just for credits, any way we had a class there yes we did lol me, Vivian, Amiri as much as I disliked him he was funny, Cassie and a few others. I also had Biology with Mr. Keegan and Cassie and Markel were there Liv was also there, but I never really talked to Liv mainly Daziel and Evander did. I had Theology and gym class with Mr. Landon man, all the girls loved him lol dude was just jacked all about eating clean and working out but one of the nicest teachers.

Geology class I had with everyone Ceaz, Amiri, Jake and his girl, Alden, Ian, mad people and our teacher was up tight but had a sense of humor and at times had a laid-back attitude, so it was overall a mellow funny environment. As the year is starting up towards the end of September beginning of October I go pass by the barber shop to see how Roland is doing, and of course Vivian is there and we are all just hanging out and Roland's mom was going to Atlantic City for the weekend so open crib lol. He tells me and Vivian is like "yea come through" but I had just left the house walked my ass all the way to 45th and Broadway lol all pun intended there lol that was pretty funny for whoever gets that joke but I was not about to go all the way deep into Caldwell for a party and walk my ass 108 blocks home drunk at that, at 2am it was just not happening. Any who back then like I said I had no cell phone no need for one and I couldn't just disappear for 2 days so Vivian let me call my mom and tell her I was going to come home pretty late because she was going to give me a ride back to my crib after the party which was the determining factor of why I went.

We get to Roland's house and start setting up and go buy the alcohol and people start coming and we start drinking having fun talked to a few girls and it was a good time. It was maybe around 1-1:30 in the morning and Vivian had to go so I was also leaving and we said goodbye she gave em a kiss and while walking downstairs there was a girl coming in I didn't realize who she was but my thought was who the fuck still coming in at 1:30 in the morning lol but it was Roland he knows a lot of people so I really wasn't surprised if people kept coming till 3am his parties were fun and crazy.

So, the weekend passes and in homeroom Vivian was asking questions weird questions and I didn't know why. The day progresses and now I am in Geometry class and I'm getting beat up with questions and I'm lost so with knowing her and how long and cool I have been with Roland she thought that I knew who the girl was walking in while we were leaving and I didn't. So, turns out that girl was his ex. Now I'm thinking awe shit I don't know if anyone is catching what happened, but I had to investigate now. So, as the week passes, I get a chance to see Roland at the shop and we catch up and he tells me that his ex- came in after we left, and she stayed the night and he slept with her. That shit killed me inside, this bothers me talking about it and I am going to get a lot of heat for this but that's ok everything comes into order next year, so whatever. So, I just didn't want to talk to anyone and there was no way in avoiding anything or anyone. So, school comes, and Vivian starts asking me what happened did I know anything, and I am just denying anything acting like I did see him or talk to him. The day goes by and back to fucking Geometry class and she starts asking me again she is like "I know you know Mikey, just tell me what happened, did he fuck her just tell me." She looked so sad and you know she was like my sister I couldn't see her like that and, I told her what happened. She became so sad her energy shifted and everything, but she has been through a lot and she is strong she just held the tears and after class I didn't really see or hear from her. A few days later I went to the barber shop and Roland was pissed so I asked him what happened and he said that him and Vivian broke up and we went out for a walk and he asked me if I told her and I said "no" and you know he trusted me you know we are like family that's my brother but he was wrong for once and he said that I was the only one he told and just asked me to admit it so I told him that I did, I did tell her because she was like family too and she was just so sad and she already knew I just confirmed it and he was pissed he told me straight up he was mad because he loved her a lot and it was true I tell you I never seen him with any other girl the way I saw him with her, but listen he was wrong this time and he told me to leave and that was pretty much the end of the friendship we parted ways I apologized but that was just not enough and it was the wrong time to apologize.

As school continues around this time Marcel starts going out with a girl at Caldwell High. Me and Marcel became good friends just that past year when Daziel was in the swim team and stuff. We were hanging out a lot and he wanted me to meet her since she already knew about me but Marcel had told me that I knew her and I was like "I don't think I know her bro" and he said "yea she went to St. Vincenzo with us but she was just a year younger or behind us," I told him "really because the name didn't ring a bell." Any who I went with him to meet her it was all good we would just walk up into the school and meet up or if she had cheerleading practice, we would go to the football field like 50 feet away from the school. So, when I saw her, I was like "yea I don't remember her at all but if you say so" lol her name was Kaylynn. As well she had a Dominican friend she tried to hook me up with so we could go out on a double date and stuff but I don't really recall why it didn't work out, I bought her some really nice flowers lmfao and I laugh because anyone that knows me knows I love flowers and giving them. Simultaneously Ceaz started going out with a really good friend of mine Lara, she was a cheerleader in our school with Cassie and Jenna and the crew, so everyone turned out to be real cool it was a good beginning to the year but when I say beginning I mean like October, November, lol.

With all this going on Basketball season was starting and Asher wasn't joining Frederick the new kid from New York and Cam, like no ballers were joining so I said, "fuck that why am I going to join just to sit out another year." So, I decided to join bowling since I already bowl lmfaoo. We'll let you tell me that was a great decision. I went to try outs and I didn't know anyone there, and I think I bowled like a 160-170 at tryouts and Mr. Landon and the rest of the team were like "yo man what the fuck why didn't you join the team last year lol," I told them I was playing bench on the basketball team lol. They laughed, so they liked me and I started to meet them and I met Melvin he was a football player for the school mad cool, and I met Joe and Joe was going out with Demi and I'm all like "oh shit I went to St. Vincenzo with her she mad cool" and we all became real cool friends lol. So easy making friends in high school lmfaoo. So, the week past and I got bowling Saturday mornings and I walk there in hopes that my teammates finally come so I don't have to bowl with a handicap every week lmfaoo. So story behind that most years I was usually alone on a bowling team because my teammates had never come it was usually random teammates for me because Elian always had something to do Saturday mornings and Daziel didn't really take to bowling so I was just left with anyone who didn't have a team on the roster in the alley they came to my team and most of the time they would quit early October or never show up. The week previous I bowled against an all-girls squad and they ripped me up lol the handicap did not help at all.

They were mad cool though I tried to go out with one of the girls she was very cute and we talked for a while just never had the time to actually go out and after they whooped my ass the first game I wasn't playing and the next two games I bowled like a 180 and 190 and won and they started calling me the one man team lmfaoo. So, this week I start bowling all by my lonesome and the three dudes walk up and start putting their shit on and I'm all like "oh shit ya my teammates lol." They said "yea I said oh shit no handicap we about to kill" lmfaooo hoping they were better than handicap lmfaoo. And let me tell you they knew how to bowl we completely obliterated them, the scores were like 180, 170, 200, 168 lmfaoo and let me tell you how I didn't feel bad at all. So, these kids were very funny great sense of humor and come to find out they went to Fairfield High. So clearly, I asked them if they knew Jonas the kid, I worked with from the Sewerage Authority and they knew him they were friends so of course I told them when they see him tell him I said what's up lol. Then we parted ways and I was just hoping they would come next week because I can finally have a chance to win one year with them on my team and not have to face 16 teams all by myself you know.

Back to school everyone is getting along no real issues and we are at gym class just stretching out and Cassie is funny she is a few people away from me and she says " ok Mikey I see that V and pack lmfao" and I'm like "hey you're not supposed to see that, that's for my girl" she said "shut up you're single" lmfaoooo you will always have a blast if you have any class with her she has high energy and is funny as hell I love that girl lmfaoo.

Any who, so Ian isn't in class this year and I think him and Janessa broke up and Janessa was looking a bit not like herself and I have noticed it for a couple days so I went to go and talk to her to see how she was doing, and shit man she opened up I didn't really expect it but I can tell she was depressed so I had to try and we got pretty cool after that. So she was going through some things so when I had the chance to talk to her I would check on her and see if she ate and slept we didn't have much communication I didn't have her number and we never hung out but we caught up every now and then in school she was a nice girl. It is just even in high school we get so complacent thinking everyone is ok and doing well just because we are and no one has serious enough problems that rumors around the school so we tend to not ever ask how people are doing and we should, or at least we should try and by should try I don't mean thinking about asking them if they are ok, I mean actually going up and asking a person I am talking about the act and even if so they don't respond it is ok to tell them that it's alright if they don't want to talk about it but you see them hurt and you hope they get through their pain or suffering and that will help them a bit as well. Trust me just them knowing someone cares is enough. Soon enough she started doing better and looking better and she started going out with Herbert and everything was getting better I won't state everything was ok but she definitely did look better day by day.

Lunch comes and we start playing pool me, Daziel, Frederick, Cam, Caesar, and a few other people I think Ceaz was there that day too. We were just having fun talking bullshitting it was a great time we all figured we had to chill someday together. So, one day after school I hang out with Caesar and I know he lives in Fairfield so whatever right. So, we end up going to Fairfield and somehow end up in the projects. Shit and all I can think about is Roland and how he warned me if I had no business there not to go there and while we are walking to his building he tells me "yo listen don't look at that dude, don't look at that dude, make no contact with that dude" and I don't really know who the fuck he is talking about so what do I do, I fucking look lol. The guy yells out "a yo my man what the fuck you looking at you got a problem little (n-word?)" Man was Caesar mad lol he said "yo don't fucking cause no problems here my mom and family live here bro I fucking told you not to look." I apologized and we headed inside, and I met his family they were nice I found out where he got his sense of humor at, they were a nice family. So we dropped off his stuff and went to hang out, but by the time we got back it was dark so he told me to take the bus or train back uptown because he didn't want me walking him all the way home because he thought they would jump me since I'm not from the area and they don't know me, so I left him a couple blocks away and walked home taking the Viaduct. When I got home everything pretty much made sense about what happened with Roland's friend and that situation, but you know I couldn't really talk to him about it at this time we still weren't talking.

As the year progresses people start reentering classes and familiar faces resurface and school actually just becomes a great place with everyone getting along. At this point I start hanging out with every as much as possible so Dennis at the Monkey Lounge which was his house were everyone would go to smoke weed and relax, I start hanging out with Sean, Vivian and Ceaz more and more, Joe I never hung out with outside of school he was a dope dude though he was a funny strong minded kid and he was understanding and protective so he always wanted to hang out with me but he knew at this time I didn't smoke weed so he said usually all he did was drive around and smoke and he didn't want to expose me to it if I wasn't involved with weed yet and he didn't want to feel like he pressured me into it because he would feel bad about it so we made the best time we could while bowling he was a good dude. I did hang out with Melvin out of school a lot and Melvin was great lol we were walking to hang out and play basketball by his house and his mom had called him we met her on 43rd and Covington across the street from the funeral home but the block was long so we were really like 2 blocks away. What had happened was his moms gas gauge malfunctioned on the BMW and we helped push the car to the end of the block to make a right turn and down the hill. Jesus Christ that is when I realized how heavy BMW's are that car had to at least weigh 4 thousand pounds because as in shape as me and Melvin were it felt like that car was not moving, so we finally got the car to the end of the block huffing and puffing and we were so tired that we forgot we had to jump in the car lol and the car started going downhill we were like oh shit lmfaoo so we caught up to the car opened the door and jumped in and damn near almost got run over in doing so lol. It was ok though there was an Exxon gas station at the bottom of the hill then his mom drove us home. We had got to his house and asked if I still wanted to play ball, I said no man not today lol I am beat, and I still have to walk home but let's play in the weekend. He said cool the said wait hold up and went to his room and pulled out a gallon zip lock bag of weed and asked if I wanted to smoke before going home lol I laughed and said no bro thanks I don't smoke but I appreciate it lol and then went home. I was also hanging out with Janelle, Amiri, Ian, Jeremiah just going around West Dover and smoking whenever everyone had time to meet up.

I am going to pause this story because today was a pretty painful day. In the previous chapters I had spoken about a beautiful young woman who is Nameless. Today is her birthday. Backtracking I explained how special she is, and the issue is I knew we weren't going to be able to spend very much time together due to the fact that life has this way with me that it just doesn't allow me to experience happiness. So, where I work, I keep a very low profile. Anything anyone knows about me is that I work and go home or go to school. These girls that I work with have this running rumor that I have a girl and like 3 kids and at first it was pretty funny but like all that shit isn't flattering I have no care in the world about any of it and I told them if they choose to talk shit and laugh go ahead just leave me out of it. So, this girl that started working with us it was pretty insane how everything came about. They had asked her if she was my girl and just started putting all this shit in her head, by any means in all honesty I don't blame her for believing it because if 15 people are telling her one thing and I am telling her another really who is she to believe. But the issue is that I am Michael, so it doesn't matter how nice I am it doesn't that I am a virgin, it doesn't matter how well I treat people, when it comes to women I only have one chance and the chances are extremely small especially when there are a whole crew of people spewing misinformation about me to a woman. So, the day that I had a chance to explain my self it just was not the place nor the time and it was just bad I could tell that I hurt her and I didn't mean to and it was never my intention. So what happened was I got off of work and it was the last time I would see her so I said " I know the girls told you I had a girlfriend" and I immediately saw that she was hurt and it hurt me because it wasn't true my ex had left me months ago at the beginning of the year but I had asked her out beginning or mid-June, so she was under the impression that I was a cheater and a player because she had the thought that I asked her out while I had a girl and I was hiding it which simply just wasn't true and I just couldn't explain it and she was hurt and she just walked away and I knew that was it that is all the chance I get and it wasn't even fair and it wasn't even the time or place to explain the situation I was in, but you know you guys could cheat on your girl and your girl would apologize for not being enough that you had to go and seek out what she was missing in another girl, you guys would hit your woman, you guys would just mistreat your woman and she would take you back any day of the week but Mikey shit man I can't even get a fair chance to explain what was going on in my life before a woman walks right on out and leaves me. The point of me asking her out was to explain to her the situation I was in with my ex, and to do something nice for her.

So, as me being who I am, I texted her at midnight because when a female is special and important to me, I always like to be the first one to say happy birthday. I waited till like 1 nothing then I fell asleep and when I woke up I sent her a direct message on Instagram and she left me on seen, and let me tell you that hurt man, and I realized how much I hurt her. Even before this I haven't spoken to her since the incident in the parking lot, which was the last time, I spoke to her and was unable to explain my situation nor tell her how I felt about her.

A week later I feel is an appropriate time to call again and she picked up and hung up, the signs are very simple to read so I called again and second ring went to voicemail, then I texted her asking if she could talk to me, then three texts popped up about what, this is her man, stop calling leave her alone, and it fucking shattered me whole. And just brought back all the memories from Kaylynn and man that was a pain that I never wanted to experience ever again, and I did, and I will live with this forever. All that rumor shit and everything that just happened over the course of those 5 – 6 months and what happened with me I truly hope I didn't ruin her. Like I told you previously she is special and we have to watch what we say, watch how we treat them because they are important to us as a society and as a whole and I hope she keeps her course and I hope I didn't ruin her because I love her very much and was unable to express it and she is so pure of heart and intentions I truly hope I didn't ruin her and this aside from everything else I have to live with this is horrible this probably takes the worst toll, I have never hurt a girl before and this feels horrible but that is just the way life has its way with me I am not allowed to experience happiness I just simply have to be everyone's scapegoat and when I need to talk or vent there's literally no one around nor available or everyone leaves me on read. So after this incident I'm cool man I finally get it I accept that I have to be alone, I literally did nothing wrong had all intention on telling this young woman what was going on in my life and how I felt about her and just fuck me right. Good men in a corrupt world simply cannot co-exist, it is just as simple as that. She will forever have a part of me that no one will ever have, and I can't even have the privilege of having her by my side, and that is just the life I live.

Back to the story and I am fucking hurting right now, towards the end of the school year everyone is pretty much broken up. Ceaz and Lara broke up, Marcel and Kaylynn broke up I haven't been to Caldwell with him in a while, I think actually Janessa and Herbert broke up too, any way I finally picked up a cell phone it was a I450 Nextel chirp chirp lol. So, I was getting everyone's number because I'm moving to Auburn and Ceaz is like "oh shit Auburn lmfaoo be careful out there the streets is hella bad lol" I'm like well thanks bro I really appreciate it. So, hanging out with Asher and Ceaz they were the ones who got me into the internet and MySpace. They opened up a MySpace for me and uploaded the pics and added friends and some of their friends who they thought I was compatible with so I actually first started talking to a girl Ceaz went to school with in Claremont, we talked for like a month lol and never had the chance to meet up.

So, at this time I had moved to Auburn and my mom was looking for a school for me and I told her listen just send me to the city high school. My mom for some reason was completely against it, but my mom didn't know that I knew how to fight and didn't care who was who because if you were bout it then we was banging, in all honesty. Upon weeks of trying to get my mom to transfer me to the public school all I had to tell her was that she was going to be saving the money she would spend on a catholic school lol that sure sealed the deal lmfao.

Chapter 11

Junior Year, Auburn

The first day of school arrives and I get to the bus stop and clearly, I am alone as in every other part of my life but this time I have no support no friends within 40 fucking miles man. At this moment clearly, I have to watch how I move, what I say, and who I talk to. I get to the bus stop because I live at the beginning of Auburn across Route 13 where the movie theater is, there is a Burger Joint and a hotel and an apartment complex where I reside. We all get on the bus and we start talking and introducing ourselves and first were Moses, and Jonas, then I met Max and Eve and a couple of other girls. They were all cool down to Earth funny people. We finally get to school and like they gave you breakfast for free and that was like a whole new experience, Moses and Jonas were like "go and get some food" I was like "really" they were like "yea the shits free dummy" lol. That was just weird lol, any who we are talking and I'm just watching and listening and for some reason the noise gets louder and louder and louder and someone threw an open milk carton in the garbage and it hit someone and splattered milk all over them.

If you know anything about high school, the first day of school is fresh day lol. Everyone looks and dresses their absolute best like a bunch of fucking cornballs to impress each other. So, Moses seems weird and fidgety and he looks at Jonas and Max and something is happening you know I don't know them, so I don't know their friendship nor chemistry, but they seem in sync.

Now Moses grabbing a milk carton and Jonas grabbing a whole fucking tray of food and juice, look at each other and I am so confused at this point. Moses looks at me and says "get down under the table" and nothing is clicking yet lol and I say "ok for what" lol and he says "watch this," he completely opens all four sides of the milk carton gets under the table and as he launches the milk he yells "FOODFIGHT" lmfaooooo the cafeteria exploded in a food fight it was crazy lmfaoo he gave me a juice and said "go ahead try it" lmfaoo man I chucked that shit so far he said "nah man you gotta do this open it up a little let people get dirty that's what a food fight is for lmfao." So, I open it halfway and launch it, it was fun man. So, they walked me to my locker showed me around the school real fast then showed me my homeroom then we went about our way.

Ok so the story has to come to a long halt, and I don't really know how to start with this situation that has me torn up inside. I guess we will start with today, I was driving to nursing class and, in my mind, sometimes is weird. So I understand the I and me and how they are aware of each other right so I am driving and 2 miles away to school my brain goes crazy and starts saying fuck fuck fuck, but like I'm driving and when I notice that like my conscious is yelling at me because I'm focused on driving I begin to think why was I thinking fuck so much, and it hit me it's going to the first day that I am actually back in that fucking school after Nameless told me she moved on. I really don't want to fucking cry about this at all it fucking pains me I haven't ate or slept in a couple days just tired of crying man. So once I realize why my mind was yelling out to me it's like I have go back to school and sit in class and I couldn't tell you why it pains me so much you know the heart wants what the heart wants and that's something I have no control over and it sucks because I'm not allowed to call her, text her, hug her hear her voice, just nothing and I am pretty much forced to be there sit in this class with all these idiots and my mind is just focusing about Nameless and it fucking hurts.

Jaylene was the highlight of my life that girl who ever she was saved my life, I never once thought it was possible to meet a woman who would ever challenge her place in my heart, I was sold on the idea it was her alone. But on November 6, 2017 Nameless changed that she challenged Jaylene's place in my heart and as a man as much as Jaylene has done for me and as much as I love her, I have to have to admit that Nameless won, she shined a light so bright on my depression I never thought possible her voice was the only thing that healed the pain. My heart and soul reached out for her and imprinted on her, and I'm so fucking hurt I did everything everything my heart and soul told me to do for Nameless and to lose a battle I didn't even know I was in, fucking crushed my soul. The worst part of the whole situation is that I'll never know what the underlying or defining factor was that made her choose him over me. How am I supposed to apologize for not being enough? Our bond and chemistry was strong and the promises she made to me then broke for him to make the decision to give him her heart instead of me well that must have been some defining factor and for that I know I have no right to be upset with her. But why didn't she tell me there was another man in her life fighting for a spot I would have done more there is no possible way that he cares for her or loves her or showed her he loves her more than I do and did it's just not possible, so what was it, what made him better than me. It's another question I will never get an answer to. I gave her my heart and she in turn gave her heart to another man. The void just got deeper. I been explaining and talking about this abyss I have been falling in since 7th grade 15-16 years later and I'm still falling it's like she shined light in that abyss I finally hit a platform picked myself up started climbing out and somehow the shit collapsed and all the debris came crumbling down and hit me and standing on that platform the weight of me and all the depression and debris of everything else going on in my life was too much and the platform gave way and I'm falling again man fucking falling and it fucking hurts so much. What do you do when you give her your all? All the letters, the flowers, the letter to her mother treating her like the queen she was knowing she was a once in a lifetime woman then for some guy just to come in and swipe her from me with such ease there's nothing else I can do and I admit I'm at a loss man. This is the turning point of my life and noticing it, I have to acknowledge it and I also have to admit that for once in my life I am fucking lost and I have no one to ask for help no one and I don't know what to do. And I have to admit it because it's the truth and I can't run from it no more; no writing will help no black and mild no alcohol will help nothing helps after losing everything again.

You know the worst part of it all, that I believe that she actually may be better off with him. She gave my soul peace, tranquility, and solace but it's not her place to fix me it's not her job to heal my void but without knowing it that is exactly what she was doing because with just her smile and voice made all the pain go away. I do believe that I deserved a woman like her, and I believe she was more than deserving of what I had to offer. And I spoke to my brother Ronaldo Williams about the situation because I can't put exactly what happened in here simply out of respect for her but he knows what happened and he doesn't want me losing myself he thinks it's a possibility and frankly he's right, as much as I hate to admit it I have to acknowledge that he is right. What am I supposed to do though, I have no choice over who my heart and soul choose to give themselves to I simply do what it tells me and I did everything it told me to no holds bar and I still ended up fucking losing her and why, why the fuck is every other guy on planet earth so much more better than me I don't fucking understand it honestly. And now I have to think about her sleeping and making love to another man and the thought kills me inside and it fucking hurts man what the am I supposed to do why is that at the end of the day I always lose like I don't fucking understand it what makes everyone better than me I just need to know I think I have a right to know but maybe I am wrong maybe I don't have the right to know and I am always open to being wrong but it's just fucked up honestly. And now she fucking replaced Jaylene's place in my heart simply split down the middle and Jaylene that woman saved my life my heart loyally gave itself to her until 10 years later Nameless walks in to my life and my heart without hesitation created a vacancy for Nameless instead of it only being for Jaylene it said come here Nameless, Jaylene will move to the left side of his heart and Nameless you have the right side and she was curing the void man just seeing her texts her name pop up calling me her voice her warm smile her hugs and just like that, the rug got pulled out from under me without warning and there's no possibility of her coming back or me being able to ever hear her voice again hold her hug her tell her how much she means to me. Just like I was nothing like we had no connection no chemistry nothing I was just left to suffer and fend for myself again I truly hate all of you so much. We really have destroyed our women and I'm over it you guys could keep ruining each other I want no part of it anymore keep doing what you're doing keep choosing to suffer and struggle other than to be happy because instant gratification is deemed more valuable than life long happiness. You guys got it you won I won't be involving myself in anyone's life anymore I won't be intervening and trying to help or save anyone anymore you guys got it I'm gone I have a different focus now and that is where my attention is going to be from now on.

    I said it before and I understand this is the turning point in my life, for one Nameless is gone, two I dropped out of college, three I received a call from a career opportunity after 2 years and I start with them on Monday so I guess this is where it all leads. After this isolated situation with Nameless I ugh I have to admit how hurt I am and I am going to put more hours in to finishing this story because people need to hear it, it will help you guys, I don't need you guys to worry about me I will be ok I always am but I help people I have given up my life for people, been in enough fights for people, stood up for plenty of people even when the odds were always against me, even knowing when I didn't have a weapon I still stood up and fought against it, all the adversary putting everyone's best interests in front of them and in front of me even if they, themselves don't care about their own interest I put everyone in front of me and I have saved several people, I showed people that there are plenty of genuine good hearted people in this world that have no agendas we simply care about what is right and your health, safety and well-being and I am here and we are here and around it's not about karma as you can see I have helped plenty of people and I have had nothing in return but heart ache and that's ok as long as everyone is doing well that is all that matters to me, I gain nothing from helping people and giving my life up to people just know we are a group of people that simply do what is right no matter the situation and we care about you and everyone no matter if I say fuck you I would never allow anything to happen to you because if I have the power and ability to help someone then by all means I have the responsibility to help and without question Mike will always be there to help just know that.

 I guess it is time to verbalize what I wanted out of life because at this point I understand after everything that has happened and all the talks with my brothers it truly will never happen but I will let you guys in on it. Without question the goal was to simply make several million dollars, the reason being that the financial independence that this amount of money would allot me to have, will give me the chance to be able to do anything that I wanted. So, what I want out of life is simple, all I want is to stay home, this gives me the chance to bond with my woman. To be able to spend years with my woman twenty four seven and bond with her, learn her past, the imperfections she believes she has, the insecurities, her strengths, her weaknesses, her thought processes why she made the decisions she made, what does she value, what are her core beliefs, what is it that she wants to accomplish out of life, how does she want to be remembered, what is the future she foresees our children having, what would she like to teach them and why, what is important to her that she would like to instill in our kids, I want to experience her love, I have never experienced a birthday, holiday, or simply a weekend or road trip with a girlfriend, isn't that crazy 28 years old and have absolutely no experience with relationships they all simply tend to just end and I get abandoned and ghosted no phone call no text nothing, they forget my birthday, or how life has always been I lose them to another man which is the common denominator here in my situation.

Pretty much every girl I have asked out said no except Nameless she was the first that said yes. How it has been working with me is that women have asked me out. Every now and then life allows me to cross paths with an amazing woman and they ask me out and the relationships are great simply imagine texting literally 10 thousands texts a month to just your girlfriend communication is never an issue I love talking with my woman and I love hearing everything she has to say because everything is important every thought every word has a meaning and I love being a part of someone's life and the massive amounts of messages on top of talking on the phone for 3-4 hours simply amazing and then the rug gets pulled like it always does and I get abandoned like I meant nothing.

To think of all the women whom, I have bonded with and to completely lose them all and have no communication with any of them I don't think you people may understand how broken I feel. And for me to wait for life another 3-5 years or possibly another 10 years for life to allow me to cross paths with another gem I simply don't see that happening again after Nameless and I understand that it is over for me and I have to accept this path that I am crossing into or merging into and take it for what is worth, I am completely appreciative of life to even allow me to cross paths with Nameless, Jaylene, Laurissa, Kaylynn, Marinella, Amelia and everyone else, just women that have helped me in ways I am unable to repay back to them so even though I have no communication with any woman that knows anything about me no one I can just call and talk to when I am down it is time to accept that and move forward with the pain and the void that simply will never heal and Nameless ripped my heart out and the void got so much more worse the pain is intense and unbearable now but people need me and depend on me and I have to put this aside and go help them simply because it is the right thing to do. And I promise I will set aside time to finish this story and get it out to you people because this will help, and it is the right thing to do. Writing doesn't heal any pain honestly, it doesn't make anything feel better but you guys need this story and its selfish of me to keep this to myself, knowing it will help you, just hang on everyone that is depressed and sad and just going through it I am here and I am here to help just give me a bit more time I will get this out to you I promise. I love you all and I appreciate you all, it is September 16, 2018 right now ok, so now you know how much time it has been taking me to write this I started in 2003 and now feels like the right time to release it and I will I promise. Be safe take care stay blessed and this will get out to all of you. I LOVE YOU ALL.

You know I must be honest with you guys here because I love you all, So I genuinely don't feel like I have very much time left here simply saying that I have given the world my all my soul my heart my mind and in all honestly I am truly exhausted, I have no energy left and frankly speaking like I said before all the women I have ever known or let me say this correctly all the women whom have known me and know who I am as a person are gone right? So, I have no one I can go to and talk to about certain stressors because really nothing ever stresses me out but situations or things on my mind I need to vent and alleviate or find alternative solutions there's no one to go to. So

I don't have the privilege like you guys to call up an ex or a female friend whom I am close with and vent to I have no one can't even say I have ever even drunk texted an ex or anything lol which actually I am pretty happy I have never experienced anything humiliating like that lol. But having such a wide understanding of life and people and how the mind works is a horrible gift because you can never be mad at people because you understand their mind, their thought process so you know the reasoning of why they did the things they did and have to constantly give them excuses and take the high road and it fucking sucks man it fucking sucks. But in all honesty, I am 28 years old and I actually can't say that I have enjoyed life, I didn't actually even begin experiencing my 20s until I was about 25 – 26 years old. So I want you guys to enjoy all the time you have left on this Earth because I haven't and I want you guys to be as happy and full of joy as possible so I will do whatever I can to put a smile on your face and I will do anything I can to put a big ass Kool-Aid smile on your face by being able to teach you things and free you from your pain you hide from everyone and you deny yourself. I will help you all. I don't want you to be like me, I will make you better and teach you how to enjoy your life you just leave everyone's problems up to me I will fix them that is guaranteed. It just hits me hard some days that all the women that are gone that mean so much to me because it is never past tense love never leaves. Everyone has heard that saying "it is better to have loved and lost than to never have loved at all' but if every woman I have ever loved I have lost what does that say about me as a man? Thus, a new question arises, because I think about all these women daily but do, they ever think about me? Will I ever be a memory anyone remembers?

Since these two women that have my heart are no longer in my life, that fire in my heart is burning out so the decision is that I will just give whatever I have left to a nice humble woman that deserves it. It may not be about love but it will be enough to me or for me to give what I have left to show a woman that us genuine men are out there and that is all I have left on the table to give after everything I have lost and I think it should be enough hopefully she would appreciate it so wish me luck. So, let me ask you all a question that has been a constant reoccurrence in my life lately. Usually with questions like this I would ask Jaylene she would just understand and know what to say and answer as honestly as possible good or bad she held no bars and was very respectful but anyways, let us say for instance well this question is for the ladies, so let us say you are with your boyfriend correct, nice guy genuine likes to help people a bit too much at times. Now it's the week end all of a sudden 2:30 3am in the morning hits and his phone vibrates, ok nothing crazy, 15 minutes later his phone vibrates 3 times back to back to back, ok now something is up then when he goes to check his phone he gets a phone call. So, the question is what would be your first thoughts? Second question what would you say or do? Third question, would it bother you? Now after you have answers to those questions I will give the background and context behind the texts and calls, first text was a girl who was depressed because her boyfriend just broke up with her and she couldn't sleep and needed to vent, second text was a girl who previously attempted suicide, the next two texts and the phone call was an old friend who showed signs of suicidal ideation and her depression is severe, the question is ladies how would you feel about these women finding comfort in your boyfriend knowing that he is the only person who was there for them during some intense times in their lives. Would you believe it is his job his duty to help them, would you be envious or feel insecure, would you feel that those are his problems to deal with and why? Would you not be proud of having a man who is there for his friends when they need him most, would you not be proud of having a man that genuinely cares about people and takes care of them to make sure they are mentally stable and physical well? Or would you convince him that those women's problems are not his to deal with and he shouldn't shoulder the weight of the pain if they actually did commit suicide because he wasn't able to help them because you asked him not to and he listed to his girl? I would like to know everyone's answers for this so when you have a chance think about it and email your answers, I would be very interested to hear them and why you believe your answers are right.

Important note, Mike is tired yall. I can honestly say I am exhausted, this situation has really taken a toll on me man, and what surrounds the situation is rough as well you know to have brothers count on you aside from the other women, you got people you need to take care of you know the alcoholic brothers, the depressed and suicidal ones, the ones with financial issues and just everyone needs me and I am at a point that I am just lost and I just can't seem to focus I don't know how to solve everyone's problems right now and it is like the time that everyone needs me most and I am fucking suffering, and as always you know I texted this one girl just simply because I just needed her just to talk and hear a familiar voice and of course I get left on read as always you know because when I actually need someone to talk to and vent that's pretty much what happens and when it doesn't they tell me if they can call me back because they don't have time and at that point it's not even worth it if I am not important to you its whatever, I have never left anyone on seen or not picked up the phone for someone and completely stopped what I was doing to help and listen and give advice and hear someone out, it never mattered if I was at work or driving I would take a break or pull over to the shoulder but you know we just aren't all built the same and just the consistencies of situations when I need someone to be there for me no one is ever there. I do have 2 people I can always rely on but there are just sometimes I need a woman around it's just that simple.

Women just are different in every aspect of life, intuition, logic, they just bring something to the table my brothers don't and cant and it's not to say anything of them it just is what it is but what can I do when there aren't any women around or they simply just avoid me. That loneliness that I have experienced is one of the reasons why I handle all my problems by myself and one of the main reasons why I always pick up the phone no matter what I am doing because I know how rough people have it and I know any moment when people call it is because they need me even if I know they will never reciprocate back what I have done for them or they will never thank me for what I have done for them I will never allow anyone to experience the vast amount of isolation and loneliness that I have encountered in my life. So, there are times in my life where I go M.I.A and don't tell anyone and don't answer phone calls unless I know it is from someone that seriously needs me. When I go M.I.A it's for several reasons that I won't go into all of them but mainly it is because I had a bad experience and there was no one there for me and the only way to overcome it was to distance myself from everyone and literally just sit and think of how to get out of the situation or how to solve everyone's problems. This is what I would do, I would literally just sit and process like all outcomes or possibilities of the situation and why they would have those out comes, I would do that for myself like the situations I was dealing with and when I would be able to understand the best scenario I would move on to the people I was helping and their problems. It was and wasn't so much as me placing their pains on me but a huge part of it was, because the way I understand people and how I care about them and place their own best interest in front of them because I know what they want out of life it takes some time to understand the best scenario for them. The issue is I understand people more than they understand themselves because people deny certain aspects of themselves and I exploit it and make them take accountability of it because if they can mature and accept that they are wrong about certain belief's or aspects about themselves how can they not grow? I get to learn about people and understand their reasoning, their thought processes, why they do the things they do, what they gain from it, why do they hang out with the people they hang out with, what do they gain from the relationships, is it personal, do they give you a higher sense of self-esteem, are they intelligent and you want to gain as much knowledge from them, or are you around them because you don't want to feel alone and all they do is fill a void a space, do you actually care for them or if they stopped talking to you would it bother you or would you go about your day as if nothing happened, what is your relationship with your parents, did you they instill certain beliefs in you that you chose to accept as your own and why, how is your relationship with your children, are you mentally capable of raising a child or are you just going about it day by day and learning and if so why haven't you taken out the time to learn about how children act when they need attention or affection or what does your child do and how they act when they need something from you, how is your relationship with the child's mother, was the foundation of the relationship simply about sex or did you actually have feelings for her, did you argue all the time or compromise and find an avenue that was common to you both and discussed things you disagreed on as two mature adults without arguing and yelling, all these are factors as to how a person thinks and the situations they find themselves in and how to find solutions to these situations and problems everything means something and plays a factor and much more it is just too in depth to get into and once I learn how a person thinks and acts it becomes relatively simple to help them solve personal issues and problems some may take a few hours, others days, others months, and others years to a whole life time. The purpose of this is to show a person to give a person enough information about themselves that they learn what they have been doing wrong and how to reverse a negative thought process, to show them that there are genuine people out there who care about them but the hardest part about this is that the person needs to be honest with themselves because if they truly want to solve a personal issue they usually are as honest as possible because they don't want to feel or experience guilt or carry that with them. Others that simply lie about everything they tell you they just usually just want to complain to someone or want someone to hear their problems not necessarily vent but they are just needy and everyone is avoiding them because those people find them annoying and usually is because these type of people put up fronts and don't act as who they are but impersonate someone because of some said insecurity maybe at home or some kind of issue they are fighting within themselves they don't want to admit to anyone, these people truly take time to deal with because the ones that truly want to change you are going to have to pull teeth to get them to admit their faults and take accountability of it and when they start to realize they been doing everything wrong their whole life you will begin to see a change but on average this has taken at least 2 years to see any progress and most friends aren't waiting that long to see people change that's why I am around because I never give up I am there day in and day out every day if you truly want to change and the smiles are always worth it let me tell you, there may not be a thank you but to see a change and acceptance it is worth the years of work and then once they have the knowledge on how to go about life the right way we part ways and I never hear from them again but knowing they have all the knowledge they need to make the best decisions for them moving forward with life that growth is always worth it and you should be proud of it.

 I really need to continue this story so you guys can meet everyone and understand how everything came together but just the constant situations that are happening it's tough and I have to expose you guys to it now as it comes. So allow me to tell you how life is funny and pisses me off right, so first and foremost this will sound weird so let me explain that and I may be the only one that this happens to maybe not but we will see, and I am very conscious about everything so all these coincidences are just that simply coincidences so don't take it too deep it is the effect of the coincidences that matter for these situations, so after Kaylynn who you will meet next year, after we broke up you know that there are things you see in everyday life that will remind you of your ex, significant other, or whatever you wish to call them, there were many things that just in everyday life would just remind me of her and how I have never met a Kaylynn previous to her then all of a sudden I met several after her which were meaningless just simply like in a store or a cashier things like that but weird because I never met one prior to her, or how annoying the number 214 came to be after Jaylene left me because that was her birthday but now all of sudden when she left I saw that number everywhere or how I had to take the bus and the bus number was 214 obviously why wouldn't it be right, just coincidences but how these minute things would just bring back all the memories and I would get really sad and depressed, and funny to how the number 99 never a thought in my head but it was the unit I belonged to in the military right but super coincidence that when I go home on leave and I drive down to Jersey would you like to guess the exit I have to take because if you have not guessed by now it is exit 99 lol but just some useless information of occurrences that happens to me all the time. To bring everything into perspective Nameless likes flowers right, her favorite to be sunflowers correct. But any who my friend who absolutely doesn't know anything about Nameless or that situation asked me today if I wanted to go to this sunflower field in Jersey so did anyone pick up that coincidence or do, I have to spell it out for yall? I told her no, clearly and I told her I just didn't want to go because it would depress me and she asked "why, do flowers depress you" lol like no girl I don't want to go to a place where it would remind me of a woman that isn't in my life and if I did go I would have the thought of her, and just no I'm cool I can't have those thoughts in my head right now I am still recovering from it all. Fucking story of my life man.

    I have to explain something because after what happened I do truly hope her and him do well I never wish bad on anyone I truly do hope he treats her well. In all actuality, if she truly believed deep down that he had the slightest potential and possibility to make her happier than I did or that I believe I did than who am I to take that away from her, maybe they do very well and have a child and get married, how would it look if I took that chance away from her, I would never do that even as down and depressed I am about the whole situation and how it was handled it is clear she cares for him very deeply and loves him, so she does deserve to be happy and if for that to happen it meant that she had to do what she did to find love then she did the right thing and I can't fault her for that. The pain will always be there, she did break her promises, but for love I have no choice but to forgive her and hope her newfound relationship goes well. It's just having this understanding of people and why they do the things they do it kills me inside like why is it that I have to give everyone excuses for their actions and it fucking sucks man I'm tired of it I am tired of being understanding and whatever this knowledge is that I possess that helps everyone is a fucking curse to me man and I don't know how to let it go and be selfish, I can't just use everything I know to just use women for sex and enjoyment because at the end of the day I would feel so guilty hurting women like that especially being that I wouldn't be here if it weren't the women I met and have helped me but I am tired man and a part of me says fuck it all women have ever done was fuck you over so go use them and make them feel that pain but that doesn't heal the void nor make it better and that is not who I am and I can't allow myself to do that with the chance that the void would get even deeper knowing how many people I hurt intentionally so the best decision I could come up with is to keep to myself and or adopt and teach my child everything I know about life and people to give them the best chance at an amazing life hoping they navigate this cruel world with the best thought process to promote self-improvement and to be kind and genuine to all the people they will cross paths with in life, and that is where I am stuck and my dilemma lies.

At this point and time I can't say that I have actually enjoyed life or well experienced it the way I wanted to, it seems to be the right time to shift focus build a career and life, my main problem has always been that I had no motivating factor because I don't have a wife or kids but I think I have to change my mindset to the point where if I do adopt I would have to have a set amount of funds to be able to take care of this child and give them the best possible life I can, and I should be using that as a motivating factor even though it has not happened yet. It is something tough for me to do because it is not here yet and is not tangible so it's tough to use as a motivating factor, but I think it's the right time to try and see where that goes. I am going to make the conscious decision to stop helping people as well, no one really cares about us good people any way and I wasn't always a good person Jaylene changed me I was a pretty shity guy prior to meeting her, you guys will see I have no reason to lie about anything and I will throw it all out there I really don't care, but to stop helping people in the sense of if I get that look in your eyes or I feel your aura down and low of life I will probably not say anything anymore and probably not confront you about it, I know I will keep doing it for a while this has been my life for more of 13 years and it'll take time but I have given up my life for yall mainly women, and placing my life in danger and the whole nine for you all on this mass Earth but Mike is tired yall, and there will be someone better to come along and help you don't think I am the only one out here fighting for you, there are plenty of people like me and they care about you as deeply as I do but I think it's time I take a rest from this and focus on building a future for the kids I don't have yet I think I owe them that and if that means I need to step aside and see life as a whole for the children I don't have yet then I think it is something I must do, but I will still be around when I see that sign that important sign of life and death I will always intervene but for now if the situation is not that severe and the signs and symptoms of ideation aren't there then I will have to just pray for yall. Mike is tired and I think it's time for some me time but I will always make myself available any day but to spend years and giving my life up for everyone that will have to cease for a while, and I have to get back to this story I have diverted from, there is a lot to cover and a lot of people you need to meet, the worst is still to come and I have to talk about it and take accountability of my actions as a man so I guess this is where I stop and begin where I left off, I am sorry for the long rant but I had a duty to explain what has been going on and why. So, I guess we will get back to it I hope you're ready for it.

Back to the story I went up and read where I left off, so we left off after the food fight on the first day of school. They took me to my locker and showed me where my homeroom was so for first day of school it was pretty nice making friends since I didn't know anyone within like 40 miles but whatever right I'm Mike just dealing with shit by myself like always. Well let me tell you about homeroom. I had Peterson, Owen, Max, Catherine, many more but most importantly the most popular kid in school annnnnnnnd the star quarterback of the football team Bernard. Oh god just writing this and reliving the memories is just funny how my life is and comes full fucking circle lol. Any who I start going to class and importantly I have class with many great people. At this point everyone already starts talking about sports and what activities are coming up to join. During lunch I found Jonas and sat next to him and he was telling me who was who and what tables were what cliques who was related and who was going out and all the couples and corny gossip because he didn't want me talking to the wrong people and getting myself in trouble and getting attention with the wrong people because the school was filled with gangs and it was just good having someone watch out for me like that I definitely appreciated it, but certain people and situations you can't really avoid in a public school but he tried his best and did real good so thanks Jonas wherever you are man. I learned who was who real fast. So the day comes to an end and guess what time it is, time to find the school bus and I get outside and to my surprise they are all the same fucking buses lmfaoooooooooo oh let me tell you how I was so not ready for public school lmfaoooooo felt like a super idiot when I stepped outside like shit my bus out here waiting for me, well man was I fucking wrong lmfaoooo. On top of that 1500 kids walking out how the fuck was I supposed to find Jonas or Moses, or Max man was I lost. The boys found me though lol Moses and Jonas both found me and directed me to the bus and laughed at me all the way home lol they showed me the pickup spot for our apartment complex bus route lol they were good dudes real funny man I miss them.

After school Moses and Max and Jonas took me to the basketball courts by the house, they showed me how to get there and back home it wasn't very far but these dudes were nice at basketball very good players and they were not just street players Moses and Max if they were on the same team you simply just weren't scoring any points that game, they had good chemistry, organization, and skills. Jonas liked playing football but he helped us practiced and played with us a lot he was a good defender and center can't take that away from him. So, after school every day they helped me get in shape and fix my shot for the upcoming basketball try outs because they didn't want to be on the team. So, after we played some games and started walking home, I asked them why they didn't want to join the basketball team and they both said, "nah fuck that shit never for Auburn." I was confused but they told me what was going on and to my surprise the same shit as Saint Bernard's, once football season comes to an end, they rally them all up and put them on the basketball team. I said oh no fuck that and they both nodded their heads yeap. It literally is Saint Bernard's all over again, so I met Peterson in homeroom and he was a basketball player and grew up in Auburn so he knew who was going to be on the team and everything so I found out when try outs were and got prepared. Throughout this whole time in this new school I became close to Owen, couldn't tell you how or why but that man took me under his wing and showed me how to maneuver around Auburn the city and the high school.

Sometimes he would take me to Burger King in the morning and just completely skip homeroom and meet up with his friends and hang out I actually met Ephram, Malakai, and Devani through him, great exceptional people and Malakai was hilarious lmfaooo boy was a lost cause man such a good guy lol dude was in love with Devani but completely clueless about everything that had to do with her it was so funny but he really liked her.

Important note two new kids came from New York, we called them the Brooklyn Brothers lmfaoooo. Somehow, they meshed so well like they weren't even transfers. One of them I had in my class his name was Nate, and his younger brother was cool too his name was Jamel lol real good guys they had good morals we got along real well. But yea that was a very important note and time, so basketball tryouts are coming closer and people who want to join have to go to this stupid study hall and do homework and class work and clearly, I didn't know anyone there. So I'm at the table by myself and I see Pete talking to some guys at the table across from me and clearly I wave over like to say what's up guys and this dude is straight grilling me just mean mugging me gave me the dirtiest look I have seen in a while like he want to fight me and he just hates me for some reason, and this guy's name is Jarrell. It just never made sense to me I didn't even know the guy and he gave me this crazy stare. Any who the try outs come we stretch run drills then we start a scrimmage match, it was me, Pete, Jarrell, and Alonzo, they all grew up together they had real good chemistry on and off the court good group of guys I had the pleasure of crossing paths with so it comes down to mid-point of the match and Jarrell is running the ball down, I juke some guy and get open by the three point line and Jarrell just looks so mad at me I will never forget it and Coach Merrick is there just watching so I am like yea you already know I'm going to drop this three pointer on them, and he passes me the ball hard and fast straight to my head I am talking to myself like dam dude I was 10 feet away and not a defender in sight no need to throw it that hard no one was going to come and steal it and when he threw it at me it felt like he threw it with the power of all 12 of Jesus' disciples because he looked infuriated that he even had to pass me the ball I was like what the hell we on the same team and I was open what this guy so mad for I was about to nickname him Kobe lol so when I caught the ball I should not have kept that momentum of just anger and strength lol because when I shot it, it was not my normal shot I put wayyyyyyyy too much power into it and it went so high it hit the cross member and supporting brackets above the backboard like a ping pong machine lol it was like ding, ding, dingdingding, lmfaoooo it felt like it took forever for that ball to come back to the ground lmfaoo and everyone started laughing, it was hilarious and I was like fuck me man they are never going to trust me with an open shot ever again lol. Jarrell just looked at me shook his head and laughed, he came over gave me a hug patted me on my head and said something in the lines of don't worry man no more threes for you lol stick to lay ups I got you lmfaoooo. From that day we have been great friends and I never understood why either lmfaoo but he never mean mugged me again he actually is a very genuine dude, much nicer than me and I don't ever say that but there are 2 more people that are my current friends that I will tell you are much nicer and much more genuine than me. From try outs I got very close with many people, Alonzo, Pete, Jayson, Abel, just everyone because it was like day in and day out it was just basketball there was no other life we go to school at 7 in the morning not to get back home till 7-8 at night. It was just a new family and it was fun.

 School became much more fun honestly, couldn't name everyone I met but everyone I met just had this protective thing over me it was weird like remember about the Saint Vincenzo kids I told you about and the Saint Bernard's kid for some reason people seem to be protective of me and I never understood why even to this day it is just weird but I won't argue over it I guess it is because of them I never really fought a lot honestly. So all the popular kids I met told me who to watch out for and if I had any problems to go to them first and not to throw punches until they straighten things out for me so I was always like ok cool but I never actually had any problems and me and the Brooklyn Brothers got real close and to find out they were Hakim's cousins, Hakim was one of the most popular kids in the high school real down to earth guy real funny but exceptionally strong he was on the football team but that man was not a dude to be fucked with at all. So when I would go home from school I would jump in the Brooklyn Brothers school bus I pretty much did what I wanted lol and I would hang out with them they lived across the highway from me so it wasn't too much to simply cross it and go home at night not an inconvenience at all and we all got cool that way and I met Pax and DeAndre in the apartments as well and Pax was the younger version of Hakim they were family but Pax was a bit annoying at times but good kid overall he wasn't our age but his mentality was there with us and he was a funny kid he just wanted to laugh and spend time with us he had a good heart. So after spending time with them DeAndre, Max, Moses and Jonas told me that I didn't have to cross the highway all the time, that if I walked through the parking lot of the Lowes movie theater there was a pathway under the Auburn / Middletown Bridge that connected the movie theater and my apartment complex so they took me to it showed it to me and boy was that thing questionable lol. So you go under the bridge and the support beams and slopped concrete are there and you can just hang out there once you walk down the concrete there is about 40-50 feet of path that leads to a Y intersection and if you follow the West side it takes you towards the back of the movie theater and if you follow the East path it takes you to my apartment complex but a gate is blocking it so all you had to do was jump the 7 foot fence which was simple enough for every average kid in high school so I loved it because I didn't have to risk my life crossing Route 13 all the time lol.

So, it's time to wake up for school and just so happens the day that all the guys from the complex woke up late lmfaoooo. Me, Jonas, Moses, and Max are all looking at each other like where's the bus lmfaoo and to our surprise we caught it turning the corner and we all looked at each other like with the same thought I am not running for that, fuck that shit lol annnnnnnd it was gone lol so I asked what do we do everyone looked at me it's a day off kid lmfaooooo. Everyone goes back home, and I just stand there thinking hmmmm if we all woke up late wouldn't it be a coincidence if Jamel did too? So what did I do lol I called my boy and he picked right up lol I said "bro are you on the bus" and he said "no I just missed it and wasn't running for it I was tired" lol perfect. So, I asked him if he wanted to go to school and Jamel is always up for hanging out even if it's a walk to school. I went to his complex and picked him up and we started walking from there well first we had to cross the traffic heavy and road rage entertaining Route 54 lol so we crossed that and on we went laughing enjoying our time and fuck ups for waking up late but this, this was cool man navigating through Auburn with a brother trying to get to school and let me tell you when we finally arrived to school that is when we realized how fucking far we lived lmfao. We lived at the beginning of Auburn and the school was literally the final block before North Auburn I never realized that the Burger King Owen always took me to was North Auburn man what a walk but it didn't really phase us as we did it so often it became a part of a weekly routine, if I didn't want to go to first class or homeroom I would tell him the night before and we would meet up and walk and hang out. Any who we got to school and went to our classes and I saw Owen and he was like "yo what's good my guy where were you today it was Burger King day" I told him I woke up late and walked he paused and said "wait wait wait whhhhhaaaattttttttuhhhhhhh" lmfao when he thinks you did something crazy or absurd he extends and pronounces his what like that lmfao real funny guy. He said "yo you fucking crazy I would never do that I would have had an ahhhhmazing nap fuck all that shit" lol so as we are walking to class, ok let's pause this for a second before this comes off crazy rude and disrespectful take what I am about to say as light as possible it's not that serious relax it is just the way I have to explain it to you the reader, so as we are walking to class there was a black kid that knew me from basketball and he was like "ayo what up Papi" and extended his hand for a handshake and we did our little hand shake and went on our ways lmfao. So at the time I was so fucking confused I turned and looked at Owen like "my dude what just happened" he said "feels weird doesn't it" lol I said "yea why the fuck he call me Papi don't they know that, that's like sexual lol like our women call us Papi for sexual reasons like I felt dirty man" he said "its ok they call us Papi like, it's their form of accepting you, we all cool here man," I said "oh ok but I never really had a problem with black people accepting me" he said "you ever look yourself in the mirror, dude you look black lmfaoooooo my guy, actually I thought you was black until you started speaking Spanish to me" lmfaooooooo I said "oh really dam I didn't even know I never actually ever thought about any of that shit I never had a problem with race or shit like that I always got along with everyone" and he said "nothing has changed no one has a problem with you now either just the weird shit they say every now and then but you can't blame them they don't know Spanish" lol, I said "oh well alrighty then" lmfaoo. So before we split up he said "yo Mikey look you don't know all the people that I know but I don't want you walking blind in this school without friends it could be a bad look to you so I got you into this party it's a 15 dollar charge at the door all you have to do is get there and tell them that your my boy, I got you I'm going to cover your charge, or call me when you get there just make sure to get there so you can meet people" I said "ok no prob thanks man." Friday comes and it's time to go to the party and

I got there annnnndddd there's nobody there lmfaoo of course how typical. So, I call him up and he talks to the girl and she lets me in and takes me downstairs and there were literally like 3 people there. I don't know anyone, and Owen is picking people up, so I have to wait until he gets there. Little by little people start walking in the party starts going I was just literally sitting there waiting for Owen to come through and then there was some girl thick cute she walked up to me grabbed me and whelp that was it for the night lol we started dancing grinding to reggaeton somehow we started drinking don't remember where the beer came from everything was going good then Owen walked in with everyone and like 3 cases of Coronas lol I swear this kid walked in with a village of people and it was everyone from school so I got even more comfortable. He came by and said, "oh my guy Mikey making friends already lol." I said what's up to everyone from school then the DJ did his thing right so he started playing Te Suelto El Pelo by Yandel so like you know it was time this was the time to get the girl you wanted go after her and get her number, everyone knows where this playlist is going so we didn't do anything for this song I helped them put the beers away and caught up with everyone Malakais funny ass was like "oh shit Mikey out tonight at the house parties it's going to be a good night lmfao ". Any who the DJ did his thing right the beat started and it was just too late to get that girl so I said fuck it I'm cool right now hanging out with guys from school at the moment I'll get another girl and all you heard from the speakers was "Its ya boy Romeo Doble Uu con Yandel" and man that was the song in high school Spanish house parties till like 09 lol. When that DJ plays Noche De Sexo either you getting her number, going to a Hotel, you guys are in a relationship now lol and if neither of the latter occurred than you done fucked up lmfaooo.

    As people may know that English is the language of power, Spanish is the language of Love, the love the pure passion that occurs when the music is on and you're dancing and connecting with someone is intense man let me tell you when we get into it that Merengue, Bachata, Salsa, Reggaeton it's just you and me baby girl it just is what it is and that connection is felt by everyone in the room when it's there, and it's an intense feeling it's a great experience. So the song continues to play, oh and for my non Spanish readers the artist Romeo, Wisin, and Yandel were the biggest reggaeton artist with a couple others but this was the song like thee song and it translates to Night of Sex, so ongoing everyone is just living it up and by the DJ this girl is tearing up the dance and she was beautiful thee baddest in the party and I didn't know who she was but I had to ask and they told me her name which I actually won't release to you guys because she actually turned out to be one of the nicest girls I have ever met and helped me walk a straight line, there were a handful of women whom have tried to keep me off the streets and have tried to stop me from walking a bad path in life and she turned out to be one of them and out of all she helped me with and taught me I am grateful to her and our friendship I mean we no longer talk but I hold her very dear to me, and out of respect I won't let her name out just for the fact that I don't want people to view her that way because that form of life she lived was very short lived and I don't want to portray her that way per say because that is not who she is as a person. So moving forward they told me who she was and after that night I never actually saw her again for a very long time until we met and became friends and even after we became real good friends it never occurred to me that she was that girl in the party until wayyyy late in our friendship lol and I don't actually recall telling her that story either so her name is a no go for you guys sorry she means too much to me I would never let you guys deface her character so sorry but fuck yall lol. After the song finished all of sudden, we hear this lady just yelling and screaming her lungs out walks right down the stairs and kicks all of us the fuck out lol. The girl who was letting us use her house for the house party her mom was extremely upset to say the least lmfaoo, she came down the steps with a fury and didn't give a fuck about any of us lol she started yelling "get the fuck out of my house now, I told ya that ya could have your fun and party all you want in my house as long as there was no alcohol involved and you guys brought it and are drunk, I gave you all a chance and you disrespect me like this no get the fuck out, if the cops come I'm not getting in trouble for anyone of you you're all on ya own fuck that." So we already upset her and didn't want to get her more mad because she would probably let us use the house again for a party after she relaxed so we up and left I got no girls numbers but met some more kids from the high school so it was a win win. To be honest as an adult now as writing this and reliving it yo, we were dumb lmfao in all honesty we live life just to enjoy the times we have and not giving any room to anyone around us we just want to do what we want without any repercussions because like no one thought about this lady right, if she wouldn't of found out about the beer and liquor and the party continued and we leave her house drunk as fuck at 3, 4, 5, in the morning some of these kids had cars and you know you weren't allowed past 11pm without an adult and you couldn't have passengers and say someone gets caught gets a DUI the cops found out we came from her house underage drinking man the works the judge would have smacked her in the face with the book man.

Looking back man it was a good time but as an adult oh the risks were not worth my kid having fun like that lol, but thanks mom we appreciate you letting your daughter host a party like that hope you're doing well P.S the party was dope lol.

School comes back around and in my Driver's Ed course I have Abel and Orrel, great funny dudes, Abel is on the basketball team and Orrel pretty much was his best friend they were real tight and funny Abel thought I was a scrub until he realized how funny I was in class then we got real cool and let me tell you that kid was a sniper on the basketball court anywhere from the 3 point line if he threw it up it was going in, he was our anchorman if you needed a 3 just pass him the ball he will make it no doubt. So our teacher in class was the Physical Ed teacher and Cross Country Coach I forgot his name but one of the funniest teachers I ever had and his assistant was this fine assistant and everyone hit on her and well I mean lol I don't really know what to say to that but we were in class and he wanted us to do some group project and hand it in before the end of class and Orrel put our names on the paper and it read Orrel, Able, and Michael lmfaooooo Abel was like "yoooo what the fuck man my name is Abel not able get it right" lmfaooo it was fucking hilarious. Then on to the next class History class and just a bunch of immature funny kids in that class, in all reality high school there was really no learning in it lol the learning was on you if you read the book we pretty much just wanted to be around our friends and have a good time. This kid that sat behind me his name was Elias and Suri was next to us and we would tear the class up Elias would start with a joke while the teacher would write on the board and have me laughing and she would turn and yell at us and I would tell Elias to relax for a bit I didn't want to get her mad and get us kicked out but what he said was so funny so I would tell Suri and then I would respond back with a joke to Elias and his laugh was so loud and funny lmfaooooo and the teacher turned and looked back and say Elias and she would yell at him " Elias get out of my class right now I am tired of you disrupting my class " lmfaoooo. He would burst out like "yo I didn't even do anything why am I getting kicked out," lol as he would walk out the class room he would be like "yo fuck you Mikey" lmfaoooo and me and Suri would just laugh the entire time and the teacher looks at us and asks "you want to follow him?" No teacher I'm all good here lol. Elias was a great kid class was boring without him, me and Suri would have fun but just wasn't the same.

Any who basketball comes up we got a game and as usual the J.V team plays first then the Varsity team and Coach Merrick wants us all professional, he played professional out in Europe and he believes in looking the manner, which I have no problem with but first we aren't an amazing basketball team I have never heard of Auburn being known for basketball like in Fredericksberg Heights we had Saint Alexander's and man listen I won't go into that I will save that for another time maybe senior year lol you guys will like how that story goes it is pretty funny. So ok I will play the political game for a while just because he is a nice dude, so we get there mount up and play and we lose he puts all the football players in for most of the game and in my head I am thinking oh no here we go again, and now Max and Moses are in my head like fuck they were right. So, the Varsity team plays, and Jarrell is cooking them on the court crossing everyone over doing his thing and then it happens, the football players curse. They just want the ball to show off do fancy shit shoot the ball in hopes they make it and Jarrell is frustrated Alonzo, Jayson, Pete the crew are all mad and I see it and it is just like Saint Bernard's. We ended up losing both games pretty normal thing for us lol.

Overall it was a good experience with the team and I learned a lot from them and the football players were extremely funny and cool so during lunch I was able to sit at whatever table I wanted to we were all just cool and they were inviting as long as you were funny pretty much you had no problems in the school.

After us losing how many games Jarrell, Pete, Beck I don't recall introducing Beck but he was a part of their crew real funny down to earth guy, Jayson, Alonzo they started taking me to play basketball everywhere around Auburn whether it was Forman Park, Davidson, Community Campus at the college and let me tell you that was when my game was at peak playing and learning from them and forcing myself to play at a higher level because these college kids were out for blood so the only option was to adapt and overcome if you didn't you got eaten alive. They helped me understand the difference the real difference in street ball and organized basketball, which I never took into account because to me it was all about scoring if you got the ball and got a shot take it but that's a no no in organized ball, defending the base line, man to man defense on teams that can shoot, 3-2 zone on teams that can't shoot and need to get into the paint it was really eye opening watching them play as a team and teaching me how they worked and watching basketball and explaining what everyone was doing and why it was fun man I can lie and we still remain very good friends until this day but it was a lot that happened but you know like I say I can't explain their story that is theirs to tell.

Back to school I got cool with the girls basketball team oh I will never forget this lol in class I had the star players and they were great girls very funny and just ballers, so one girl stops the class and says "ayo teach did you hear what happened this weekend" the teacher responds "no what happened?" She said "the police found a decapitated body behind the school by the trash bins" he said "WHAT!!! I didn't hear anything like that I will have to investigate after class," she said "that's not all that happened," He said "there was more" she said "yea they actually found the head in the trash bin" the whole class got quiet because not one of us heard that news and we are all in school knowing someone was just brutally murdered outside, the teacher was like "no way" she said "yea and they found a note in the guy's mouth" the teacher said "what did it say" she said "the note said I DON'T NEED NOBODY "can you guys please tell me and explain to me how I was the only person in the class that started laughing LMFAOOOOOOOOOOOOOOO and what was the funniest part, everyone was so serious that it didn't click in their head for what felt like 5 minutes and all of a sudden the teacher gives her a look and now the class gets it and you could hear our screams down the hall that shit was sooooo fucking funny lmfaooooooooooooo. I can't really lie to you guys I really miss Auburn and High School.

On a better note I have to jump back to Lexington City so Junior year was like I guess looking back at it was like a turning point of who

I was as a person, I mainly went up to hang out with Jeremiah, because we were close and I felt at the time he needed me around more than Daziel did and Daziel was with our other best friend Adrien, and Adrien was just a down to earth kid real funny very respectful just a good dude overall and we were all like family. So, to put it into perspective if I went to Lexington City 4 times in a couple months 3 out of 4, I would be with Jeremiah and the other times I would be with Daziel and Adrien. Jeremiah pretty much what we would do is go to house parties every time I went up there or help him fix his car or help him with some essays or something for college you know we were brothers we always watched out for each other and his mom really pushed me to help him get into a decent college he was, well is a smart kid but like I said none of us really eh paid attention in high school like that it was more a social thing and college was just another step for most of us, well them I didn't take the college route until way late in life lol. I would sleep over his house and then take the bus to NY Port Authority because that's where the bus I had to take was then back to Auburn NJ it was really crazy that I had to go to NY to go to where I wanted in NJ it was an insane bus route.

 Back home the school week starts back up and we have a basketball game coming up and this girl who was cool as hell her name was Thalia and I always messed up her name and the tall one which her name was Taliah man was I always confuggled lol and honestly I can be confusing their names right now lmfaoooo ohhh man I am so sorry if I am because they were both my home girls love them to death. So lunch comes up and I sit on their table its Thalia, Taliah, Hakim and his girl and Thalia's boyfriend, and that dude was grilling me hard core and I was so confused as to why, but so I was extremely far from popular right but everyone sees me with everyone I don't form cliques or anything like that every day I am on a different lunch table and everyone says what's up to me and Nate walks into the lunch room and sees us we were right by the door and he goes up to Hakim and is like oh shit "my boy Mike is on your table that's what's up" and Hakim cool as fuck he said "yea we all cool Mike is funny as hell" we had all hung out and played Manhunt by their house Nate forgot he was like "oh yea Mike was there I forgot we all hung out" lol so Nate sat with us and dude man Thalia's boyfriend was just grilling me down it was so weird, as lunch breaks I walk with her and asked her why her boyfriend was grilling me I didn't know he had problems with me if he wanted to talk it out or whatever let me know, and she said "who" I said "oh no no hold up lmfaooo ya women are horrible" lmfaoooooo she said "that's my ex" I said "when did you guys break up" she said "it doesn't matter I told him you my boyfriend now" lmfaoooooo I said "wait what lmfaooooooo I think I should know if I am anyone's boyfriend you know" lmfaooo she stopped me and said "No I just wanted to piss him off because he got me mad when broke up with me so I told him you were my new boyfriend to get him mad" I said "yo relax lmfaoooo dude looked like he wanted to slit my throat if it weren't for Hakim and Nate knowing me he may have" lol she said "no he wasn't going to do anything I just wanted to make him mad so you my boyfriend whenever he around" lmfaoooooooooooo I said "oh ok lol." So Thalia she ran cross country well fit beautiful girl and I couldn't tell you when people that don't know me see me talking or walking with beautiful girls they give me the stare and till this day I never understood why so if anyone can explain that to me please provide me with an explanation lol because I am at a loss lol.

Well the day comes to an end and its basketball time lol so we get on the bus and Jarrell gets on the bus then Alonzo, then me and all I hear is "OHHHHHHH SHHHHIIITTT yo yo yo wake up wake up and someone yelled shit I think he dead he aint waking up" so we get Coach Merrick and the other coach that one of the basketball players Landon looks like and they get up and we found this kid blacked out on the bus how sad. It wasn't about the fact that we were going to be late to the game, it was the fact that a bunch of high school kids woke up this innocent kid that fell asleep on the bus and not one of his friends or classmates woke him up and the bus driver didn't check to see if everyone was off the bus before coming to pick us up man and it was so heartbreaking the kid woke up scared and disoriented and we packed up all the ballers and took this kid home instead of back to his school to get picked up by his mom the driver just called the school and told them because his house was on the way to the basketball game so it wasn't really off route and we dropped him off and that poor kid had to be scared he knew none of us but we took care of him pretty well and dropped him off home.

So we finally get to North Auburn for the basketball game and they hate us for whatever reason and I never looked into the rivalry because I never cared for it any who J.V starts playing if I remember correctly and I probably don't lol no no I do I do because they were infuriated that's right so unraveling the story Varsity plays and it's a head up match this game is good Jarrell is cooking people the footballers are actually making their fancy shots but we just can't take the lead it's just back and forth back and forth, so the fourth and final quarter come and we start pulling away 2 points 4 points then they catch up and it's hard to keep the lead then our hearts break they drop a 3 point shot and take the lead by one with 5 seconds left. Anyone guess the play yet? Well if you didn't let me tell you pass the ball to Abel lol Jarrell brought the ball up passed it to Abel by the half-court Abel crossed and shook the defender a bit but he still contested the shot and the ball was up in the air hit its peak the buzzer rang and guess what the shot went in of course lmfaoo I tried to infer it earlier, I tried to prep you for it I hope you paid attention to the boring parts of the book lol well the tension of losing back to back and the rivalry and the buzzer beater do you think they were upset well yes they were lol and the entire crowd ran down on us it was like breaking open a beehive it was crazy they started fighting on the court so we ran on the court and got as many people as we could out the cops were there already made a blockade and escorted us out to the bus it was bad but no one was hurt I think we actually knocked a couple of them out from the Varsity team, it was just way too many people to see what happened and man we let the jokes fly on the bus lol and couldn't go back there without a police escort it was a good night.

So, the weeks progress in school and what happened was I was not doing so well in Science class. I was put in remedial, which is sort of like after school the Science teacher has a 45-minute block for extra teaching if you were borderline failing. Well what did I do all I did was sleep an extra 45 minutes in the remedial. I didn't care I was going to pass anyway but there was this girl there and well she had a big booty to say the least I was very attracted to her so after class what did I do I went and got her number and we became real cool she was actually a really nice girl so Valentine's day was coming up and what did I do, bought her flowers and chocolate of course this was like my first real Valentines right. I get off the bus and head to the cafeteria and I saw her and we sat and talked until the bell rang and we were just hanging out didn't care that the bell rang and we had to go to homeroom, I do what I want and I gave her the chocolate and flowers and she was shocked and surprised and then the thing happened, she told me she had a boyfriend aww man but why she aint tell me before now what do I do lol well I will tell you since you asked so nice, I didn't do anything she actually accepted the gifts lol her boyfriend actually didn't do anything for her on Valentine's day and the only gifts she got were from me, hmmm wait a minute writing this that was pretty familiar, I wonder if this is where it started I doubt it but now I have to make a mental note of this and reassess somethings wow that was weird but when I get into the later chapters I do get thanked a lot by girls who have boyfriend's on Valentine's day that was really weird to see and acknowledge but ok moving on you guys will read it later. So, she accepted the gifts and we were really good friends, but I backed off because now I know she has a man even though he was a chump but any who that was Valentine's Day lmfaoooooo.

Now I hate cold weather and it's the weekend around March now and I am with Jeremiah and Kabir and he had some beautiful home girl with him and we went with a couple people to a party Jeremiah found out about by Burger King on 32nd street in Lexington City. As we are walking there we are getting to know everyone mixing it up laughing just enjoying time with each other, and that is the thing about the people I am always with they accept everyone as do I because I know their persona as they know mine and the people we keep around are genuine, honest, and humble and will help you and be there for you in a heartbeat no matter what time day or what they are doing we just have it in us to go and help we will all stop everything we are doing to lend a helping hand just, I don't know I love these dudes man always glad to have them in my life. So, we get to this party and its wild so fuck that smoking shit I wasn't really known for smoking weed at the time I did it a couple times but party time is party time and drinking time to me fuck all that. The party is taking off I know absolutely no one in that party Jeremiah and Kabir were nowhere to be found so I step outside to make sure everything is alright, and it was so cold and quiet you could hear a needle drop or clock ticking. So walking in it was like two houses connected by a gate and a driveway that lead to a parking plot on 4 sides just empty spaces until people parked their cars and you simply just see the second level, supporting pillars, empty parking spots and a door to your right where the party was, so I thought well fuck it he has to be inside there's no one out here and all I hear is someone rushing to me heavy breathing in my head I'm like what the fuck, I turn around and its Kabir, so I ask him "what's up" and he's out of breath telling me that his friend is inside and he doesn't know but something is wrong, so to me when I hang out with my friends I don't know where it stems from but like I protect them make sure they are ok because like I know my fighting ability I know what I can take and who I can take out and there aren't many that I would have a problem fighting, my high school years were bad I thought I was invincible I didn't care how big you were if you wanted or had problems we were throwing fist no talking no questions right, so I go inside and check on his home girl and dam I kind of don't want to paint this picture but there's no way around it, I went in the party and the girl was black out drunk she was gone, she couldn't even keep her head straight up and these guys at the party were groping her and tossing her around at the party, I said oh hell no I stopped that shit real quick I went in there and grabbed her up and took her out of the party and people didn't stop me I guess because they thought I was going to do something, so I brought her outside laid her on the steps and Kabir was shook he thought she was drugged but I can tell she wasn't and he was freaking out so I had the solution it wasn't a good one by any means but you just have to know that sometimes putting your faith in people is a chance you have to take just remember that there are good people in the world it will never steer you wrong and it hasn't failed me yet, so my best thought process at the time was to call her a cab home there was no way she was staying with us and I was going to make sure she got home safe, Kabir didn't know her address but she started to wake up but still semi- conscious and she told us her address I called the cab and put her in the cab and told the cab driver make sure she gets home I wanted to take her myself but Kabir wouldn't be able to get back and Jeremiah was nowhere to be found. The cab left and I told Kabir to stay by the steps because I knew the people would be mad but I had to go find Jeremiah kid was a lost cause right now, and we had to leave, so I make a right and once I turn that corner let me tell you every guy in that party was out looking for me it was like 18 to 20 dudes mad as all hell ready to fuck me up, in my mind I am already checking myself into the hospital lmfaooooooo but Lord knows that I am knocking at least 2 of them motherfuckers out before I get my ass jumped by 20 guys fuck all that lol so I knuckle up ready to get my ass beat and in my head it's an ass beating I will proudly take to save a girl from getting raped so as long as the hospital take care of me and the girl made it home safe that's a win, win for me fuck the rest lol. The moment comes and now we are like 10 feet away everyone is squared up and all I hear is "YO YO YO what the fuck is going on here what the fuck happened" and Jeremiah comes out of nowhere and completely stops my ass from getting jumped and stomped out, the head of the crowd was like "Yo Jeremiah that's your man's right there" he said "yeah that's my boy Mikey what's good what happened" the guy said "for you my guy I aint going to pound his face in, that (n-word) aint welcome here no more get em the fuck out of here." Aye what lol aint got to tell me twice I grabbed Jeremiah and told him "yo we out of here my g, we got a long walk home and we have to take Kabir home I will tell you later" Jeremiah said "alright bet lets go." So I explained the whole situation to him and Jeremiah's funny ass was like "dam you really ready to get beat up huh I mean what you think you were going to do against a gang of dudes" lol I said "get fucked up what else could I do lol but I was going to take a few of them with me I wasn't about to get stomped out alone" lol. He laughed and him and that guy are no longer friends but you know that wasn't even a question Jeremiah just doesn't associate himself with people like that I can't tell you anyone I know who does we are just different Jeremiah is good kid with a good heart grew up around some questionable people but his personality will always be him just an intelligent, caring, genuine, honest, dude that's Jeremiah man have to respect him and love him that's my brother man.

I am home by this time and Jeremiah and Kabir hit me up and explain what happened because I needed to know if she got home safe and they called me up and like 8:30 in the morning and said she got home safe she is good and she said thank you and she was sorry that I had to see her like that the first time we met and hung out but none of that mattered, if she just wanted to have a good time she could have just told me I would have watched her closer until I knew it was time to stop drinking and I would have told her to be careful but that wasn't the case of course with Mike and women it's always deeper, so the residual issue was that she was alone, her mom passed away with AIDS and I am unsure if that is too personal or not because I don't even remember the girls name and the only people that know about this situation is Jeremiah Kabir the girl and I explained to Nameless but beside the point I don't think anyone will be able to pinpoint her from this story any way but yea, and she lived with her grandmother who didn't really care for her or about her and all she had was her mom but she wasn't with us anymore so that day was her breaking point and we all have one so I didn't want her to be embarrassed just because it was our first time meeting but like I know there are roots real deep there it was just a different form of intoxication and its ok we are all human she made it home safe she wasn't raped and she learned and grew from the experience and simple enough as long as she is safe that's all that matters her mental health will stabilize she won't be depressed too much longer and I have actually never spoken to her again since that day so I hope you're doing well girl keep your head up you made it out the adversity so stay strong.

On a side note just because we are on the topic, I was at party with my very good brothers and his girl was there, so my brother is well he considers himself an introvert and I don't because he is very social he just needs to be nudged so if I push him a bit like hey just talk to her or ask that question you know he will open up and get into great conversations he's a very smart guy just one of those people you need to push a bit there's nothing wrong with that. So, at the party I saw his girl grab a drink then another one and she got to her third and in my head, I was like ok hold up that's the limit there. I basically watch out for everyone not many people have the experience I have with women or society or have the thought process I have, I see and analyze situations so quickly and I see all the outcomes fairly associated with that person so since I don't want anyone getting in trouble and I know peoples personalities, families, wants, needs, vices, problems, body language, and add it all up in a fair amount of time within the ongoing scenario I make a decision with the best options with the best outcomes for said person. So I walked up to my brother and said "uh bro come here real fast" he said "what's up bro" I said "it's time for your girl to get home man she had too many" he listened we drove her home and gave her water to drink and he walked her home and we went back to the party. The next day he told me that her parents spoke to him and thanked him for bringing her home early because she seemed drunk and they appreciated that he took good care of her. Then he asked me how did I know, I told him "first off you're my brother, secondly you and her started going out so it would not have been a good look if she went home at 3 in the morning heavily intoxicated her parents would have never trusted you, and I have never seen her drink but after the second drink I can tell that was her limit by how she was acting it was clear she is not a drinker that is why I brought her the water and took the 3rd drink from her and told you we had to get her home." He said "yo thank you my brother I appreciate that I didn't think or notice any of it" and I said, "I know but that's what I am here for man we are here to take care of each other." They had a pretty good relationship they learned and grew together so it's an experience that is going to stick with them both even though they aren't together anymore they had a good connection, she never had a person in her life as good as my brother and my brother has never experienced a woman such as her and you know life had its way and they went their separate ways but there was no animosity they ended it well as two mature adults in a working relationship as they should. They helped each other and grew and learned and that is life what can I say.

 In all honesty I am treading pretty lightly because talking to my brother Ronaldo Williams yesterday I actually realized where I was in this story and the next chapter is Kaylynn and I didn't realize how fast I got here and I am wasting paper because I don't want to relive this and it hurts and the next chapter is where my life just took a spiral downward and I am like literally recovering from it now after all these years. I have been at peace with everything that happened until recently when Nameless came into my life and just crushed what was left of my soul but that's ok I forgive her but any who I don't have much time left to finish this story and get it out to you so I have to keep chucking along.

At minimum at this point I guess I haven't apologized for the writing all the horrible punctuation and grammar but understand that this story is told in format of where I was in life and school and how ignorant I was back then and how much I didn't give a shit about anything but spending time with my friends but everything will be much better after the next couple of chapters punctuations, grammar, sentence structure but the lols and lmfaos they will be staying sorry I remember certain things and they are still very funny to me, hopefully to you as well.

I guess we shall continue, so being on the basketball team clearly I met what you would consider or people who you would call thugs, or gangsters or whatever label you want to place on them, so this common occurrence and theme in my life has been I really don't give a fuck what set you represent, what gang you're in, who you don't get along with none of that shit matters to me because I know you, I know who you are when you're alone, I know why you choose the vices you choose I know who you are when no one's around and you aint that gangster, well to me anyway because people respect me, to you I used to know kids that if you simply looked at them the wrong way they had no issue punching you in the face. But me being who I am is like why like to me that is not reason enough to get into an altercation but the people I used to know they didn't give a fuck they were throwing fist just because, but what was the underlying factor and where I am in life now I completely understand the front they put, like I knew before but I wasn't able to articulate it as well before as I can now so I used the word respect, but it simply wasn't that. Now allow me to explain a very small circumstance, living in Auburn and going to high school in Auburn gangs were all around and everyone knew who they were. So playing sports and getting to know everyone I met quite a few, there was this thing one guy he was relatively short but stocky always acted tough around everyone unless it was just me and him hanging out then he was so relax not tense and funny so I was like well I grew up with these dudes nothing new here so I knew how to break him and get him to trust me right. So we hung out several times and at this point in my life me and my mom's relationship wasn't at the best I didn't see the point in ever going home after school to an empty home it just didn't make sense to me I didn't want it to be like Lexington City all over again, so I would do whatever the fuck I wanted to do and many people in Auburn didn't have that privilege they had to be home at certain hours, check in with their moms, the whole nine right. Some people felt embarrassed about it that they couldn't hang out late like all the gangbangers get home at whatever hour so they put this persona on to showcase that they are tough and not to mess around with them but hiding this little fact that they lived in strict household with very strong women as their mothers and they knew they couldn't go home late or they would get their asses beat and mom didn't care in the hood. She would go out to the most common hangout spots and grab your ass by the throat embarrass you in front of your friends and take you home, so to not let any situation ever get to that point they built this wall this tough guy fighter persona so corny but I get it man, I get it and whenever it gets late to that point they make up an excuse to go home before momma dukes comes out to hunt.

So the time comes for another party go figure lol so all of us the ball players are in there me, Jarrell, Pete, Baren, Alonzo, Jayson, all the kids from school it was a good party and there was this girl of course beautiful I wanted to get to know her and she looked kind of familiar, then I saw her walking around with my friend from school we shall call him Cam, and I walked up to Cam and he introduced me to her and he asked me if I knew her because she went to school with us and then it hit me that's where I seen her but I believe she was a fairly new transfer she was dope funny and she was from Argentina so I stuck with them the rest of the night because we were just clicking having a great time and we didn't even drink that much honestly we weren't even tipsy, so for some reason we leave the party and its just us three and we start walking and heading home but let me tell you I was all the fucking way damn near Salinas and just so you guys can gather the distance imagine Pennsylvania being 12 miles long and I lived on the East end and the party was 12 miles away on the West end that's how far I was at like midnight 30 in the middle of Auburn it was not a good look just thinking how far I had to walk home. So, my thought was that me and Cam would drop off home girl clearly so we knew she would make it home safe and we would go our separate ways and meet up in school on Monday. Man was I wrong you know Mike always alone always got to do shit by myself man. We walk maybe 2 miles just walking talking having fun when Cam gets a call and when he looked at his phone he didn't notice what time it was and said Oh SHHII-ITTT and picked up the phone and you just heard this lady screaming at him and we got to a corner and he told home girl he had to go home and fast because he was late. He turned and gave me this look straight into my eyes and said "Mike you make sure she gets home safe" I said "yea of course bro I wasn't about to walk home and let her find her way home alone like the fuck" he said "that's not what I meant, Ima tell you again make sure she gets home safe" I said "I got you I won't let anything happen to her I'm walking her straight to her door no issues brother" he said "you damn right." So if anyone could guess where she lived, she lived by one of the worst streets in Auburn at the time, and now since we were not on the far west side of the city we were as south as you can go, now at 2 in the morning I had to walk this girl all the way North past the gang infested streets of Auburn just what a night man. So, we start our hike and just talked all night and I learned so much about her who she was a person her background it was just good deep conversation and we became good friends for a while. So, we finally go to her house surprisingly without any issues, she thanked me and on my way, I went to go home. I think I got home at like 4 am I was tired man.

 Schools back in session and I saw Cam in the hallway, and he said, "thank you for taking her home and getting her home safe I appreciate it not many people would have done that." I said "what did you think I was going to do, she was with us she was our responsibility I wasn't going to let her go home alone in the middle of the night in the middle of Auburn that's kind of against who I am and I actually had thought we were going to drop her off together it would have been bad if I got jumped by myself at least with you I would have a fighting chance but what happened that night?" He said "nothing I had curfew and forgot and my grandmother called me bugging out I had no choice but to get home and I knew if I left her with you she was going to be in good hands," I said "oh I didn't know you had curfew I thought you were a blood" and he replied "no I'm not a blood everyone thinks I am because the people I grew up with all became bloods and I'm always around them because their my friends but don't let none of that gang shit fool you these cats aren't all living that gang life like they portray and act in school they just act tough but thanks again I appreciate you taking care of my home girl she said you were real nice and respectful," I said "no prob man anytime I got you," In an explanation of the after party and walk home the point is that as thuggged out as these kids may seem as tough as these kids may be I experience everyone's and I mean everyone's vulnerabilities and I don't share it I keep it between me and said person and they just seem to have this high level of respect for me and even to continue the story almost finishing the conversation cool guys came and one said "yo Cam what you doing around this chump" and Cam said "yo relax he aint no chump this a cool as (n-word) so if you got a problem with him then I got a problem with you" and dude just said "yo relax I was just joking bro but if you riding for him like that then he cool in my book Ima catch you later though" and I told him "you didn't have to do all that I know him to I know he just acting tough he jokes a lot," Cam said "yea but that guy gets annoying real quick even though we grew up together he not built like you" and I said "I got you bro anything you need you know I got you just ask" and we went our separate ways to class.

Towards the end of the day I saw Jarrell, Alonzo, Baren, Pete and Jayson, and they were like "ayo Mikey you coming to Franklin Park today for ball," in my head I was like ehhh I am beat and tired I just want to go home and go to sleep, so I just told them "nah man I'm not feeling like balling today Ima bit tired Ima just go home" and Alonzo always funny ass "nah man you pussy you don't want them Franklin dudes cooking you on the court" lol Alonzo funny as hell love that kid and everyone laughing and I say "nah have ya fun I don't want to score all the points today I'll let you guys have it today" lol, and they all laugh and we go to our classes. The day comes to an end and I just get on the bus and go home and go to sleep it was just a long week already.

The next day comes and they all coming at me, Pete in home room like "yo it was you right you set us up right" lol I was at a complete loss and I see Jarrell in the hallway and I walk up to him and I'm like "yo why Pete so mad at me lol he out here saying I set you guys up" and Jarrell just starts laughing and it makes me more confused I'm like "what the fuck happened yesterday?" Jarrell said that they were in the middle of a game and some guy got mad and pulled out a gun and just started firing shots and we said fuck that and got the fuck out of there as fast as possible, I said "see good thing I didn't go lol and I'm glad yall didn't get hurt man what the fuck that shit is crazy." He starts laughing he says "yea that's why Pete saying you set us up lmfaooo because the one day you didn't go we get shot up" lol Pete funny as hell and Pete came out of nowhere and Jarrell said "yo Pete why you telling Mikey he set us up" lmfaoooooo and Pete starts laughing and says "yo he was shook right ahhhhhhh gootttt eemmmmmmm" lmfaoooooo. Man, I love those dudes they are some of the funniest people I have ever met in my life man great sense of humor just out of this world and the chemistry they share they are family they are my family I love them dudes. So Junior year comes to an end and it was good had no complaints, throughout the summer I was usually with Jeremiah, Daziel, or Adrien, and Dennis, just good people to be around overall, we are all still very tight till this day.

Chapter 12

Senior Year, Kaylynn

Kaylynn, Kaylynn, Kaylynn I love you and miss you dearly and I shouldn't even be saying that knowing you're married now but there was never any love lost, I always knew you would make for an exceptional wife and mother I hope everything continues to go well for you, for it is much deserved.

Senior year rolls around and just thought this was it college next year so let's make the best of senior year. First day no food fights greeted everyone from last year even though we all hung out all summer it was good being in school and seeing everyone all together. It was a good way to start the year. Jarrell and the crew are planning on joining basketball you know; basketball is a part of who they are, so I completely understood, and they asked me and I said no lol. I just didn't want to get involved with all that bullshit and let the football players take over and I just wasn't about it, so I decided I was going to join the Bowling team but there was like absolutely no information about it, so I didn't really know what to do about it, maybe just taking a year off of sports was the best option but, I didn't want to do that.

Any who the weeks start to pass by, and I had history class again with my favorite people Elias, Suri, and Arabelle. In class I had actually never spoken to Arabelle but we knew each other because in class

I was the annoying one with Elias and she would randomly laugh at our jokes from across the room she sat on the far opposite side from us and I asked Elias who she was and he told me, that was Arabelle. They knew each other from previous years of going to school together I said oh she funny and cute well beautiful she was, is beautiful. Well one day after class I was walking around taking the long road to my next class because I didn't want to go to class lol, I saw Arabelle talking to Jarrell by his locker, so I went to go intervene lol. Any who was it a bad idea to say the least, well no it turned out to be a very good idea, so I went over there and Arabelle was in the middle of inviting Jarrell to a youth group that she tends to, Jarrell was like nooooooooooooooo thank you lmfaoooooo and he said but you can ask Mikey I don't know if he up for that type of stuff and sure enough I was lol. In high school I didn't care what we were doing as long as I was out the house and laughing was involved then I was always going to say yes and Arabelle was funny so it was going to be a good time but, going to youth group by myself and I barely knew Arabelle well that was a no. So, after school where did I go lol straight to Jamel and convinced him that it was a good idea and Jamel said sure why not.

Friday comes and we get there right, everyone is all sitting in a circle and as Arabelle is walking us up to where everyone is sitting, I saw this girl lol well you know with me there is always a girl. These girls are exceptional when my heart eyes them right, she was just simply beautiful and a smile from ear to ear I tried to not look at her very much but I couldn't help it any who, we sit down and we go around the room introducing ourselves which at this point I cared less about I just wanted to know that girls name lol. So we meet Rylee, Mabel, and Max which in fact he was the football player from my homeroom cool to see a familiar face and then her, her name was Marinella, and the person who was hosting or in charge per say of the youth group was Austin. Man you know like I feel like I can't get away from shit lol it all hurts because like Nameless' real name is the same as Marinella's first name so just me talking about these stories bothers lol but it's all good man I'm healing so we are all gravy lol and Marinella just had a baby and to be honest I was really sad inside but very happy for her and her healthy child and her relationship with her boyfriend is going well I couldn't honestly say I have ever seen her happier than in the pics she posted with her newborn and her with her boyfriend so my prayers are out to them I am very happy for the both of them, and life goes on. Austin you know since he is the leader he explains life situations and what are the right courses of actions to take in certain scenarios how to abide by God and do good by him and I was like thinking to myself, oh it's this type of youth group I don't know if I can continue this even on the first night I felt it wasn't for me, but I couldn't disrespect Arabelle by leaving and a part of me wanted to get to know Marinella so I was like let me not dismiss this maybe I can actually learn something from this guy and these peoples stories so I will give it a couple months I mean why not. Then Austin starts talking and tells us to look at each other and gives us some stupid ass statistic that one of us is going to die and not make it to 18 because whatever study and statistic said and we pay no attention to it well me and Jamel didn't you know this isn't the first time we are hearing this shit everyone tells us this lol. So the meeting comes to an end and we are cleaning up and me and Max start talking while we are helping put away the chairs and then we go down stairs and let Austin close up the church well we used a part of the church on the side so up on the third floor there was a reception section that they used for fundraisers for the church and the school and they allowed us to use it for youth group every Friday. Any who Arabelle said thanks for coming and she introduced me and Jamel to Rylee and Marinella which were the girls she hung out with outside of church the most. We were familiarizing ourselves with everyone and they asked if we were coming back and hesitantly, we said yeah, we will be back next week.

 The next week comes and we are back at youth group and it was actually good you know hearing people's stories how they overcame adversity and how they proceed to stay positive and keep their head up. It was nice well not knowing that other people were suffering but knowing that they didn't allow certain life situations to get the best of them and they made the conscious decision to overcome it and better themselves. At this point we are getting along with everyone and there was this thing coming up in Concord like a church event and they wanted us to go to. Alright so me and Jamel said we would go.

    School is ongoing and Jamel hates a class and he wants to get out of it so I told him I was in this Piano class and it was pretty dope I never played the Piano or any instrument of that matter other than what Elian taught me on the guitar so he asked if there were any cute girls in the class and I said there's only one girl in the class lmfao he said ehh ok if it's an easy passing grade I will go. He spoke to his counselor and the next day would you know it he was in my class and it turned out to be a horrible idea to have us in class together lmfaoooo poor teacher. We didn't make her life hell there was another kid there that Jamel had nicknamed him Virgil lmfaoooooooo this funny kid who was short black had short dread locks and Jamel said that he looked like Static Shock lmfaooooooooooooooooooooooo you guys don't even understand how funny this was because it seemed to be that the artist for the cartoon Static Shock got his inspiration from this kid in our class it was like a complete doppelganger lol for the rest of the school year the kids name was Virgil lmfao. So Virgil was a very overactive animated kid he would just joke all day long and just didn't know when to shut up which I didn't care because he took the heat off of me and Jamel and when him and the teacher went back and forth that was my time to go and talk Amelia and get to know her and try and get her number, and we actually became very cool she just wasn't giving out her number man I tried I spit my C game, B game, A game, I improvised, man I threw everything I had in my book at her she just wasn't budging lol, but she was so beautiful and cool and down to Earth.

Jamel one day comes up to me in lunch and says "yo you sure Amelia doesn't have a boyfriend?" I said, "no she never mentioned anything to me why?" He had a look on his face and said "look look" I turn and look and see her holding hands with this dude and I knew him and I was like "oh shit" Jamel said while he was laughing "yo you better back off and stop trying before ol boy beat you the fuck up" lmfaooo I said "hey bro we never speak about this ever again to anyone I will step back and he never hears about this" lmfaooo we both laughed and I kept that shit to a minimum with her just hi and bye, how you feeling, how's your day going lmfaooooo.

Friday comes and we get to youth group chat it up a bit then Austin comes in the van and picks us up and to Concord we go. It was fun we got pretty close and I don't remember Max being there I actually think he had a football game to go to so he couldn't attend but he's usually there with us. We get to Concord and me and Jamel just look at each other and we knew we just knew man. Looking out the window of the van and dudes walking down the street with their blue bandanas hanging out the right side back pocket and me and Jamel had the same thought, yo no trouble today none avoid it at all costs we were with women and it's just not worth it. So we get to church and it's just man, no respect out there dudes in church walking in and singing in the choir with their blue bandanas hanging out and I just had enough I felt extremely uncomfortable, so I walked out, I acted like I went to the bathroom and walked out took a break, Jamel followed behind me and we talked outside and we had the same feelings just uncomfortable and he didn't want to go back to the youth group after this but I couldn't just leave you know I respected Arabelle very much and me and Marinella became close but he didn't like Austin well he did there was just an aspect that he was our leader and very religious and Jamel just didn't like that he would say all this stuff but then he smokes like he felt it was a bit hypocritical but Jamel was my brother and he would never let me go someplace alone especially knowing I had to walk all the way back home by myself he was just a solid dude he's from the streets so you know we clicked we know how the streets work. Any who the night ends Austin drives us all back and we get home.

Me and Jamel got out by the church and Austin had asked us if we wanted a ride home and we said no we would walk, and we decided to venture out and see what good old Auburn had to offer us. We found ourselves walking on Keene Ave and you know the College kids were out and about tearing up the streets of Auburn all drunk and shit so what did we do. It was time to go find a party. We come up on the corner of Keene Ave and Leonia and there was this house a couple just walked out of and some guy on the back patio, me and Jamel looked at each other and had the same thought just walk up in there but so we took the path in between the bushes and felt kind of bad so we looked at the dude he was drunk and asked him "hey is this a private party" he said "nah man come on in" and didn't even second guess it. We walked up in through the back door and it was the entrance to the kitchen which was actually pretty big and there were a few people there and to the left was a bathroom with the door open and two girls were making out and we knew this was it this was a good idea right, some guy tipsy walked right up to us and said "yo you guys new here?" We said yea Freshman at the college lol I love how me, and Jamel just have the same thoughts and answers to people without even talking about it before.

The guy said "yo welcome my names Jack this my place you're welcome here any time you want and the party is downstairs free liquor for everyone all I ask is that you don't go upstairs and we are cool man do whatever you want and have fun man everyone is cool here." That is when our friendship with Jack started. We walked downstairs and man it was intense and we didn't get the basement yet man we felt the energy and boy my glasses fogged up real quick lmfaooooooooo had to clear that up before I got down there lmfaooo can't be looking stupid in front of college girls now can we. We get down stairs and to your front is just the wall so you had to make an immediate right and the basement opened up and 20 – 25 feet straight you had a bar which took up about a quarter of the left side of the basement and in front of the bar was a dance floor which lead way to a stage with a pole in the center, behind that was a wall that separated the front and back parts of the basement, and the back part had a ping pong table then a couch and a tv with room on every side to host enough people it was great, a massive basement free liquor, women, a stripper pole oh the endless possibilities of fun. Me and Jamel went our separate ways and just started clicking with people dancing having fun drinking and I kept going back to the bar and the bartender asked me "yo you like Jack Daniels" I didn't know who Jack Daniels was at the time but oh boy did we become the best of friends from there, I said "sure do brother" and he pulled out this massive jug of Jack poured me half a cup and I kept going back all night. I lost track of time and Jamel, I went out looking for him and found him upstairs with a couple girls, so I had to go and help him out lol. He saw me coming and he was like "hey ladies have you met my friend Mikey yet?" Lmfaooo and that was the beginning of that line and everyone loved that line for some corny ass reason and well safe to say we got a lot of numbers and I couldn't tell you how. The night comes to a rest and we go up to Jackson and ask him if he hosts parties every weekend and he said "every weekend what? We start Thursdays and end Monday mornings before class lmfaooooooooo, yo people and my friends loved you guys you're welcome anytime you want man." Me and Jamel looked at each other and said "yo we will be back next week" lmfaoooooooo. So we had this longgggggggggg walk home, and for some reason maybe because we were kind of intoxicated we decided to walk up through the college by Dover Street through the mall to get home we thought it would be easier and it seemed so long I think I got home by like 6 – 6:30 in the morning. I didn't wake up till like 1 in the afternoon lol.

Monday comes and me and Jamel are chatting it up about the weekend we didn't really talk or see each other after that party. We get to Piano class and Virgil just I don't know man I guess this kid was one of those that anything that came up in his head he would just say it right lol. So we're all laughing and having fun and our teacher was so strict she had no humor in her it took me and Jamel some serious jokes just to even see a smirk or smile like we had to continue for the whole block of class to get one laugh out of her lmfaooo and Virgil while we were talking said "Voulex ous voucher avec moi bitches" it was a part of a Lil Wayne song and Lil Wayne was just everyone's favorite rapper except me everyone knew I was all about Joe Budden all day every day, but when he said it our teacher had literally just walked into class and heard him say it and she was pissed she was like "WHAT DID YOU SAY ? DO YOU EVEN KNOW WHAT THAT MEANS? WELL DO YOU BECAUSE IT MEANS DO YOU WANT TO HAVE SEX or something like that I was going to google translate it but ehhh whatever not important lol any way she was pissed lmfaooo and she was going to send him to the principal's office but just kicked him out instead and looked at me and Jamel and said "did you tell him to say that" we said "no we didn't know what he was talking about" lol that was thee longest block of Piano class ever and Amelia was like "yall funny but are a bunch of idiots" lmfaooooo Amelia was dope as fuck lol. Any way on a sad note because this broke my heart, lunch comes and I got my plate and I was eyeing the whole cafeteria scanning seeing where I was going to sit today and I looked all the way to the left and saw this table empty in its entirety, and this girl was sitting there I couldn't see who she was and she had curly hair I was like why she sitting by herself and I go, and I see Arabelle aww man did that break my humble heart man, I said "yo Arabelle what are you doing here sitting by yourself," and she told me how she lost pretty much all of her friends when she started going to church and I said "why that's weird" and she said "yea well I guess they weren't really my friends per say honestly" and it hurt me man Arabelle was the coolest funniest girl around how are you just going to abandon her just because she goes to church that's fucked up so I sat with her so she knows she wasn't alone I had to make sure she never felt alone she was my friend I can't allow that ever especially with her she has such a warm, caring, genuine heart it wasn't right and anytime from there if I ever saw her sit at a table alone I didn't care who of my friends sat at lunch Arabelle came first always.

Friday comes and its youth group time me and Jamel go but we go better dressed than usual lol. About halfway in I tell Arabelle that me and Jamel had to go somewhere, and she thought it was weird but she's my home girl so without any disrespect I told her, and we left. Where did we go? Anyone want to guess lol? We went to Jackson's house lmfaoooooooooooo oh boy was it a party you guys are about to learn something. So we get to the party we drinking I'm already drinking my Jack straight up and Jackson sees us and I love this dude he gets so excited when he sees me and Jamel and he walks up to us and is like "yo you guys really came man that makes me happy yo enjoy yourselves" and he introduced us to these two girls he was like "yo these two dudes are legit get to know them," listen man they were gawgeous and I was not walking away from this girl she was super fly I stayed with her all night getting to know her lying to her about every question she asks me because I was 17 and not in college lmfaooo then it happened the got dam lights went out I don't know if it was Auburn or just our block but there was a black out, no music everyone mad everyone sobering up because they are upset. So me and Jamel looked at each other and looked up and there was the exposed ventilation system and we started just playing beats on it and someone had a strobe light flashlight and put it on and me and Jamel became them dudes man people requested to have us at every weekend his boys and home girls loved us because that one night lol so Jackson was like "yo yo take it easy lol I'm renting" lmfaooo so after we stopped like 2 minutes later the lights came back on and we started drinking again and that girl wouldn't leave my side it was great but me and Jamel went to go refill our cups and Jackson was leaving I was like "yo Jackson what's up you leaving?" He said, "yea I have to take my girl home" I said, "wait wait you good to drive you want me to take you or go with you?" He said "nah man I am good I know myself brother trust me I would ask you if I knew I wasn't good, just stay here and entertain the guests I appreciate it though you're the only one that asked me thanks man I will be right back" I said "ok man no problem I will be here waiting just to know you got there and back safe" he said "thanks brother." Me and Jamel are at the bar and we are talking and looking around and I see this girl in the back playing beer pong with her boyfriend and I was like "Jamel I have to go get her number" and he said who, "I Told him 3 o'clock beer pong table" he said "she with her man," I said "yea but she gave the look bro so I have to know what she about," he looked again and he said "yea she definitely looking over here and she aint want to see me," I told him "yea so what's the plan," he said "fuck me man I don't know I can't see who they playing against but I got you." So, we walk over there and start playing stupid "Hey you guys who got next on the table?" While getting past the door we saw that there were actually two girls on the other side of the table so that was a simple equation for Jamel I knew that was no problem for my man, I was just focused on coming up with a plan to get her man out the fucking room so I can have some time to talk to her lmfaoo. So I saw that she was the only one with a cup and it was a see through one which is very important to this story so follow it, and her stupid ass boyfriend was done he was drunk by all senses of the word and now I am reading her body language while trying to get this chump out of the beer pong table. So, I'm like "yoooo anyone thirsty, anyone want a drink?" This is important because the more people that need drinks the more time this man spends at the bar the more time I get to try and get her number lol well that was my thinking back then

I didn't think it was that bad of an idea especially him being drunk hopefully he spills a drink and has to go back and get more lol. Her boyfriend says "yooo get me a drink," I countered with "wait man you been hogging the beer pong table let me play a game and you can get us drinks" lol he had a pause and said "yea sure who else wants drinks?" Jamel already knew and said "yo get one for us 3 man" and he asked his girl and she said "no babe I got one already" he said "ok so four five" I said "yea 5 sounds right man" lol and he said "ok be right back and this is my girlfriend she'll play with you for a moment while I am gone getting drinks." So let me learn you something, she had a clear cup with Jack on the rocks, her body language was not telling me that she wanted to be there so as her boyfriend walked out of sight I looked at Jamel and bam fuck beer pong aint no one wanted to play bum ass beer pong with these beautiful women here fuck that shit lol. So he started talking to the two girls always a simple task for him and I started talking to this girl, I said "why you not drinking I can tell all shit is water what's going on," she said she isn't really a drinker and she didn't really want to be at the party because she knew how her boyfriend gets when he is drunk and she doesn't want to babysit and on top of that I just sent him to go get more drinks lol. I said, "I sent him to go get more drinks so I can separate you and him so I can talk to you" she said, "oh really why is that?" I said "because I think you're very beautiful and I would like to get to know you" she said "well if that is true here call me sometime" I said "I will lovely" and her boyfriend came back and we left back to the other side I heard him say "hey babe what happened why you let them leave they were cool" lmfaoooo oh man have to love the chumps sometimes. So to learn you something back then I wasn't able to articulate everything my mind saw and add it together which now it takes me seconds when I walk into a room usually I can assess an entire class room of kids by the time I pick my seat and sit down I know who is who, who has problems and what they are man shit is so simple to me today. To explain what I was seeing and couldn't explain at the time, this girls body language was yelling saying that she didn't want to be there at that party, the confirmation was the drink she was holding because man you women are so smart that's probably why I love the small subtle things you do that go unnoticed until I walk in the room. She had Jack on the rocks and the bartender was not stingy with the Jack so what she did since it was on the rocks she would just hold on to it and let the ice melt and dilute the drink so she wouldn't get drunk man just those small things man I wish I was that smart at times lol because back then you didn't waste Jack around me I would just finish it for you lol I loved Jack but that is beside the point just how everything she did that added all up and I couldn't explain it but I knew because I saw it, and now you don't want to play the games now that I am an expert I would crush every signal, false signal, body language, oh man it's just too easy but I don't do that anymore I stopped all that partying and shit lol but oh was it fun oh so fun especially back then that I didn't really have respect so my mouth was real slick lol.

 The night continues and I went back to the girl Jackson introduced me to and we were just feeling each other that girl was dope like heroine. We had so much fun she was one of the only girls that I got her number and stayed with her all night. My main part about all this partying was to test my skills against all these older mature women. All I wanted to do was get their phone number nothing more, I just simply want to test my game and communication and response I had absolutely no intention on talking to any of these women after a party night lol if you see my phone and I may still have it, oh shit I don't I gave it to Fabyen fuck lol you'll meet him next year good guy, well any who my phone contacts list looked like this Jen from college, Jennifer from college, Rachel from college, Jess from college, Janessa from college, Michy from college, Michelle from college lol it was so confusing I didn't know who was who I couldn't put a face to any name so there was no point in even calling or talking to these girls again anyway lol my whole phone list was crazy. So me and this girl are dancing the night away and Jackson comes in and the party is ended and good to see him though which meant he made it there and back safely and he definitely wasn't drunk and he was like "oh you guys really got close huh" and the girl said "yea he was super cute and funny better give me a call back" and I said "of course love" but clearly had no intention of calling her back lol and I remember her, let me tell you she was gawgeous super thick short ahhh man body of a goddess and Jackson gave me and Jamel the look and yea of course well be back next week lol. He said "yo next week Halloween party" I said "what does that mean" lol he said "Pajama party stupid" lol me and Jamel said "oh word we be there early man" he said perfect "Ima buy a bigger gallon of Jack just for ya" I said "what perfect" lol. Me and Jamel went on our way home lol good night to say the least.

So the next day Arabelle called me and asked what happened and I love Arabelle, I couldn't lie to her and I told her that we left to go to a party our friend invited us to, and she was mad and it bothered me I didn't want to make her mad she was important to me and she had told Marinella and Marinella oh boy I heard it from her too I felt really bad.

So school comes around homeroom just a beautiful day to get fucked up before classes even start so, I go to homeroom and I go to my seat far right of the classroom second to last row second to last seat and in front of me is this girl Catherine, the seat in front of her to the left is Owen and in front of Owen is Max and the first person in my row is Pete and next to Pete is Bernard right, star football player one of the biggest dudes in school probably the strongest at the time if not arguable. And what happens so he was playing around with Catherine and threw her book on the floor and it fell next to me on the right and the seat was empty and I didn't care right I wasn't getting that shit. Well so I thought first off, clearly in all the places in that room the book had to land next to me of course why not, second being all nice everyone knows me because I am nice Catherine turned around and asked me to pick it up and I said "sure" right it's just a book, well fucking wrong answer, Bernard said "don't pick it up" and I was like oh ok they playing he going to give it back to her and she asked me again so I can tell she was annoyed and of course the nice guy in me is like fuck it just go get it, class about to start I don't want to hear anyone bickering in the morning so what does good ol Mikey do, I just went to go pick it up and Bernard said "yo Mikey don't pick it up" and I didn't care so I went to reach for it and all I heard was like a fucking stampede chair flipping just mad noise coming at me so I get up turn and look and Bernard is right behind me, and now the class was all quiet like the world was in silence waiting watching to see what comes next. What people don't understand is that I don't give a fuck who you are, how much you weigh, how much you bench, how strong you think you are if we throwing hands we throwing hands, a lot of people respect me for it and some people think I'm crazy for that trait but I simply just don't care you're not going to stand there and try and bully people because you believe you're strong, well not believe because that man was like 90% muscle lol I would have got fucked up but that's not the point I don't care about getting my ass whopped it's the point that I won't allow it I have no problem getting my ass handed to me but I'm going down swinging, and the teacher couldn't do anything teachers were scared of him and Owen wasn't going to do anything because Owen knows if it's a fight if I don't get jumped there's no jumping in Pete and Max weren't going to do anything it was just me and Bernard while the class stood and watched and so the awkward thing was that I was still reaching for the book and he was in my ear saying "yo don't pick it up man I'm just trying to fuck with her man" I said "yo but it's too early for all shit man" he said "come on please man I just want to fuck with her" so I stood up and we just looked each other in the eye and as soon as I sat down the bell rang and Catherine went to pick up the book but she thanked me and I still don't kind of understood why lol but any who Owen was like "yo I was waiting to see him throw you across the room" lol I said "oh jeez thanks bro lmfaooo you aint got no faith in me" he said "helllllllllllllllll nooooo not against Bernard" lmfaooooo I said lol "I know I was ready get my face beaten in man but he wasn't going to do it" he said "how you know" I said because he told me he was just playing with her" but in the classes eyes I got punked which as a man it's kind of demeaning is that the word like it takes your manhood away if you allow yourself to get punked but in this situation it was ok because he was the star quarterback for one, one of the most well-known guys in city and another reason I can't put on here lol and on top of that no one in that school would have stood up to him and it was weird because after that I didn't really get looks or anyone trying annoy me lol it was weird but any who we start the day.

So I get to class and Jarrell is there and I didn't have class with Jarrell so I walked back out and walked back in and I was like wait what this my class "yo Jarrell lol what you doing here" lol he looked at me and gave me the shhhhh sign lol in my head I was like what's this kid up to lol. Man, I love my friends they are fucking hilarious and we all have balls of steel lmfaooo. My teacher walks in and is like "hey everyone, wait JARRRREEEELLLLLL what are you doing here?" Jarrell said with a smirk on his face "what do you mean I'm here to see you of course, why else would I be here" lmfaoooooooooooooooooooo she said "Jarrell you better get to class right now" he said "I will be back later my love " she said "you better not" lmfaoooooooo fucking Jarrell man love that dude. So class ends and I am headed to my next class and I find myself cutting through the cafeteria to get to the other side of the school and as I get out the cafeteria a fight breaks out so I go and see what was going on and it was by the security officers desk and I go up the small flight of stairs and Landon is squaring up with some guy and oh if Landon is fighting it's going to be a good fight fuck class I wanted to see this lol. What we did was block off a circle so the security couldn't get through you know we had to let them fight it out as men whatever the situation is as men we had to resolve it because if security came in and broke it up the tension would still be there and they would take it out of school and it'll just get so much worse so rather it be handled then and there. So they start teeing off and Landon dodged a punch and stepped back and he got upset and all I saw was Landon take a running start and just speared this dude lol it was great lol and as he speared him like a football tackle he picked him up and just body slam him all in one move I was thinking to myself, whelp mental note don't get on his shit list lmfaooo then the security guards finally broke through and broke it up but the fight was over by then the guy didn't get up for like 5 minutes lol, then I went to class and my teacher was like "why are you late" I said "well mam there was a fight and I couldn't get past it" lol, she said "you better not be lying" I said "no mam it was a good fight" lol.

I forgot what class I had but it was with Alexander he was a real good baseball player and his brother was the star running back for the school's football team and we would talk all throughout class and I tried and tried and tried to get this kid to like Joe Buddens music the kid would just not budge man lol he loved that tough guy rap and shit, he was kind of tough more funny though good kid always was able to see through the persona and I can't tell you why he had the front on but his brother told us and it was ok it was understandable but you guys see it as embarrassing and there is a double standard when it comes to the situation depending how popular you are which is fucking stupid but whatever this kid was cool as fuck just didn't want to listen to Joe Budden lol. I told him "man just listen to Mood Muzik 3 you will never go back" and he said "yea yea yea whatever" lol. So the day ends and me and Jamel go hang out with our home girl Genevieve she was this cool ass girl that lived across the street from the new apartments and her mom was like never home like ever me and Jamel started to believe that she lived by herself, and we would just go and hang out smoke a black and mild and just talk shit we literally just like spending time with people that was just our thing we loved to laugh and relax so most of the time we would be out it would be with a group of people just laughing the night away we really weren't delinquents lol. So the night was coming to an end we had to walk back home and Genevieve was like you guys want another black and mild for the walk we said sure how can we turn down a black and mild lol well we got on Route 54 which was a few blocks away and unwrapped it and started smoking it and just immediate death, Jesus Christ I never coughed so much in my life and when we looked at it, it was called like a Black and Max or some crazy shit like that and it had a red tip we were like yooo what the fuck this girl just tried to kill us, the next time we had a chance to go to the store we asked for one to see the ingredients it was like 100% pure tobacco we looked at each other and had to go talk to Genevieve like if we couldn't smoke more than one pull there was no way on Earth she was so we had to know where she got this shit from. Next time we saw her in school we talked to her and she said that it wasn't hers she never smoked one before and we were like oh well what the fuck lmfaooo that shit almost killed us don't smoke that shit ever and she laugh and said she was having people over and if we wanted to come by we could later that night. You know me and Jamel always down for a get together, so we go and well safe to say it wasn't a get together lol well it was but not lol. Our homeboy we shall call him Mark was there and me and Jamel just got there and when we walked in the vibe was weird and awkward and we both felt it and Genevieve gave us a drink so we all started talking and Genevieve and Mark went to the kitchen and after a couple minutes it got quite so me and Jamel turn around and Genevieve and Mark out there in the kitchen tounging each other down me and Jamel looked at each other like yooo what thee fuck started laughing and we knew our place lol so we walked right up out that house lmfaooo. Probably one of the most awkward moments ever she could have just told us she wanted to be alone with Mark we would have never went over lol.

School is back in session and I find myself in class with Alexander and guess what, he listened to Mood Muzik 3 and he said "yo did you hear what he said on Family Reunion" he said "you can go home and just Chris Benoit, yo Joe Budden my guy now" lol and I said "see I knew you would like him even though that wasn't the best line on that song but see man now we can have more in-depth conversations about rap" lol. Lunch had come around and sitting on the table with Jonas, Max, Moses, and DeAndre I told DeAndre "yo I finally got Alexander into Joe Budden it took me a while" lol he said "what how did you do that" I said "I told him to listen to Mood Muzik 3 and his favorite line was go home and just Chris Benoit" DeAndre said "wait what that's not even the best line " I said "that's exactly what I told him" he said "so what's the best line my guy Miiiiiikkkkeeeeyyyyyyy" I said "ride or die or do both (and DeAndre started rapping too) ride to the death I'll acapella the whole left side of his chest" and we banged the table at the same time and finished the verse. It was a great moment, it was so corny, but it was a great moment, Joe Budden bringing people together lmfaooo.

So, the day ends, and everyone wants to go trick or treating so we wait for night fall and then leave the apartments and we go the back route because there are a lot of houses and I didn't have to cross the highway. We see a group of people walking and I think I know them so I yell out to this one girl that kind of sort of looked familiar so I just yelled the name of the girl I thought it was lol I was like "ayo Sabrina" lol and by all means it was her lol she said "is that Mikey" I said "hell yea" and she turned around and ran up to me and jumped on me and hugged me I love that girl she was super funny great personality beautiful we got along great and I haven't seen her in a while so we grouped up with them and just went trick or treating with them. It was a fun night overall hung out with great people I haven't seen in a while and tomorrow was the pajama party, so I wanted to get home early for that I didn't really care about school.

Friday comes and Arabelle sees me and asks if I'm going to youth group and I told her no because there was a party and my brother Daziel was coming down to hangout for the weekend and she was upset, she really didn't want me out in the streets partying and getting drunk every weekend her and Marinella really tried to stop me from doing that because they knew the people I was out with and they knew their past and it wasn't such that they were bad people it was more that they didn't want me going down a bad road they talked to me a lot they took really good care of me and I tell you there were times where I wouldn't do things or go hang out with certain people because I knew they would be mad and I loved them and I appreciated them so I didn't want them to worry about me so I just wouldn't go because I couldn't lie to those girls. So, she was upset but she really couldn't do anything about it but let me be, but she didn't give up and they both kept trying and I will always appreciate them for it.

Night comes and Daziel gets to my house and he already knew Jamel we all smoked together with Adrien once last year and played Super Smash Bros afterward. We all link up at Jamel's house and walk to Jackson's so we get there and Jackson always super excited to see us and said "yo what you guys wearing man" lol we "said pajamas bro that's what you said" and he thought we knew what he meant and it was weird so in laymen's terms for a college pajama party that means girls are just wearing bras and panties and guys boxer shorts with or without a pair of shorts with flip flops, no t-shirts lol so we were overdressed to say the least, so what did we do clearly just take off our shirts, that night we got super drunk one of the few nights I forgot how we got home. For the rest of the weekend me, Jamel, and Daziel all hung out together and just had fun man.

School comes and I'm talking with Arabelle and she wants to hang out and go to Woodbury mall after school and Marinella and Rylee are going to be there, and I was like sure why not. So the school day passes and Arabelle pulls up to the back of the apartments in her Hyundai Elentra Hatchback didn't even know they had the hatchback versions it was dope and we went and picked up Marinella and Rylee and went to the mall and Arabelle and Rylee were out walking about and I was just talking with Marinella and I am going to be real honest well this whole book is honest but beside the point, I actually fell in love with Marinella she was very important to me but I couldn't bring it out of me to ask her out like I felt bad because I wasn't a very good person back then and I didn't want her falling for me and feel like it's her responsibility to keep me out of the streets because I was her boyfriend or what not and I didn't want to drag her down I just couldn't do that to her she was very important to me and she tried her best to help me and keep me away from people she believed would be bad for me to socialize with she tried to stop me from partying every weekend as well and like I said these women were important to me so there were times were I wouldn't hang out with certain people because I just didn't want to lie to them about it I couldn't bring it out of myself to lie to either Arabelle or Marinella. Marinella in all honesty was probably my only regret, I do regret not ever asking her out but I just knew that I couldn't break her heart my mind was just not where it should have been to be able to make her happy and I knew that and I acknowledged it and that was the reason for the decision to not ask her out. But if you ever ask me do I miss her well the answer will always be yes, she had a good heart and soul and I hope she is doing very well for herself and I have no doubt that she is I love you Marinella thank you for everything hope you're doing well.

 It comes down to the weekend and we are at youth group and Austin is late which is weird dude was never late for one meeting and he came in all in a suit and we all looked at each other like what the fuck are we going somewhere because we are all underdressed and Austin said no and apologized for being late because he always preached about being on time and always for God he would never be late and things of that manner. So he told us he got hired from Verizon and he prayed for it and there were people who were well more apt and experienced but they gave him the position and sometimes he works late and he tried his best to make it here on time but he just couldn't and he apologized which I didn't care nor did Jamel but whatever. At this time him and Mabel got together and they were doing well, but me and Jamel just didn't feel comfortable that night so we left and Arabelle and Marinella were pissed they told us it was like rude and disrespectful if we were going to leave in the middle of the meeting just don't bother to come at all and I felt super bad so at this point we kind of stopped going but we went to Jacksons house and that was a crazy night the last thing that I remember that night was going to the bar and asking for another shot of Jack and the bartender told me "dude I love you this is like your 17th shot Ima save the rest for you I will tell everyone we are out of Jack" and bam the night turned black. I woke up having a heart attack I fell off something on to the floor I didn't know where I was, I was so confused and when I walked out of the room I walked into a living room and I realized that I was home. Had a huge hangover, headache the works and after a couple days I recuperated I wasn't even thinking about Jamel then I remember he was my friend so I got nervous and I called him he didn't remember what happened either he said he woke up at his house too and we just realized we drank wayyyyyy tooooo much. That my friends was my breaking point, just realizing that I didn't remember what happened, or how even we got home and we had to get through Chambers Ave, cross 2 highways to get home it was just bad and that is when I decided to stop drinking alcohol, and to this day no one could tell you that I am a drinker people will laugh and call you a liar if you told them this story they would say I have never even seen Mikey drink a full beer, I just don't I stay away or at most I would have 3 Blue Moons a year when I hang out with Adrien we usually go out to eat and I would have just one Blue Moon each time and most of the time I wouldn't finish it.

At this time, I started to change and just relax, Marinella saw it and she continued to help me such a wonderful woman she didn't give up. She took me to church with her mom and little brother and like I said I am forever grateful for crossing paths with her such a genuine caring soul I will never forget her and always appreciate it. We talked a lot and I was just attached to her but couldn't just allow myself to hurt her and I knew if there was a small possibility that I could hurt her I couldn't chance it she just meant that much to me. I stopped partying and I started going to more basketball games and that was a nightmare the basketball team was just getting blown out every game and they ended up going up against Saint Alexander's from Fredericksberg Heights remember I mentioned them previously and that was bad lol the halftime score was like 50 – 2 and the game ended 98 – 12, I had no idea why Auburn would even play such a high level school like that it just didn't make sense that schools entire bench were division one college players once they graduate guaranteed.

I would go to youth groups every now and then and then Arabelle and Marinella told me and Jamel that Austin was in the hospital so we had to go and check on him see if everything was alright and well Austin had cancer, and it was bad it was extremely sad seeing him in the hospital like that just laid up no energy tied to the intravenous lines and all it was a sad site. We didn't really know what was going to happen but we kept visiting him and eventually he got discharged home and we would go and check up on him at the house to see if he was ok, it was a really rough patch in his life but he did have us and Mabel and Rylee and his family, so he had support.

Everything actually turned out ok with the aggressive chemo and stuff and from last time I spoke to him and Mabel and the whole crew he was just on close observation and that was pretty much the end of that relationship because me and Jamel never went back there weren't really any more meetings without him recovering and the change started to get better.

At this point with everything that's going on with me I start to pay attention in class more I know it's too late but in my head I was thinking well I got a few more months of class left I am not partying anymore just let me focus and give it some type of effort until school finishes. So, in math class I have all the funny football players Max and Karter then I have Sabrina and Arabelle and of course I sit next to my home girl Arabelle. So we are all laughing in class and some lady in a suit comes in and interrupts our jokes and tells us to quiet down, just wow the audacity of this lady lol so Karter don't give a shit dude is like 6 foot 1 like 200 odd pounds and keeps telling his jokes and we are all laughing and the lady said "excuse me I told you to lower it down" and Karter turns around and says "well who the fuck are you" lmfaooooo and the lady goes "I'm the new Vice Principal and we are going to have a talk in my office rite now get up" lmfaoooooooo when she said she was the new VP the whole class got quiet and when she left we all started laughing lmfaooo not one of us has ever seen her in that school not once.

Our teacher was like "dam you guys messed up pretty bad today" lol he wouldn't joke very much it took us all year to break that guy to make him a part of our class and joke with us. So Karter comes back and says "she didn't want anything she just introduced herself and wanted me to know who she was I didn't get in trouble but she told me not to disrespect her again I told her I didn't know who she was" lol. So the class starts over again and Karter sits in the seat behind Sabrina but one row to the right and Max sits to the left one seat back and one row back and Max looks at me and says "yo Mikey you one ugly motherfucker" lmfaoo and everyone starts laughing and in my head oh it's time to start the jokes bet lol so I say "yea I'm ugly but you always see me with the beautiful girls I aint see you with one yet and the years about to end" lol the class blows up and Max says "oh look at you Mikey got jokes today" lol then he quietly calls Karter and points to Sabrina and Karter says "yo Sabrina you know what the most addicting drug in the world is" and Sabrina says "no what" and Max yells "Craaaaaaaaaaaack" lmfaoooooooooooooooooooo and Sabrina started blushing and was like "oh my God I hate you guys, (while pulling up her pants) yall could have just told me my ass was out" lmfaooooooooo. She couldn't pull it up sitting down so she just got up and pulled her pants up it was hilarious the thing was every one of them they all grew up together they had this sense of humor and chemistry which was good to experience I learned a lot from being in that school.

Well I guess it's that time to introduce Kaylynn I just didn't really want to and I been avoiding it because I know where this topic and path leads and I don't want to cry but also I don't have very much time left to complete this and I will finish it fairly quickly it's just all downhill from here and you know what I heard an enlightened man once say, "do what you want to do be at peace with yourself because at the end of the day as much as we ignore it and don't acknowledge it, time, Time is undefeated."

March comes and everything is going ok, I stopped going to youth group me, Arabelle, and Marinella still hang out and spend time laugh a lot they were good to me they kept trying to keep me on a straight path. A couple weeks into March I get home and usually I would just get on MySpace and A.I.M and catch up with everyone from up North and that's how really me and Cassie kept in touch for a while boy, was she mad when she found out I left to Auburn and didn't tell her I felt so bad she was an amazing friend I apologized very frequently for that for a while. So this one weird day this weird screen name popped up on my friends list and I was like huh who the fuck is that and all of a sudden they messaged me and as confused as I was I responded and we started to talk and she told me her name was Kaylynn. To my recollection it hit me and I knew exactly who this girl was and we start catching up and talking like ohhhhhhhhhh hey how have you been the whole nine right, then she sends me her MySpace profile and that is when I realized I had absolutely no idea who the fuck this girl was right the face that I put to that name was not her. So when she told me her name was Kaylynn in my head my mind went back wayyyyyy back to Freshman year in Spanish class to Jeremiah's cousin Kara right and that is who I was thinking she was this whole entire day we were talking and nothing clicked then all of a sudden she starts asking me about my boy Marcel and it was the weirdest thing just ever I was so confused and lost and just didn't understand how she knew him or what was going on so I played along because I was just lost in my head I was like oh you know he is good we don't talk too much but every now and then we hang out very rare circumstances and whatever so the days flying by me and this girl just clicked and hit it off it was amazing. At this point A.I.M is getting annoying the conversation is getting way too good so what happens she asked for my number lol it was great, and we spoke on the phone for hours until we fell asleep.

The next day comes and first thing in the morning she texted me and that's when everything fell into place we just seemingly meshed into one it was a great feeling and we did not stop texting at all, all day long until she had to go eat dinner with her family and the we jumped on the phone and talked until it was time to go to sleep.

Now comes the first week of April and my mom got the phone bill and sheeeiiiiiiitttttt let me tell you I did not have unlimited texting lmfaoooooooooo my mom was pissed she was like who the hell you sending 1000 texts to the bill is 700 dollars lol and well I had to find some way to pay that shit off I was not about to let this girl out of my sight for 700 dollars we had an instant connection and bond that I had never felt before so I told my mom I would pay it just change the plan to unlimited texting because you know after 7pm it was considered unlimited nights and weekends so minutes weren't being used so that's when we started calling and talking until we fell asleep lol. Then something happened it hit me, like all at once all the conversations just everything she has ever said to me the past two weeks, the lightbulb finally hit and I thought to myself oh shit this girl is Marcel's ex and I didn't even notice it. That's when my heart broke because I never knew how they ended or what happened between them I just never went back to Caldwell High or saw her again and then I realized I had to talk to Marcel about this he is my friend and this is his ex if he is uncomfortable with the situation I can't allow it you know morally speaking it would be wrong. Then that day she had asked me out and of course I said yes lol what the fuck can't say no to a connection so strong. I made it out to Lexington City and hit up Marcel and talked to him and I told him the situation you know genuinely speaking I didn't really know who she was and it didn't click when she was asking me about you, and he said its ok man no worries it's all good. Actually writing this out is pretty funny because I blame my horrible memory on the accident that happens in a few months but writing this down holy shit my memory was bad back then too wow that's fucking weird man I swear I am about to start taking Namenda for memory loss lmfaooo.

Any who she asked me out to the movies and our official date was within the first week of April of 2008 the date is not important to you guys, so it doesn't matter. So I get there and Daziel, and Jeremiah, and Adrien had picked me up because I didn't have a car so they were going to drive me annnnndddddddd the awkwardness was that someone had told Marcel and he came but the guys didn't know my past with Marcel and Kaylynn so I didn't blame them they knew nothing of the situation but any who they drove me to Rivers Ledge theater and they sat down to the left I went to go look for her and she was with her brother and her brothers girlfriend so I met them and it was pretty cool man her brother such a good dude love that guy he let us go to our own separate movie while him and his girlfriend went their own way to another movie coolest thing ever. So the movie finishes and ours ended before theirs and it was good I was able to spend more time with her, everything just felt so good with her around I just held her and she stood on my sneakers some brand new Air Force Ones low tops lol and we just started dancing swaying and talking until her brother and his girlfriend came out and they caught us in the middle of our dancing session lol and I walked them out and stayed with her until they brought the car over and I gave her my sweater actually because it was pretty cold out that night and then walked her to the car opened the door gave her a kiss told her brother thank you and said goodnight to them. Well fuck the goodnight we were already texting by the time I closed the car door lmfaoooo.

Everything was just great with her man had no complaints other than it took me like 2 and a half months to just get her to forget about her ex-boyfriend that was the toughest thing ever but we just meshed everything was just in place with her and our thing was we stopped texting around 7pm and just stayed on the phone and our thing was that George Lopez was on at 10pm and 10:30pm it was two episodes and after that is when we went to sleep and who ever woke up first texted first and that was our whole day just talking about this is when I tell you texting was pretty infrequent and newish and when the bill came my mom came into my room and said "who are you texting 10 thousand times a month this is ridiculous" lmfaoo like yea shits real when me and a girl just bond and connect that's just how it is and I think our max was like 12.5 thousand texts a month and the one thing that was weird that I experienced with her was like after I first saw her and met her at the movie theater and we hung out like literally after I closed the door of the car it just felt wrong it felt weird and she felt the same thing as well so she explained it to me as sort of a separation anxiety like it felt wrong not being around her and not having her in my arms and I would catch myself just feeling like empty it didn't feel normal if we weren't together it felt wrong if she wasn't in my arms like this bond that we shared was intense and I shouldn't really tell this part of the story because she is married and has her own life and

I highly value her and respect her but what she had taught me about myself and about life well how can I not thank her and show my appreciation for her and towards her no matter how we ended you know and I apologize if any of this gets back to her but I am forever grateful for having her in my life the short period that she was there she will always be a part of me and I will always hold her near and dear to my heart there was never any love lost.

Back to school we were in class and all of a sudden the fire alarm sets off and what fuck yea lol so we all go outside and I am with Arabelle and I call Kaylynn and the best part about her is she does not care what is going on where she is she will always pick up the phone it was just any chance I had to hear her voice and talk to her I would and she would do the same, so she was in class and the phone rang twice which was unusual she usually picks up first ring, but clearly different scenario because she was in school and she picked up eventually and was worried and I said no babe don't worry we just have a fire alarm that went off and I just wanted to hear your voice and we were talking and I told Arabelle say hi to my girlfriend lol Arabelle was like "hellllloooooooo Michael's girlfriend it's nice to meet yoooooouuuuuu" lol. I love Arabelle so much lol she is so funny lol.

Kaylynn was great she knew all my friends and I knew plenty of hers not all but many because I had grown up with them so it was just a great relationship. So I let her go to get back to class and the fire alarm was over and I was just bored at class because Math was over so now I had to go to Mr. Devonte's English class and I didn't want to lol he was a great guy and he advocated for us all the time. In this class I had Max, Pablo, Coal and some others and we were all talking in class and Mr. Devonte goes "Coal is that your real name" and he goes "why yes Mr. Devonte" and we all looked at him lol and Pablo is the star running back of the football team and he goes "really Coal I had always thought we called you Coal because you black as coal" lmfaooooooooooooooooooooo and Coal was like "oh hell no" while he looked around the class and asked everyone he said "yo Max you not going to tell me we grew up all this time and now in senior year of high school you are going to tell me you never knew my name was Coal" Max was a part of the football team from my math class and said "well yea (n-word) you black ass hell I had always thought that was your nick name" lmfaoooo and the class had just burst out laughing and Mr. Devonte says to Pablo "what are you laughing at gold skinned" lmfaooooooo that was Mr. Devonte's nickname for Pablo because he had this caramel complexion lmfaooooo then Coal looks at me and says "wait wait wait oh hell no, my (n-word) Mikey you not about to tell me this too" I said "well Coal I was a new transfer last year and I heard everyone call you Coal and I was always under the impression it was because you black ass fuck" lmfaooooo he said "oh I ma fuck you up Mikey" lmfaooooo and we just sat there for 10 minutes just laughing. I decided I was done for the day and I was going to leave lol I texted Jamel I said "yo outside in ten I'm cut class" Jamel replied "bet bro." So I told Mr. Devonte I was going to the bathroom and he said "did you complete all your work" I said "yes" and handed it to him and he said "because you did your work like usual I will mark you here and let you leave" Pablo was like "what that's not fair" lol Mr. Devonte said "shut up gold skinned you think because you have gooooldskin you have some privilege" he said "what no only you call me gold skinned" lol he said "and you never do your work so shut up and finish if you complete it before class is over I will let you leave too" lol he said "ahhhh man come on Mr. Devonte I will hand it to you tomorrow" and Mr. Devonte said "you always say that and I am tired of your lies gold skinned" lol he ended up letting him leave too lol. Man Mr. Devonte such an exceptional guy, leader, mentor, just a genuine man who cared about the kids of the school and community may his soul rest in peace a lot of class discussions and topics I had the privilege to hear him speak about and learn from. Happy to have been a part of his class and pick his brain, we need more of him which we won't because there was only one Mr. Devonte.

 I meet up with Jamel outside and we just took a long stroll home and Jamel was asking me what I was doing this coming weekend and I told him I had to go support my girl at her school play and probably fight this kid and he asked why I said because he grabbed my girls ass at school so I told him to meet up I was going to be there Friday to beat his fucking face in and as always he said "cool just be safe and make sure he remembers not to touch your girl again" I said "of course Mikey is always safe and that guy is going to know who I was simple as that" lol. Any who its prom weekend well for my fellow brethren and sisteren from Saint Bernard's so I go to Boulevard East and hang out with them for a while until they head out on the buses and seeing everyone Ceaz, Daziel, Jeremiah, Adrien the girls it was great to spend time with everyone again made me realize how much I missed them. So I had to leave to not be late to Kaylynn's play and I said by to everyone so pause for a second writing this out I realized dam I traveled mad far lmfaoo Caldwell was no joke that shit was deep up North lol well any who I get there and I call her and she meets me at the door and I don't know if I am allowed to say this but anyway without any disrespect to her husband, man listen she was dressed in all white just looking beautiful as always like just wow she gave me a kiss and showed me where to sit and so while the play was ongoing and I was sitting in the seat everything hit me all at once, so when we first started talking and she was asking me about Marcel, then Marcel telling me she went to our school but was a grade under us and then it hit me it was her. As weird as it was like if you remember the story I told in Chapter 7 in Saint Vincenzo when we were walking through the hall and I saw that girl and Roland didn't want to tell me her name this was her, and man did I just fall in love with her all over again my heart got so warm lol how corny right lol any who she did an amazing job nonetheless. So on we go and her brother is waiting outside and so we are walking to the car and there is this car on the opposite side and she said "I will be right back babe" I said "wait what is that your friend" she said "no that's my ex" man that shit hurt just to spend all that time trying to make her forget about this fucking guy and then he pops up out the blue and there she goes hopping over to him to greet him and honestly I just went to the car and I am very respectful so I didn't get in the car because I don't really know her brother that well so I just waited until she came back and got in together and I was just lost honestly speaking I didn't know what was happening and I just felt bad like I felt like shit like if she was still that happy just seeing him like what was I to her? I don't know if that was a valid question you know and I understand you know she was the star cheerleader of the school and he was the quarterback of the football team how cliché but I didn't give a fuck about all that it was just the fact that everything she told me about him and how I spent all that time just going up there to support her and show her how much I cared for her and loved her then to get there and this happens and honestly I don't think there is a girl that would be able to tell you that I have ever got mad or a girl that has ever heard me raise my voice it's not something I ever did nor believed in. I just don't believe in raising your voice or you hand to any woman for any reason and in all honesty I was just lost I didn't really say a word the whole ride and she would grab my face and make me look at her and of course I'm not going to shrug her away I don't believe in that either you know she's my woman and you always have to listen to you woman but I guess I was just really hurt man and weirdly enough like she asked me what was wrong and I didn't say anything and I went to look away and I caught her brother looking at me and listening to the conversation and he knew I was hurt man it just sucked being open and vulnerable in that situation and you can't really do anything about it you're just at everyone's will until you leave and it really wasn't much about that I was always respectful it was just the fact I had no words I was really hurt. Her brother dropped me off at 32nd street of course I said thank you and told them to have a good night and Kaylynn kissed me and I just went on my way and as always once I closed the door she immediately texted me and wanted to talk and I just didn't have words man I was really really hurt, and I got on the bus and it was a long ride home and I didn't know what to think, I honestly felt like a part of her still felt like she wanted to be with him.

So I took the bus to Fredericksberg Heights this time my cousin told me it would be faster and cheaper and I was just hurt and I wasn't really paying attention to what I was doing, so I got to the Path train in Fredericksberg Heights and I was just hurt and I walked down to await the train and it was me and another guy there, this guy was fucking drunk as all shit, intoxicated dude was out of it and he has extremely unsteady gait just wobbling his way around and he starts to cross the yellow line and my mind isn't right so I'm not processing things so quickly because my mind is on what happened that day. Then he gets real close and balances on one leg tries to catch his balance by spinning 180 degrees and he tries to step on the platform but guys let me tell you there was no platform there it was the train tracks and I just saw dude disappear so I ran over there and there was a train coming so fucking stupid like why today like why after what just happened with my girl I have this happen and if this guy dies it's on me and I was already sad so I ran over there and he was like help, help extending his arm at me and guy had some weight on him so I don't remember if I jumped down on the tracks to get him or lifted him up with both hands either way the train was getting fucking close man and I got him out of there before the train came and I asked him "man what the fuck is wrong with you" like there was no need to ask him that he was drunk and didn't understand me so I sat him on the steps and took the train.

Now on this train is moving and nothing is looking familiar I don't see Harrington station I don't see water or a bridge then all of a sudden, the conductor says World Trade Center last stop everyone please get off the train. I said wait what the fuck happened, oh man was my thought process so fucked up man I couldn't think for shit so I ran and found someone and asked how to get back and they told me I had to purchase another ticket and get to the other side and quickly because it was coming and it was the last one of the night. I ran over there got the ticket and it just came and I jumped on it. Finally got back to Fredericksberg Heights and then took the last Path to Greenville Penn Station and when I got there I looked at the time I was already late it was like 2-3 in the morning and the next train was the last one and I had like 5 minutes to get the ticket and run across to the other side of the station and boy let me tell you I made it sweating and all and on top of that I still had like a 5 mile walk back home I was just tired I didn't want to deal with people if someone would have fell off the platform again I would have let them hang there to dry honestly I wasn't having it anymore it was a long night.

So it was just weird because this was my first relationship so I didn't really know what was ok and what was not, I didn't think it was wrong for her to go see her ex-boyfriend you know they experienced each other they shared moments and loved each other and I thought that was perfectly ok to go and say hi I don't think there was anything wrong about that you know you just don't forget about people that you experienced growth with welllllll unless it's me Mikey then aint no one give a shit what we shared and experienced together the only option is to cut me out their lives as quickly as possible without telling me about it but in due time you guys will understand that. The issue was how she went about it because she could have just dismissed him for the reason being she would see him around school or whatever or maybe he told her he wanted to support her just to see who her new boyfriend was I have absolutely no idea but the whole hopping over there and looking excited that is what fucked me up and I honestly felt like ok if she isn't or hasn't moved on from him then maybe we should take a break and when she finds her closure we could try this relationship out but I just thought it wasn't fair especially that I took my time to go and support her knowing I didn't live in Somersworth or Lexington City I lived 35 miles away and whatever man it doesn't matter anymore. So, we spoke about it and she apologized, and everything was ok.

During school you know Arabelle saw me really, really sad and wanted to know what happened to try and help and I just wasn't in the mood to talk and she kept insisting she was so sweet and I just didn't want to be bothered so I just sat all the way on the other side of the class in the last seat and the teacher was like "oh shit you guys ok" Arabelle said "yea" yea well for some reason many people thought me and Arabelle were together because we were just so cool but like days like this I look back and realize how shitty I treated her some days because of what was going on between me and Kaylynn and I felt super bad and after everything blew over I apologized to her she knew I had no intentions on hurting her I just needed some space and I couldn't skip anymore classes because I was on the verge of failing so I had to go and be around people but Arabelle man I love her so much I am forever grateful for her she is one of the main reasons why I have so much patience that is what her and Marinella taught me patience so you guys make sure you thank these women for teaching me so much patience because if not and I stayed on the road I was heading a lot more people would have had their faces punched in for being ignorant. Any who so my prom comes up and she wanted to go but she didn't know that my party days were numbered after that night I got black out drunk I just couldn't be around any party or liquor and even Jackson was hitting me up he was getting me in to 21 and over bars in Fairfield and Fredericksberg Heights and I just straight up lied I told him listen man I partied way too much this year and my grades were lacking I had to catch back up and I had a ton of essays to do and Jackson was great he said "oh shit my bad man yea your academics come first brother just know when those grades come up we all will be waiting for you and Jamel to come back yall always welcome man you already know that" I said "thanks bro I appreciate it you know when I have a chance I will be there but my grades are hurting so for now I have to calm down" he said "no problem man good luck and be safe." On top of the not partying anymore Auburn just, I don't know it just wasn't me I felt that it was their prom for all the kids who all grew up together this was for them and I wasn't a part of that and Jarrell and the crew and Owen all tried to convince me to go I just wasn't up for it at this point in my life I didn't want to be around a lot of people I just wanted to be with my girl just me and her and they knew and it was ok. Kaylynn was really sad about it and looking back like I told you this was my first relationship so I didn't see it as a chance to show off my girl and introduce her to my world because well she was my world but I don't think that's how she saw it and I never understood it until later. We didn't go to prom, but we did spend time together I would go to her house and we would watch movies and walk and talk and it was just good I had never experienced that. Let me define "that" so when I say or said that in the previous sentence I say it to mean to have a woman invite me into her home and have her and her family welcome me as a part of their own was an amazing experience that I will forever be grateful to have.

School is nearing an end and I was at gym class and there was this kid me and him got real cool, he was I guess what you would call a thug or gangster whatever call it what you want, and me and people never get along at first unless they see me hanging out with certain known personnel around the city and me and him just got mad cool so I told him "yo yo hold my phone Ima go play basketball for gym" he said "fuck I look like lol nah go ahead I got you" I said "word thanks bro but if my girl hit me up come get me" he laughed and said "ok now you asking for too much my guy" I said "ok ok lol I will be back." So I finish playing basketball and dude is just dying of laughter I say "yo what's good lmfaoo why you laughing so much you read my texts" lol he said "my guy who the fuck is My Baby Shrimp" lmfaoooooooooooo that shit was so funny, I said "dude give me my phone back that's my baby girl that's my nickname for her she so small she fit in my back pocket so I called her My Baby Shrimp" lol he said "yo bro go find her a new nickname that shit funny as hell" and well like I don't know any better I thought that shit was cute as fuck and she loved it and I probably should have taken his advice and asked her lol but whatever that's my baby girl fuck out of here lol.

Ok so next week comes and we have the Physical Education test which was weird as fuck because in private school we aint do nothing like that, when Physical Education was done it was done. So we went outside and all we had to do was run a mile, I said "what that's it" the gym teacher said "yea fuck else you want to do Mikey" he was the driver's Ed teacher last year and a coach for the track team, so I said "well if that's it ok then" he lined us all up and said go and started the timer, man listen when all the kids that played track took off it was like seeing the Olympics I thought I was fast these kids were gone but, the kids in my class weren't the distance runners and what did I do I catch them man did I catch them I was at my peak running in high school all I did was play basketball and condition I crossed the finish line and the Coach said "yo Mikey come here let me talk to you for a minute" I said "wait what did I fail I came in second what did I do wrong" he said "your time was 5 minutes" I said "ok is that good or bad, did I fail" he said "no" I said "so what's the problem" lol he said "you are not about to tell me that you been running 5 minute miles and throughout your time in Auburn not one year did you join the track team, what the fuck is the matter with you lol, why the fuck you been hiding this ability for man we could have used you this year and you here hiding man, what the fuck" I said Coach "I didn't know I ran that and I didn't even know that, that was a fast time" and he shook his head turned around and waived his clipboard like he was in shock or something lol I said "so am I good Coach" he said "yea man in a really annoyed voice, go change get the fuck out of here I can't believe this shit lol."

On to the next week my boys are graduating, so I go up North and support my boys graduating they my brothers we spent the weekend together it was fun. My mom had to go drop off my sister to school she went to Franklin Roosevelt wayyyyyyyy up North lol so she picked me up and since I was in the area I called my baby girl and I asked her if she was home if I can go see her for 5 minutes and give her a hug and kiss because I missed her and she said no. She was hanging out with her friend that had gone to the military and he was back for a couple weeks and it was his last night there and her and her friends were all together and I was bothered a bit by it you know I don't live close by and I just literally just wanted to see her and hold her and give her a kiss and tell her I loved her I didn't see it as such an out of world inquiry from my girl. Well to conclude I didn't see her and I was with my mom so I told her to forget it and we just went home and me and my mom didn't have the best of relationship you know so she was just trying to get me mad and talking shit. So well before I explain the conversation let me tell you the chemistry we had so whenever there was just an off vibe like me and Kaylynn were very close and it was felt it was such a weird amazing experience so to say like if I texted her and was watching tv and some time would pass by and she didn't text me and I didn't realize it because I got into the show for some reason I would have this minny heart attack my heart would just start pounding all of a sudden real weird and in my head is like yo where's baby girl at and when I grab my phone it would vibrate and she would be texting me at that very moment it was so weird but great and to even dive deeper when I looked at my phone at the time of the text it would be literally only like 30 seconds would have passed by but that's so you understand how much we texted day in and day out 30 seconds felt like 30 minutes without hearing from my baby that's a no, no I must be around her all day long I have to know what she's thinking how she is feeling every minute of the day its important that's my woman. So I am not going to explain it more than that you guys are probably thinking weird shit already not many people experience a bond, or feelings, or communication like that and others call it clingy and ya will continue to label it all you want which is cool but I hope you guys experience it one day it's a great chemistry and great feeling. So we were talking and she texts me "babe what's wrong" and that's my woman I can't lie to her and she knew something was wrong and she was just amazing and while I was texting I guess in her mind was like fuck that shit so she called me while I was in the middle of texting and we spoke and I told her what my mom said. At this point in her life she wasn't getting along with her mom very well they shared their problems and she didn't tell her mom about me until like now June when she was finishing school and I won't go into that it's not important it was a mutual decision anyway not to tell her mom. The issue was that she hadn't met my mom yet and now she has issues with her mom, and she is under the impression that my mom doesn't like her, which was not the case, but I couldn't explain it. She was upset because she thought that I didn't fight for her or back her up and that just wasn't the case I tried to explain to her that she shouldn't take my mom's words to weight because she just says shit to say shit and she didn't care all that was on her mind was that I didn't defend her, which was completely understandable but it wasn't that serious because I know my mom and she just likes to say shit to get people mad and well my girl was mad now and I didn't know what to do. The dust settled and we spoke about it again and I realized she was right I should have defended her but still understanding that this I my first relationship I will be making many mistakes and learn how to correct them and I think that is an issue that I had no relationship experience before her and she did. I didn't really know right from wrong and there were many variables I was just learning and I don't think she took that into consideration sometimes but that was it she taught me a lot so it was like balanced because there would be days where she would sit and talk to me about what are the right things to do and right courses of actions to take in a relationship but I don't know maybe it wasn't enough. Then we have to I guess well get to this portion of the story that is the turning point of just everything I didn't want to talk about because not only is Kaylynn on my mind but Jaylene, Amelia, and Nameless and I am starting to feel the pain again I just really have to finish this story man it's just been too long.

So the week of finals is upon us and I am sitting with Jamel in the cafeteria, laughing relaxing eating cereal and then something starts happening, at this point I don't know what is going on I am going in and out of consciousness and not noticing and Jamel woke me up and asked me if I was alright and he walked me up to our Accounting 2 class and our teacher was cool he loved me I was one of his best students and Jamel told him that I wasn't feeling well and the teacher told me if I wanted to sleep during the class that I could he would let me and I passed out I didn't remember what happened, I remember Jamel waking me up scared as all hell him and the teacher said that I wasn't responding to them when they tried to wake me up. The teacher told Jamel to take me to the Nurses office and he took me and the Nurse had said that I was ok that I probably slept wrong and they called my mom from out of work to pick me up and I didn't remember much of that I remember going to the car and trying to give my mom directions to Robert Wood Hospital and I remember I felt like straight shit and I felt myself passing out and my mom yelling at me and I had thought whelp this sucks if I'm going out like this and all I thought was I hope Kaylynn would be ok without me I prayed that everything would turn out ok then I completely passed out the next two things I remember were waking up in front of the ER in Elkton Medical Center in Agua Dulce I walked myself in and didn't remember what happened from there, next I remember waking up in a room and a doctor yelling at me about some bullshit anesthesia and man this shit hurt, so the anesthesia didn't work my body didn't take to it and I guess the word would be rejected it or they either under dosed me so what happened, well folks since you asked so nicely, I felt him slice me open by my rib with his scalpel and I just yelled "I FELL IT I FELL IT" and that was that. Eventually I woke up in just pain man just pain I didn't know what the fuck was going on and all I wanted was my fucking phone to talk to my girl, and my mom wouldn't give me my phone and I remember her telling my cousin Zade to take my phone and I was fucking pissed and whelp guess what I passed out again lmfaoo.

Let me tell you how annoying it fucking is to not have control of your consciousness per say I just couldn't stay awake every damn time I passed out I thought I was dead it was fucking crazy and I still didn't know what was happening. I really don't feel like explaining the rest of the scenario tonight I am pretty tired and I feel like crying and I just don't want to do it tonight I will be back tomorrow I just need some mental rest right now before I break down crying. So have a good night ya and be safe.

Yea so I am not really in the mood to talk very much today just pretty sad and I will try and write out a few pages hopefully. So I woke up just in agony and pain and I was finally coming into a real state of consciousness and it was a really bad time for that to happen because the effects of pain meds I guess had worn off for better or worse, so I finally wake up and I am back to myself mentally and I see I am attached to the intravenous bag and the fucking intravenous line was painful I am unsure of as to why I was just feeling everything it fucking sucked and I felt so much pressure in my chest and my side I couldn't really move and my left arm was above my head and I was confused I was thinking what the fuck was wrong with me and I put my arm down and I felt something and I looked and I had this just huge tube sticking out of the side of my chest and it hurt oh that shit sucked and my mom was there and I just wanted my phone I just needed my girl and I knew she was worried I haven't spoken to her all day I had to let her know I was in the hospital but I was ok for the moment and my mom just wouldn't give me my phone I was so pissed then I passed out again. I woke up in the middle of the night and my phone was left on the table and I texted Kaylynn and told her what had happened and we spoke for a short time before I passed out again and my roommate had his family members there and they came to check up on me and I apologized for raising my voice earlier because it wasn't really like me I was just trying to stay awake and talk to my girl and they said it was ok and they tried talking to me but I had passed out.

The morning comes and I finally wake up like I am ok now with the pain but it was bearable and the nurse came in and told me what happened and she said I had a Spontaneous Pneumothorax and that translates into a collapsed lung and they asked me all these questions and no one knew what happened I told them everything I remembered and they pretty much confirmed it was spontaneous just fuck me rite my lung decides hey I don't want to work today forgetting that I need oxygen to live and survive like just fuck me right. So this time I didn't pass out I just fell asleep because I was tired and I woke up in the middle of the day and I was alone alright my mom was at work cool, but my roommates family members were there I heard them all crying I didn't know what happened then I passed out again. I woke up a third time and I was just by myself and I asked the nurse to pass me my phone because it was just too far for me to reach at the time and she did and I started texting Kaylynn she had left hundreds of messages and on walks in the family of the guy of my roommate and they came in and brought me KFC chicken and I felt super bad they didn't have to do that for me I barely knew them but they said they felt bad because no one was there for me that day since my mom went to work so of course it meant a lot to me and I asked what happened and they told me that their family member had passed away while I was asleep and I felt soooooo bad I apologized and gave them my condolences and they said they would keep me in their prayers and hoped that I got better and recovered. At this point all I care about is when my girl is coming to see me I just needed her there by my side I just needed to hold her I needed to see her and she said that her dad was going to bring her to come see me and I said ok and just knowing she was coming made everything feel so much better.

I fell asleep and when I woke up, I had a new roommate like cool at least I wasn't by myself and my mom and my aunt came over night, but my aunt left early because work and my mom stayed a bit later. My roommate was this elderly woman if I remember correctly and her family was so nice to me too they were great and I had fallen asleep now its day three and I woke up in the middle of the night and my roommate wasn't there and the nurse had come to draw some blood so clearly I asked her what happened annnnnddd she passed away too. At this point I felt bad like was it me, was I like stealing these peoples energy to keep myself alive or am I just a bad luck roommate my thought process was so weird that week and it was late and I didn't want to text Kaylynn I didn't want to disturb her sleep or anything but it didn't matter I passed out again. By the time I woke up I had a new roommate this guy was a middle aged guy real funny he told me a few jokes and all I remember from that day was getting up and going to the bathroom because they wanted me more ambulatory throughout the day which I didn't understand how but any who on an important note I didn't have a catheter which I was super stoked about lol I didn't know what that was till I looked it up after I got out the hospital so whatever I didn't have anything up my urethra lmfaoo. Then I got back to my bed and fell asleep so by the time I woke up sometime at night they took me to get an X-Ray and I came back to an empty room confused so I asked the nurse and she gave me the look like fuck that's 3 days and all my roommates died what the fuck. Then she proceeded to tell me that they wanted to take out the tube in the morning with the doctor and I said ok. She left and I started texting my girl and seeing when she was going to come and she said that her father told her he was going to take her when he had a chance and I said ok, I guess it was just comforting at leastknowing or having in the back of my mind that she would show up eventually so it was something nice to look forward to.

I woke up on day 4 new roommate and all then they took the tube out and that shit was crazy the pressure was so immense and I don't remember if my mom was there or not and several hours later they took me to another X-Ray and I get the results, you know what the results said, it said staff you done fucked up my lung collapsed again fuck me right I was just in hell and my girl wasn't there I could barely breathe at this point I told them and everyone to fuck off, well not like that I was still very calm but I told them and refused re-exploratory surgery to place a new tube in, and no one could tell me different, good for me 2 months earlier I turned 18 and now I am legally an adult and could make my own medical decisions, the only thing they could do was give me a Spirometer and the doctor said I had to get it above this line and improve every hour do a new X-Ray later in the day and see the progress. Man did I do that shit, fuck yea I did I was not about to die or get surgery again fuck all that shit. So with all this nonsense going on lunch comes and I could barely eat I think I ate a jello and I hear something from my roommate and I think to myself what the fuck that doesn't sound like my roommate and when the lunch person leaves I start talking to my roommate and she was there for alcohol induced psychosis and I asked what happened to my roommate and I don't know if you guys want to guess but they passed away too so I lost all my roommates one every day for each day I was there and I just felt so bad you know now I started thinking like why did they die and I didn't, and to point you guys in a decent mindset for this thought process, if you know anything about Pneumothorax, there is a limited time window that you have to get to the hospital before you die, with the lack of oxygen, cardiac mediastinal shift and jugular distension, tracheal deviation, the works, so with all this I started the calculation in my head that I could remember, so I passed out approximately at 7:45 in the morning at breakfast, went to my first class lost track of time from there, by the time my teacher asked Jamel to take me to the nurses office, then treat or diagnose or just tell me to go home, call my mom from work she worked in Middletown well over 6 miles away, my mom getting ready driving to come get me, pick me up, drive through Auburn because there were 2 competent hospitals there but she didn't know how to get there, drive allllllllllllllllllllllllllll the way to Agua Dulce to Elkton Medical Center then to get me in diagnosed then tube me in the Operating Room, how the fuck was I alive a lot of things didn't make sense then having my lung collapse again after they extubed me I didn't know if I was just lucky or what you know.

One more X-Ray and my lung was reflated and no more collapsed lung was seen so they wanted me to continue this Spirometer thing and I was not playing with them I said no doubt I won't stop it and I was looking for my roommate and there was no one there and I was so alone that day and night and I asked the nurse and she said the person was discharged and they were moving me into another room so they moved me into the room next door and I asked why and she said that they decided to give me my own room because they were worried that all the roommates I lost was going to take a toll on me and they wanted me to be positive and I said ok so just stick me in a room by myself and they said it was better than being in a room with everyone dying but you know at least I could talk to people I wasn't alone and everything was just hitting me at once my mom wasn't there, my girl didn't come see me I spent a whole week in the hospital most likely getting discharged tomorrow and I had no one there and it was such a lonely feeling man, I will never allow anyone to ever experience ever and I guess it's a part of the reason I am who I am it was a long lonely night.

In the morning I called my mom and told her they were going to discharge me and she came while I was signing the papers with the nurse and I think she brought me McDonalds or some shit and we left I don't think I ate for like 3 days but any way day 5 I get discharged, 4 roommates passed away, I was alone for a couple days, my girl didn't come see me, it just wasn't a good feeling man not at all. So graduation was up in the air for me I had a meeting with the principal and he told me not to worry all I had to do was get a letter from the physician that did the surgery to clear me to walk and that was tough finding him and getting that fucking letter man they just wanted their asses secured because I still had my stiches in and just got discharged.

So graduation came and the day previous I asked Kaylynn if she was coming for sure 100% because if not there was no reason for me to even walk I didn't care but she said she was going I told her Jeremiah and Adrien were coming and they live near her they wouldn't mind just picking her up and taking her along to the ceremony and she assured me her brother promised her that he would take her and that was my baby girl I trusted her word. So the whole ceremony started and mid ceremony she texts me and I knew I just felt it was a bad text, and I look at the text and it said she wasn't going to be able to make it, and I was just hurt man I didn't even want to be there I still had stiches in I felt like I was still learning how to breathe again it fucking sucked man and I was so hurt it was the first time I ignored her and didn't text her or call her back all day. That says something because I have never ignored any woman's phone call or text in my life like ever I just find it rude and disrespectful even if you're hurt mad upset but I felt I had all the right to be hurt it fucking pained me man and maybe I was wrong I don't know that's just how I felt after not coming to see me in the hospital then the reason I am even in graduation is for you to see me graduate and you tell me you aren't coming I don't know maybe it's me but I was just hurt man and I didn't want to talk to her until my mind was ready. After graduation we are all hanging out outside and Marinella and Arabelle come up to me and congratulate me and give me hugs and Marinella asked me where my girl was and Arabelle man Arabelle, Arabelle, Arabelle she said she's not here if she was he would have introduced us to her before anything. Arabelle just processes things so fast I don't think I could ever thank her and Marinella enough for always being there and keeping me off the streets and away from bad affiliates just genuine women man I love them so much. When Arabelle said that it just hurt more, and I was hurting for a while.

Afterward we went to eat and just hung out with Jeremiah, Adrien, and Dennis and I, was just sad the whole day just after the month I had and still not being able to see my girl I was hurt, and at this point I had stopped drinking and smoking marijuana all together after the incident that put me in the hospital so there was no going back to that fuck all that shit, so I spoke mainly to Adrien about the situation and he told me that I should just tell her how I felt, but it just didn't feel right because I know that she felt bad and I didn't want to add on to it I know me and her both have our sensitive days and we take everything personal when we have our days and just I wasn't sure if I should tell her how I felt it just didn't seem like the right time. So as we are walking to the bus station right outside the turnpike exit for Auburn I see them off and appreciate that they came out you know I love my brother I always appreciate everything they done for me and I could never repay any of them back and just thought about it. After some time passed throughout the night I called Kaylynn and spoke to her, and I took Adrien's advice and I told her how I felt and safe to say that wasn't the course of action I should have taken, and even though I felt I had a right to be borderline upset but I just don't get mad I was more sad about the whole situation not mad I just missed my girl I wanted to see her I needed her and I felt that she just wasn't there for me, I mean she was there but not physically there for me, it was just this time I needed her at the hospital I needed her to hold me and tell me everything was going to be ok I felt like I was just out there fighting it by myself and it was tough a part of me thought I wasn't going to make it out the hospital especially when they told me my lung collapsed a second time, then her not going to my graduation everything was just piled up and when we spoke she got really upset and started crying and saying that she tried to come see me at the hospital she did her best, and she tried to come to my graduation her brother promised her that he would take her but I just didn't want to hear it like don't make me a promise because someone made you a promise that's just not how it works you know and just hearing her cry made it all worse I didn't want to make her cry I didn't want her to feel bad that wasn't my intention I just wanted her to understand where I was coming from that is all and from that point on I learned more of consciously placing my feelings aside to spare everyone's feelings and that wasn't a very good attribute to have I learned later on in life and I won't get into all that in this autobiography / memoir because it doesn't really matter but what the fuck ever any way, we leveled everything out I just couldn't have my girl crying it just hurt me more, I don't believe in it to me you should just be genuinely uplifting your woman, making her feel that she is a priority and that she is important and special to you in your life. As we talked through it all I had forgot that she was going to have knee surgery, so I asked her if I can go with her to the hospital and her parents denied me that. They said I was able to see her the day after surgery so whatever I will take what I can get you know. For those that don't know which I don't think I explained previously, her parents didn't know that we were together, she had just got out of her last relationship months prior to meeting me and she didn't want to get them mad because they wanted here to focus on her school and grades which was perfectly fine with me. She had the surgery and at this point I am still fresh from the hospital I still had the stiches in and everything and knowing I had to travel all the way up North on public transportation I knew it was going to suck and I was just hoping trouble didn't follow me just not this day I was way too weak to be fighting with anyone. So I take the bus to NY, then take the bus to Lexington City then took another bus to a park closet to her house and walked all the way down to her house which was so weird because to get there I had to pass 2 Cemeteries and I was like I don't know if death is just being condescending like out of all the places she lived in the world she lives by 2 Cemeteries oh the humor lol. Any who I get there, and I greet her parents they were extremely nice and welcoming wonderful people and her father knew what had happened if I remember correctly, he was a retired EMT super smart guy I had a lot of respect for them. I saw my baby and when I saw her smile everything was just ok man everything felt ok and I gave her a huge hug and just held her, man did I miss her that separation anxiety was no joke man that was just an experience. So when I saw her though give me a second I am trying to think about it like walking into her house where she was sitting what side the cast was on and I believe she had if my memory serves me correct which I doubt it, right knee surgery and she had like an immobilizer and I felt super bad, like it hurt me seeing her like that and she was a fighter her pain tolerance was very high but it didn't change the fact that my baby was hurt and I spent as much time as I could with her and there were some small things that happened which aren't important to the story so we will just dismiss it, we pretty much just watched her childhood videos and talked all day and that was all I needed just simply to be around her and know that she was ok and hold her and kiss her and tell her how much I loved her, I really hope no one experiences separation anxiety it is the weirdest shit in the world it is extremely hard to control your emotions it's just a different experience and if you don't know how to deal with what you're feeling just call me or shoot me an email I will help you out as much as possible I will tell you Kaylynn really fucked with my emotions and it took me years and the help of Jaylene to learn how to grab control of my emotions and today I am truly happy how I managed it with my past and the women who have helped me and guide me. Any who I can't over welcome my stay I just met her parents, and she just had surgery so she needed to rest and I felt super bad when I saw my baby using crutches it just broke my heart man so fuck that I had stiches in and I was recovering fuck all that my baby girl needed me so of course I was there for her.

    A couple weeks pass by and her birthday is coming up and that's my baby girl I have to go all out for her. Her parents still weren't too fond of me, I knew they liked me but I just wasn't there yet, Kaylynn had told me that for her birthday it was going to be a family thing which was cool no issues be with your family as long as I can have a few hours to be able to spend your birthday weekend with you I was happy. She said yes which was either a Friday or Saturday I can't remember, any who the day comes and I had got her like 6 gifts lol I don't remember them all it was a Happy Birthday Card, A small necklace, I took her out to OutBack and we had dinner in Rivers Ledge. Prior to all this as I am making my way up there to her house, I stopped by Carvel in Altoona and I was packing lol I had my duffle bag with all my stuff and a change of clothes and all her presents, and I went in there and bought a birthday cake for her and candles and I was able to get them to put Happy Birthday Baby on the cake it was great, well at the time I didn't know they were able to do that stuff so I was fucking ecstatic that the worker did it for me and walking out, there were a group of girls and they said what the hell why doesn't my boyfriend do that for me and that is an important quote per say because what I do for women all women whether it be from school or some randomness I always hear women say that so it helps preserve the good in me it helps me and reminds that you know what maybe I am doing good by these women and I am doing the right thing because when I help out a girl usually I don't get a thank you and I don't do things for a thank you I do it because it's right and I do it because I know what said person is going through and I now I have the ability to help so at times I don't know if I am doing right by them or not because I don't get a thank you and they disappear forever so I am left with the thought that I hope I have helped them and I hope I have given them the tools to solve all of their problems by themselves without me and when I hear something like I wish my boyfriend did that for me or I hope my boyfriend does something like that for me it allows me to think I stayed on the right path and haven't diverged off it too far.

 Moving forward, after Carvel I start making my way to her house and I get on a Immy bus and I get off at the park and walk down through the Cemetery cut through people's houses lol down the big ass hill then I get there and she was upstairs and her dad opened the door as I was walking to the kitchen I heard her quickly coming down and in my head I was like "oh shit oh shit I can't let her ruin the surprise" lol I asked her father if when he picks us up from Outback if he could take us to Boulevard East so I can cut her the cake and sing her happy birthday. He said ok no problem in hopes that he would remember to bring the cake, candles and lighter lmfaoo. Kaylynn finally came down looking beautiful as always and we got in the car and he took us to Outback so we ate conversed clearly and I don't remember if they did the happy birthday thing for her I don't recall all that but we finished and her father came picked us up and as we were driving she was confused she didn't know where we were going and her father dropped us off by Boulevard East and handed me the cake and it didn't melt lol it was great. We sat and it was a clear night beautiful overlooking New York and it was definitely a nice night, so I sung her happy birthday and she blew out the candle and cut it her father brought a knife because I clearly forgot about that lol and it was perfect she loved it her smile was from ear to ear I knew I did the right thing and her father was great I appreciated it I had thought he was going to tell me no, you know he barely knew me but I chanced it and worse scenario I would have cut the cake at her house which would have been nice as well but this was better.

The night was coming to an end and I had to get back home before I missed the train because the bus had stopped running already. Her father offered to take me to New York and I couldn't accept that it was just too much but he wouldn't take no for an answer and me and Kaylynn got in and he dropped me off at Port Authority, super nice guy I appreciate everything he has done for me. Me and Kaylynn start texting as always, and I went to Penn Station and took the late train back home it was an amazing night and she loved it.

By this time, I started going to school at Lincoln Tech in Winchester and it was great everything was going great. In school I was in class with a variety of different people so the first week of school man that shit sucked, I had to get to the Train Station the grab the bus through Milford and Winchester just to get to school it was annoying. Then I found out my man Owen was in school too. So, he offered to take me to school every day just give him gas money once a week and hell yea I did it was great. Now school is ongoing and we are meeting people and I am in the back of this class and this kid was sitting next to me so I was like of course let me get to know everyone in school so I started talking to him and he told me his name was Damien, cool ass kid man funny as hell so we start talking and I ask him where he's from and he's from Lexington City I was like oh my new brother lol that's where I'm from so I knew he went to Dickerson everyone but me went to Dickerson and I was like yea, and somehow we started talking about girls and he said his girl went to Caldwell and I don't know many girls from Caldwell other than my girl and so he showed me a picture of his girl and I was like "wait I know her" and I said oh shit that's well we will call her Denise and I looked at him and he had this stare like he was going to murder me and my head quickly got into process and said yo you better tell him how you know her and I said "nah no worries I grew up with her she was my neighbor next door to my crib when I lived downtown, cool ass girl I haven't seen her in years though how she doing." The face came right off lol in my head I was like sigh good thing I cleared up the air so fast I was about to get killed in school lol bad way to die, so let me learn you something if you don't know someone and they show you a picture of their girlfriend don't say that you know them lmfaoooooo bad idea bad bad idea lol. So I was like well at this point I have to show him a pic of my girl too lol so I showed him and he knew her too lol such a fucking awkward day lmfaoooooo his girl and my girl were friends lol how life comes in circle was weird lol. Now all of us had class together it was everyone we met in one class it was great it was Fabyen, Damien, Ameer, Sohan, Cullen, Me and Owen and Walton. Me Fabyen, Damien and Owen sat in the back of the class and started talking and all of a sudden Fabyen starts speaking Spanish and we are all like what the fuck lmfaoooooooooooo dude was black like a crayon lol and Owen looks at me and it hits me Ohhhhhhhhhhhh I understand now lmfaoooooo and man was it a great class we got in trouble a lot but we all had fun and learned.

During break we would go outside there was a basketball and empty field some of the guys would play football and that would be the day just go to class have fun on break and back to it till the end of the day. Once the week ended, I went to see Kaylynn and we would just spend time together and take a walk and just enjoy the time we had. I had got home, and she texted me what I thought about her joining cheerleading and I was not liking the idea and she told me her parents didn't want her to join and I thought they were right. I mean I didn't really care if she joined or not I knew that was her passion simply speaking I said I didn't like the idea and I didn't want her to join because she really is accident prone, that is how she hurt her knee and she had previous injuries before meeting me and that was my baby girl and seeing her in that knee immobilizer it really bothered me I couldn't see her injured or hurt any more so I disliked the idea honestly I didn't want her to get hurt that is why I said she shouldn't do it. So, we spoke a bit more and that was it.

Around this time in school I saw this kid Abel and I was so surprised to see him he is Arabelle's cousin he went to Auburn too, but we didn't hang out that much in Auburn, but we were always cool me him and his sister. He got me a job with Primerica or something like that he wanted me to check it out, so of course I said why not.

School was starting up for Kaylynn and things just got weird really fast. The first day was great we spoke a lot like usual, then I just don't know honestly. The next few days I barely heard from her, so going from thousands of texts a month and all those hours spent on the phone daily to just nothing is such a small-time frame almost overnight, it hit me hard she was all I had. I hadn't mentioned that I completely shut out all my friends. After the whole hospital thing and right after graduation I haven't seen nor spoken to any of my friends, I just wasn't in the mood to talk to anyone other than my girl, she was my life and to not hear from her at all I was really hurting. So at this time I was hanging out with Abel who I don't recall introducing, he was Arabelle's cousin he was in Auburn High with me and everyone else and I met him again in Lincoln Tech as I was going for my Automotive Certificate he was going for HVAC and he got me a job with Primerica and I was going to get my Insurance and Realtor License so the first class was on a weekend, and I just didn't know what was going on with Kaylynn, we had finally spoke and she told me she joined cheerleading and I understood that's why we weren't talking she was out practicing and working with the squad. So to explain the thought process, it wasn't the fact that I felt she went behind my back it's her choice if she wants to join cheerleading again that's fine the concern was that she just upped and did it, many people will think or choose to believe it's a control thing maybe I don't really know nor do I care, the issue was that from the last conversation we had she never decided or expressed to me that she was going to join. Now I am going to be just worrying about her getting hurt because as much as I hate to say it she is accident prone and she has had previous injuries and she just had knee surgery a couple months ago give yourself time to heal and I didn't want her breaking a leg or falling on her head that was my problem and I would just be worrying day in and day out how could I support it knowing she was just going to get injured again that's what hurt I didn't want to see her like I saw her after her knee surgery it bothered me you know you never want to see your woman like that. So the weekend comes and I am waiting for Abel to pick me up so we can go to this Primerica meeting and I was just really hurt and thinking and we were texting and I called her and just told her how I felt and I thought for the moment that we should just take a break and she just broke down crying and that hurt me even more, hearing her cry and knowing that I'm the one that made her cry shit destroyed me inside but I just couldn't do it with the cheerleading thing I was just thinking about the betterment of herself, and we spoke for a while and it was pretty much our first argument per say but not really because we were adults there was no yelling or screaming we just talked I don't yell or scream at women but that's not even the point she has never yelled at me either but we just spoke honestly and decided to not take the break. After I came back from the Primerica meeting, we spoke, and it seemed ok everything seemed ok, so I thought.

    The month is progressing, and day in and day out I am hearing less and less from Kaylynn and it is getting really difficult to contact her. She stopped texting me, I would call her house phone and her mom would pick up and she just sounded frustrated when I told her it was me and she would tell me that Kaylynn was busy doing homework and that's it. I didn't know if like she told her mom something about me, but that lady hated my blood and I just never knew why. So, around the beginning of October since I couldn't get into contact with her or get her to talk to me too much it would pretty much be a couple times a week and I was just hurt man and I wrote her an email. A part of me told myself not to send it so it was just sitting in my draft, and me and her were talking on the phone one day and I asked her if she received the email and she didn't clearly because I didn't send it and she said to send it again and I actually sent it and safe to say it was a horrible idea, I was just really hurt when I wrote it and we weren't talking very much and I don't remember it and I don't have my AOL account anymore they deleted it but from what I can recall I was hurt and I wrote her and it was kind of had the notion that I was like attacking her like confrontational like because she didn't go see me in the hospital and she didn't go to my graduation and like everything was about her and man did she just break down crying and hung up on me, I called her back and we spoke for a while and kind of started fresh a new per say. I thought we were ok, and that's when I completely stopped hearing form her all together. At this point when I would call her house her mom would just tell me she wasn't there, or she was studying. I didn't know what to do I had no one to talk to and calling her, well I was getting nowhere with it.

At this point I started working for Office Depot good old Office Depot in East Auburn before it closed. After school I would have to walk all the way on the highway just to get there and my manager would give me a ride home every now and then when he worked. Everyone was real nice over there. On my lunch break I would try, and call Kaylynn see if I could just get a response and try and get her to talk to me and oh, I got a response, she would pick up and just hang up on me. Let me tell you that shit hurt man and I just don't know what happened I didn't have answers I just needed to talk to her and see what was going on and she just wouldn't talk to me. This time in life social media was still MySpace so I went on MySpace and tried to talk to her friends and ask if she was ok if she was doing alright because I had nothing to go on. She was pissed all her friends snitched on me. Around December she had finally picked up the phone and let me clarify I wouldn't be blowing up her phone, I wouldn't call her 50 times a day, I got the message after I called the 2nd time and she hung up on me I would call back every few days or call her house and when her mom told me she was busy that was it, so she finally picked up and she was with her friends and what happened was she blew up on me she cursed me out yelled at me the whole nine and man that shit hurt I didn't know what to say and she said stop hitting her friends up asking about her and I just couldn't talk or get a word through and I was trying to talk to her I wasn't yelling or anything and you could hear her friends telling her to hang up, and she didn't hang up and her friend grabber her phone and hung up on me and that was the end of us. I stopped calling and everything after that, man that shit hurt I don't know what to tell yall, but it hurt. As I wasn't able to spend any holidays with her and I didn't know how she was doing, well clearly she was doing fine but Christmas was coming up at the end of the day I still wanted to do something nice so from what I can recall I had all of our ticket stubs from every movie we went to and what she used to do was write me poetry and in my phone I had locked the messages because I loved her writing she was very good at it and I had typed it out and laminated everything and printed it out on purple paper and put it in a box and I think I had another gift as well and man, Christmas week one day after I got out of work I took the bus up to NY then to Lexington City and I couldn't find a bus to Somersworth for my life so what did Mike do, I walked all the way to her crib form the bus stop and man was that shit cold and fucking far, and honestly I shouldn't have done it but I did and I think I got to her house somewhere around 10 o clock at night and her father answered the door and I guess he felt bad for me and let me in and she came down and I gave her the gifts, man was it embarrassing I broke down and started crying and her mom and dad were there but they let us sit and talk for some time but it was late and I felt bad and I left and we started texting and talking again but for a short time.

Now January comes and I am at work and my brother Daziel calls me, he tells me he is in the hospital and his girl is about to give birth and he wants me to be there he needs me for support so what yea that's not even a question so I told him I was on my way. I talked to my manager and she said no, because he wasn't my immediate family and he wasn't my biological brother, I said I just need to leave early this once and granted I did go to work late a lot because I had to walk across that freeway just to get there because school finished late and there were no buses at the time but I explained all that at the time of hire and she was ok with it, but now after all the hard work I did I couldn't just leave early once well now go fuck yourself, well no I never gave her an attitude we were adults, so we spoke and she said "Michael if you leave early and walk out don't come back because you'll be fired," I said "that is ok, that's my brother and I am sorry for leaving you without extra help but he needs me and I have to go." I said good bye to everyone because they all helped me and Jonas helped me prepare and laminate the gifts for Kaylynn super nice guy I told him thank you again and the other two guys helped me all the time giving me rides home and explaining to me how retail worked and I learned a lot from everyone they weren't mad at all they all said it was ok and to not feel bad. So I grabbed the next bus to NY and called Jeremiah and Adrien and we went to Hackensack and once we got there we found Daziel and everything was all good man the baby was healthy his girl was in good health it was a good night, I don't care if I lost my job they'll be more jobs, bills will forever be there, money comes and goes but this, this I couldn't miss for anyone or anything this was important to us and we needed him to know we were always there.

 I had recently spoken to Kaylynn sometime in January and she had some personal issues and that was that I never heard from her again and at this time in school was pretty annoying to I was just really frustrated. In class there was this kid who just wouldn't stop talking shit so we called him Big Pun I can't tell you the reason but whatever and he was just annoying and really tried to piss me off this kid was about 5'9, 5'10 maybe 250 pounds he said he was around 270 but I am unsure and he just wouldn't stop talking shit to me and class ended early and it was me, Ameer, Sohan, Walton and the rest of the class and we were just in a circle talking shit having fun and then Big Pun just thought it would be cool to try and get me upset or mad and talk as much shit as he could so I just waved him off and told him to shut up and he said "what you going to do your like skinny as fuck" and I said "bro relax before I fucking drop you" and he said "man you can't pick me up" back then that was kind of the wrong thing to say to me because I didn't care about proving people wrong I had absolutely no mercy when it came to a fight if we ended up throwing hands it was going all out and I just dropped my back pack I picked him up and lifted him up in the air and the whole class went quiet and I body slammed him on the floor and the class just erupted and I was standing over him and I threw a punch because now in my head it's a wrap for this kid he is going to learn to keep his mouth shut because it's not about the talking shit it's about the principle now that I told him to relax and he kept going like it was a joke and Ameer came up behind me and locked me up and said "yo, yo, yo my g relax, relax we're in school you're going to get suspended" I told him "alright, alright I'm over it I got it brother thank you." Big Pun got up and what's the first thing he did, would you happen to guess he started talking shit again. At that point I actually felt bad because I realized he actually had mental problems and then I felt super bad for body slamming him but that was after the fact and Walton was like "damn Mikey I didn't know you had that in you" and I said "yea I just don't like to fight man not anymore" and we went our separate ways.

To explain Ameer was a newfound member to my family of brothers so was Cullen and Fabyen and Damien and Eugene but those dudes are another story we will get to soon. Ameer was a Joe Budden fan so every day for lunch we would go to his EM1 which was a 2000 Civic SI and we would listen to Mood Muzik 3 and the track of choice would be no other than the best song Joe Budden has ever written, All of Me. It would be an everyday routine well until his car battery died because we listened to it so much lol.

As the year is progressing, I had to move out of Auburn and lived in Agua Dulce for a small while and I got a message from this random girl I didn't know. She introduced herself and told me she was Kaylynn's cousin, I was worried and asked if she was ok and she was, just had personal issues she was going through that aren't important to you guys and we started talking and she told me that she thinks Kaylynn had hated me because she felt like I was acting like her parents and trying to keep her away from cheerleading so I explained that I wasn't and she said I should try to reach out to her again and we kept talking and I explained you know everything that happened until then and she said that she believed I was obsessed with her not in love with her because I knew the times and dates that things happened, you know fuck me for having good memory when it comes down to people and certain situations but I guess it's more of a curse.

As the year progresses Eugene had got me a job in Pepboys in Middletown and by this time I moved out of Agua Dulce and to my aunt's house in Middletown, Pepboys was not that far from me. Then me and Kaylynn started talking again not very much but it was good having her around here and there. Day to day after school Eugene would drive me down in his Civic hatchback to work and that car was great and he was an exceptional driver I learned a lot from him, as we were making our way to work he would point out things about peoples driving habits and tell me what to watch out for while driving little subtle movements of the car tell you a lot about what the person is going to do and what lane they are going to next and he just knew and I picked it up from him, Ameer, Adrien and a few other guys I took what I learned from them and became the driver I am. So while heading down to work we were just driving speeding on the Parkway and there was this SUV and from a distance Eugene saw he wasn't going to get around him and he wasn't a crazy driver he wouldn't use the shoulder and do crazy shit like that but gaps and holes in traffic he would see them before they opened up it was good seeing him drive and his thought process so he called out this SUV and said watch he's going to brake check us, and I was confused I didn't know how he could tell we weren't even behind the car yet, and we finally got behind the SUV and the car parallel to us slowed down and there was an opening to get into the lane on the right and sure enough the guy brake checked us but at the time he did Eugene had already started merging to the lane on the right and the guy almost crashed in to the car that was behind us in the lane and we look and the guy had a mean mug face on while brake checking us and when he realized Eugene had already switched lanes his face changed so fast lol it was so funny like it took me a while to understand how he knew but what he saw was the guy maneuvering into the front of the lane and didn't want any one in front of him and he had seen us coming from a far and Eugene caught on to what he was doing but the guy didn't take into account the car next to us that slowed down and created an opening it was great lol, as we get to Route One there was construction and all of a sudden the car shut off on us and we didn't know what happened. The car came to a stop and we got out and looked under the hood and the timing belt snapped so we called our manager at the time and he had a Ford F150 and towed us the mile to work.

Our manager was great so he didn't care that Eugene worked on the car, we got the car to an empty spot and lifted it with a jack and I took some of Eugenes cars did their oil changes and tires while he worked on the civic, real fast changing the timing belt and then came back to work and the workload wasn't bad I was fast at the time because Eugene taught me all he knew and I will forever be grateful for meeting him and appreciative of all that he has done for me that's my brother he didn't have to do all he did for me. Just like Owen he would wake up and take me to school even if he didn't want to go he felt bad because he was my ride and he would just go for me, fucking exceptional guy man I owe them a lot and I will never have the chance to repay them for all they had done for me but I would just like them to know that I truly do appreciate all of it I am always grateful for crossing paths with good people. Also, Eugene's cousin Vince I learned a lot about cars not just Hondas but cars in general because of them I truly do owe them a lot I miss those guys.

    The next week Eugene was driving us to work and we get on the Parkway and we only made it a few exits and he tells me "Mikey look behind you" so I look and this Nissan Altima is just speeding through traffic just recklessly and Eugene started pointing out certain things about the drivers habits and said "oh they definitely running from the cops you can tell" then a couple minutes later we got in to the far right lane and they had lost control, flipped the Altima went into a ditch flipped again and slammed into a Exit sign, then they all got out and started running. They didn't crash into any other cars or anything and we made it to work. We actually made it to work early and if I remember we actually clocked in early but had time to spare, in the plaza where Pepboys was, there was an Army recruiting station and we walked up in there and just talked to the dudes and well we definitely lost track of time and we walked back into work and our manager was pissed he was like where were you, you signed in early and were not here at work don't let it happen again as if we don't close every day and spend extra time cleaning up for everyone and we don't get paid for it and he was upset we signed in early once literally once it was whatever. Work starts and the whole time at work we were wondering what happened to the guys that crashed, and we are almost closing and this Mazda RX-8 needed an oil change. Eugene walks up to the guy and asks him if I can drive the car into the shop because I needed to learn manual and he told the guy he helped me practice on his car, and I never drove Eugene's baby lol, what happened was that Ameer told me to YouTube some Asian guy in a Miata because he had 3 different camera angles and explanation on how to drive manual and sure enough I found the guy on YouTube and practiced all day in my imaginary car at home lol then a Cobra Mustang came into the shop and that clutch was like stepping on bricks you just couldn't depress it and after I stalled it once I called Eugene over and he said it was like a stage 6 clutch ridiculous for no reason and so I didn't feel so bad at the time he had trouble himself getting it in but he didn't stall it, so he told me when there is another better car coming in he would let me do it because he wasn't going to be at work all the time for me to depend on him to get the cars in, sure enough the guy in the RX-8 was cool he said sure go ahead don't worry about burning the clutch I will get a new one if I have to, and he let me drive it around Pepboys and into the garage watched me do the oil change pulled out the car and gave me and Eugene a nice tip guy was cool as all hell and there began my manual car days and since then I never looked back. So, since it was the last car, we cleaned up mopped put the tires in the recycle pile closed up and Eugene was driving me back home. We just literally got outside of Pepboys at the light made a left to Route One next to the Mercedes Dealership and the car just shut off. It was weird it wasn't like it lost all electrical power, or like the car stalled it just bogged out and died so we broke that car down as fast as we could before the Ray Catena dealership called the cops on us and guess what happened to the car, somehow the rotor in the distributor broke in to a million pieces and until this day I have never seen anything like it lol I swear if it wasn't for Eugene and his special problems with that car I wouldn't know all I know about Hondas lol I can't explain the other incidents but they were just weird car part failures lol so he called up Vince and Vince drove from Greenville with a new distributor and took 3 minutes to put the new one in started right up and on we went.

Kaylynn was talking to me little by little at this point and we were getting along ok, she had told me when her graduation was and it was pretty important because she wasn't doing well in a Math class so if she walked it meant she passed and I knew she was going to that girl doesn't give up on anything and it was gearing up towards the end of the year, her cousin believed I should try and talk to her about going to prom, at this point I knew that she was or had someone in mind she wanted to go to prom with but the people that I knew had told me about him and cool if you want to go to prom go ahead and enjoy yourself but not with him, he was disrespectful and when I found out he had called her a bitch I was heated man I wanted to rip that kids head off his shoulder and so I told her what he said about her and she got mad at me, like I was so confused I was just trying to watch over her and protect her and keep her away from people like him and I shouldn't have done that because she was just fed up at that point and told me to leave her alone and to forget about going to her graduation and that was the last time I heard from her. Her cousin tore me a new one too like I just wasn't understanding I was just trying to keep her away from getting hurt in cheerleading and on top of that when she started speaking to me again she was recovering from a concussion that happened at cheerleading practice because the girls didn't break her fall and catch her and she fell and hit her head and I was so sad when she told me man you don't even understand all I fought for and tried to keep her away from and she got hurt, then how hard I fought to just get her back in my life to just lose her trying to keep her away from a bad influence and everyone is under the belief that I am obsessed and whatever when her ex-boyfriend would just stalk her and stay outside her crib waiting to see if she would leave or not and all I was trying to do was just get her back in my life and protect her and love her and I end up losing her and she ghosts me again and her cousin don't want shit to do with me and that was the end of us and I will never fight for another girl the way I fought for her because at the end of the day I can't explain all I have done to try and get her back and protect her but I did a lot man and I know my faults I know I fucked up but I acknowledged it and tried to right my wrongs and tried to get her back and all I got in return was just being called names and belittled and rejected and ghosted on with no reason no phone call no nothing other than me and my thoughts it was just a horrible end to my first relationship as well as no closure so I didn't know exactly what I did wrong so I wouldn't do it again I just knew that this girl that once loved me hated the blood that flowed in me and I had no way to make things right and I was just lost, this connection this bond this communication the secrets we shared promises we made in a moment all just faded away like it meant nothing and being Michael I didn't have a chance to explain myself or get answers to questions that I had and that was just the end of us.

Soon enough, well looking back at it now as an adult was probably the weirdest thing, I have ever done in my life aside from the intentions that paved the way for it. Kaylynn's graduation was a couple weeks away and working at Pepboys I think it actually was on a Saturday I may be mistaken but I talked to my manager to see if I can get the day off and he said no. So to me in my mind the thought process wasn't to go there and try and get her back I was just going to see if she walked because if she did that meant she passed her Math class and that's what was important to make sure she passed and she progressed and graduated with the class she came in with and with her friends because I know that was important to her so it was important to me to. At work I didn't care my manager said no and I said ok I am putting in my 2 weeks. I walked out of his office and I told Eugene and he was upset and I know he was you know he got me the job there and now I am leaving but we all had problems in that shop and not giving me a one day off which I had never asked that, it was just time to go man. Graduation comes and I go and the graduation was at the football field and I went and sure enough she was there and she walked and got her diploma and graduated and it made me happy knowing she didn't give up she's just not that type and looking back on it now yea that was probably some creepy ass shit lol and like I am joking now because I can think back to my thought process and I know and understand why I went, it was all for her and I didn't see her or give her a hug or her family and I just left but man if I had my thought process now I would have never had went lol just that whole year was so difficult with her I just didn't know how to control my emotions or thoughts and let me tell you something, when your judgments are cloudy, whether it be because of love or good intentions, you tend to believe all your irrational thoughts are justified, and going to her graduation was just not justified no matter how much it meant to me or to her I shouldn't have gone and it was wrong of me to go but that was the last time I saw her, I actually wrote her a letter apologizing for everything I did wrong or that I believe I did wrong from what she was mad about and what I know I did wrong but her mother answered the door and just did not want me there and that was the end of us. I tried I gave my all and as usual I fell short, I just wanted to clear the air, I didn't want her to hate me, at the end of the day the bond we shared the connection we had it was just not ok to end things the way they ended but I learned from this experience that it is always on the woman once she gave up there was no turning back there was no reason to fight and I don't want people to think wrong about this situation. For one we were both young, I had absolutely no experience with relationships and that was a huge problem, I know all the things I did were wrong even if some people believe otherwise because of the buildup of frustration that occurred after the whole hospital thing. At the end of the day I was in the wrong and I can take accountability of all my actions with whatever prejudice, bias, or consequences come my way I admit all my faults and take my hits like a man and at the end of the day listen in all honesty I was wrong man it is what it is I am truly sorry. Kaylynn was well is an amazing young woman, we all have made mistakes its life and we grow from it the love was never lost she will always be a part of me and I am forever grateful for crossing paths with her, I am grateful and appreciative of her welcoming me into her family and her family treating me like one of their own, I will never forget it and I hold such experiences very close to my heart, I may not have had the opportunity to take my girl to her first day of college or work and other experiences that we will soon get to but I am forever grateful for all she has done for me, as well as she was a huge factor in me not being in the streets, she did an amazing job keeping me away from drugs, gangs, street culture aside form Marinella, Arabelle, and Melina, Kaylynn was there for me and I have to show my respect and appreciation the right way because if she didn't come into my life when she did and we didn't have that connection and bond and shared some amazing experiences that I will never get the chance to experience again I really don't know where I would be if she wasn't around, I love her very much and she will forever be a part of me.

Chapter 13

Jaylene, The Girl That Changed My Soul

This woman who I will introduce you to was, well is extremely important to me and was the single most important woman in my life for quite some time, well until Nameless came along but I will not disclose very much information about her or things we have been through because I just won't allow anyone to speak ill of her or any woman in this story for that matter but for all she has done for me I simply cannot allow it so I will do my best to tell the story to the best of my ability without disclosing very much information about her in which I actually don't have very much but that's neither here nor there but understand that she is very important to me and how I developed such an in-depth thought process about people in general to be able to explain all that I have explained until now and further coming. The love will always be there. It was always love, and it will always be love.

I really honestly don't want to write this part she just means the world to me, but I guess if we are letting it all out then this needs to come out as, well right?

After everything ended with Kaylynn and Pepboys just wasn't working out I thought the best option was to go and join the Army. I had bills to pay and I wanted to venture out on my own aside from my mom telling me I was a piece of shit and I needed to get a job so fuck it right what's better than jumping states and getting paid to fight and train right simple enough. My stupid ass thought process lol. Every day I would run 2 miles to the park in front of McDonalds in Agua Dulce and just go do Suicides on the basketball court, pushups, pull ups on the basketball rim, sit-ups and take a cool down 2 mile walk back home and I did this every day at 7 in the morning because the Sergeant told me I had better start running and after my lung collapsing the doctor told me that it could potentially happen again spontaneously within the next 3 years after that I wouldn't have to worry anymore, so I believed him I had no medical knowledge back then, and I knew what was going to happen in the Army with all the weight load I would be carrying for how many miles and the running I had to get in to some type of shape because I had not worked out all year while I was going to Lincoln Tech. At this point I had already told my mom I joined the Army and she was pissed but oh well, I needed to get away and she told me to get a job, so I did both lol.

Around the third week of August I just I guess still feeling pretty hurt about the whole situation with Kaylynn and knowing I would never talk to her again and stuff I put up a status or comment I forget how MySpace worked and throughout the day I would just talk to friends and add people and just talk. All of a sudden, this girl had commented on the status I posted, and her name was Jaylene, and the comment she left caught my attention it was just intriguing. So, I responded, and we started to talk from there and the conversation got real in-depth and real good real fast, she asked me for my number and called me.

At first clearly, we introduced ourselves and she had such a sweet soft-spoken voice man I miss hearing it, and then we had started talking and one of the first questions she had asked me was have I ever used a girl for sex. The question was so left field from our conversation and it was great she just didn't care what was on her mind she just let it out if it felt right no matter what it was. I told her no; I have never used a girl for sex, and I am a virgin. She was shocked like all guys are evil or something and we just all use women for sex and for our needs. From there we just didn't ever get off the phone until like 2 in the morning because I was just super tired and had to wake up early to go work out. The issue was that well lol she was from California, Los Angeles for some better understanding of Time Zones and this is where I learned Time Zones in detail and she had told me that she was 3 hours behind so it was 11 pm for her when I had fallen asleep, and she had told me to call her when I woke up to go work out, but I felt extremely bad after learning the Time Zones but she insisted that I called.

The next day I woke up to go work out and I don't usually bring my phone but I woke up stretched and I called her and it was like before 7 in the morning for me and I knew that it was like 3 or 4 in the morning for her and let me tell you the first ring didn't even complete before she picked up and it was weird, I don't know it made me feel like important to her I didn't understand why she would pick up for me so early we barely know each other and just like that she just picked up and she sounded tired but when she heard my voice, like she completely woke up and greeted me so sweet and I don't know man I just felt like important and special to her and I thought she wasn't going to pick up I thought she was just being nice then we just started talking and I started walking to the park and she asked me about my girl and I told her I didn't have one and she said why what happened to you and your ex and that was the beginning of that, I literally told her everything that happened both good and bad my side and Kaylynn's side until she stopped talking to me in October and then the here and there briefly talking and everything just everything that happened. Jaylene she just didn't say a word unless she didn't understand something so I didn't know if she was just letting me vent it out or was actually really interested in knowing what happened but soon enough my phone was dying so I turned back around and ran home put my phone on the charger and continued the conversation and she opened me up man. That girl grabbed my soul and made me vulnerable man and she protected my soul she brought it out of me and held it gently in her hand and took care of me. As the conversation was on going what happened was she was asking me why did I do certain things with Kaylynn or why did I act certain ways and I really didn't have an answer honestly I just didn't know what to do, it was my first relationship and I didn't know how to take care of someone else's emotions as good as I can take care of a female friends. It such a different environment with an exclusive relationship and Jaylene told me what I did wrong and what I should have done, and that woman did not judge me she just I guess guided me toward the right path. She just always knew what to say what to do how to fix the situation and I didn't know how much things I did wrong with Kaylynn until Jaylene pointed it out to me. I felt super bad about everything with Kaylynn and I saw how I was able to fix things at certain points of our relationship but it was way too late you know she was just gone but knowing that I fucked up and how I did, it actually really helped me grow and understand certain aspects about life and relationships with people.

As that conversation ended, we actually had to get off the phone because she had to go and pick up her sister's kids from school little Malakai and Janessa which aren't their real names so don't go too crazy. When she got back we started talking again and she just had all sorts of questions for me and we just talked man and she was talking to me about like the fights I been in and just why was I fighting or why was I so upset with people to the point in which it resulted in a physical altercation and again I had absolutely no answers for her and she man she was just a god send. She just literally talked to me about it and pretty much made me take accountability of the shit I did wrong and the people I hurt and I just felt super shitty but it was just her she was just there simply just guiding me through it all and I just didn't know why, and I was very grateful and appreciative of this woman that came out of the blue and made me acknowledge all the stupidity I have ever don't wrong and even though there was no chance of making it right, knowing that it was my fault and knowing that I had the choice to change and get on a straight path was welcoming. There was just no malice no judgments nothing she just wanted me to do better and to treat people better and for her I did I learned so much she taught me so much she is a huge reason why I am the way I am today she is the reason why I know myself and are conscious about all the decisions I make today, she is still the reason why I don't use women for sex, would you know how disappointed this woman would be in me if she found out I turned into just a horrible human that I could have because I really didn't give a fuck about anyone or anyone's feelings until this young woman walked into my life and straightened me out.

Throughout the rest of the day we just spoke about everything and it was just good, we spoke, and she was 18, she was still in contact with her ex and whatever cool I didn't really care honestly. So, what happened is that she had told me that her pictures were taken and this and that right, so people actually know this girl right, her picture at the time was all over the internet. She had sent me pictures and they just didn't coincide with her profile and I just didn't care, I confronted her about it and she stuck to her lie cool whatever I didn't care honestly I just needed this girl I was talking on the phone with I didn't care about anything else at all nothing mattered I just needed this girl whoever she was that was on the phone that is who I needed.

Towards the end of the month well the phone bill came lol and it was up at about 500 dollars and I was dead broke and I couldn't just let this girl go man she was all I got and she cared she actually cared and so I told her and she had offered to pay for my phone bill and I said fuck no, that pride is just I don't ever allow women to pay for anything doesn't matter how small it is I just won't allow it, Adrien hates that lol it's so funny when we hang out with our female friends from high school we will go out to eat and he says, are we splitting this one to and the answer is yeap lmfaoooooo, it's not so much a bother for him it's because we know them so well they will try and take the check so I always ask for it before they do lol, I don't know I just can't it's a weird thing it's not a man thing or anything like that I just feel if I invite you out its just to spend time with you, I just want to be around you and I don't want you to worry about the spending because it's not about that its simply just spending time and being around your presence that's all. What had happened was Jaylene had invited me to California and she said it would be on her dime she didn't care she just wanted and needed to see me and I just couldn't allow it at the time it was like 800 dollars for the ticket and allow me to stay in her place and I just couldn't do that I thought that it was just too much, and in all honesty I regret it to this day. I really wish I would have gone and just payed her back later for it. For everything that woman has done for me it was just priceless and how could I repay back something that's priceless.

After the whole phone bill conversation she had to go pick up her sisters kids and I awaited till she got back and she called me but she actually had to go run an errand with her mom and so we got off the phone, then I received a call almost immediately back and I said hey babe everything ok, and I just heard her singing she had an amazing voice, she would sing to me when I asked but she was pretty insecure about her voice so I would have to beg unless it was night time that was like when she sung me to sleep, and so I just listened to her sing her pretty little heart away while she was talking to her mom and I was just on the line it was great just when you catch a girl off-guard and know that they are and have the same persona you understand and believe they are to be and I just sat and listened then like 15 minutes later she checks her phone and guess who was on it lol me lmfaooo. She was so embarrassed lol she said wait you were on the line the whole time you didn't hang up I told her I did and she butt dialed me lol you have to love an accidental butt dial lol it's a good feeling when you get butt dialed you know the booty misses you lmfaooo any who she was like you heard all that I said yeap and I heard you singing so now you have to sing me to sleep lol. Nighttime had come and we were talking, and it was time lol I asked her to sing me a lullaby so I can go to sleep, and she sang to me, so our thing was we actually never got off the phone. When we first started talking the bond was just there it was felt mutually and we just I don't know it just felt weird not talking to her and after a couple of days when we first met she asked me not to get off the phone, I didn't understand what she meant at first and she just explained to me to simply just stay on the phone while we slept and I said ok and I understood why like it wasn't weird it was that, that's the closest we would ever be and it felt intimate and it was just a great experience, so if she would wake up in her sleep she would wake me up and we would talk or I would help her go back to sleep and if accidently she or I hung up we would just call each other back ask if everything was ok and go back to sleep and it was just a pleasant experience it was really amazing that was my baby girl man my soul my heart just attached itself to this woman man it was great to experience a woman like her. She made my soul feel safe.

    Coming to September, September 11th to be exact well her father had passed away. What had happened was that she was at the hospital when it happened, she was close to him and after he had a conversation with her, he passed shortly after, it was really, really sad. Me being who I am you know I had to check up on her make sure she was ok and I called her you know not to be too much of a bother I know she was grieving and she was just crying her eyes out man it fucking hurt I tried the best I could to change the subject I just couldn't hear her crying it hurt me so bad man, I had asked her if she ate and she said "you care if I eat," I said "yes I know you're grieving I know you're feeling bad but you still have to care for yourself and since you're not doing that because your mind is off thinking about your father I will take care of you and check on you to make sure you're ok while dealing with the loss of your father," and she like stopped crying and promised me she would go get some food and call me back after wards and we spoke and she told me the relationship her and her father had and how they were close so I understood why it hit her so hard you know.

So let me tell you a bit about this girl, and I really don't want to, I have decided to cut this a bit short because I realized there are many things that I cannot talk about and there are people I actually don't want to talk about its just not important honestly that weight doesn't wear me down so it's not really necessary to put it here either way Jaylene was a pretty wild child man. From going to a party in LA to somehow her and her friend end up in the middle of the desert in the middle of the night trying to find their way back home, they just weren't normal party stories lol I am just glad she was safe, but oh yea and she taught me a lot of slang so a get together in Jersey is considered a Kick Back in Cali language which was so weird to me but Cali people are so chill I love them man my heart will always be in Cali honestly. So, she wasn't really into marijuana her choice of drug was Ecstasy and that was a no go for me man. So after her father passed away she wanted to turn to the Ecstasy and the issue was not only the Ecstasy the issue was her and her best friend loved Ecstasy so much they had bought a bag of 600 fucking pills just fucking wild man, man when she told me that shit I told her go to that fucking safe of hers and flush all that shit in the toilet and tell her friend if she wanted to yell at me or make me pay for her half I would but she simply was just not taking it anymore or being in the possession of that while I was in her life fuck all that shit. Girl was like addicted to that shit and at first it had like a control over her, but she did she flushed it down the toilet for me and she never took another one again. After some time had passed by and she went to her dads funeral he was buried in Mexico and that was pretty nerving for me because I had never been to

Mexico but she would take flights alone and meet her family there so I wouldn't hear from her for a few days until she came back and that was my baby I couldn't just be a minute let alone a day without talking to her and we got through it and little by little day by day it got better and she was ok to the point that she accepted that he passed and when she needed to vent I was there for her just an exceptional woman man I really miss her and writing this and reliving it is like 50 50 it hurts but it feels good remembering the conversations her soothing and welcoming voice her laugh it was just good times I really, really hope she is doing well.

So the time comes and it's time to leave for the Army and it sucked man because I just wanted to be with Jaylene so bad and now I know I wouldn't be able to see her until sometime next year, and my mom I really don't know, I guess she thought I was joking about joining the military and mentally she just broke she just fell into a depression and they had come to pick me up to go to the airport and my mom was in the hospital and they didn't want to let me go see her before I left I told them to fuck off because Sergeant V6 brought some idiot with him that I didn't know and he was talking shit saying if I went to go see my mom I wouldn't go to the Army or some shit like that like my guy I signed the contract I take accountability I told you I will go so I will go but I'ma go see my mom first dick head and Sergeant V6 told me to relax because he was going to take me and he did and I said bye to my mom and on I went.

The flight was from JFK Airport in NY to I believe Columbus Georgia or Atlanta any way we had to go to 30th AG which was basically reception for military personnel entering basic training where we go and get all our shots and they get us ready for basic. Any who that bus ride was the longest bus ride I have ever taken in my life. It was like 2 and a half hours to 3 hours long but felt like forever, it was so quiet and dark the roadways in Georgia don't have highway lamps so it was just a dark environment overall and once I got on the bus what did I do I called my baby girl and of course she was waiting for me first ring didn't even finish and we just spoke nonstop for all the hours on the bus and man like I just appreciate it man knowing how much she was there for me how much she supported and cared and cherished me she really left a void in my heart when she left. Coming to the drop off I can tell we were getting close and she just started giving me advice telling me you know not to give up and just keep going she was just my heart and my soul man.

Soon enough well let me tell you a lot a lot of shit happened at 30th AG I was simply not prepared for lol both gooooooddddd and baadddddd and that's just not to be discussed but I remember it all simply because we are on the subject matter. We are a day away from going to Sand Hill and Charlie Company was my unit up there where I was going. All the Sergeants had us all in this room in 30th AG talking to us and just smoking the living dog shit out of us, so smoking for the civilians reading this book is just when the Sergeants make you do physical activity as punishment or just for the sake of absolutely nothing so we were all getting smoked doing pushups till our arms fell off and they stopped us and left, so while we were all sitting there talking this kid goofy as all hell real funny guy from Texas was talking us we were just getting to know everyone, he was telling us how where he lived in Texas was a small community and they had to take their horses to school because there were no cars or anything and he was just a good story teller man just real believable guy even if the story was so farfetched he just attracted you to his story by the way he was telling it and he was like yea we park our horses outside of the school they feed em and all lol. Everyone was like really and he was like no you dumb fucks where do you think I live; I live in Texas damm it lmfaoooooooooooooooo that shit was so funny let me tell you. So aside from that story the Sergeants came in and we were just ready to get smoked again and they said at ease and oh baby at ease it was that meant no smoking session lmfaooooo they came in with a box and gave us our cell phones back because they were going to take them tomorrow and told us to make our last calls before tomorrow and this is when things changed. So I called Adrien, and Adrien is an exceptionally huge part of this story and I may not be able to express all that he has done for me but know if it wasn't for him and all he has done for me and supported me as his best friend I would be completely lost, so I always show my gratitude and appreciation for him every chance I get. So I called him and no answer, then I called my mom no answer, and we were on a time limit and my thought process was if I call them real fast let them know I am ok I can spend the rest of the time talking to my baby girl. That process got really fucked up huh lol so I called my baby girl and as usual I don't think it even got to ring once and she picked up right away man I fucking love that girl so much there's really only one person that understands the love and meaning she has in my life. She picked up so fucking fast man with such pleasure and joy in her voice MY BABYYYYYYYYYYY fucking love that girl she was so excited to hear from me such a great mutual feeling, she was actually shopping for clothes with her friends and we talked and I told her she won't be hearing from me for almost a month but prepare for longer I really don't know and we had spoken about this previously I had asked her if she was prepared to be in a relationship with me because I was going to be in the military so our communication was going to be pretty rough for a while until I got out of basic and sure enough she didn't hesitate she was there by my side from day 1 and the support the love was so intense I could just feel her next to me and the Sergeants came in and we had to give our phones back she gave me more support and besos (kisses) and I had to hang up and it hurt hanging up man it really did.

So, November 13 which I believe was Friday the 13th we got on a yellow school bus on our way to Sand Hill for Shark Attack. Getting to the lot all I could see was all the Drill Sergeants lined up waiting for us to get dropped off and this fucking bus driver dropped us off right in front of them lol literally parked and the door opened to the first Drill Sergeant in line to hem us up lol. Let me tell you how much that shit sucked on top of getting fucked up and smoked you had all of your duffle bags man and you haven't moved in yet so they were packed to the fucking max oh man run here run there while they are yelling at you about how much a piece of shit you are and you have no friends in there yet so you can't even joke around or laugh and shit it's all serious and it just gets tiring real fast like the yelling the screaming off the top of their lungs and you just think while your sweating your fucking balls off how much fucking energy do these fucking guys have man they have to let up soon I just can't deal with all that yelling shit man they going to have an aneurysm because they blood pressure so high lol and let me tell you they did not let up. So after the initial Shark Attack and getting the balls smoked out of us we had to find our bags and run all the way the fuck upstairs because of course we lived on the 3rd floor of the building and they had made us drop all our bags in a pile and with 3 different bags you had to find it in a pile of over 70 fucking bags and go upstairs because you had to run there was no such thing as walking in training ever if you get caught walking you getting smoked and on day 1 your especially fucked. I am going to stop swearing real soon so guys relax please it will be ok I promise for those that are upset lol. So, we go up and no one knows whose bunk is whose. The Drill Sergeants come upstairs and yell toe the line, well I don't know what the fuck that meant and I am assuming everyone seen military movies and I don't ever recall that shit so I am out there trying figure out what the fuck that even means and I see everyone standing in the middle of the room so I go there and the Drill Sergeants gave everyone their assigned bunk and a Battle Buddy, so your Battle Buddy was your bunk mate and if he got in trouble either everyone in the platoon pays for it or the Sergeant singles you out for him fucking up because you're supposed to watch out for your Battle Buddy. After that they smoked the shit out of us again just an all-day event then it came to eat dinner, just running everywhere it was annoying and we had to do pull ups before we got to the chow hall then first dinner eat what they gave you, find a seat for no reason because they just get in your face and tell you that you have 30 seconds to finish your food and get out the chow hall then once your run outside and open that door bam another Drill Sergeant like got damn how many instructors they got working holy shit man, and once you stepped outside you got smoked and sent straight back to the football field with sand instead of turf it's a sand pit, so hence the name Sand pit but the size or a football field so 100 yards of just sand, and that's the place you didn't want to be it was just hell all day long and you weren't leaving there were no breaks from smoking sessions once everyone reached muscle fatigue from one muscle group it's time to change to a different exercise and they were smart literally they changed exercise every like 50 to 100 reps so the muscle group stayed fresh and you can go back and reuse the muscle group and smoke you longer it was total bullshit lol like how did they know how to do all this shit, then run to the back of the sand pit, and you had to fire man carry your Battle Buddy as if he was injured and good thing I was in decent shape my Battle Buddy Urias good fucking guy man good guy I miss him, he was only like 170 180 pounds at the time and I was in shape carrying weight wasn't an issue and they said first person to finish gets a break until the last person passes the line and I grabbed him up and ran as fast as I could but with all the exercises we had done already I was just beat and I collapsed at around the 50 yard line and Urias was like "yo get up get up the Drill Sergeant coming" I said "oh shit oh shit" I forced myself to get up and well we definitely didn't finish last but we still got smoked until the last person passed the line, so this guy's last name was Bruce they nicknamed him Brute lol, dude was like 300 pounds and his Battle Buddy was a short kid I forgot his name he was a good kid but had little man's syndrome but the issue was he was small and weighed probably 110 pounds so Bruce had to carry him and that was no problem he threw him over his back and hit the sand running and finished first but the issue was on the return they were Buddies so the kid had to carry him the way back and we all finished and what did that mean we had to get smoked until they came across the line and man that shit sucked fucking sucked but the kid made it and I feel really really bad for calling him kid and I don't mean it in a disrespectful way I just forgot his name and we were all family in there except a few idiots that caused us a lot of problems so I mean my apologies brother I love you.

After the day smoke session it was time to go back upstairs and take a shower and these Drill Sergeants did not let up man so we were given these baby sized towels like the waist was literally a 29 I had to rip that shit a bit to try and tie it around my waist any who we line up and all I hear is yelling and in my head I was damn we don't even get a break for a shower fuck man but they couldn't smoke you in the shower because of the risk of injury, and everyone is coming out so fast I am so confused so the closer the closer we get I hear better and better and fuck man lol all I hear is you got 10 seconds and they are counting down you can barely get soap on and it was going one, two , four, seven, ten get the fuck out nowwww lmfaoooo and it is funny now at the time going through it that shit was fucking annoying and I was pretty much on autopilot just doing whatever I was told because there was absolutely no other option, and so when the last person got out we were already toed in line and they smoked the living shit out of us, shampoo, and soap and water all over the floor man and like I said before with these neonatal towels they fucking gave us what do you think happened they fucking fell off during the smoking session lol so like half of us were ass naked no socks on getting the shit smoked out of us man oh man I didn't need to see all that shit lol.

They finally left us alone and gave us 15 minutes to clean up all that soap and shampoo and water off the floor and well it was over 50 of us in there we got it done fast by the time they came back it was already done we rested for like 5 minutes literally. The Drill Sergeants came in and taught us how to do the hospital corners and all that and get ready for bed so we got ready for bed they turned off the lights and left man was that a sigh of relief from the whole platoon lol everyone fell asleep but had to be no more than 15 to 20 minutes all we hear is the Drill Sergeants desk getting thrown across the room and that shit was so loud it woke us all up and the yelling and screaming just started man that smoke session I would never forget shit was crazy I won't discuss it though lol but we all jumped out of bed to see what was going on and this fucking dude fucking massive dude shorter than Bruce but bigger I didn't know how this dude got through the fucking door man and he was dressed as a Drill Sergeant and we were like man how many fucking instructors do we have I didn't see this guy all day today what the fuck and he smoked the shit out of us, all while explaining the policy of sleep which he said legally they have to give you 4 hours of sleep a day then went on to say that the law didn't specify that the 4 hours of sleep had to be continuous and man did that wreck my soul lmfaooo now I knew what they were about with the games and shit I knew it was going to be a long 5 months and there was no turning back you only had the option to hit it head first running, so he said we would get 30 minutes of rest sporadically throughout the day to add up to 4 hours and if we so happen to stay awake and not sleep that it is our problem not theirs and shit man the first month was just absolute hell and hell week which we won't discuss either well me and Urias hadn't slept for like 3 days straight it fucking sucked man.

 Any who that was day one lol and a lot more happened but there's no discussing that it isn't important to you or the story I was just show casing what is was like when I got in I don't know how things have changed by now. So Thanksgiving comes and they are giving out mail and they start calling names and throwing the mail into the center of the room and in the center of the room is a huge logo of our platoon and unit so we aren't allowed to step in the middle of the room like out of respect for everyone who has come and gone which was completely understandable I didn't mind that at all. So they called up Bruce's Battle Buddy and he did not move lol we all awaited his response lmfaooo so he looks at the mail and looks at the Drill Sergeant and the Drill Sergeant says "what the fuck private you going to get it or not do you want it" he replied "Drill Sergeant yes Drill Sergeant" the Drill Sergeant said "well go fucking get it" he said "Drill Sergeant Roger Drill Sergeant." When he took that first step into the mural on the floor the Drill Sergeant said "oh you want to play fuck fuck games do you, you just want to step on to the center of the floor no man's land well then give me 25" and he had to do 25 pushups, and as he got to 24 the Drill Sergeant called his name again and threw the letter to him and he tried to reach for it and stepped again and another 25 pushups lmfaoooo oh this shit was a setup and it was going to suck for everyone, then all of a sudden he called out his name 6 more times and that was a lot of fucking pushups so the Drill Sergeant said "oh people really love you huh, well since you have so much love coming your way give me 200 and call it a day for all your mail" lmfaoooo fuck. In my head was like well aint no one give a shit about me so I aint doing no pushups lol. So what started happening was we adapted people wouldn't step on the mural they would lay down and reach for it and the Drill Sergeants said "oh you guys are smart now huh, its 50 for each now since you guys want to adapt we will adapt too" lmfaooooo man the fucking games they played like these Sergeants were fucking smart. So it got to my name and the Drill Sergeant said Rodriguez, Rodriguez, Rodriguez, Rodriguez man fuck this give me 250 since your whole fucking family wants to mail you shit, man in my head I said what the fuck they don't want to pick up the fucking phone but everyone will individually write me a letter what the fuck man when I call them I'ma have a talk I aint doing pushups for that bull shit lol. When I went to go get my letters there were like 3 brown ones with turkeys on them from my family then the real letters I saw, sent from Cassie man how much I love that woman and her family, Fabyen from Lincoln Tech my fucking brother man, and Roland, I don't recall telling you that we became friends again after we reconciled after what I did but any who I went to see him a year after what happened between him and Vivian, and I admitted my fault about telling her and I told him he was wrong for it and he as the man he is acknowledged he was wrong and we spoke and everything was all good that's why I like dealing with adults who know themselves and who can acknowledge their own faults and take accountability for it because when things go wrong we can be humane and discuss shit like mature adults any who I love them all such a big part of my life these people were and supported me in ways I could never repay honestly I owe them a lot.

Now we finish all this, and the Drill Sergeants are feeling nice, so they allow us to use our phones and gave us 15 minutes because the next time we were going to be using the phones was on 2-week exodus when we weren't there anymore for vacation. What did I do, well if you haven't guessed I called baby girl of course lol. As usual before first ring ended, she picked up oh my how I love her so. She was just always so excited to hear from me that was my baby. We spoke for like 90 percent of the time then I told her I had to go and we would talk again around Christmas and of course she always asked me if I was ok or needed anything and we spoke about something I will disclose in a bit anyway, I called Adrien and spoke to him then called my mom and clearly she don't pick up lol so I left her a message and told her to tell the family no more letters I was not doing pushups for their generic ass cards lol. If you haven't gauged or understood by now I have no care for political bullshit or generalized shit, like don't give me advice like everything will be ok, or you know the dumb generic shit everyone says because they don't know what to say about the situation because if you don't know that about me now well we will get in depth about it soon enough in the coming chapters so you will see I don't deal with that bullshit I tell everyone to fuck off with that generic shit and throw it out the fucking window if you don't know what to say don't say shit.

At this point with Jaylene I had missed a lot, she was going through a lot and she needed me and I was not there for her, she keep on a straight face and supported me when it should have been the other way around and I kill myself for it every day, and her mom started to dislike me very much at this point, and the weird thing was that she hadn't given me her address so I wasn't able to write to her but I wrote her as many letters as I had the time to write and till this day I still have them and they are locked up in my safe I still have to burn everything from these women and I will after I finish writing this story everything is getting destroyed it's just time to move on man it's been too long and none of these woman are in my life anymore they have all decided that I have no place in their life and that's perfectly fine it's a decision that I must respect.

December comes and we had already started shooting and qualifying and the Drill Sergeants started to trust us and talk to us and they could make out the mature people from the immature idiots and my Battle Buddy was out here in the barracks selling candy lol and he got a big ass box like a care package and it was filled with candy and all of a sudden the Drill Sergeants came up stairs and there was contraband every fucking where and so we did the best we could to hide it all and Urias had rolled up the rest of his candy in the his Ranger Rolled T- shirts and put the money in his drawers on him lmfaooo and the box we folded it and put it under the mattress lol. The Drill Sergeants found a pretty hefty amount of candy and said "oh we thought we were on track doing good with you guys so someone's going to talk" and we all stayed quiet no one snitched lol, bad idea though they fucking hemmed us up for it they were pissed all lockers were cleaned out everything was thrown into the center of the room on the floor all mixed up and it was horrible because even though we didn't have an incidence of Staph Infection there were some dirty ass dudes in there man and it sucked had to double wash all my shit man we got the living dog shit smoked out of us for the rest of the week. As Exodus comes closer training was getting less and less and we were cleaning more and more because we had to leave the barracks spotless until we returned because no one would be there so that and getting smoked was the last week before Exodus.

I get home and me and Jaylene were talking I was on my way to Adrien's house and I don't know what happened man, she started crying and she had told me that she wasn't who she said she was, which was already clear but then she admitted she wasn't as old as she said she was either, and that crushed me man, so she was 17 but I was 19 at this time, so I quickly broke things off like that shit was just not happening so she agreed but, the problem was that she lied about almost everything but we were just too close I couldn't lose someone that my soul was so attached to and how she helped me grow as a person and as important as we were to each other we spoke and decided that it was the best idea to wait until she turned 18 which was a few months away. So, this girl, her friend / sister that she was living with she, I guess the right way to say would be looked up to because of her beauty and success chose her to impersonate because I don't know for whatever reason. At this point after she realized how disappointed and hurt I was, and she was going through it with her mom and another situation with some guy from school I guess it just all hit her at once I mean I got clarification from all the situations. It had turned out she was older than me she was actually 21 and graduating college. I can't discuss the situations honestly because they are extremely personal but comes January I am taking the train back to the airport and she is just not responding and I don't know what happened but something was wrong it wasn't just that, she wasn't picking up but she just I don't know it was weird man. So, we got back, and the Drill Sergeants let us make a phone call before they took our phones till like Easter, I don't know I don't remember but I called, and she didn't pick up and now I was fucking worried man.

    A few days later my friend from Cali his name is Lyal he just wanted to talk to his girl but the phones were locked in the Drill Sergeants office so Cali people man I love their mentality they are just so mellow and think outside the box and just don't care about shit lol well he came up with a plan to break in by not going through the door and get his phone so he asked if anyone wanted their phones and 2 other people did I left mine in there fuck all that getting caught with that shit. He broke in and retrieved the phones, and what happened was he let me use his phone and try and get in touch with my girl she was just M.I.A man and I started texting her telling her it was me from a friends phone and I got a message from her mom saying she was in the hospital and in a coma at that, that shit crushed me man and she told me she didn't know what happened. She eventually woke up and started to text me back and she told me that she had jumped off a cliff and tried to kill herself because she couldn't be with me. Ummm well this is an extremely painful memory and so as supportive as this woman has been, as much love as she had for me and has shown me aside from lying to me, as she had never asked me for absolutely anything except to come see her and I didn't because of my pride to not allow women to pay for anything ever, as much as she needed me because I was the only person there for her when I was able to be there day in and day out, as close as a connection and bond we had, I was not there for her when she needed me most I was not able to be there and protect her, I was not able to be there when she needed to talk to me and vent, I simply was just not there for her as she was there for me and she needed me, my woman needed me and I wasn't there for her and I have to take full accountability of that and I wasn't there for her to the point where she felt so alone with all her problems she couldn't run to me about it that she thought her only decision was to try and ease the pain by jumping off a cliff, and for the readers to help you understand, that is something I have to live with forever. That is one of the main reasons why I never leave anyone alone even though that trait was always a part of me I have never left anyone alone ever, but when I see the signs of suicidal ideation I quickly intervene to show people and remind them that they aren't alone, that is why I constantly check up on people, that is why I am always there for everyone at all times of the day no matter what I am doing, I have literally paused my life and given up my life for people to help them understand that they are not alone that there are genuine people still walking the Earth people that genuinely care, people that genuinely want to see you do well and don't want to see you in harm's way, I have created safe environments for women where they wouldn't have to worry about being physically or verbally abused by family members or significant others but at the end of the day doing all of this doesn't take away the fact that I was the reason my woman the love of my life my rock my support my strength tried to take her own life away, and for that I could never forgive myself for. This is where we end writing for today, have a blessed day you guys and be safe, it's always love.

I am back I haven't really written anything in a few days which is bad but I'm back. So with everything that has happened to this point you know, you start to understand how feelings, emotions, bonds, connections you make with people can change a person's life, I mean you know and you understand but when it gets to a point where people are taking their own lives because certain things are not going the way they should and they have no escape, they have no one to go to, the void the loneliness the pain envelops them and in their head the decision is already made and no one can alter the outcome of their decision and to know it to hear about it is completely different than to be a part of the reasoning of such a tragic event and the level of understanding is set to another tier, and the fact that this was my woman the love of my life and it was part my fault was the worst feeling in the world. I was just happy that she turned out ok because she did come out of the coma and fully recovered. The worst part of the whole situation was that when her mom found out that I was a part of the reason for that and she tried very hard to keep her away from me which it came to a point where if it was for the betterment of her health mentally and physically then how could I be upset about her mother protecting her if the situation was reverse I would have done all I could to protect my child as well so I wasn't upset about it but it came time where I just wasn't hearing from her and the pain came from knowing out of this whole situation, nothing changed I as a man still could not be there to support her, hold her, tell her I loved her, tell her everything was going to be ok and I will never allow myself to make my woman ever feel like that ever again, work will never be a reason why I can't spend time with my woman especially when she needs me I just simply won't allow it.

At this point the Drill Sergeants had found out someone broke into their office and snatched several phones and they were exceptionally upset. So, what happened was that next to the sand pit there was this Pavilion sort of to explain it is a massive Gazebo with benches on both sides, we usually go there for training of weapons and things of that sort. The Drill Sergeants were so upset they made us grab all the bunk beds and wall lockers and move them down to the Pavilion and gave us 12 hours to do it, I don't think you understand how many beds and wall lockers that was and how fucking heavy the wall lockers were and on top of that we had to be up extra early for training the next day so with all this shit on my mind not really knowing how my woman was doing or feeling, not being able to talk to her and then Lyal losing his phone which was my only source of communication with her I was just sad man and it came to be 1700 around that time and we still weren't finished moving. The Drill Sergeants came in and smoked us for an hour and told us we had to move everything back in and in case you guys forgot we were on the 3rd level, and they gave us till 2200 which is ten at night and it was an all-day event just to get 75 percent of the barracks down stairs how were we going to manage that and after just getting the living shit smoked out of us man. Me and Urias just looked at each other we didn't know what to do. With all the people we had living with us we got it done but around 1 in the morning so we got smoked for not finishing in time then had to be up in a hour to work another 72 hours straight it just sucked man and it was good for the moment because it did help take my mind of Jaylene but she was a part of me and it hurt not knowing how she was doing and worst of all I couldn't do anything to help her my woman I couldn't do anything for her and I felt like such a piece of shit man it just sucked honestly.

    I don't really want to talk about that situation with Jaylene anymore so I am going to change the subject either way, after the training week comes to an end we were told to go back to the barracks wash our clothes and clean the barracks it was weird like the Drill Sergeants tone and all so what ended up happening was all the Drill Sergeants came in at once it was our 3 main Drill Sergeants and they sat down and called us to toe the line just a weird day because it just usually means they will all smoke the shit out of us so when one gets tired of yelling the next one start smoking us you know do pushups till my arms get tired like what lol and so they told us to sit down and that was even weirder we didn't know what was happening.

The Drill Sergeants started to talk to us and explain the process of what they were doing, Our main Drill Sergeants were, Drill Sergeant Hiru Drill Sergeant Ren, and Drill Sergeant Dante, Drill Sergeant Hiru was theeeeeeee absolute worst man when his little ass walked in off the bat from the get go you getting the living dog shit smoked out of you for 5 hours minimum, so after some time he opened up he told us he was a recovering alcoholic and what happened was that he walked in on his wife cheating on him, he was from the 82nd Airborne Division and after he broke it to us because he had a rep there we had thought the guy just fucking hated us but he turned out to be a honest genuine guy man he told us his brother had died in front of him is Iraq pretty much saved his life and to come back and walk in on his wife he just lost it, so he explained to us that he was hard on us because the day is going to come where we will be in country (that's the term for going into a combat zone also known as theater) and it is only going to be you and your brother there and you have to do everything you can to watch each other's back it doesn't matter how tired you are how much weight you're carrying your job is to make sure your brother gets back home and it's his job to make sure you get home and I didn't understand that till I was in Afghanistan. Drill Sergeant Ren was former Special Forces he was the most level headed man there he was pretty much the head Drill Instructor, he was explaining that he was hard on us because while in theater there is no option to give up, to quit nothing its simply to adapt and move forward because the enemy doesn't care about you, your family, your brothers next to you, they don't care about rank, nothing all they want to do is kill you and it's my job to prepare you well enough so you guys have the basic knowledge to make the best tactical decisions while in combat. Drill Sergeant Dante was former Ranger he was in the 3rd Ranger Battalion and he would just fuck you up for any minor detailed mistake, he would keep you up for 3 days tell you to get dressed and if something was out of line he would fuck you up and tell you if you don't pay attention to detail you will die. So all in all they sat us down as men and talked to us about the reasons of why they did what they did and from there it wasn't basic training anymore, we came to a mutual agreement as men and they did their job and kept their word they still smoked the shit out of us but simply when we made a mistake on the range or in training and they didn't really train us by the book what I loved about them they trained us in real life situations, I mean clearly they had to do things by the book but when we got done doing book shit they taught us real tactics thinking out of the box how to maneuver around an enemy that's flanking you in a direction the book doesn't tell you and that's when training got fun and we kept our word no more fucking around no dumb shit I mean we still broke in and stole the phones but put them back in before they came back in the morning so they never noticed but other than that we didn't fuck around because they started treating us as grown men and most of us there had very mature minds we were mainly street kids some business men some cops but we knew the rules as men and we abided by it after all was said and done. I miss them man we had a very good group of guys Urias he helped me a lot drop my run time and get my pushups higher he actually protected me too during a lot of the training just funny shit was just happening to us during training and he was a good guy sad story he lost his hearing at a gun range and had to reclass to a different job but his hearing was saved as much as possible I believe he had hearing aids now but at least he's not in the front line so its ok he had a big family a lot of people depended on him that I can remember, Lyal, Vander, Wyatt helped me with my run a lot as well they never left my side they would fail with me they would pass with me just to make sure I was pushed and doing my best, my lungs were still bad a year later but they did their job as my brothers and I will always appreciate them for it. Greyson was a police officer that wanted to join the military, so he gave up his civilian life to serve if I recall correctly, he was married as well just a good dude.

Harlow was this ripped kid German he went to military school as a kid and this kid would push out 100 diamond pushups for the fuck of it and even teasing him like hey what you doing you can't afford a diamond that big he was close his hands in more and do 50 more just because, this dude was fucking strong for no reason lol. Robinson was a fucking nice guy man he would never get mad just a swell dude lol. Rodolphus was a nice dude as well fucking intelligent guy. Rastas man one of the nicest guys ever fucking sad story man he lost both his legs in Kandahar Province while deployed I was pretty sad about it; he is a really really nice dude. Sev was a great buddy during basic training he helped me out a lot as well he actually came with me to New York but that's where we separated. Everyone except a select few were just amazing men I couldn't have asked for a better group of guys to be in basic with man and that was us we were the Hell Hounds of Charlie Company Fort Benning.

Now it's time for the Field Training Exercise, so we drive like 3-4 hours out of Fort Benning and we finally get there set up all the beds equipment then training started right away they told us to go outside and line up. Then all of a sudden all these grenades and flash bang grenades were going off everywhere alarms just the disorientation was fucked up run here run there, there was absolutely no reason for it and after hours of this game went in and took a shower then had to go take an objective at night with your squad and land navigate it out get there, attack the objective, reload, get attacked the flash bangs going off the grenades going off man was it fucking fun but just days of no sleep and just getting attacked the rendezvous point 100 percent security we did not get any sleep for like 3 days and when we did it was like for a hour then back to running through the forest getting to the objective but this certain objective was far as shit man, so we had a rally point and left 2 guards with our ruck sacks (backpack containing sleeping equipment hygiene equipment etc.) the rally point was attacked we had to go back clear it then locate a secondary rally point and tackle to objective, that mother fucker was far and it was a stealth operation and we had to low crawl mother fucking low crawl 200 meters (greater than 2 football fields) through a fucking rose field we were sliced up from head to toe bleeding to tackle this objective on top of that the objective was another 75 meters away through an open danger area. So you guys may not understand what I am saying but I do because I was upset because I didn't sleep throughout all of this lol anyway, so we had to run through it bounding get there and attack the buildings as quickly as possible and I am not sure if anyone is reading this is understanding how tired we are at this point past exhaustion and have to maintain performance physically and mentally to correctly make tactical decisions to not get anyone killed during the training exercise and it was a great learning experience.

We finally took the objective went back to the rally point set up security and on to the last day of training, we had to take an objective in all honesty I believe we only slept like less than 10 hours if that at this point and we are on day 7 barely eating or sleeping and in all honesty the platoon was very well adapted no one was really making mistakes or anything we were doing pretty well, and if I haven't told you guys which I don't recall since I am Mikey what do you think the weather was, well ladies and gentamycin if you can't guess, it was one of the worst recorded winters in Georgia lol of course since it's my time to be in basic training why not make it the worst time to go, so while attacking this last objective you couldn't see 10 feet in front of you we were in the middle of a blizzard attacking this objective and we got through it, it was rough but we got through it and the Drill Sergeants gained more respect for us they almost completely stopped smoking us just maybe here and there for like a hour max because they didn't want us getting too comfortable before going to our units. So graduation was coming and we found out the units we were going to and the Drill Sergeants had us on the floor and were calling us and our units and so where does Mikey get called and ordered to huh anyone guess since I did my very best to get as far away from Jersey as possible, Drill Sergeant Ren says "Rodriguez, 10th Mountain" and in my head I am just thinking 10th Mountain, 10th Mountain, 10th Mountain, fuck that's New York. That destroyed my whole mood man, it's like there is nothing I can do to get away from Jersey it's like this black hole for me man I just can't get the fuck out of it.

So Graduation day finally comes and doing rehearsals and all we get to the field and they do the whole show and shit and we give a half right face in full green uniform and all the Drill Sergeants got down with us and started doing pushups with us and it was a nice moment honestly the Sergeant or Drill Sergeant in the military that smokes you and does the exercise with you that's the one you want because you know he will never leave you behind and plenty of times they have all smoked themselves while smoking us and that's why they always had my respect. At the end everyone's families had come to the field and took pictures and all so seeing as how I never mentioned it. Here comes my family from where I don't know, how I don't know, I never gave them the date or anything of that matter but my mom, sister, and both aunts came to the graduation and I had never said a word and this is important so hold on to this certain situation which I was very grateful for but I really just wanted Jaylene to be there and I haven't heard from her so at this point I was just wondering how my baby girl was doing.

After all was said and done, I had to go I couldn't miss my plane, so I was put on a bus and to the Airport I went.

Chapter 14

Deployment, Afghanistan

I got on the flight to Fort Drum, New York and it was pretty lonely and I don't really know what else to say about it, there was a lot going through my head that I can't remember at the moment but I just didn't know what to expect, literally all that was in my head was going to some foreign country and fighting my heart out and trying to make it back alive. So we finally land in Syracuse Airport in New York and well there was no guidance which I don't need guidance I'm an adult I will find my way to base somehow but finally paying attention to detail there was a person with a sign waiting for all military people getting off the planes and I was literally the only one there. They had taken me to the USO which is pretty much a military liaison and they help transport you to base and give you some cookies and chips. I'm there by myself in the middle of the night I believe it had to be around 1 in the morning at this time I even believe it was on a Friday, we were waiting for one guy whose plane just landed and then they were going to take us to base. The kid makes it and we get on a bus and it was just us two on the bus and we sat in completely different seats. At this point there was no Jaylene, I didn't know what was going on with her I haven't heard from her in a month and I'm not sure what is wrong, but something was wrong. The drive was extremely long, quiet, just lonely dark there were no highway lights like Jersey and after driving in Georgia I had come to conclusion that only Jersey has highway lights which I realized I had taken for granted after jumping and driving through all these states. We finally get to the gate of Fort Drum and it was just weird honestly I didn't know what to feel or how to feel so I didn't really feel anything I was just tired and wanted to go to sleep I didn't care if we just booked a hotel because knowing the military I know I have to do this and that and the run around just to get a room and I wasn't in the mood for all that.

    The bus finally comes to a halt, and there it is 1st Brigade Combat Team, we go in and since it was a weekend no one was around really other than the security and people awaiting us to check in. We checked in and got our assignments we were assigned to 9-99 Infantry Regiment and none of this made any sense to me at the time, in all honesty I didn't even learn rank until I was pretty much in Afghanistan. At last I learned this kids name and his name was Edwin, they gave us our room and barracks and it was located in Triple Deuce and that name didn't even click in my head for months, every time someone said Triple Deuce barracks I just said ok because it never made sense to me, I am telling you guys I was literally on autopilot for a while man a while just simply not paying attention just going with whatever they said because you really couldn't question anything any ways so what did it matter. Any who its zero dark thirty hundred hours and of course we get to the barracks and guess what, well our room was on the last floor and guess what more, no fucking elevators, yeap had to carry all 4 bags up one trip the whole ordeal was just tiring man the run arounds the hurry up and waits the unnecessary bullshit like I had thought we were grown ass men but I guess not then to be so tired and bam go climb up 8 flights of steps with 100 plus pounds to your rooms and do this paper work because if somethings broken in the room and you don't say anything it becomes your fault and you're paying for issues that need to be fixed.

Saturday the day time finally comes and we had absolutely no clothes, no soap, no toothpaste, no tooth brush, no car no nothing so what did we do, we went to the mall in Baytown NY, bad idea bad bad idea, getting the looks hearing the bullshit and you can't fight anyone here just not the time to get in trouble in a military city just not the place. We buy a set of clothes ate and left.

Now we are meeting people and we find out that we are ordered to meet at the back court of the 9-99 barracks Monday morning at 6:30 in the morning for a Rear D formation, D stands for detachment I didn't know what that meant until someone explained it to me that since our unit has left to Afghanistan several weeks ago the people left behind are called a Detachment platoon because several issues whether it be non-deployable, retiring, moving to a different duty station, new soldiers there are just various reasons, so ok no issues at least now we know what's going on now we have some information.

Monday comes and we wake up and get to formation and there is an abundant amount of people there and mainly everyone is waiting for formation smoking cigarettes by the pavilion. Some sergeant comes and starts formation, his name is Staff Sergeant Seamus and he tells us that we will be deploying to Afghanistan in two weeks after we get all our equipment sorted out, go to the range and zero our weapons and for the moment while we are here we are to be reporting to Specialist Yuko and Sergeant Pen, so we get situated and start working out before the workday starts. They then release us to get breakfast and we eat and go back to morning formation and it was a fucking smoke fest man I mean I thought we were grown men already like no they still treated you like shit and everyone was just fucking mad for absolutely no reason and it was just stupid man and worst of all when the work day ends and you're not married and you live in the barracks the work day may end but the smoke session doesn't you live there with them all day long until they feel like releasing you at 2000 hours just a fucking smoke fest man. So, I still couldn't get in to contact with Jaylene by the 4th day me and Edwin went to the mall again and I just bought myself a baby computer just so I can try and contact her. What happened was I, was getting messages from her brother about a situation that had happened with her and it was sad nothing you need to know about but by the end of the week we finally got into contact with each other and spoke and she was back and her mom had it out for me and you know I understood man I did but I had no intentions on hurting my girl I love her I need her and I need her to be ok and I need her to be safe her safety and wellbeing mean the world to me I know I live 3 thousand miles away and I have no way to help her or hold her or hug her but that doesn't change how I feel about her my heart my soul are attached to this woman one just doesn't simply break that bond. It was difficult it really was she needed me and I just wasn't there man I wasn't and I have to own up to that as a man, it doesn't matter how much I tried to be there for her the fact of the matter was, I was not there for her. Knowing that she was ok and safe was a huge relief because I was just thinking the worst and with her I had to be prepared for it she was a wild child she made many mistakes but we got through it and she listened to me my word and opinion meant a lot to her, as well as I have helped several of her friends with problems of their own to the conversations we had I just don't know how to explain it to you I wish I could girls been through it and mentally she was well above what she should have been and I was happy for her, I mean the situations she has been in are horrible but it molded her into an amazing woman, and I don't recall introducing her sister to you guys but I did not like her sister probably one of the only women on this planet that I can say I disliked, I can't really discuss why but daily or weekly there would just be random guys at her house just fucking weird man and I really didn't like that at all just don't bring any weirdos around my girl man that's all I asked and it was just constant, listen it doesn't matter or concern anyone at this point but I had my baby back.

After week one had passed by moving on to week 2 they pushed the flight back another week because we still had to get some things done, at this point we just made friends with everyone so our IRO platoon which was just a replacement platoon was made up of 70 people, we had just received a guy who was prior service his name was Specialist Ramses fucking great guy he was a man, honest, genuine, a great father and husband he is one whom you should always pay attention when he talks because he will tell you no lies and he will try his best to elevate you to believe in yourself just a fucking great human man, we also had Watkins which was my fucking brother man, another honest dude and I respected more than I respected anyone in that platoon other than Ramses and Sawyer, Sawyer was our California kid straight baller and just always had a smile on his face he never worried about anything just a smart intellectual guy, real good guy, Noah was another California kid he was a runner, Airborne kid good guy also, Thaddius, no one knew how to pronounce his name and Sergeant Seamus just called him alphabet lmfaoooooooooo kid had like every letter of the alphabet in his name but dude was strong as fuck man never gave problems just a good guy, Chase was a good kid funny as all hell, you will always laugh when you're around him, Harvey man Harvey loved that kid just problematic man, Miles good kid just wasn't cut out for the military, and Farryn the only girl in our platoon she was cool.

Around this time people started getting comfortable and coming to formation minutes late and it was fucking annoying standing out in the cold and rain waiting for people getting smoked fucking sucked man people just couldn't simply act like adults and you payed the price for it because the army believes in capital punishment and not the soldier taking accountability of his actions fucking idiot man I swear. So every time someone showed up late to formation the next day's formation was 30 minutes earlier, like that made sense yes they couldn't wake up for 6:30 formation let's make it earlier and leave work later so they still can't make it, it sucked for Ramses because he lived a hour away in Syracuse with his family and boy let me tell you these fucking idiots couldn't just wake up it literally got so bad we had to be there at 3:30 in the morning for first formation get smoked till 6:30 then start working out before work it was just insane you guys couldn't imagine it because I won't go into all the details.

Any who it came down to a time where everyone was ok and we were doing good as a platoon so one day at the end of the day they let us play basketball to end the day and guess what fucking happened, everyone and their got damn spit bottles for the chewing tobacco left it and didn't clean it up and there were 2 bottles left. They lined us all up and said there are 2 bottles on the floor and you guys left it there and Sergeant Pen is pissed now because we left trash in the area and now he wants 2 people to confess and you know you were just going to get the shit smoked out of you so no one wanted to confess for it fucking shit bags man and the longer we stayed there he was just going to smoke all of us and at this point we had moved out of the Triple Deuce barracks and into the 9-99 barracks then moved again into the 2 floor barrack and my roommate became Watkins now. So what happened was I was tired of the bullshit and Sergeant Pen was fucking heated now I didn't want to wait longer because if he smoked all of us it was going to be a fucking smoke session of a life time, so of course I stepped up and said it was my bottle I apologize Sergeant I forgot it, and Watkins my fucking brother stepped up right after me and said me too, good guy man he wasn't going to let me get smoked by myself for something I didn't even do, the integrity on that guy the honesty I just have a lot of respect for him he really is a honest human love that kid. Everyone was released from formation and the screaming and smoke session begin pushups, flutter kicks, run 10 laps, mountain climbers, squats, just nonstop then the audacity of Sergeant Pen to make us bear crawl building to building man that's just a far bear crawl I didn't want to do lol but any who we did that for 10 minutes alone I had a 20 pack of abs just from that exercise alone lmfaoooo but seriously that was like the longest hour of my life. Sergeant Pen stopped smoking us because he saw we were bleeding and we didn't even know what happened he felt bad he just made us throw the bottles away and released us for the day and yelled at us some more, and when me and Watkins are walking back to the barracks I told him thank you, you know because I appreciate that he stepped up with me he didn't have to but you know he's a real one that man, and we talked for a bit and walking back blood was just dripping and we didn't know from where and what happened was while we were bear crawling there was a broken glass bottle of Snapple and we ran right through it we both had glass in our hands but it wasn't to the point we needed stitches we just showered and took the glass out. He was a very good roommate man we would go grocery shopping opposite weeks he would shop then I would we just split shit it was cool man.

Now we are a few days away from being a month in Fort Drum our orders were canceled, what had happened was that there was a volcano that erupted in Greenland and we were not cleared to fly over for another month so we are looking towards May now for our fly out date. The weekend comes and for every anniversary it's fun because me and Jaylene talk and it doesn't really matter what's going on between us, I just love hearing her voice and hearing her talk that's my baby girl I love her but this anniversary was different it was my birthday as well. So we were talking and I asked her what day it was, it was a little inside joke of ours and she said our anniversary and well she wasn't wrong but she forgot my birthday and like I felt really bad like really, really bad because she's so important to me and I know she was going through a lot and I understood how something like that slipped her mind but I was just hurt so I just didn't say anything because if I did I know how sad she would get and I didn't want her to be sad she had a rough start to the year and I was barely around and I never want my woman to be sad so I just didn't say anything but her being my girl and how well she knows me she knew something was wrong. This girl is the only person that just knows me to a level beyond comprehension, the difference between her and Kaylynn well in this certain aspect was that when Kaylynn was sad I would clearly know so I would ask her and she would open up like a book and we would talk, with Jaylene she would just straight up call me and be like baby I am sad, and I would say why baby talk to me what happened and she would just release it all from there for hours and it was great the bond was great it wasn't anything to be forced out we just flowed like a river so smooth man so that day we didn't sleep over the phone I was just super sad, and she called me super early the next day and asked me what was wrong and I didn't want to tell her because I felt bad I felt like it was kind of selfish in a sense because I knew what she was going through so, could I the person she depends on make her feel worse than she does already with this situation going on in her life I couldn't do that I was supposed to be there and support her that's my baby but I could never lie to her and she asked me again and she never asks me twice like ever its unheard of so after she asked me the second time and I didn't answer, she wasn't going to ask me again that just wasn't our relationship she just knew something was wrong and being who she is I just told her I said, you know what yesterday was and she said yea babe it was our anniversary and I said you know what else it was and she said no what and I told her it was my birthday and just like I know her so intimately just what I thought happened she broke down and started crying and I tried to talk to her I told her it was ok I know she was going through a tough time so I wasn't upset I don't think I have actually ever been upset with a girl even to this day but it hurt me man like once I heard her start crying because she said no yesterday wasn't the, whatever date is my birthday because I just don't ever tell anyone so yall will never know and she hesitated and started to think and she just broke down crying, and I can't have my girl crying that shit hurts me so much inside man and knowing I'm the reason she's crying made it so much worse like I felt bad that's why I didn't want to tell her and she hung up on me and just wouldn't pick up the phone the rest of the day and I know she just felt like a shitty girlfriend and I was trying to explain to her that she wasn't she was the greatest gift I ever had I mean well other than the whole lying part but aside from that what we shared what she taught me how she treated me her choice of words how she spoke to me it was so special and means so much to me and for your guys reading this let me tell you because of Jaylene she definitely saved several people from getting punched in the face and getting beat the fuck up simply off the principal of respect but I just couldn't lower myself to that person anymore and even today everything that girl has taught me and how she has treated me I have kept and the promises I made to her and it's because of her I am who I am today if her and Kaylynn didn't come into my life fucking lord knows where I would be today but I just couldn't bring it to myself to disappoint such a wonderful soul and I keep her very dear to my heart and still base certain decisions I make off whether if she was still around would it disappoint her or not and I am human I do make mistakes from time to time but very rare and the mistakes aren't crazy you know I would just lose my self and disrespect someone and realize I was very rude and would apologize after and that's how far that goes.

So quick side story, this girl Kallie I had met her while working in Amazon last year, fucking amazing young woman, very beautiful, booty was well never mind she was very beautiful and there was a situation that happened between me and my supervisor who was new to Amazon and new to the work environment as a whole. So I'm walking her back to her station and she said "you ok" I said "no this dumb ass supervisor messed up I swear she's fucking stupid" and I don't ever swear in front of women but it happens from time to time and she caught me at an annoyed state and she stopped me and said "hey Michael, stop we don't talk about women like that" I said "wait what did I say, I didn't call her a bitch or anything I never have ever called a woman a bitch seriously" and Kallie said "stop it doesn't matter we don't talk about women like that" and she was right I don't ever disrespect woman in any way and I needed that just for her to check me like that I appreciated it I love that girl we had some very long long conversations, she is a super sweet girl and she finally got promoted and bought a new car for her and her family I was very happy and proud of her super sweet she definitely deserved it she really went through a bad time I hope I was able to help her a bit she took some advice but she had a family so it was bit different environment to make decisions because her family was automatically in the equation so she had to take into account some variable changes but overall super sweet and smart very proud of how she succeeded you go girl I miss ya.

Jaylene was my world man and I just simply won't get too in depth into everything simply speaking because there's just things that are for me and her to know and I keep those very special moments and conversations very close to me so I won't allow you guys to pollute them. At the platoon level everything is getting better Specialist Yuko and Sergeant Pen have grown an appreciation and respect for us because any time they tell us the main people to do something we don't hesitate we don't question we simply just do it and once they realized we were there to work and learn they stopped smoking the shit out of us daily unless we really did something stupid, which was completely understandable. Simultaneously speaking we received new soldiers to our IRO group, platoon, detachment whatever you would like to call it and they were medics that were going to deploy with us to Afghanistan next month. So we begin learning new techniques for treatment and evaluation of gunshot wounds and what to do in case the medics are tied up with another wounded soldier, we would have to take care of each other, which was pretty reasonable and common sense you know there is only one medic per platoon and if one guy is wounded that's almost a squad down and inactive in the fight already so if someone else got wounded who would treat them, us obviously. These two skinny kids walk in and they are both Asian and a clear thought process is well these guys weigh about 90 pounds wet ok that's not an issue I weigh 155 pounds soaking wet and I am capable of doing a great many of things but and that's a big but because I like big butts and I cannot lie lol that pun was pretty funny lol any who seeing these guys and watching them work its very clear they are not physical people which is ok but at minimum with full equipment we are weighing automatically 50-70 pounds heavier and that depends on what your job in the platoon is and what equipment you are carrying so if someone gets shot and we have to eliminate the enemy who is carrying that wounded soldier away because I know for sure they are not and it does not matter how intelligent they are if they can't move a wounded soldier to a secure area for treatment while we try and eliminate the enemy they become a liability to us as well but that was a thought process I was going way too far in advance for because that's a situation you pretty much deal with when you cross that bridge.

Training begins and we are learning about gunshot wounds that penetrate the armor and cause a sucking chest wound and when people were teaching the class, they talked so fast that it sounded like sunken chest wound lol I was like what the fuck lol. So these guys introduce themselves and the entire platoon is reading their name tags and we are all thinking the same shit, one guy's name the tall one was Specialist Ikie, ok pretty weird name the other guy was called Private First Class Dye pronounced die lol see where this is going lmfaooo. Staff Sergeant was like "wait what the fuck is your name PFC Die, listen man if I am ever shot don't come to my rescue because the last thing I want is for a medic named Die to come and treat me and when I wake out of consciousness all I see is your name tag that says die and now instead of trying to fight to stay alive I am thinking I am going to die because of you lol just stay the fuck away from me" lmfaoooooo. It was so funny because the entire platoon had the same thought process and Sergeant was the one who said it and it was fucking great lol. PFC

Dye went along with it for the jokes and when we wore the jokes out, he told us his name was pronounced Deeyee lmfaoooo he ruined it man the jokes were great lol. So, we are coming close to our departure date and we got called in for a formation, they had mentioned to us that whatever happened with the volcano was cleared but they had to push the flight back again. Clearly we asked again what happened and now some civil war broke out near an Air Force Base in Kyrgyzstan where we were supposed to land to and they wanted to let it play out before sending us there and possibly causing a new war but the Air Force Base wasn't attacked but they wanted to secure the surrounding area before letting us land there, so to await another month before flying out to Afghanistan.

Time passes by and we are coming close to our expected fly out date and there were no changes this time, this time it was confirmed we were flying out the beginning of June. Everyone is getting all their paperwork ready, their powers of attorney, wills, everything. I go home and Adrien was my go-to brother, I entrusted him with a box, and we don't ever talk about the box. The box was a safe that I bought and stored it in his house throughout the entirety time I spent in the Army. This box was something we never discussed and if I ever had to go into the box it was an exceptionally bad day. The box held several important documents of legal importance and other personal important items that don't need to be discussed but if anything were to happen it was for him to open my will was in there and things of that matter, but the latter doesn't matter. He had the key and most importantly I had given him my phone. I had kept my phone on while in Afghanistan just as a source of communication for Jaylene so if she needed to talk to someone Adrien was there so there would be weeks that go by when we were on mission and clearly couldn't talk to anyone but we will get to that. Me and Adrien spoke before I headed out and I told him and my family they wouldn't hear from me for some time while traveling to Afghanistan we didn't know how long it would take to get there and we didn't know the time difference either so it was ok I told Jaylene when I gave my phone to Adrien and it hurt like I felt super bad like I was leaving her again and you know Adrien is a super nice guy nicer than me so she would talk to him and ask him if he has heard from me while traveling and it took almost the whole month just to get to Afghanistan and Adrien just being a genuine human as he is he would reply back to her you know he had his life to live as well but when he would get home and checked my phone he would reply and talk to her and calm her down and tell her if he heard from me he would notify her immediately.

So the day comes, and it was just a weird fucking day man, it felt so quiet my thought process is so far ahead right now because the situations I have to discuss that are up and coming so I am trying to control my thoughts to explain Deployment day and it's a bit difficult just give me some time to think it through and organize my thoughts give me a second.. I am just trying to reorganize and think this through person by person..........................Ok so the first person I can recall is Chase, fucking Chase man. Good kid, so the previous day I helped him ship all his items back to his girlfriend and kid because he didn't have enough money at the time and we went to UPS together so I spared him the money and he never gave it back asshole lmfaoooo good kid though love him. Secondly, this guy Sebastian tall kid goofy as all hell extremely funny just great to be around, he let me keep all the household items at his house with his wife while we were deployed and I appreciated that, kid had heart man great guy. Watkins's girlfriend was there for the goodbye, she was super nice. Tyrus was this Turkish kid real fucking smart and funny I don't remember who was there for him but let me tell you that man lol well nothing it doesn't matter he was one of the smarter kids of our platoon real good guy. Edwin's family was there for the goodbye as well if I can recall correctly but don't quote me on it. Sawyer was just with me his family was from Cali, so no one was there for the goodbye, but we had each other lol. Specialist Ramses family was there and he has deployed before he was from the 82nd Airborne and he was a great mentor, the most honest straight up man there was had an exceptional amount of respect for him and he always tried to get me to go to school while in the Army and he guided me in every aspect to get my degree before I ended my contract and I never listened to him and I kind of regretted it when I actually went to college lmfaooo and I told him that and he laughed he knew he did his best and tried but I told him he was right and I appreciated that he did try even though I didn't listen he was a good man and a great father and a great husband. Well the saddest part was seeing Noah and his wife separate man, it was pretty sad she was the worst she was balling her eyes out they had a real good connection you could feel it they really did love each other and I felt the pain of their separation when we got on the bus, I know it, that separation anxiety kills but worst off being as young as we were and going to a war zone I understood her emotions I know what she was going through but not one of us thought we were going to die either. To us the thought process was we go there do our job and come back we knew what we were getting into we knew we were there to go and fight but no one prepared us for what was coming and it's no one's fault it's not something you could prepare for it is literally something you deal with while you are currently in the situation and adapt to it as well as possible to overcome what life throws at you at that exact moment but any way the general consensus of war was very well understood within our platoon except for 2 people. The week before departure Private Miles, he decided he did not want to deploy to Afghanistan and left us, he went AWOL which is absent without leave or permission and they did not find him until the late months of our deployment. The day before we departed Private Harvey decided he didn't want to deploy either and thought it was best to buy a plane ticket back home on the day of departure and Staff Sergeant Seamus found him at the airport and brought him back to base and what happened from there I don't recall.

For whatever reason we did not fly out of Fort Drum, we took a 8 hour drive South and flew out of a civilian airport which was fucking annoying because all the laws and regulations so the way we had to pack, where we packed it, how we were legally able to transport our M-4s it was hell going through a civilian airport so much extra unneeded work. We finally got on the plane and flew another 8 to 9 hours to Europe, we landed at an airport there and had a lay over four a couple hours and let me tell you that country and airport was super nice very beautiful. Once the lay over passed we got on another airplane and got to an Air Force Base well clearly I am unsure if I can release the information about the countries and flights we took and common sense tells me I can't because operational security but any who none of the countries or flights matter but the countries were beautiful and the Air Force Bases, huh well I understood where all the Air Force jokes stemmed from because those bad boys are super nice and they have some amazing chow halls lol. Once we settled there and retrieved our luggage we awaited for a plane, it was crazy I think we took somewhere in the amount of 8 to 9 flights just to get into Afghanistan it blew my fucking mind. Any way we make it to Kuwait and waited lol. Once we landed there, I completely understood the Kuwait jokes as well lmfaooooo. So to inform you readers there are an abundant amount of jokes in the military about the Air Force, Kuwait, the Marines and the Army we just go back and forth with jokes but I have never understood them until I experienced it for myself lol it's more of inside jokes you won't get unless you experience it for yourself so if I say all the jokes here only military personnel will understand it and that's not fun for you guys and you guys will just skip over it and not read it so I mean it's not really important but its funny lol. Moving forward we finally got out of Kuwait and finally landed in Afghanistan, I think I have been to like 5 different fucking bases in

Afghanistan I was super tired. When we got there the next day we had to go to a formation because some 2 Star General wanted to talk to us about you know politics and what to expect in country and this and that bullshit and listen I told you I don't put up with that shit.

In the middle of his rant, conversation or what the fuck ever you want to call it I interrupted him, yeah fuck that bullshit. While he was talking I heard him say something so fucking stupid so I cut him completely off, I said wait wait wait wait, and everyone got quiet and looked at me with these big ass eyes because god forbid I interrupt a dumb ass 3 Star General in the middle of his bullshit ass political speech. So, I questioned him about what he said because it was just so out there, and everyone was either soaking up the bullshit or playing along and I simply don't play along fuck you. Edwin and Watkins looked at me with these big ass eyes, and I won't lie I thought I was going to get the whole entire IRO Platoon smoked lmfaooo and I did not fucking care lmfaoooo. The General completely dismissed what I said of course because he knew he was bullshitting and after formation Edwin and Watkins and Noah came up to me and said "yo if we would have been smoked for your dumb ass comment and interrupting that General I would have fucked you up, but that shit was fucking funny as hell lmfaoooo you got some balls man." I told them "no fuck that shit you know I don't play that political ass bullshit man keep that shit away from me." They replied, "yes but you're in the Army now and you have no say about anything unless you want an Article 15 for disrespecting a Commissioned Officer." Clearly, I didn't because I forgot about that lol. This was a weird time in the military if you looked at a Non Commissioned Officer wrong or did not salute a Commissioned Officer they could write you up and give you an Article 15 which is 45 days of extra duty and 2 and a half months of reduced pay, and they abused that power if you simply challenged them these NCO's would just write you up like be a man grab your balls and admit you were wrong but people have too much pride and the military gives them way too much power and they could ruin your career in the Military because they simply don't like you.

So, diverging off of the story because I have to, yesterday was November 6, 2018 if anyone remembers that date was when me and Nameless met. The past couple of weeks she has been on my mind and I been pretty sad. I am over what happened and all, but I just couldn't get her off my mind and something happened. Things I don't really want to explain because they are extremely personal and I won't name the people involved but, I have to explain this and go back some years as I have stated before this story is about shit I have to get off my chest and to do so I have to explain how my life has been and how people have helped me and how they have affected the outcome of the person who I am today. Many years ago, there was a beautiful woman in my life, and she meant the entire world to me she will not be spoke of and you will not know who she is, and I will not release her name. To continue, we were very very close, and I was the only person she trusted in her life. This is tough, so one day I suddenly stopped hearing from her, and it just felt wrong the whole day was weird and off and I just couldn't pinpoint what was going on or who in my life was having issues. Every now and then this happens and I won't describe the other situations simply out of respect for the other people involved but what happens is I get these extremely weird vibes and feelings I can't control and I just simply know something is wrong to the extreme that someone is not doing well so when these very rare feelings come I jump on my phone and literally call everyone I know who has problems and ask if everyone is doing ok. Calling is important because I am able to hone in and listen to their voice vocal patterns or vibrations or whatever you call it and when I catch an inconsistency, I know who lied to me and I can break them down and talk to them. Furthermore, this woman did not answer the phone and I couldn't get in touch with her. Coming to find out that she tried to commit suicide and had written me a letter. I won't explain the rest of the story because it's not important to you but as my world and life continue to come full circle this similar circumstance had repeated itself yesterday with a very close friend of mine, and it was a very painful situation and I cried a lot man it fucking hurt. I didn't cry in front of her when she was explaining the weeks leading up to attempted suicide and the attempt because she needed me to be there for her she needed me to be strong for her and I tried, I teared up a couple of times but it took a lot out of me to just not cry it was extremely sad and the memories of my friend came up and it all hit me at once. This was something I had to take accountability for, this was my fault, I could have prevented it and I missed all the signs because I was down and sad about the situation with Nameless that my thought process and judgment were not on a straight path these past couple of weeks. Like I fucked up guys I did.

It's so painful some days I hope you guys don't understand because if you do that means you have been through this situation and I don't ever want anyone to be in this situation that I am in, it's just the way life my life comes back full circle and there's just no getting away from it. I'm human but I'm not allowed to have off days, the one time I just lose my self being sad about a situation that happened to me, while I know there is an ongoing situation and person I have to care for the one time I don't pay attention the one time I slip up and missed the signs it almost cost me a very good friend and I can't forgive myself for that. After she spoke to me I knew what my mind was going to do, automatically it goes back to all the conversations, all the times we spoke and I gauge her voice, body language, words, phrases every minute detail for the past months gets drawn through my head without my consent and I saw where I was losing her, I could pin point the distance, the sadness in her voice, the conversations we had that topics changed and I missed it all because I was fucking sad about the whole Nameless situation and I almost lost someone important to me. I didn't acknowledge the signs I dismissed them I fucked up and for that I have to take accountability for, this one was my fault I didn't make her feel wanted, or loved, or appreciated I fucked up man I admit it I fucked up. I feel so fucking bad and hurt and like the selfish part of me that has lost everyone every woman that has ever come into my life has left me and to think that she almost left me too made everything worse and it hurts even thinking about that simply because this is not about me other than the fact that I fucked up and missed the signs she was sending, this was about a beautiful, intelligent, amazing young woman who is important to me whom I love dearly who almost succeeded in taking her own life because she felt alone and I wasn't there for her. I can't allow that to happen again. There's times where I am just exhausted and I am just tired of it all and I just want to be by myself and stop helping people because after all these years I have got nowhere with it and everyone is just gone simply gone so what do I have left, I just have to focus on adopting and being selfish and thinking about myself for once but when I do that this happens, so the question is when does the road end? The answer is never, after this situation it pretty much solidified that I can't stop, stopping is not an option, I have to give this woman meaning again I can't allow this situation to repeat itself ever, she's an amazing young woman and she has been through some very trying times and more over is doing very well for herself but just because you're doing well doesn't mean that you're not struggling internally. So talk to the people you surround yourself with please I admit that I fucked up and look it almost cost me a very good friend and this isn't the first time this has happened to me nor the second and I as a man have to own up to it I fucked up I take accountability of it and I won't ever allow it to happen again. Guys listen man if you just feel that someone is going through something and they won't discuss it with you just send me a message I will talk to them we can't be losing people we love and there is no apology for this situation and there is no way to apologize for not being there and allowing someone close to you to feel alone there is no excuse either, but simply put we have to do better man we have to this is unnecessary pain it could have been avoided if I would have acknowledged what was going on, being sad about a situation isn't an excuse for not paying attention to those closest to you and I take accountability for that, I have failed her as a friend, and it won't happen again. I am sorry I truly am.

Back to the story, we finally got out of Kuwait and into Afghanistan we flew and just more jumping from base to base until we finally reached our F.O.B which is a Forward Operating Base, and that was in Kabul Afghanistan, I believe that is all I am allowed to tell you I am unsure so I won't get into the names of villages I will change that for this story and either way it's not important to you. We report to base and I had orders to go with Alpha Company 9-99 Infantry Regiment and was placed in 1st Platoon 3rd Squad. I met my Platoon Sergeant who was Sergeant First Class Pierson and we were waiting to see where I was going to be placed in the platoon, and up comes this Gator which is a small ATV with a bed in the back. The guy driving the Gator pulls over next to us because my Platoon Sergeant waved him down and we started talking he got out and introduced himself and his name was Sergeant Nicodemus also known as Sergeant Niko. He liked me and told Sergeant Pierson he's mine he's apart of Lion Squad now I want him, and that's how I ended up in 3rd squad. Sergeant Pierson said "you just want everyone in your squad huh" and they started laughing and Sergeant Niko said "hell yea and he looks like Tiago" mind you I didn't know what a Tiago was at the time mentally I went through my entire vocabulary and tried to figure out what a Tiago was while they were talking and laughing and I couldn't figure it out. Any who I get on the Gator and we drive away to the tent area so he can show me where we sleep and he described the layout of the guard towers and FOB and said that we were waiting on another expansion for the FOB so there were going to be more towers and another tent area but that's for the months ahead.

We were driving to the tent area and saw a soldier that Sergeant Niko needed to talk to. We passed by his Tricon which is a storage unit, in the civilian world you guys know them as shipping containers that go on boats or that Semi Trailers carry on highways. Any who he was fixing the Tricon and Sergeant Niko calls him out and yells "hey Bradford come outside I need you." Bradford comes out and says, "who is this guy," Sergeant Niko replies "he is our FNG his name is Rod." Sergeant Niko couldn't pronounce my last name, so he nicknamed me Rod, for your information an FNG is a Fucking New Guy. So, Bradford says "hey where are you from, are you Dominican?" I reply "yea how did you know" he said "I knew it man, so you're good at baseball right" I say "well yea I played baseball for a while and stopped when I got to high school but I do play every now and then." We all started laughing and that is how I met Bradford and he was one of the funniest guys I met in the Army, real good guy very humble and super funny. Him and Sergeant Niko went on to talk about an empty supply box Sergeant Niko needed for storage and Bradford had an extra one to give him but it was in another Tricon so he had to wait till later to get it because he was pretty busy at the time. So we finally reached the tent area and he showed me which one was our tent and as I was getting my bags from the bed of the Gator a female soldier walked by and started talking to us and Sergeant Niko had asked me what was the muzzle velocity of the M4 and I said 2300 feet and he said "no crazy, its 2970 feet per second you were close but you get no points for being close here, give me 50 then take your bags in the tent, what are they teaching you in basic lol." I thought to myself, well fuck me I never learned any of that shit in basic. The soldier leaves and Sergeant Niko says "hey Rod, you have to make friends everywhere so when you need something they will help you out" I replied "I will Sergeant, I came from IRO Platoon we had cooks, supply, mechanics I know people everywhere" he said "fucking A man." Thinking to myself when he called me crazy, it was funny because that was Urias's word in basic it was funny and all too familiar.

I walk into the tent and the entire platoon is in there, they all stopped and looked at me, it was the weirdest vibe ever lol. Sergeant Niko walked in behind me and introduced me to the platoon and then left, he said he had to go back to SOG duties whatever the fuck that meant. I rest all my stuff and I was top bunk from Thurlow if I remember correctly which I probably don't lol but I will tell you once you walk in from the front door, to your immediate left there was a bunk laterally and in front of that bunk there was a bunk and I was that top bunk, so whoever was under me I don't recall. I put all my bags away and this kid his name was Deegan, he asked me what did AVPU stand for and I didn't know what the fuck that meant either I was like a lost cause man. He was upset and said, "what the fuck are they teaching you in basic these days man?" I had absolutely no answer because all we did was get the shit smoked out of us go to the range and do ruck marches. Then this Corporal his nickname was Conner so Corporal Conner short guy mean face but technically he's a NCO and I got the vibe real quick that he's an asshole kind of power hungry so I was like ehh fuck I have to listen to this guy, he seems the type to just write me up for anything. He starts asking me medical questions I have no answer to any of it and he got upset and said, "you better learn your shit real quick or you're going to start doing a lot of pushups this deployment." I was just getting hammered left and right, but it was expected because I was the new guy so whatever. As it seems there were several people on guard duty, and it turns out that it was mainly my squads turn to be on guard. This one kid his name was Gerardo he came up to me and told me he would help me study all the medical shit we needed to know because Sergeant Niko was big on combat medical care so he took out his computer and started to help me study.

Sergeant Niko came back a couple hours later and asked me if I had spoken to my family and let them know I was here, and I told him I didn't. He told me to go buy a 25-dollar calling card call my family then come back to the tent. So, I went to the computer lounge bought a calling card and started calling. You already know my baby was the first I called, and she didn't answer, and I was really really sad, but I left a message and told her I loved her and hoped that she was doing well, and I missed her. Then I called Jeremiah he didn't answer either, well to be frank aint no one answer that day I just left like 5 messages and it was weird that no one answered.

Anyways night was falling and everyone started to come back and I started meeting the rest of the platoon, so there was 1st Squad Leader Sergeant Zebediah, he was a work out stud always had a huge smile on his face unless it was time to do some dumb ass unnecessary shit, 2nd Squad Leader Sergeant Corbin, always had like a pack of fucking dip in his mouth no matter the time of day good dude, and 4th Squad Leader Sergeant Curtis, and Sergeant Curtis looks at me and says "Rod huh, you ever fuck a guy before?" I laughed and said, "what no lol" he said, "well how do you know you don't like it if you never tried it?" I said "because I'm not gay lol" he said "well you know what they say, try anything once, then try it again to make sure you don't like it, and try it a third time to confirm that you really don't like it" lmfaooooooo I said "wait what lol" he said "Rod are you a virgin?" I said, "well yea" he said, "ok well then it's your loss lol." Man, I have never been so confused in my entire life I didn't know where that conversation was heading and right after he was done talking, he started talking to Sergeant Niko like normal, so I wasn't sure if he was serious or not I was so lost lmfaoooo. Sergeant Pierson walked in and gave report about up and coming missions and he asked Sergeant Niko if I was going on mission with them and he said no because he hasn't zeroed his weapon, yet he goes tomorrow. Sergeant Pierson said oh ok then and on top of that my team leader at the time was going on his 2-week vacation back home so I would be under Team Leader Extraordinaire PFC Lionel. Sergeant Pierson said, "hey Rodriguez you better hurry up and do what you need to do we need more people out there we are short we have a small platoon." I didn't mention to you guys that the entire fucking platoon lived in that one tent it fucking sucked 24 fucking guys with 3 bags each body armor and all in that tent, but once the expansion was done we were going to be separated and cut down to one squad per tent hopefully.

On to the next morning everyone leaves for mission and I had to go zero my M4 and went and couldn't zero for shit, no one knew what the fuck was happening. I get back to the FOB and Sergeant asked if I zeroed, I said no, we didn't know what happened somethings wrong with my M4. Sergeant Niko said, "what the fuck Rod you suck at life let me see your M4." Come down to an investigation my front site post is bent so with all his connections he gave me a new one and a makeshift tool to help change windage and elevation. The next day comes and bam 7 to 9 rounds I was zeroed. This actually sucked because there was no reason for me to go back to the range since now, I had finished everything.

We got back to the tent area and there's no one there I just waited until Sergeant Niko comes back and check in with him and then went to call my family again I told him I didn't get in touch with anyone and he said "oh it's probably because no one recognized the number it's a weird like 11 digit number." I said "ahhhhhh that makes sense." So, I went back and called baby girl again and right away she answered, man do I love that girl. She said that she tried calling me back when she heard the voicemail, but the call wasn't going through, so she called Adrien and he said that he missed my call to, but he would tell her if he heard back from me. We spoke for a while it was really nice hearing her voice, her voice was very soft and warm, hearing her voice was the only thing that ever relaxed me and calmed me it was such a weird experience with her and I loved every part of being with her, the love, the support she was just amazing man she will always be a part of me. We hang up because I have to get back to the tent and have to call Adrien and my mom, so I spoke with Adrien and he told me that Jaylene called and I said thanks I had already spoken with her and you know I appreciate all that he is doing for me and taking care of her as well when we all can't talk, Adrien's a real good dude man we are still very great friends to this day. I spoke with my mom and then went back to the tent area.

The next day I started my guard duties because I was zeroed, and the platoon was on mission and guard fucking sucked ass honestly. It was literally like 20 hours on duty 4 hours off every day for 5 days. At this time my Team Leader Specialist Walter had left for his 2-week vacation, and the platoon was coming back for a reup then out for another mission. Now this is the first week of July. The platoon resupplied and Sergeant Pierson asked Sergeant Niko if he thinks I am ready to go out on mission with them. Sergeant Niko said, "Fuck yea he's apart of Lion Squad he's ready." Sergeant Pierson said, "alright if you think so, we leave in the morning." On the Morning of July 4th, 2009, my squad had taken me to the motor pool and taught me how to prep the trucks for mission, with all the necessities and test and ready all the radio equipment. The 4th squad they were tasked as heavy weapons squad, so they mounted all the weapons on the trucks, and we helped if they needed it or if when we saw them struggling and that wasn't very often, they were very competent. This PFC Rico and Bernard were some strong ass dudes let me tell you they would just carry the 50-caliber machine gun in a book bag or by hand all the way to the motor pool climb up the truck and set it up within minutes. While they were doing that PFC Orian was teaching me everything I needed to know about the trucks and going out on mission what to watch out for and things of that sort. He also introduced me to the translator and his name was Malakai. Before Malakai met us at the motor pool something very weird happened and I told Orian I won't discuss it but I was just at a loss I didn't know what happened or what to think about it and right when it happened Malakai waved at us with a huge smile on his face and for some reason he was wearing his helmet and we weren't even leaving for another hour lol it was so funny. To be honest with you guys I am just fluffing this part of the story I really don't have to put all these details in at the moment but something happened and with the week I just had I am not really in the mood to discuss this topic that's about to occur and we as a platoon don't ever talk about it but it happened and we will get to it.

After setting up the trucks and seeing how all the leadership reacts and stresses to time deadlines, I can tell it was going to be a long year. The trucks are finally set up and we meet the Lt, his name was Lieutenant Maverick. He catches us up on all the reports for the week and weekend and we get into the trucks and out we go.

Orian, Lionel, and Tiago are teaching me the path and routes we take to our district headquarters which was some odd miles out off the Plateau, and we are making a right hand turn to one of Afghanistan's only paved roads in the country and what is the first thing I see aside from paying attention to the locals and all that military shit I have to pay attention to. I see a huge sign that reads, Amelia Airport. Like what a fucking coincidence, remember how I told you in my life when I meet someone all of a sudden just random things pop up that I have never seen before and it just reminds me of them, well this sign ladies and gentamycin was one of them. As how I don't recall introducing Amelia to you and no not the one from piano class in high school. Amelia was the girl that Jaylene pretty much was envious of and wanted to be I guess if that's a fair statement. So, when she told me how old she was and what she was majoring in school and all that, that information was taken from Amelia. These women all lived together, in that household were Jaylene, Amelia, Coralyn which was Amelia's sister, Nadine, their brother Alexander. So as we all know Jaylene didn't exist I never found out which sister she was and they all rejected to tell me the truth so till this day I have absolutely no idea who was this girl who stole my heart and changed me for the better, but I will always be grateful to have had met her and had her in my life aside from the whole I guess catfish situation if that's what you all would like to call it. Any who me an Amelia became great friends, but we had an extremely bad fallout in the years to come. Aside from that we continue driving and pass the little shopping district and reach a long stretch of road, at this point they tell me that we are getting close to a choke point and historic sight. I had no idea what a historic sight even meant, and they tell me that it is an area where no matter what time of day you pass through you will get harassing gunfire or ambushed. We pass by and don't get targeted, then we come to the bridge and cross it then we finally get to our District Headquarters. Stationed there are the Afghanistan National Police, German I believe at the time it was 3rd Coy and us 1st Platoon Alpha Company but we were detached to Delta Heavy Weapons Company.

We dropped off our equipment and we had actually forgotten something back at base, which wasn't really a hassle for us we weren't that far from base. We packed back up but lightly because we were staying the week. We made our way back and actually in time to eat dinner which was pretty sweet for 4th of July. We picked up what we forgot and then we headed out again. Driving back, it was turning dark, so it was time for the night vision goggles to get put on and after we did that, we came to this road we passed by twice that day and the road was getting dug up. When dismounted and searched the area for IED's which are Improvised Explosive Devices. None were found and we made the decision to go around then we made it back to the DHQ fairly quickly. At the time we unloaded the trucks earlier, so all we did was just remove the rucksacks and assault packs into our living quarters.

To explain the blueprint pretty much was simple, we had a large enough room to fit the platoon in and enough space to fit all the food and water but when it was all said and done there really wasn't very much room to walk around in you know space was taken up fairly quickly and the rest of the building the Germans stayed in it and they pulled over watch guard. The Germans guarded all the towers. To the building left of us is where the ANP stayed, between our building and the ANP's building there was enough space to park our 4 vehicles there which were mainly MATV's and a Cougar, they are just massive vehicles. The Germans Tanks and other vehicles were parked all over the place because they mainly stayed there.

Side story, so you know these past couple of weeks been rough man, and to make it worse I just got bad news. It's not really bad news overall, it's just the sequence of events that are up and coming have now changed. The issue with that is, now I am forced to be the person people look up to for guidance and understanding. Now I again have to grab my balls and man up and sometimes I wonder when it is going to stop, like when am I going to be able to just take a vacation and be at peace and just simply not deal with things. You don't understand like mentally I am an extremely strong minded individual but at what point can I take a break, at what point can someone take over and take some weight off my shoulder. It's not about me asking for help I can handle all the situations that are ongoing in my life simultaneously but listen my man I need a break, I been strong for too long for everyone and I am telling yall Mike is tired man, I need a fucking break. It's not even like I can just go to my woman and talk to her about this because there is no woman I don't have anyone to go to and in an understatement as previously stated I can handle it but like fuck man I need life to stop throwing me strikes at some point. I'm sorry for diverging off the story I just needed to rant and get that shit off my chest because the sleepless nights and everything that await me and now I have to face it with extra weight because I don't want anyone to fail is just a bit much with everything else I got going on but fuck it right, Mike got it he be good right.

Well yea but that doesn't mean I can't use some days off like fuck

I'm tired of being strong sometimes, sometimes I just want to be weak.

Back to the story, sorry again about that. SFC Pierson went and had a meeting with the Police Chief and NCO's about tomorrows mission. Orian was tasked to teach me about the radios in the trucks and guard duties. Orian comes and says "hey Rod come on we have to go listen to the radio" I said "oh cool what music we listening too" Orian replied "no music dummy we have to listen on the company channel and wake up the LT and Sergeant Pierson if there is any enemy contact lol." So, he taught me all about the radio frequencies and our company channels we have to maintain communications on. It was time to switch guards and get some rest for tomorrows mission, and on to sleep we went.

Morning comes and it is extremely early, clearly we get up earlier to do hygiene before anyone else which is what I learned when there is limited space and an abundant amount of people living in this limited space, just wake up before everyone and do hygiene brush your teeth shave before anyone gets to it. As we are packing for the mission 3rd Squad was made to be the head of the movement and we needed to carry the WALK kit which is the Warrior Aid and Litter Kit, essentially it pretty much houses our litter for a wounded warrior and medical supplies for the medic. Sergeant Niko voluntold me to carry it which I had no problem with. Sergeant Curtis said, "hey Rod you sure you can carry it" I said, "roger that Sergeant I can carry whatever you give me" he said, "alright Rod it's your responsibility now." Before anything as we rally up outside and await for everyone and the trucks to be prepped the Police are all on their phones and it's not even 6 in the morning yet and I always found that weird but that was explained to me that the Chief was the Chief and he was an important person so he was always on the phone and speaking in military terms I understood what they meant. Now we begin movement out the gate and make a left on to the main road and I can't explain our tactics and reasoning for what we did so I have to skip ahead a few minutes. PFC Team Leader Extraordinaire Lionel was the head of the Platoon, then Tiago, then Orian, then me, and the rest of the Platoon that I won't outline the formation just this is important for now. As we walk toward our objective, every culvert we pass by we go down into and check for IED's. The Taliban where we were worked extremely fast placing and removing IED's it was pretty insane how fast they could dig one in place and remove one.

Now we are in the midst of passing the Afghanistan National Army's District Headquarters and all of a sudden, we see a mass of people exiting and leaving this small village ahead of us. We get to this Y intersection which is either go straight and go to the bridge that takes us back to the FOB or make the left into this village where everyone is evacuating. In this crazy scenery that we are seeing and we all knew what this meant, I mean does it take a highly intelligent person to understand if a village of people are evacuating their city at 6 o clock in the morning in a country at war mean anything else than a fight awaiting us than I don't really know what to tell you guys. Incase if you guys forgot this was my first mission and it was very easy just adding up all the pieces fairly quickly. So, we see these two kids a boy and girl just running for their life with their Donkey by their side just full on sprinting and Sergeant Niko tells us to stop them and tells Malakai to ask and translate what is going on and why is everyone leaving. The kids tell us that there are 10 Taliban on their way to the village ready to fight us. Well fuck if an entire village is scared of 10 Taliban, they must be some bad ass Commando Taliban lol. Walking up the street there are complex's per say but not really, it is simply on the right was a 2-story house and an indention which had a small garden and ditch and to the left was just a wall. Moving up a bit more we encountered another Y intersection which we made the decision to send Sergeant Zebediah's truck with the M240 Bravo machine gun and Sergeant Corbin's Squad up and to the left and we would take the right, because we had to take in to account any ambush and reinforcements. Now moving to the right through the Y intersection we had Bernard and Sergeant Curtis's 50 Caliber Machine gun and truck, to the left of the road was a rice patty which is just a field of crops and about 100 meters away was a tree line, to the right was a wall with a small ditch but big enough to drop into. As we keep walking the rice patty ends at a stretch of wall and to the right side of the street the wall ended, and a massive rice patty was there. Also, there was a 3-foot wall which dropped down into a ditch with crops. Sergeant Curtis stops the truck because we hit yet a Third Y intersection and Open Danger Area, to our 10 o'clock was a two story house with a window directly facing our position, where Sergeant Curtis Stopped the truck there was a 8 to 10 foot wall and to the right side of the wall there was a small leveled ditch with a pile of rocks and Sergeant Niko tells me and Orian to take position there.

Me and Orian look at each other, I tell him I am taking off the WALK kit because I can't really move my head around and assess my area, he tells Sergeant Niko and he's ok with it as long as it is within arm's reach. I look at Orian and he looks at the building and looks back at me and says "I know this is a bad fucking spot to be bro." We could directly see in the building through that window, I mean it was dark and the building was about 175 to 200 meters away, but it was a direct line of sight. All of a sudden it became really quiet, like the wind stopped and just seemingly everything and everyone stopped. Then a 3-round burst of gunfire, me and Orian took cover immediately behind the rocks we quickly put our heads down and it was on for sure we both heard it. We look around and no one is fazed like no one else heard the gunfire it was weird, then we heard the mortar and it simply just exploded about 60 to 70 meters in front of us. Me and Orian looked at each other and said, "shit this is a bad fucking spot man we got to get out of here." So I grabbed the WALK kit with one arm and slung it around my back and as I was crossing the street I saw

Sergeant Curtis hop out of the truck and take position by the 8 foot wall with Orian as another mortar hit and now shit is just blowing up everywhere there is debris hitting us Bernard was up on the 50 Cal letting rounds go down range and hitting the building, then all of a sudden automatic gun fire was hitting us we didn't know where anything was coming from aside from the building and the mortars were getting closer to us we were getting bracketed in and all the mortars were landing on the road aiming straight for the truck and then the 50 Cal malfunctioned and we all look at each other and just know this is not no fucking 10 guys this is a massive ambush and its only about 15 of us counting the guys in the trucks this got bad real quick. I was on the opposite side of the street as Orian, I was now with Sergeant Niko and Lionel by the wall but now we couldn't just walk on the street we were exposed to a Linear danger area in the middle of this shoot out, Sergeant Pierson is calling for our QRF which was our Quick Reaction Force or people on standby to help our troops in contact, and he couldn't get them on the radio.

At this point Bernard was getting his other weapon to begin firing, since he couldn't get the 50 Cal back up and the bombs just kept on dropping the AK's, and PKM's just wouldn't let off like these people just didn't fucking reload like they had just an infinite amount of ammunition inside of their magazines and belts it was insane. So they started reversing the truck way to late because they were trying to give Bernard a chance to get the 50 Cal up and we started hearing gun fire from where Sergeant Zebediah was positioned and now we knew we had to get the fuck out of the area before we got over run. Sergeant Niko looks across the street and says everyone get over the fucking wall right now and Lionel jumped right over that wall, then all I saw was Sergeant Niko's feet split and clear the wall and he was gone. I ran right after I saw him take off and crossed the street and the WALK kit was still slung on one arm so when I thought I had it cleared I threw the bag underhanded with momentum to try and clear the wall and it didn't it got caught on the wall but by that time I was midair clearing the wall myself I misjudged the distance and I got all scraped up and I was hanging on to the WALK kit and I was still trying to get it over the wall and Sergeant Niko yelled "Rod leave that shit and get over here now." I drop it and actually that stupid little fucking 3 foot wall we jumped over, led down to a fucking 6 foot ditch I fucking rolled down that little stupid ass ditch, got up started running towards Sergeant Niko and Lionel and fucking tripped, would you happen to guess what I tripped on right behind Sergeant Niko I tripped over fresh fucking produce lol a fucking massive sized watermelon, you believe that shit lol had to be the size of my torso it was massive lol. Any ways making our way back the truck was reversing and we caught it so we jumped on the passenger side and walked side by side so we wouldn't get shot but they had problems backing up so Sergeant Niko told us to bound back while they helped reverse the truck.

It was me, Tiago, Orian, and Doc, if you are trying to understand where we are now, we are located between the wall and the massive rice patty on the right side, moving towards the rice patty on the left side and the wall on the right side it may be a bit confusing for you but you have to understand we are reversing this huge truck so I am telling you the blueprint of the street in the eyes of the truck driver. Tiago starts to bound back with Orian and if anyone knows anything about war and fighting and shootouts the one thing you don't want to do is be in front of a wall while getting shot at because they can see where the bullets (rounds) are landing and they can easily bracket and adjust the rounds in to hit you because they know where they are shooting and where you are located. Now Tiago and Orian are using suppressing fire to give us cover to bound to them and as we are running we almost got hit several times, a 4 to 5 round burst of bullets hit inches away next to my foot and Doc was in front of me and the rounds were just hitting the wall behind us above our heads and dust was everywhere and he jumped over Tiago then Orian then I jumped over him and he wasn't shooting yet and I didn't understand why until later, but I landed next to him on the right and now the rice patty was directly in front of us. At this moment at this very moment I heard Ka chunk Ka chunk and man how painful it was to see both M249 Squad Automatic Weapons go down almost simultaneously. To know we had absolutely no heavy weapons in this fight was the worst thing possible we were outnumbered out gunned and to mention the bombs never stopped dropping it was fucking intense and when I heard both 249's malfunction I started letting rounds go, at this time if I recall correctly which I probably don't so you would have to ask Lionel, Tiago or Orian, but about 100 meters away you could see the Taliban bounding as well I believe they were dressed in all black at the time, so I kept firing until they bounded back to me and Doc and when they did we just sprayed the fucking tree line until the truck came then we took cover behind the truck. Until we got to the Y intersection where the Platoon split up and Sergeant Pierson started guiding the truck to turn around so we could exit the village. At this time we were awaiting for Sergeant Zebediah and Sergeant Corbin's Squads to get back but Walther and me were in the small garden by the 2 story house watching the window to make sure we weren't ambushed from there and simultaneously as Sergeant Pierson was reversing the truck the truck went too far back and broke down a wall and an insurgent was behind him and fired a RPG which missed Sergeant Pierson and hit the pile of rocks to the left of him and the insurgent fled and at this time, we had a moment of peace. It felt like a lifetime me and Walther looked at each other and it was so quiet like everyone just packed up and left, both trucks were turned around and we rallied up. Then the bombs started dropping again, we couldn't get in touch with QRF, all heavy weapons were down. The decision was made to get to the Afghanistan National Army Outpost down the road, so we started running and there was the lead truck then we ran behind it and had the rear truck protect us from the back.

We got to the ANA Outpost and they wouldn't let us in. So, we decided to call the rest of the guys at our DHQ and told them to bring an extra truck down, so we didn't have to run all the way back to Headquarters. Right after we made the call the ANA opened up their Outpost for us and we took cover in their compound, but as soon as we did that within 5 minutes the firing stopped, and the bombs stopped dropping. SFC Pierson called again for QRF and listen guys they didn't believe we were in a fire fight they had thought we were lying about it, so they didn't release QRF to us. It was insane just imagine being handed a asswhooping so bad you had to call for back up and the decision maker is like well you guys never been in an actual firefight other than some harassing gunfire and a RPG that disabled your vehicle we can't waste our resources on you. At this time all the NCO's are pissed as fuck, and up comes the Cougar Truck and we round up and head back to our DHQ. Once we get there we reset, re-supply and run a review of what happened. All the NCO's were in agreement that what happened was pretty fucking well-orchestrated, because in fact the truth is there was no possible way that they fired those mortars on our position so precise for being the first time, they said that it was pretty evident they got set in weeks prior and dialed the mortars in when they set up because for the first one to land damn near 60 meters away from the truck is not luck. We made a pretty good decision not to move forward but anyone with any basic mindset and basic training knows not to walk into a fucking open danger area with a 2 story complex overviewing the entire location with no foliage or terrain obstructing the view that's why we decided to stay behind the wall.

While hearing all the stories what happened was that, while we were reversing the truck after the mortars were coming down and we were getting bracketed in, Rico was the ammo bearer for Sante who was the M240 machine gunner were at their over watch position were taking fire as well and unbeknownst to us, was that the Taliban were firing 30 millimeter grenades at us as well as RPG rounds. They got hit with a 30mm grenade but did not explode, simultaneously Sergeant Zebediah's truck was getting hit with rounds and I forgot who was the gunner at the time but they had the M240 machine gun up there and that malfunctioned and was down and the truck was getting hit with rounds, the gunner took the M249 machine gun and started firing back. At this point Sergeant Zebediah and his team and the team on the ground started taking mortar fire as well, if you know Sergeant Zebediah, he doesn't not like mortar fire. He told us when they started taking fire he was all for the fight, but when he heard and saw the bombs start dropping his facial expression changed and he said "oh shit fuck that we have to get the fuck out of here lmfaoooo." There were a multitude of situations happening simultaneously and putting two and two together if Sergeant Zebediah and the squad on the ground didn't split up and take the left side of the road, we would have been ambushed from both sides but that is exactly why we split up to cover the front and rear incase and insurgents wanted to flank us and attack and they were going to until Sergeant Zebediah and the ground squad prevented it.

After the whole review of the situation, guess who comes on in and knocking at our headquarters, well you guessed it our QRF backup came 2 and a half hours after the fucking fight. Can you believe it, and this being my first day out, we get into a massive fire fight and to see that we have absolutely no support from our own people. Can't believe what was going on in my mind, like fuck it, what happens when we go on mission that's over 10 miles away and we get ambushed and attacked like this again, what happens then? We just die out there alone. It was insane.

Aside from everything that happened we spent a lot of ammunition, so we needed to resupply. We went back to the FOB and resupplied, during this time SFC Pierson, LT Maverick and some of the NCO's went to the company's headquarters and briefed First Sergeant and the C.O about what happened. At the tent everyone called me the good luck charm because they haven't really been in a real fight like that until I got here so we pretty much got the experience together and they thought I did a pretty good job considering I just came out of basic and haven't trained with the Platoon yet. Everyone was pretty happy that they are getting their Combat Infantryman's Badge, which indicates that you have been in and experienced actual combat and returned fire on the enemy, it's like a badge of honor when people see it, they know, and they respect it. Also being that I got my CIB before my own team leader was a pretty weird feeling considering he has been there months before me and has rank over me and he doesn't have it, he was actually pretty upset about the whole situation. I was the first one out of my IRO Platoon to get one as well.

This is a tough situation, but we are out in the open right. Things went sour real fast, SFC Pierson walks in the tent and we have a meeting. He tells us that we have to go back and fight, the Company Commander and First Sergeant were upset that we retreated. He stated that they received Intel from the German ISR that was in the area, they reported that there were 80 to 95 insurgents during our fight and there were another 15 to 20 insurgent reinforcements coming from the City Naahlehu to the West of our location at the time. Mind you it was about 15 of us on the ground alone with two trucks running skeleton crews. Does everyone start to understand the people we are working for and under? Do you guys see how ridiculous this was? We had absolutely no chance at winning that fight, on top of all our heavy weapons were down, at the moment if we didn't make the decision to retreat, we were fish in a barrel. Yet they wanted us to stay and fight without authorizing QRF backup because you had thought we were lying about being in a firefight when you could see the smoke of all the mortars they dropped on us from the Plateau, oh but wait your fat ass is sitting behind your desk at the base, of course you wouldn't be able to see the fight we were in. The best part about this wholesome situation was that SFC Pierson said that the CO wanted a written statement from me explaining why I dropped the WALK kit because I was going to be invoiced for losing it and it costs 1500 dollars. The day got better and better and better. Just imagine you're in a place of war getting fired upon and not only do you have to make certain decisions but you also have to take into consideration hey I need to run faster, and the only way to do that is to drop weight, ahhh wait fuck if I drop this they are going to charge me for this, well it's not worth it let me carry this run slower and the risk of me dying increases exponentially. Man, if you don't get the fuck out of my face with that bullshit. We are in war go send the invoice to supply and get us another one you piece of shit, so my people reading this you think war is all about fighting and let me tell you it really is not, on top of that the wall that we broke down trying to reverse and get out of the village, yea, well we paid for that shit too. I can't really explain all the politics of war and I don't and will not get into it but it's insane the shit that I found out during my time in.

Well ummm on a more important note, SFC Pierson starts to tell us about enemy casualty updates and how many insurgents were killed in action and wounded. Then his voice changes and it's something pretty serious and the tent gets quiet and he says "well guys there were some children running around in the area we were fighting in later in the day, and 3 kids started playing with an Unexploded Ordinance which was an RPG that they fired upon us but did not explode. While the kids were playing with it, it did explode, and all kids lost their lives." This was a reality of war no one considered nor expected. The tent was just quiet, that was just something we never thought to expect no one warned us about that. You know and understand how horrible it is to hear about a suicide bomber setting off a bomb and everyone in the surrounding area women, children, fathers they all die and pass away and that's more understood, it's not ok but it is understood that it is a reality that we may encounter and deal with but this, this wasn't.

....
....
....
....
....
....
....
....
....
....
....
....
....
....
....
....
....
....
....
....
....

SFC Pierson broke the silence and went on to tell us that we are going back to fight them, but that I was staying behind and pulling guard on the towers to give some of the vets in the platoon a chance to go and experience the fight and since I was the newest guy I didn't have much experience with the platoon or train with the platoon so he made the decision to take a more advanced person. Sgt Niko fought for me, he was mad about the decision he said it was bullshit but he couldn't do anything about it, and it pissed me off at first, you don't want your brothers going on and fighting without you. I did what I was told I stood back and pulled guard.

I started my guard shift and they mounted up and left and took the whole entire company. This new mission was to regain honor or some bullshit like that because weretreated, so they took the whole fucking company out. After my first guard shift, I went back to the tent and slept my 2 hours, then back to a 20-hour guard shift. At the end of my second guard shift I had enough time to make a couple of phone calls and of course I just called my baby girl. We started speaking and she knew something was off, so I told her everything was ok, that I just missed her. That was the only time I had lied to her. How am I supposed to tell her that I was the reason for the death of innocent children, directly or indirectly I was one of the reasons that those innocent children are not walking this Earth and enjoying life whether all they wanted to do was go outside and play with their friends, it was because of me and my brothers that they are not around anymore, and that, that shit hurt. I was scared honestly what if she didn't want to talk to me anyone, what if she left me because of this incident. What was I supposed to do, how do I even start a conversation like that, and to this day no one knows about this situation and above that this wasn't an isolated incident every time we got into a fight, innocent children lost their lives and I won't get into how many because I just lost count after a certain number and just started expecting it and literally just took a minute or two and just prayed for their young souls. Casualties of war are expected but innocent children aren't a casualty of war, if you want to fight we can fight all night long, we can take it to the extreme but children, innocent children they are off limits, and they have nothing to do with what is going on. Jaylene she would have known what to say and I know she wouldn't have left but I know she would have been disappointed in me I just I don't man I don't, I just couldn't tell her, and she knew something was wrong but as intellectual and intelligent and as much as she knew about people and emotions and everything she understood she shouldn't ask and she didn't but we knew things just weren't ok. Innocent children losing their lives changes everything. I don't think you guys actually know how much I love that woman and miss her dearly she will forever be a part of me.

As the week progresses the company got into the fight and I don't know how it went I just heard it over the radio on guard, and I just hoped everything went alright and everyone was ok. After all those days on guard it was my last day and I got off duty and I had to report to the motor pool because our guys got back from mission, so I had to help them unload and resupply. After we finish unloading SFC Pierson got to the tent and talked to us about our next mission to Naahlehu. SFC Pierson said I was good to go this time round and Sgt Niko gave me my packing list so I had to hurry up and pack it was already fucking 0 dark thirty I am tired as fuck from 5 days guard duty just got off to help them unload and we had to be up by 4:30 in the morning there was no sleeping for the next 2 days. So I quickly packed and got my shit together cleaned my weapon and now me and Orian had switched so I turned into the SAW gunner and Orian was a rifleman, but became the squads M320 gunner which is a detachable grenade launcher, you can use it by the weapon system itself or attach it to the M4 which ever was more useful to you. So off to mission we went. I will not speak about every mission in depth and honestly, I will not speak about this one in depth either. For the fact being that when I arrived and started going on mission with the platoon, we got into a firefight every single mission we went on until the end of September. To put it in perspective we got into so many fights that we used up most of the Battalions ammunition. We used up so much ammunition they told us we had to be conservative and stop using so many rounds in the firefights. Can you believe that bullshit hey you guys need to go to war but when you get shot at don't shoot back so much. I am not going to discuss all the political bullshit that happened in my time in the military but it was a very big reason for me getting out of the military and what happened in the time I spent in Afghanistan and how it was handled I was very disappointed in what I saw. Nonetheless we went on mission and got into fights and came back but more important we will talk about the next fight.

After the Naahlehu mission some time had passed, and they were not satisfied with Naahlehu. What happens next, they decide they want to go back to the Village of Naahlehu. All of Delta comes with us, Engineers come with us, it was a big mission we had actual support. We start out at DHQ and 3rd Squad is leading the company on this mission. Recalling this I can't lie to you guys I miss it so much. You know 0 dark 30, and we are making our way and the CO is with our platoon. Navigating through the villages in the middle of the night onto the objective that's just what we live for, Ruck Sack, Heavy weapons, Ammo bearing grunts it's just what we do. At this point and time respect is established and we know each other very well, we know who is most likely to fall in the shit water because he is clumsy as fuck, we know who is going to trip and their muzzle is going straight into the dirt and they have to hope we don't get into a fight getting to the objective so they have time to clean their weapon. It was, it is a great bond I loved my guys. Navigating the terrain, jumping creeks and rivers, helping your squad leader so he doesn't fall into the shit water. Let me explain it in a sense of I watch your back, you watch his back, he watches their back, to the point where it's a 360 degree field of view and everyone is watching everyone's back, but also in this sense of security you never have to worry about yourself because someone is already watching your back so this whole selfless lifestyle is immediately instilled within the brother hood. You never have to second guess if your brother is watching your back because he will without question because he knows someone is watching his back, we all understand that our brother has to make it home alive to his wife and kids and family. Of course at times it will be just you and one other person and times will get tough but you never act selfishly because if there is a hint or a scent of it you will be left back on the FOB, there are too many lives at steak to not pay attention or act selfishly.

Now we are at a halt and we allow the vehicles to move into position before our platoon takes the compound. We get to the 2-story compound, we were going to force our way in, but the owner just opened the door and we went and cleared it. At this point the whole platoon was split up because it was a pretty fucking big compound. Now at the entrance through the door to your immediate left, there were a flight of stairs going to the second floor I forgot what squad took that. To the immediate right was a patio area and a bathroom, when you walked into the patio to the left was another house. All that was left of the platoon at this point was me, Tiago and Sgt Curtis. Sgt Curtis breached the house and me and Tiago went inside, and it was completely empty but there was a danger zone to the left which entailed another room. At this point this was very very bad, due to the fact that me and Tiago are both SAW gunners, we clean our weapons exceptionally well but at the end of the day it's still a SAW. Me and Tiago stacked up at the door and we looked at each other and said we're fucked lol I love you bro, I love you too man lol. Tiago breached and I went in and took the far wall and he took the close wall cleared it and there was no one there and no one under the bed and we said, fuck man we dodged one on that. For you guys reading that don't understand the SAW machine gun is very well known for malfunctioning several times during a fight. So, the one thing that you don't ever want to happen is breaching a compound with two SAW gunners leading the pack because if there are insurgents and both SAW's malfunction minimum that's 3 casualties worst case scenario. In a time of war where you have a massive compound and are running a small platoon to clear the compound, well things like this tend to happen and you wish for the best because it is war and you will fight but you're hopeful that your weapon doesn't malfunction at the worse time possible.

Moving forward the platoon found the owner of the compound upstairs and we told him that he had to go because we had to clear the village of the Taliban. Once we got upstairs, we cleared it and there was a massive window which was great for an oversight position of the woods, which we knew that's most likely their avenue of approach to come and fight. We quickly kicked out the iron window fence. Sgt Niko and Sgt Curtis took care of that and broke that shit out fast. We stayed overnight no contact the next day the trucks moved and took a different position now they were directly to our left at about 200 meters away. Soon enough the fight started, our position was just taking rounds and we were fighting and come to find out we were the only ones engaging the enemy.

When all of a sudden, the compound starts moving, shaking, vibrating immensely, we didn't know what was going on. All of a sudden, our heavy weapons truck fucking Delta Company idiots were firing on our position so at the time we weren't only engaging the enemy we were taking friendly fire that was not so fucking friendly. We were getting hit with our own 50 Cal rounds and Sgt Niko and Sgt Curtis were yelling through the radio like what the fuck, and SFC Pierson LT Maverick were trying to get a hold of the CO to let them know we are in the compound like they fucking came up with the mission and the buildings we were going to overtake how the fuck your dumbass forget where we were. Luckily Sgt Niko had this massive 10-foot VS-17 Panel and hung it out the side of the compound and they finally stopped shooting at us, finally.

It was great being on mission with support because now we had fire support from our mortar platoon and fire support from both fixed wing and rotary wing aircrafts and when that Raptor came and did a gun run with the 30mm cannons it was a pretty sweet sound knowing you had support aside from the friendly fire lol. Continuing the firefight SFC Pierson disseminated some information about the insurgents having a Recoilless Rifle. A Recoilless Rifle has various sized projectile the Taliban in our area were known to us an 80, 82, or 84mm Mortars that can be shoulder fired, and boy did they use it. It blew a massive hole right next to the compound that the heavy weapons truck was located. At this time with all the friends I had, my dear friend Coleson was on the ground at the point of impact, a few of his squad members were also hit but there was no shrapnel or injuries other than minimal concussions, but everyone was ok. We had a flyby by one of our Rotary wing aircraft I forgot the call sign, but it was a Warrant Officer she was real cool and she unleashed a couple of Hellfire Missiles and took out the insurgents, our fights were pretty intense.

After the fight we had to go and do a Battle Damage Assessment, and we were in for a night. Third squad went out and it was me, Sgt Niko, Orian, Lionel, Tiago and I forget who else. We head out to where the insurgent's position where they were firing us from, and we came across this rice patty. We tread lightly and someone almost falls in the shit water, but someone grabbed him before he fell and we all gathered ourselves again and I don't really know what to say about what happened next, none of the squad does. So, we have our Night Vision Goggles on and all of a sudden, we all came to a halt and took a knee. We turned off our lights because we all saw the same things almost simultaneously and we all knew what to do. After we took the knee we all looked and saw 3-5 lights strobing, so if we can see these lights strobing that is not a good sign, that means for one either Special Forces is doing a Recon or some type of mission and no one notified us and we were going to get into a very very bad fire fight or two the Taliban had access to our equipment which was not feasible but several years prior to us going in to Kabul, Army National Guard lost a MK 19 which is a 40mm Grenade Launcher and several Night Vision equipment. I say Special Forces for the reason being that we did a couple missions unaware that we were used to clear villages for Special Forces entries. No matter what way you look at this, it is a terrible scenario. Sgt Niko made the decision to await clearance and we never got word if SF was in the area or not, so we quickly did our assessment and got the fuck up out of there before causing a massive fight with unknown personnel. We arrived back at the compound, asked if they got word of any operations in the area and they said there wasn't anyone operating in the area and we never got an answer but it was best that the decision was not to engage, and we all stood by that decision behind Sgt Niko.

Moving forward we pack up and move to a different position overnight, we overtake a one level house with roof access. Let me tell you that this house was made of dirt, mud and feces it was a pleasant experience to say the least. Walking in from the front entrance directly in front of you was a mud stable for some animals couldn't tell you which ones, because the only ones there were chicken at the time, but it was big enough to house two horses or two cows. It was an empty room with just hay and above it was the roof and to the left of that entrance was a latter for roof access. To the right of the main entrance was a room with stairs to the roof. This small compound was big enough to fit our platoon, so we fortified it by putting sandbags lining the edge of the entire roof. Other than that, it was just clear skies the compound itself had no roof which is usual in the Middle East. Above the per say Cow shed or room whatever you would like to call it we placed the M240 Machine Gun on over watch position because from the entrance at the 2 o'clock position there was a crop field and approximately 400 meters away was the beginning of the tree line where we knew we most likely would get attacked as well as at the 12 and 1 o'clock position there was a 2 story compound and the building was fortified with walls and ceilings and a roof and a small wall on the balcony which was directly facing our compound so the 240 gunner had those 2 positions to over watch. From the 11 o'clock position of the main entrance was an avenue, crop field, and a series of complexes, so we placed a M249 on over watch in that position next to the M240 on that same roof.

Moving to the living quarters the room with the stair case to the roof we placed a M14 sniper on over watch covering a part of the sector of the M240 and on the right side of the roof at the 9 o'clock position there was a continuing stretch of tree line that we had to over watch for insurgent reinforcements as well as a road (unpaved because there are not really paved roads in Afghanistan) stretching to the entrance of where we walked into the village. You know I would really like to use some military words because it would make this story so much more concise and easier but you guys wouldn't understand it so forgive me for trying to explain things at such a detailed level because to me I feel that anyone can just pick this up and read it and understand the blueprints of the structures we were in, lol well I hope so if not my apologies lol. Along that stretch of road, we had several trucks from Delta Company, so we had heavy machine gun support and this time they knew where we were so no friendly fire lol which isn't funny but damn some people are stupid. We finally settle in, to let you guys know again there are certain things I can't discuss tactics wise so when I am telling this story and battle you guys will be able to understand what I am saying but the tactics behind the fight and how the enemy maneuvered pretty much only military will understand what I am saying they will be able to infer very quickly once I say certain words and when we were attacked and how so you readers will understand it but the military personnel will grasp the intelligence of what was going on so again my apologies.

The next day arrives and as the sun was setting, we started receiving small arms and harassing fire. The fire was coming from the tree line by the 240 and that was good old Boyde's, Ricos, and Santes position and they sent as many rounds into that tree line as possible. The 50 Cal gun trucks from Delta Company were firing away and the Taliban did not like that at all, but they stayed and fought the only thing that scares them when they are fighting from that far is when we request gun runs form airships. It finally got quiet and died down, so we collapsed people on the roof for good reason we didn't want the roof to cave in and the fight was over for the night. We wake up and it's my turn to get on the roof but there was no activity, so I went to the roof with the sniper and M249 and I left my 249 downstairs with Bryson. On the roof it was me, Bernard, Lionel, Sgt Niko, and at the time one of the Scouts Snipers were on the roof with us also, at this time Sgt Niko indulged us with some information that him and Sgt Curtis saw, at the tree line in front of us, they could see a 4 foot wall behind the first row of trees, so when we engage try to bring the wall down which means let as many rounds as you can fly.

As quiet as it was Bernard asked me if I was ok and I said yea I just propped up the bipods on the 249 to reach over the 2nd row of sandbags and I was good, and he said ok and went downstairs to eat. Moments later all hell breaks loose, we start receiving fire from every position. Then we just let loose on every position we saw them firing us from. The 240 was firing very well no malfunctioning Lionel was on the M14, I was letting rounds fly from the 249 and the Scout was having at it with the sniper. Then they bracketed us in, and the scout was taking pretty close fire, so he got down from the roof, the sandbag that I was shooting over was creating a massive amount of dust, so I just pushed it off the ledge and continued to fire. All of a sudden everything went quiet and when it goes quiet it's time to just reload doesn't matter if you reloaded already put a fresh nut sack on the 249 and fresh magazines in the weapons. A nut sack is just a sack of ammunition that can hold 100 rounds of 249 ammo. All I hear is Bernard yelling at me "Rod you're cleaning my 249." I thought to myself well shit I almost got away with it lol I fired as many rounds as I could knowing damn well it's not my weapon so I don't have to clean it lmfaooooooo you guys don't understand how funny that is lmfaoo.

We received no contact for the next half hour, so we rotated personnel. I swapped 249s and let mine go to the roof since I had to clean Bernards lol I cleaned it very well to say the least.

Some time passes by and the Taliban resupplied I guess and started firing at us again and another massive fight broke out but this time air support came and helped and that fight was over pretty quickly after the gun runs, well in all honesty no one likes getting shot at and even less to get shot at by a bullet the size of your hand that if it hit you would take your entire arm with it. At this time, it was shift change, so I went on the other roof with Tiago and Boyde, and that was my section for the rest of the stay. We settled in for the night, Orian and Sgt Zebediah were telling me that Sgt Zebediah was walking outside and right when he hit the door all of a sudden, a sandbag fell from the heavens lmfaooooooo. I said oh sorry that was me lmfaoooo, Sgt Zebediah said "hey Rod I almost died man, you know I want to go home and see my wife and kids" lmfaooo. Aside from that guess what fucking happens, well you guys know I'm from Jersey I don't know anything about the fucking Desert lol. We got over taken by the most immense sandstorm ever and not just because I never been in one, but boy when I saw that wall of sand heading toward us from the roof I said aww shit just my luck, because in my head I know it's a fucking sandstorm which means whoever is on the roof is staying on the roof no rotating shift tonight it's a 24 hour plus day baby. It was a long night I couldn't even see my hand in front of me. Sgt Hammond climbs halfway up the ladder and yells at me and says turn around and pull guard, I said I couldn't see shit, and he chewed me out. I didn't mean to be rude, or disrespectful, or to talk back but what you want me to do I couldn't see shit. Up all night looking at sand trying to entertain my mind lol. Morning comes and I am pulling guard and all I hear is some guy yelling at me and I think to myself what the fuck who is that. I look back while on the roof and these two dudes are looking directly at me have my direct line of sight like who the fuck let them in there, how did they get around our security and bam, I got taken off the roof and decisions were made. A couple squads were taken to clear the whole fucking village again and guess who were the squads, well ya guessed right 3rd squad and 2nd squad, haven't slept ate but at this point I am so used to the war life it doesn't faze you at a certain point, especially now knowing you were going to be up another 24 hours lol. We cleared the village and came back. I got back on the roof and now I was on the 240, Boyde's 240 and Sgt Curtis advised me where the insurgents were firing from so position the 240 at that area. We stayed on watch for a while and nothing was going on, but I had a feeling it was coming soon it was just tooo quiet. I told Sgt Curtis "hey I have to go use the bathroom," he said "ok, fuck you want me to do hold it for you lol," I said "no I have to go and defecate but I feel like we are going to get hit soon," he said "well Rod make your decision because we have Boyde downstairs he could just cover you for 10 minutes," I said "you sure," he said "Rod just go nothing's happened yet nothing is going to happen." Boyde came up and relieved me and I went downstairs and right as I started to use the bathroom all I heard was PKM's, AK's, all the small arms going off and then the 50 Cal's and I said man fuck that shit I knew I shouldn't of came down, oh well it's their problem now lmfaoooo. The fight stopped and I went up and took position next to my brother man from another mother man!!! I love Tiago that's my brother for life lol. It was quiet for a moment I grabbed up some water next to Boyde and it was just us three on the roof Tiago didn't want any water he had and Boyde was on the 240 and Tiago was laid the fuck back next to his 249 and someone got a picture of us and it was a great shot and well shit I haven't even told you guys about the NY Times guys that came on mission didn't I? Damn well I have to go insert that somewhere or I may just tell you later that story.

    Any who another fight broke out and this one was just more intense than the others and they didn't care about air support this was a fight. There are just a multitude of guns and bombs going off it was just intense. Then all of a sudden me, Tiago and Boyde start taking heavy fire and it was pretty damn accurate. Sgt Curtis caught on to where it was coming from because he came back up on the roof and told me it was coming from the 2 story compound 4 to 500 meters away with the balcony and at this point you have to know your weapon systems and target because when we ranged it out by eye that distance was pretty accurate because the weapons system while you are shooting the bullet at 300 meters rises up instead of drops and my rounds were not hitting it I couldn't see any dust from my rounds hitting the compound so I knew that I had to aim lower and when I did I tore that balcony up, you couldn't see shit just dust and that's all that mattered at this point because if rounds were coming at me, Tiago and Boyde that means that rounds were flying by the rest of the platoon and that was a no go and Tiago unloaded a whole 2 nut sacks at the compound as well we were trying to bring down that house at this point but the 249 has baby bullets it wouldn't have brought down the house like a 50 Cal lol. Then we just hear massive explosion and overhear on the radio that a Buffalo Truck and MATV hit 2 massive IED's. later on, reported that one hole was 20 feet wide and 10 feet deep and the second hole was 15 feet wide and 12 feet deep just massive IED's.

At this point the mission was almost over and we had 2 vehicles down, so the decision is made to breakdown the tactical sites. The 2 downed vehicles were blasted on the 2 main roads we used to enter the village. The decision was made that during the breakdown of the tactical sites, we were to save the sandbags and put them in the MATV and fill the holes with them so the rest of the trucks can roll through. I don't think you guys understand the work involved in what I just said. As tired as we were there for 2 weeks living in Cow shit, barely sleeping and now someone's bright idea is to take all of the sandbags and fill these holes with them like our trucks can't go off road like they were built to do, but hey it came from up top so we need to do it. A truck sets up close to our compound and we start dismantling our site and from the fucking roof we set up a chain or try to and unload as many sandbags as we can. I am out here sweating, tired, dying and I look to my left and I see Tiago grabbing sandbags and they are just broken unusable and Sgt Niko says, "fuck it Tiago leave it if it's broken, we can't use it." I think to myself what the fuck he is lucky as shit how is he getting all the broken ones. I take a sand bag and throw it down and wipe some sweat off my eye and go to grab another sandbag when I catch Tiago going to get a sandbag, but he kneeled real fast and picked it up and said "Sgt Niko got another one down." Sgt Niko says, "fuck it you know what to do." I think to myself this is craziness lol, so he went to get another sandbag and what I saw was ahhhhhmazing lmfaooo. So Tiago had his knife on his right hand and kneeled with his right knee and stabbed the sandbag lmfaoooooooo so inconspicuous no one noticed and when he got up to grab it he saw me and put his finger to his lips and said shhhhhhhh lmfaoooooooooooooooooo I fucking love Tiago man lmfaoooooo. I went over there and "said dude what if we need those," he said "fuck that they aren't going to need those, the whole entire battalion is out here and we are the furthest from the IED site, they will have more than enough sandbags to fill those holes it's just unnecessary work for us and we have to head out to the Scouts position after this work out and get back to DHQ fuck that shit they will be alright." Turns out he was absolutely correct, three quarters of the way to breaking down our site, we got the call on the radio saying that they had enough sandbags to fill the holes and they didn't need the sandbags anymore. Sgt Niko said we still needed to breakdown the sight, so the Taliban didn't have a fortified fighting position, so he wanted us to take all the sandbags down. I looked at Tiago and looked at Orian we all knew, start stabbing every motherfucking sandbag fuck all that shit lmfaooooooooooooooooooooo. Sgt Niko said, "what happened to all our sandbags" we replied, "I don't know Sgt Niko looks like the Taliban had good aim this time they all shot up," and Orian said "that and motherfucking Rodriguez shot them up with the 249." What an asshole lmfaoooooooooooooo that joke has remained so constant with us as friends and it will forever be funny lmfaooooo.

We were making our way to the Scouts position when contact broke out, so we had to stay in position. We hear over the radio that our brother Kawa was hit in the head and was being medevacked out, well if I remember correctly they put him in the truck because we were in the process of exiting the village until the fight broke out. The fight quickly ends because at the time the Taliban didn't fight very often at night, they didn't have night vision capabilities, so night firefights ended pretty quickly. At this point we move to the Scouts location and when we get there, we understand how Kawa was shot. You know sometimes I completely understand that I am not the smartest guy but to give you a breakdown of where the Scouts were positioned by our higher ups it went like this for my strategic fighters, 200 to 250 meters at your 12 o'clock position is a tree line, from you to that tree line is bare space, grass a completely Open Danger Area. 10 to 15 meters behind you is a wall, the wall where Kawa was shot and you and the entire scouts are spaced out evenly on the road a Linear Danger Area and all you have, all each person has is 3 to 4 sandbags and that is it.

Sometimes I wonder how we all made it home with these college scholars setting up this type of position like it is intelligent I can't shake my head enough. The thing is when we got to that position and we all knew how horrible it was it was just insane that it was even allowed, all the NCO's, SFC Pierson, LT Maverick the whole entire platoon man was just in awe, that is just something you don't do, it is not smart at all man.

We set in for the night and let them fill the holes with the sandbags. As morning approached, we met up with the Scouts and the Scouts took the lead from us to start the Company's movement out of the village. They were a pretty far distance ahead of us, and now as we are heading out, we are moving fairly quickly. We hit this Open Danger Area and about 100 meters to the 12 o'clock position where we had to pass through was this massive Opium Farm, and let me learn you something, these Opium plants were massive they were well over 6 feet tall, we all ran right through them well part of the field and when we came out the other side of the field we took contact. We found cover and settled in, we didn't know where the fire was coming from and who was getting shot at. The radio starts exploding with traffic and what happened was the Scouts were heading out and were actually being followed by the Taliban. The explanation was, they were being Paralleled by them and came to a Y intersection and met and the Scouts took them out as quickly as they met and kept it moving through the village so the fight ended as fast as it started and we were a good distance behind them and we followed their path and went through the village.

We came to the main road to our District Headquarters, and on the main road is a compound with roof access where we were to overtake for an over watch positions while the rest of the company exits the village under our watch and we would take up the tail end of the company once everyone has exited. We get in the compound and find the owner, we clear the whole compound and find a really, really nice shot gun lmfaooo but we also found a manual to build hand grenades and that was a no go. The higher ups questioned him in the compound with the translators while we set up over watch on the roof. Sgt Niko wanted me and Tiago on the roof as the 249 gunners and I forgot who else from the platoon was with us on the roof. The trucks become visible at this point now and it's a good sign nothing has happened, and we are almost there being able to just get to the DHQ regroup and head back to the FOB. The trucks are about 200 meters from our position on the roof and to the left and right are Open Danger Areas and Forest, so that is what we are over watching to make sure no one gets ambushed.

    The Buffalo is the head truck and is slowly making its way to the main road, when all of a sudden it hit a IED, and this IED was massive it threw the Buffalo about 12 feet in the air the truck flipped and landed on its side and the worst part was we had soldiers on the ground near it. We were absolutely helpless at the time but right when it struck the insurgents attacked simultaneously. We were taking rounds in from every field of view and we fought for about 1 to 2 hours before the sun settled in and we stopped taking small arms fire. Me and Tiago looked at each other thinking the same thing, like ehhhh we kind of may need those sandbags now lmfaooo, but by this time we got reports of minor injuries but everyone was ok and a few soldiers were going to get tested for Traumatic Brain Injuries when we got back. Since the lead vehicle was a Buffalo, they didn't carry any sandbags because they had no room. The trailing Vehicles had enough remaining sandbags to fill the IED hole and we just awaited the Wrecker Truck to come and get the inoperable Buffalo, it took all night. It was a 100 percent security from everyone that night but at about 2 in the morning all the trucks made it across the IED hole and made it to the main road and we exited the village without any more casualties and got to the DHQ pretty quickly after that.

    Just an insane 2 week mission, and we found out that Kawa was ok and the bullet had hit his night vision goggles but the impact sent him to the wall and knocked him out that is why we all thought he had died but he was ok and he is a nice dude man let me tell you, I am glad he actually didn't get shot. After getting to the DHQ we packed up and headed to the FOB for resupply and After- Action Reviews. We had it pretty rough and we had some tough missions coming up. At this time, I was sent to Bagram Airforce Base with a guy from the supply unit and his name was Bartholomew. We became great friends from those 2 weeks at Bagram, I completely forgot what we had to pick up, but I learned the reasoning behind all the Airforce jokes and man they were accurate lol. Great people overall though very welcoming. Just to reiterate, we had a lot of fights and I wasn't involved in all but most and I won't be discussing all of them because that is an entire book by itself so we will be skipping ahead and the fights will not have the depth and detail as the others above. After the detail I had at Bagram Airforce Base I came back to the FOB and on a weird note everyone was there and playing videos games like such a rare day. Oh, and they hated when I played video games with them.

This was the prime time for Call of Duty Modern Warfare 2, and I would pick my character and run around with an AT4 Rocket Launcher and just demolish everyone and when they got annoyed, they would kick me out the tent lmfaoooo it was just hilarious. At this point everyone was getting ready for one of our biggest missions of the year and I was highly upset I wasn't going. I was put on guard duty for 2 weeks and I was upset. You know just not being by your brother's side and fighting with them it sucked because if anything happened to them you know you could have helped out, so you just hope everyone is on their tips and sharp.

The mission was to take over this Taliban strong hold in Kuala. While on guard duty I overheard all the radio chat of the TIC which is Troops in Contact. This was a very big mission and some people went with the company while others stayed at the DHQ since no one was there they needed security as well. From what was told to me by the platoon and the After-Action Review they went into the village so quickly that there wasn't much of a fight but the fight that erupted was a bad one. The Taliban had an automatic 30mm grenade launcher as well as the Recoilless Rifle and those are 2 weapons you don't want to fight against no matter that we have the 50 Cal and Mark 19 because the Recoilless Rifle could take out the entire truck itself with one direct hit and render it inoperable with an indirect hit. Upon that there were Intel reports of a Dishka which is a 14.5mm round (bullet) which is bigger than our 50 Cal and that round is deemed an anti-aircraft round. The company was getting hit hard and simultaneously the DHQ was getting hit as well it was a pretty well calibrated attack but we always have contingencies in place for that and Tiago, Sgt Niko, Deegan, Orian, and Lionel almost died but they could tell you what happened better than me explaining it and during the fight and they called in air support and the air force flew by and dropped 2 or 3 J-Dam bombs which were approximately 500 pounds each bomb. The fight was pretty much over after that, which is when they went to investigate the rest of the village to clear it out.

At this point they were reporting holes in the wall and some detached detonation cords and they found out that the Taliban tore out all of their IED's that they planted. They tried to take all of them but upon the next mission that we will discuss in a bit, they left several of them. To everyone's best guess they had taken them out to not waste it on us as in regular Infantryman. Previously stated Special Forces were doing missions in Kabul and no one really knew anything about it which should be the way clearly but you have to understand that the Taliban also know who they are fighting it is relatively easy for them to know regular military from covert operations and many people will say yes that is obvious but in reality it is not. If we decide to do a night mission and overtake a village it is not easily discernable regular Infantry and Covert Operations because tactics and platoons are different but but as fast as we move and as fast as we clear villages you the regular person will not be easy to identify which is which and I can tell you we regular Infantryman are far from Tier 1 or Tier 2 Operators the way they talk and carry themselves the way they train it is a completely different lifestyle and that lifestyle overflows into work and they deserve the status because let me tell you there are guys that just don't want to leave the FOB because they are scared they will die or something will happen to them and those people are how to say, would selfish be the correct word. We all sign up we all know what we are getting ourselves into and many people have families as well you know so for you to verbalize that you are in fear of your life, well we don't want you on missions with us because now you're a liability and pretty much are just a security guard, doesn't matter if you're a NCO, or Commissioned Officer all of you can go fuck yourself.

Aside from that rant, everyone came back and had to clean up and pack up for another 7-day mission back to Kuala. I pack up and the next day we head back, this mission was a different one we had a Joint Task with the Germans to search for IED's. If I remember we took the village and the Germans took the south side and roads.

We dropped off trucks and walked into the village and pretty much questioned as many people possible. The Intel started coming in and there were plenty of IED's and mortars left in the village. We set up a perimeter and waited for EOD to come which are the Explosive Ordinance Disposal unit. They arrived and took the IED's and mortars and I collapse my security and Orian is next to me and the EOD guy is just walking right past us real nonchalant holding two 81mm mortars taped together with yellow tape with wires sticking out of it, me and Orian look at each other like what thee actual fuck guy.

Really like go put that shit somewhere and blow it the fuck up why you walking around with it and talking and explaining what you found lol but to be fair after meeting some EOD guys and learning about the explosives I really didn't care anymore lol like go ahead pick that shit up and throw it in the garbage for all I care lol. The EOD guys blew it up and it was a pretty fair-sized explosion from those small bombs. We walk out the village to meet the Germans and get report from a villager that doesn't want to be seen talking to us that there are other IED's. We took the Intel and went on our way to search for the IED that he spoke about. This was a bad boy IED, the main issue about this IED that we found was not only was it found on the entrance path of the village and not only did we walk over it 3 times but the main problem was that it was daisy chained to 3 land mines, and the only reason it didn't go off was because the safety pin was left in.

Moving ahead for a moment in the story the guy that told us about the IED was fingered and was killed because the Taliban had thought because he told us where the IED was that we didn't walk over it and that's why it never exploded. The Afghan National Police took the IED which was a yellow jug (the yellow jug which was a 5- gallon jug is very common in Afghanistan and that is why mine detectors don't pick them up because they are made of plastic). We followed the ANP and it was worrisome because they were in their Ford Ranger with a 5 Gallon Yellow Jug full of homemade explosives driving off-road at 40 mph hitting every bump they find. We placed so much distance between us and them because they were just driving reckless and you didn't know what explosives were in that jug which means you aren't really sure how stable the chemicals are. We arrive at the Germans checkpoint and they take possession of the Jug and we exchange information and all in all throughout the day the total IED's found with the Germans we found about 14 IED's so it was a very successful day and none of the IED's exploded prematurely they were controlled by EOD which is a plus.

Throughout this time many things were going on with Jaylene and as you can understand we didn't have very much communication and even Amelia tried to get in contact with me via video chat and it just wasn't happening it was a pretty rough patch in our relationship because like I stated previously I was her man and when she needed me most I couldn't be there for her and that is what hurt most. The way that woman cared for me supported me appreciated me and loved me I just wasn't able to reciprocate back and as much as I wanted to I wasn't able to and that was my woman she was, is my heart and soul I owe a lot to her and I can never repay her for it. No matter what she was with me on every mission just when we left DHQ I had no choice but to leave the relationship there I couldn't take it with me on missions, you just simply can't do that and no one teaches you how to place your life on pause it is something you learn on your own. There were many things that happened that it's not to discuss just small instances where loss of life could have been tremendous or simple situations that was a lack of communication but the thought of mass casualties lingered and we realized that complacency even for a minute in combat could cost life.

A couple of small examples, we were resting in the FOB and all of a sudden, we are getting mortared. As we all know the Taliban can't really calculate mortar fire very well and we just came back for a 2-week mission and were tired. We hear the alarms go off and the bombs dropping, and we wake up but just stay in bed. We ask around the tent anyone getting up, Lionel says "man I am tired if we get hit and die, we die fuck it." Orian and Tiago both don't care either and I say "I didn't hear shit I am sleeping" Sgt Niko says "you know I really don't care guys but if SFC Pierson comes in and sees us here and not the bunker he will start his bullshit." We all replied "yea but fuck that lol" we all start laughing and everyone is like "yea we should just get up before he comes in" and bam right when those words were said all you hear is "what in the fuck are you guys doing here even at that still in bed, what the fuck do you not hear the mortar alarms going off right now get your shit and get to the bunker like fucking yesterday." So, we did the lazy drag and got to the bunker and 5 minutes after we got there the mortars stopped, a fucking waste of sleep time like we all knew. This situation leads to one that happened at the DHQ. We were sleeping when all of a sudden a massive explosion woke the entire platoon up and we jumped up and were in kit weapons loaded ran out the door in 30 seconds all a while we were checking ourselves for injuries, we had thought the worst we had thought we were hit. We set up outside everyone in fucking shorts, t-shirts, no socks just fucked up but armor on Night Vision Goggles up and weapons at the ready. What happened was the Germans were on a recon mission and fired a

155mm mortar illumination round from the DHQ and didn't communicate with us about it and we had thought it hit us we thought we were dead at that point. Other scenarios include a VBIED (Vehicle Borne Improvised Explosive Device) suicide bomber that was aiming at our DHQ but the Afghanistan National Army the ones that didn't let us in quickly during my first firefight intercepted the vehicle and the vehicle drove straight into the ANA outpost and completely demolished ¼ of the compound it was bad.

All this goes to show you that there is no place for complacency in war. Our Platoon was very lucky that we had no incidents and no casualties, but our company did, and we will get to that a bit later. You just learn how to leave things that will distract you on mission in safe places mentally. It was safe to think about Jaylene at DHQ and at the FOB anywhere else would have been a liability, and it's not to say that your woman is a liability but the fact being that if you ever want to see your woman again it is important to not think about her or your family during operations because it may be detrimental so as a man you have to make the decision on how to change your mentality and focus and it is difficult especially when no one tells you how to but you learn and you learn real fast.

Since we are on the subject let me explain something that per say civilians have a problem understanding. So during my time outside the military back in college which we will get to speak about, being around all these young kids and when I say young I need you guys to understand that my definition of young is kids of ages 17 to 28 that have never left their house and are highly opinionated on parts of life they have never experienced nor ever will. I have no problem conversing with anyone at all but when all you have done with your life is go to school, go home study, never go out and socialize or if you do you don't leave your small 3 mile radius of your city, you have no experience with diversity or simply people of other states and countries and the common problems or misconceptions other than what you see on tv. This was a big problem to deal with in college. On a small concise anecdote, I was in class and the subject of the military came up and when it does, I never speak about it nor let anyone know I was in the military because it gets bad. So, one kid said that people only join the military because they want to be heroes. At the time I didn't really care I heard the kid talk in class and it was apparent that he never left the house, walking down the hallway I over hear him talking to his friend and the conversation went something along the lines of he failed out of Seton Hall because his grades and his friend asked why what happened and he said just dorming man, I didn't have my mom to wake me up for class it was difficult for me. I was just so disappointed in life at that point, like this is what we come down to, needing mom to wake you up for school and you're 19 years fucking old like really if I would have put that kid in his place he probably would have called the cops after calling his mom that I yelled at him. In all honesty that's just one example another is when I went to San Diego to try out for the San Diego Police Department, we were at the physical fitness exam and this kid next to me starts talking to me and I could just tell how young minded he was and he confirmed it, he said yea I fucking hate military personnel I been trying to get on the force for 4 to 5 years and all these vets get the job before me so I have to keep retaking the exam and I'm like yeah sure sucks dude and I walk away. Like these are people that not I have to work with alone but have this major biased mentality of military personnel because they have vet status, and on top of that on routine traffic stops have this stick up their ass and when they pull over military personnel they will take out all their anger out on them every single time and just all of the situations I been in that can explain and just won't there is no reason but for the note coming up, I told this girl that I was military because she asked and it seemed like she could tell even though I don't carry myself like that at all. I confirmed I was military, and she gave it to me man, she threw the book at me I hate all you guys, you are all wife beaters, womanizers, alcoholics, drug addicts the worst people in the world. I just walked away like there was a time I couldn't catch a break; I have heard all the names in the book and all I did was keep to myself that's it. Then you have the group of people that say the military isn't hard I work 80 hours a week this and that and I barely see my family. That is completely understandable and I get it I get everyone's point of view trust me I do but some of the shit you guys say is outrageous and I am happy you guys take it out on me because you will meet someone that does have very high pride about being in the military and they unlike me because I am very sympathetic and empathetic and I don't fight unless absolutely necessary because I deescalate every situation because I don't want people getting hurt, but man when you find the wrong one you will know what it means to feel pain, so be careful with what you say and your dumbass opinions because it will get you fucked up. Most of the time it's not worth the fight but when you ask for it, people will give you the fight and you will not win that is guaranteed.

So on the topic of discussion I understand you may work 80 hours a week whether you're an entrepreneur, truck driver, teacher, CPA whatever your job is how many hours you work I understand believe me I do I see all sides I know people in every aspect of life and I am not small minded I get that you're tired, I get that you miss your family and all you're trying to do I get it, I am not saying this about me I am saying this for the general public because this is important, we all come from different walks of life even in the military we may have the same job go on the same mission but have different experiences because we get separated and have different roles to play during the mission so even though we all go to the same place everyone has a different story that is why I tell my story with the people I was with at that time even though we were all there. Now we have to discuss the difference in views, so allow me to paint the picture for you. For the civilian not isolating anyone this is a generic painting per say for conversations sake. You wake up at 5 or 6 in the morning you make your breakfast, your coffee your toast whatever you like for breakfast. You walk into the bathroom, and your wife, girlfriend, mistress, boyfriend, husband, is there getting ready for work now as well as the kids are getting up and getting ready for school. At this point everyone is downstairs eating breakfast while you pack up and leave. You get in your car and you get stressed because the traffic and you're almost late for work and you know you'll hear your boss complaining about it again but it's out of your control, but you know they don't care. Then you get to work and have all this mail, unread e-mails, overload from work that wasn't able to be finished last week and you realize you have a long week ahead of you and you can't afford to procrastinate because it is a lot to do. Then its 6pm you try to leave but have so much work to do so you try to get ahead for tomorrow then its 7:30 and your spouse calls you and tells you that you missed your daughters cheerleading competition and sons baseball game and now you're all stressed out because you genuinely forgot but this isn't the first time and now your spouse is highly upset and you know you're going to hear it when you arrive home. So you pack up and leave work and upon arriving home you catch a flat tire and it's just one of those days but you think well its better than catching a flat on your way to work tomorrow so in your head you have leveled out and thought it was for the best today and not tomorrow but Triple A takes a ridiculous amount of time to reach you and now its 10 and you're still not home and you're spouse is calling your phone but it died while you were waiting for Triple A. It is 11pm and you finally arrive home and your spouse starts an argument asking where you were because you arrived so late home and your spouse has unresolved insecurities that stemmed from childhood and past relationships, even though you have never made them second guess your loyalty or love and with the day you had you respond because you have to let your anger out as well and it blows up in to a heated argument. Now you're both mad at each other and well you're on the couch because you're a liar and because you said some things that you didn't mean but at this point it doesn't matter because it's 2 o'clock and you have to be up at 5 for work. You wake up at 5 and barely slept because you know you hurt your spouse's feelings and feel really guilty and bad and you're just trying to figure out how to apologize because you love them. Everyone is awake and you go to the bathroom and catch your spouse getting ready and have a talk and you both apologize and make up and you get to work and write a post it that you have to pick up flowers on the way home and it was just a hectic way to start the week but happy that problems got resolved quickly.

To explain the military side, it's not starting at waking up at 4 in the morning, you have been at work the past 10 days doing 18-hour shifts and today your company gets back and you're not allowed to go and get rest. Your job is to wait for them to get back and help them unload and clean the trucks. After you unload and clean the trucks you have to clean the weapon systems because no one sleeps until all weapon systems are cleaned so you might as well help out even though yours is clean. All the weapons are cleaned and now it's 5 o'clock in the morning and you can rest, but you have to be up at 8 because you have to lay out all the equipment in the trucks. This means you have to be up at 6:30 in the morning to even be able to get to the bathroom and take a quick shower before the layout because the layout is at 8 which means that is not when you start that means that is when all the equipment is supposed to be out in front of the trucks. You and your best friend go quickly to take a shower before 500 people line up for it and grab some peanut butter and crackers for breakfast run to the truck parking lot and start laying everything out. Your Sergeant is walking towards the trucks and you and your best friend are looking over making sure you got everything and you're so tired that everything looks right, and you say fuck it, it looks good and you both agree. Now your Sergeant is in your face yelling at you because he can't find the fire extinguisher for the truck and now you're doing 100 pushups keeping in mind that you now have to locate a fire extinguisher for that truck and your Sergeant gave you 20 minutes to find it and you weren't even on mission with them the last 10 days because you were on guard duty but Sergeant is having problems with his wife at home and decides to take it out on the stupid private that doesn't know any better. The layout is over, and you have 10 minutes left to find the fire extinguisher. You rush to the tent because you maybe have one there and catch your Sergeant there and he asks you if you packed for the 2 week mission coming up tomorrow and you say no because you were at the layout all morning and now you get belittled and demeaned because you're a piece of shit private that can't do anything right and now you're doing pushups for talking back to a Non Commissioned Officer. Your Sergeant tells you that you have an hour to pack and you honestly ask him if you should pack first or find the fire extinguisher. Now he is highly upset because he tells you that you were being condescending in questioning him and he is the NCO and should never be questioned and now you're doing more pushups and getting called all the great names in the book and at this point you think to yourself well fuck you I hope your wife is getting pipped by another guy because if I was her I would leave your dumbass too but, you're not allowed to say that because if you do you are getting written up and losing 2 and a half months pay so you just keep your mouth shut. After a 45 minute smoke session he tells you to get up and pack because you have 15 minutes to pack from the hour he told you and says you should have found the fire extinguisher yesterday but we all know what that means just find it ASAP. You pack and remember you have a good friend at supply and run over to him before he closes for the day and ask for a fire extinguisher and he gladly helps you out and you show it to your Sergeant and he asks if you stole it because if you did you're doing more pushups and you tell him no but that you tactically acquired it and you finally get a smirk out of him because it was funny and he tells you when you're done putting it in the truck the rest of the night is yours. You go and put the fire extinguisher away and run to the computer lounge to call your girl and catch up because at the end of the day it doesn't matter what happens in the platoon just that you're able to hear your girl's voice and know she is doing well and that's what matters to you. You call her and she picks up and as soon as she said hello you knew her voice was different so fuck everything else and jump right into the conversation because baby girl has to be ok or nothing is ok. She tells you that her grandmother just passed away and you know how close she was to her, and now her grades are dropping because she is depressed and you're not around to hold her and tell her everything will be ok. You try to comfort her as best as possible but as humans you understand that sometimes you just need to be by your significant others side during hard times because words are just not enough they need to feel you to feel safe, to feel comforted, to know that you weren't lying when you said you would always be there for each other but you're not and you cant. Now it's 1 in the morning and first formation is at 4am but the trucks have to be ready before you guys go to first formation because after first formation you guys are in the truck going on mission. What do you do now because your woman needs you? Your woman is always first so you stay there and forget about sleep for the next 2 weeks, and you comfort her as much as you can and you feel something else is wrong because aside from all of this she seems distant and it's a weird feeling but you cannot address it at this time because the situation so as a man you make the decision because you trust your woman and dismiss the feeling.

With this whole conversation nothing was about you and you weren't able to relieve any stress and now have more stress on your shoulders and its not to be selfish but it was just this one time you needed to vent and let it out and it was at the worst time possible and she is about to fall asleep and you tell her that you love her but she doesn't say it back and you tend to understand under the circumstances you know she is hurting so you wish her a good night. Now before leaving you check your Facebook and immediately regret it. Your best friend messaged you saying that he saw your girl hanging out with a male friend. When he described this male friend you immediately knew who it was because you asked your girl to stop talking to him because you deemed him as a threat to your relationship because you could see he was making small gestures to your girl and your girl simply believed that they were simply friends and he didn't mean anything by it. Again you have to man up and take it easy because you don't want to confront your girl at this time and decide to wait after the mission to talk to her and of course you trust her she never made you question her but the thought of her hanging out with another man is still very bothersome. Its 3 in the morning now and you rush back to the tent grab your stuff and run to the truck line and set up the truck with your brother. Your brother knows something is off and starts asking you questions but you haven't slept in days and now you have to worry about your woman with another man and you give him an attitude and he tells you to relax and you know you were wrong so you do and tell him you'll talk about it later. You pack up and have your mission brief at 4 and now leave for mission.

 At this point you been on the road for 2 hours and all of a sudden all you see is a wall of dust, and immediately hear gun fire. Your truck just hit an IED and you guys are getting ambushed, the truck seems ok and everyone is fine. The gunner on the truck is firing back and now it's an all-out firefight and for some reason the truck isn't moving. You guys have to dismount and check the truck, so everyone dismounts and returns fire while checking the truck and notice a tire is blown out. Your Sergeant calls for QRF and a Wrecker to come and haul the truck out. After your Sergeant made the call you start taking mortar fire and you guys have to move and get out of that location. The decision is made to tow it out of the red zone or ambush area.

So, since you're the driver your Sergeant tells you to get back in the truck and be prepared to move out, while him, your brother and another guy from your platoon are setting up the tow bar and get back in the truck. The tow is working, and you guys are moving the mortars stop and the gun fire stops. You guys get to a safe location and finally QRF and the Wrecker come and lock up the truck and take it back to base with you as the security convoy. On the way back to base you hear of another Company in a firefight and that is where all the air assets went the fight was closer to the FOB and the fight was worse it was an all-out ambush at the checkpoint. Hours later you return to the FOB to pick up a vehicle, but you have to drop off the inoperable one at the mechanics and take everything out of the trucks for now until they fix it. You get to the truck line and your Sergeant asks to talk to you and for the moment you know you just simply don't want to hear shit from him and are in a bad mood especially from being blown up 4 hours ago. He pulls you to the side and tells you that the base is on blackout, blackout means no communication at all to the United States because someone was either severely injured or passed away in combat and they have yet to locate the family and tell them. You start thinking well what does the blackout have to do with me I mean I am sorry for what happened to the person, but this situation doesn't make any sense. You start to connect the dots and rethink the day, and you remember that there was a company in a firefight and you recall hearing it was Bravo Company and you start going through names in your head of all the friends you have in Bravo Company and you come across your best friend that you went to basic training with who was a super nice and genuine just a great guy to be around with and back in the States you guys are always together hanging out he was the only person you trusted and vented to. Your Sergeant confirms that your best friend had passed away in the firefight.

Your day is over at this point, they won't allow you to go anywhere near the computers or anything because they don't want you calling his family but on top of dealing with the past 12 days, not sleeping, not eating, nearly died, not being able to talk to your girl because she is going through her own issues and then the possibility of your girlfriend cheating on you. Your mind is going crazy and there is no way of stopping it and no one teaches you how to deal with all these situations that are ongoing and you can't even talk to your best friend about it because he passed away and it still hasn't hit you yet even though you know he is not around anymore. Your Sergeant gives you the night off, but it doesn't matter because you have to go on mission tomorrow and now with the night off, you're alone with your thoughts and memories and that is thee absolute worst thing possible at this time. With no knowledge of how to deal with everything going on we revert back to what we know and that is displacement. If all I do is work, then I can't think about my problems and if I can't think about my problems then the illusions introduce itself because I think that they have resolved since they are not on my mind anymore. So, the next day comes and you go on mission and everything is much better because at this point reality is virtual and false. I don't have to face my problems because I have none because the only thing on my mind is my job. After the week goes by and the mission is over, trucks lined up clean, weapon systems cleaned, all those thoughts and problems come running back as quickly as they left. Some time is left in the day and you go and call your girl because you need her fuck the thought that she was hanging out with some guy you dismiss it because you just need to hear her voice and talk things out with her.

    You call her she picks up and her voice is off again, and she tells you that you guys have to talk. You know her voice when she says that it is something serious. She tells you that she moved on from you, she tells you she found another man and she is sorry but when she needed you, you weren't there for her, she then tells you to take care and hangs up. At this point you're completely speechless holding the phone now you have lost both your best friend and girlfriend and it's the lowest part of your life and you have no one to talk to or vent to anymore. After it hits you and you hang up the phone walk back to the tent lay on your bed your mind goes into depressive state and start thinking and adding things up you're awake all night morning comes you get up for formation you get to the bathroom and this one day no one is there except you.

With tears coming down your eye you man up and tell yourself everything happens for a reason and everything will be ok, and no one knows what is going on in your life and you have to carry all this weight by yourself. Then you come to the realization there are 10 months left on deployment.

To everyone that is the difference between military and civilian life. No matter what happens at the end of your workday or workweek you will be guaranteed to go home no matter what. Military cannot, we can't fix the problems like you are able to, we are 9 thousand miles away, we can barely support our women and children, words only help so much. Yes working 80 to 90 hours a week being away from home traveling days at a time it sucks but all in all you can go home at any time you can hug your woman you can hug your children you can say fuck work today I am taking a sick day and stay home and spend time with your kids. The lifestyles are completely different and that is what I am getting at, please broaden and expand your mindset from what you see on tv and what you believe from movies this lifestyle is not of the norm. I completely understand the people that say well you chose to sign up well yes you ignorant fuck and I decided to punch you in the face too does that mean the decision was wrong or right now we both chose different paths in life to take and that should come with respect itself simple as that, there is no need to argue about career paths no one person is better than the next we are all here to help each other progress so can we all just put the bullshit aside and move forward? Can we just live without stigma? Can we just appreciate each other's job? Is that so hard to do as adults because if it is then we as a society do have a lot of work to do and I am all open to hear how we can accomplish it and help out. We can do better and I think we must for the future generations.

At this point in the deployment, Jaylene wasn't doing very well she had a lot of issues going on and as usually she needed me, but the good thing was that we were winding down because deployment was almost over. I spoke to her as much as I could but it is not possible to fix every problem over the phone, you do need physical contact, you need to hold your woman, kiss her, show her affection, tell her that you love her and these were things that I just couldn't do. I was very grateful to have her in my life during these times she was my rock and honestly even writing back and forth with Cassie, Melina, Roland, Fabyen, talking to Adrien it was only so much they could help with. I appreciate all of the letters written and just the support everyone has given me throughout my life trust me it is greatly appreciated and I make sure to tell them every time I see them knowing I have absolutely no way of paying them back for all they have done for me and I wish I could I really do.

While deployment is coming to an end, our main mission now is to make sure we have all our equipment and do accountability or do a layout, so we don't leave anything in Afghanistan. One day on a layout someone went out to the hole in the wall without full equipment, which was a massive hole in between the Hesco Barriers or fence which was the construction area for an expansion of the FOB. Chain of Command brought the issue to our Platoon Sergeant which was SFC Pierson and he relayed it to all of the Squad Leaders. Here comes Sgt Niko and smokes the living dog shit out of us, and we got smoked for a couple of hours and Orian had to go to guard duty and after another 30 minutes of getting smoked we are all standing up and Sgt Niko is just looking at us and says "Orian, kick rocks." So, what does Orian do? He starts kicking all the rocks on the ground lmfaoooooooooo. Sgt Niko said "Orian what the fuck are you doing?"

Orian says "kicking rocks Sergeant." Sgt Niko says "that's not what I meant; don't you have guard duty crazy? Get the fuck out of here lmfaoooooooo." At that point it was just too funny he couldn't smoke us anymore the serious moment went out the window lmfaoooooo. The next day we had a Truck layout, because we were turning over trucks to the new unit and had to make sure they had all their equipment. A serious call had come in about an explosion in our district. What happened was that our District Governor had been executed via suicide bomber. The issue is that the Germans were down on manpower and we weren't doing missions anymore for the moment because we had to get the new unit ready and the Taliban took advantage of the low security and took out the Governor, previously we talked to the governor and did some protection services for him he seemed like a good guy and that's what happens in war, you change units and during the change the enemy sees an opportunity for an attack and they go for it and in war you can't predict or train for everything you know. I think it was Moltke that said, "No plan of operations extends with any certainty beyond the first contact with the enemy or main hostile force." You just simply cannot account for every situation and it sucks we started losing a lot of people during the unit change it was horrible.

The next issue was a serious one to our platoon it hit us hard and I simply don't agree with the actions taken but there is only so much you can do as a dumb private. In the military you learn very quickly that as enlisted personnel you are deemed a level 1 individual. Level 1 means that you are expendable. Just like in the civilian world you can work at a job for 20 years and all of a sudden get laid off like you didn't invest your entire life into that job and if that doesn't explain what a level 1 individual is then I got nothing for you. What it seemed to be for me and I am speaking for myself is that we don't go out on missions after a certain point because if something were to happen to us or if we were to put some Afghanistan civilians at risk it would be the fault of the Company Commander and First Sergeant. Due to the fact that it was so late in the deployment what justification would they have to their supervisors if something were to happen to us or a civilian if we got into a firefight. To explain the situation, our brothers the Germans were doing a mission riding in their tanks and hit a Historical Ambush Site and were ambushed. The issue with this fight that erupted were the Talibans equipment, they carried RPG 7's which are armor piercing Rocket Propelled Grenades. The round went through the tanks armor and some of the Germans passed away, just a gruesome way to die. The ambush and firefight came down to our communications and our platoon was not able to go and help out we were told that the platoon was going to stand down. It bothered all of us, coming to a point and time that in all honestly if the Germans didn't come and help us out with their tanks and equipment we wouldn't be here right now. Plenty of times we would get harassing gun fire and wouldn't be able to fire back because the Taliban would be hiding in a village with women and children and as any Escalation of Force if there are innocent civilians you are not allowed to fire back, so you are literally just sitting there behind a wall for a hour getting shot at, but when the Taliban see the Germans and their Tanks rolling through all the gunfire seemingly stops. Also the Battle at the Abandoned Mosque I wasn't able to fit in the story we almost lost all of our Sergeants, and Lieutenant on a Reconnaissance mission due to RPG fired at them that Sgt Niko called out and everyone split up and caused a decent firefight that the Germans helped us with, it was just very upsetting that the one time they truly did need us we weren't able to help and as a Private you don't have any type of power or say in what the Platoon does and it sucks, but I pray for them and the ones we lost there really isn't much else I or we could do honestly.

I don't really want to discuss this next part due to the entire situation as a whole was just an extremely sad situation. So, towards the end of the deployment leisure becomes a luxury. You are allowed more freedom since you're not on mission anymore you are in this giant clamshell tent waiting for a plane to begin your travels back home. At this point our platoon was in the clamshell and all we did was work out or watch The Unit. At times me and Tiago would go to the Computer lounge or go eat at the chow hall. We didn't really let anyone know where we were going and Sgt Niko was pissed me and Tiago got the living shit smoked out of us for it. We finally got the message and just stayed in the clam shell and watched The Unit with everyone else. The countdown is almost done we have 3 days left before our flight back home. We went to the chow hall and someone asked if we wanted to go call our families and we said not at the moment. Fuck you guys I'm not doing this anymore today I had enough of the day today.

....
....
....
....
....
....
....
....
....

My apologies I just wasn't in the mood yesterday, but I am done with this chapter I'll finish it right now for you guys. Me and Tiago went back to the Clamshell and moments later there was a huge ruckus we didn't know what was going on. So out of respect for everyone and their families I am not going to explain how anything happened but the end result. Our fellow brother Weston was shot and passed away. I knew him through my IRO Platoon brothers they introduced me to him and he was a good guy man a genuine guy and sad that we were literally days away from being home and one of us didn't make it back it was a sad day and Sgt Zebediah was there and he did the best he could to help but there was just nothing anyone could do, but they tried and just a sad situation as a whole.

We finally boarded our plane it was a quiet ride until we landed in Germany. After many, many hours we finally landed in Fort Drum, NY. Of course, it would be snowing when we landed such a welcoming gift. When you land there are a multitude of things to do before you are able to go back to your apartment. I won't go into the details of all the bullshit it is really fucking annoying but aside from that after we do everything we get to the gymnasium. When soldiers arrive back from a deployment, they hold this reception I guess the right word would be. Where they have everyone's families in the gym, and we have a formation and First Sergeant, or Command Sergeant Major I forgot how the whole thing went and I have been to several, but I never cared for it other than when my brothers came back. Any who they hold this formation and welcoming back party and when they release you from formation then you go and pick up your bags and head out. Formation was over and everyone's families met them on the court and me and two other guys walked right up out of that gym and left. It was literally us three that didn't have any family or friends that came up for the welcoming back. Part of that reason was that I didn't tell Adrien or Daziel or Jeremiah, aside from that there was a secured information clause.

You weren't able to tell your family the exact date and time of your landing for security reasons but they were able to find out and just like I didn't tell them when I was graduating and somehow they ended up going to that and graduation I didn't care about that but this I would say bothered me and the best I could tell them was that I was going home in a couple days and which a couple is 2 but that's neither here nor there its past no one was there and its over but let me tell you it was a long walk to the barracks. Cold, snowing, carrying 3 duffle bags and a ruck sack and assault pack, being alone, getting to the room while everyone was spending time with their families and girlfriends and wives and there was just no sleeping that night. The heater didn't work, no bed sheets, no pillows, no phone to be able to call Jaylene and go to sleep with her on the phone, Weston was gone, and I was just trying to put the deployment behind me. It was a long cold lonely night I will never forget.

That will be the end of this chapter I can't go in depth on certain situations that happened but it's not important to you guys. Rest In Peace Brother Weston.

Chapter 15

Amelia

Before beginning this chapter let me explain a few things. For one I feel as if I just need to remind everyone here reading this, that this is a conversational autobiography, journal or whatever you would like to name it. It did not start out like this. For the readers, this was not intended to be like this. When I first began writing I did not know what I was doing, I just go by my feelings. If I feel the need to do something I do it, in which the feeling was to begin writing and that's how the first chapter was. This isn't a diary or journal; I felt the need to express certain things that happened in the day in a story formant. Then it grew to be, well since I don't have anyone to talk to let me write my thoughts down and as I write it down its more of a conscience or conscious thing I don't feel like checking the word usage on that at the moment but as I write things down I can see where I made wrong decisions and learned how to analyze and see all available options and consequences of such actions and be better at making hasty decisions in dynamic situations and that's how I learned to be so fast making judgment calls on the fly. Before I used to stay up all night thinking about what happened in these scenarios and how was I able to have a better turn out if I made a different decision or if everything could have went south if I made a bad decision with serious repercussions or consequences and it has taken me many years of bad experiences to get to where I am today as a man.

As stated before I will not talk about everything in this story as it turned out to be because I feel that you as the audience may benefit from my past mistakes and how I have helped others I may be able to help you with the advice I will leave to you on the back of this book. This story is mainly just things that are weighing on my chest that I have to get out and to do so I have to tell you the main parts of my story but I will not tell the story as a whole just the important parts that bring everything together because everything aside from that is irrelevant and I don't care nor think about.

As this year continues to just keep going downhill, I just don't care anymore honestly. I have chosen a career path that will enable me to help others and now I have to consciously make the decision to stop helping everyone I bump into on the street that needs a helping hand because I do have things I do want to achieve in my life and just helping everyone I meet has taken its toll on me and compassion fatigue has set in and as a man I can acknowledge it and make the decision to finally be selfish and place my own needs and desires first which has taken well over 15 years and Mike is tired yall. The reason to reexplain this is because Amelia who you will meet or I will reintroduce, we had a very bad falling out. In that sense I will not explain the whole relationship and I won't explain everything that happened in the years we were together or not together and this will hopefully be a quick chapter very sad at times there were a couple hospitalizations and friends I lost but I will try my best to compact it and make it concise so please bear with me I will give you the most genuine advice you have ever received in your life because I love you all and I care about you all but it is time for me to move on and trust me someone better than me will take my place and help you all out maybe not like I have but there will be someone there for all you just like I have been but I must focus on the life I have to build for my family that I don't have yet. Seemingly that is the motivator and I'm still not sure how that is supposed to motivate me but its time I focus on myself, after putting my life on the line multiple times and stopping people from committing suicide, beating up men that hit their defenseless girlfriends and wives, bringing people back from a depressive state, getting people jobs the sleepless nights from everyone calling my phone at all hours of the night to fix all their problems I feel like I have done a lot I can't really discuss any of these situations but for the moment that's what it was and more, and it may not have been enough but I feel like I have helped out society a bit and I need to take some time out to work on starting a family of my own and to teach my kids valuable information to be able to navigate this world when I leave because remember I can't live till I'm 150 years old, time is undefeated folks and I feel like I did ok for society and I just need to focus on building a family of my own instead of fixing everyone else's. Well to start a family I am going to have to have sex one day lol there's a little humor to brighten up the grey clouds but please be patient with me.

That night back from Deployment was a long, cold, lonely night honestly and I have had some real lonely dark nights but that one is up there at the top with them all. The next day my great friend Sebastian brought all my clothes and comforter and pillows from his house. I was so grateful to him and his wife, Sebastian was a good dude one of the most goofy guys on this planet you will ever meet but he had a pure heart and pure intentions guy wouldn't hurt a fly, would never get mad even when he tried to lol his face would turn red and he would forget to breathe then burst out laughing because he forgot he wasn't breathing lmfaooo. I was able to get internet within a couple of weeks because Deegan my roommate got it and gave me his password so I could use my computer and me and Jaylene started talking again but things were just different. I didn't really know how to talk to her anymore honestly the connection was there but so much was different with her. So, Amelia was one of the sisters in the house, this household of questions. There were I believe 3 sisters and 2 brothers or 4 sisters and 1 brother I don't recall very well. Amelia had told me that Jaylene cheated on me, that completely crushed me. She did admit it to me, and it was just like I mentioned before, Jaylene was always there for me since day one and she did a lot for me and I will forever be grateful to her and for her. She explained to me how she felt that I abandoned her. She went to a kick back, in Cali that's what they call small parties with friends here in Jersey we call them get togethers and there was guy there who had a crush on her and smooth talked his way and they made out. My problem was keeping her away from all those people, you really couldn't comprehend how many negative people she was around I told you she was a wild child and I won't explain what she has been through but it was all bad and she had asthma and her friends were smokers and it was difficult but how much could I have done from three thousand miles away I couldn't do anything and then she cheated on me. It was just all bad.

It hurt a lot because at the point where I just wasn't able to just be there for her just once with the exception of her father passing away, I wasn't really there in the relationship at all. It was simply her supporting me through all these years and it was unconditional love and support until she just couldn't take it anymore. That, that was my fault and there was no exception for it but also there is no exception for cheating either but I completely understand both sides so the question becomes, can I truly be mad at her? I don't know the answer to that I really don't I was just really hurt man truly hurt. It came to a point and time I that I know I wasn't any good for her but to the point where we couldn't be without talking to each other we would still talk a lot honestly we just remained friends which was a weird atmosphere and didn't last long at all.

On May 2, 2011 as everyone knows Osama Bin Laden was killed. How this situation affected us is that, our unit Alpha 9-99 was placed on GRF which is the Global Reaction Force. From reading this story you know that QRF is the Quick Reaction Force, well unless its me and my brothers in a fight, so when a company is in a firefight and you are the QRF for the day you get dispatched out to support your fellow companies in that fight. The same goes for GRF, if something were to happen in Afghanistan and they needed more soldiers on the ground we would be going back. GRF lasts an x amount of time, this time is added to your reintegration time back from combat, so we are not allowed to go home for an x amount of months. Reintegration consist of the obvious psychological exams, medical exams, the stupid test that examines you for Traumatic Brain Injuries or TBI's like really one of the questions is like what is 11 plus 22 well hmmmmm I don't think its 33 because I have taken exams before and that's too obvious and too simple so there is more to the question so you reread the question a gazillion times then realize wait what the fuck this is real what the fuck am I doing it is 33 lol then the time runs out and you fail and then think fuck was it 33 lmfaoooo we really hate the stupid test.

After the reintegration period they allowed us to go home for a weekend. I couldn't possibly tell you how I got home I honestly don't remember if I took the bus or train. The first house I went to, was no other than my brother Adrien. I spent the night at his house, and we talked and caught up gave him thanks for everything he has done and how he supported me and took care of my girl during my time across the pond. I went home and saw my baby there; my baby was the first car I actually bought but didn't buy lol. To explain I had purchased this vehicle while I was still in Afghanistan. The car was a 2001 Blue Honda Prelude 5 speed and she was beautiful. Let me tell you the faith I have in people, the owner of the car was from Virginia after a couple weeks of back and forth talk and pictures I decided to buy the car. My mom went to bank and withdrew the money and the guy drove the car from Virginia to my house and talked to my mom for a bit parked the car and left back to Virginia with his father. I didn't know the guy from a hole in the wall and to give my mom the amount of money I did to meet a stranger well you guys get the drift you would think that's pretty shady and wouldn't trust anyone but in all honesty I asked him to give me his word the car was good and he did and he drove it all the way from Virginia and gave my mom the excess money I put there for gas and he didn't want it he was a super nice and humble guy and till this day has been one of the best vehicles I have ever purchased, well until I crashed it lol that's beside the fact lmfaooo. That night me and Adrien and a couple of friends went on a drive and just caught up it was great.

Back to good old Fort Drum I go to start this Garrison life that Orian warned me about. Before we even started training things just got really bad at the Barracks. We started losing soldiers left and right. Every day we would wake up to the Police at the Barracks, guys would be overdosing on Cocaine, K2 Spice, I believe Heroin as well it was just bad. Charlie Company was getting hit really hard. The people I knew from Charlie Company were doing fairly well but it's never ok to lose someone in your Battalion and it was just bad man. So, when we get home you believe you're coming back to your old life and many people didn't. Some guys gave their wives General Power of Attorney and they came home to an empty house with a Foreclosure Notice, the car sold their wife with another man it was all bad news and how do you handle that after being in war for a year. Then you have the guys that went home and walked in on their wife having sex with another man and there goes a double homicide, those first few months back were just not good I don't know how else to describe it without describing the scenarios and horrific images that will stain your mind but how do you deal with all that?

At this point in time my very good friend Malcolm asked me and Sawyer to help him move into his new apartment with his wife. So of course, we said yes, and we met them at the new apartment just as they parked the U-Haul. We opened up the back and he showed us the path to the apartment just simply pointing to it. Everyone grabs some furniture and Sawyer and I grabbed a couch just to get it over with quickly. As we are walking toward this path, we all see this yellow tape blocking the entrance way and as we got closer, we all noticed it was Police Caution Tape, we all set down the furniture and looked at each other. We didn't know if we were trespassing or not, but it was the only way up to the apartment. We cut the tape and headed inside, while inside it was a beautiful apartment but a weird feeling. We started noticing things like the carpet in the living room was brand new, the kitchen wall cabinet looked repainted and something was wrong in the bathroom I forgot what it was. We are all in the apartment looking at each other and we are all wondering the same thing. Sawyer and I asked Malcolm and his wife if someone died in the apartment and they said they didn't know they were never told of anything. After moving all the contents of the truck into the apartment we tried doing some research and couldn't find anything. Several weeks pass by and finally something came up that there was a homicide in the apartment complex but didn't have any more information than that nor what apartment in which the murder occurred but after the very clear evidence from day one we concurred that it was their apartment that this took place lol and it was fucking creepy lol. They moved out soon after finding out the truth. We were very happy they decided to leave the apartment lol.

    Throughout this time, I was not talking to anyone, friends, family, Amelia, nor Jaylene. I was so down about what happened, and that Jaylene cheated on me and the worst part about the whole situation was that she was pregnant with the guys kid. I was so hurt man and I just didn't know what to do or how to feel so I just stopped talking to everyone and bought another car and started street racing. I bought a K20 EK Hatch, which translates to a 1998 Honda Civic Hatchback with a 2004 Acura RSX 2.0 Liter Engine. The car made 222-wheel horsepower and 180 pounds per foot of torque. For my non- automotive readers this means the car is pretty fast for what it is. Mainly on

Friday nights I would go out and just take a drive it didn't really matter where I had no purpose but to drive the car and test its abilities. One Friday night I made my way to downtown Baytown and found a group of cars hanging out at Audio City and that was the beginning of the crew's friendship. It was a lot of us, Jake, Baron, Jaron, Dontae, Rhoderick, man it was a lot of people we were maybe 10 to 15 cars. That is aside from when we would hang out with the Subaru Crew and when we would go on a car cruise it would be anywhere from 20 to 35 cars it was a lot man a lot it was a good family they were all good people in there and the couple that started the Group which were Cara and Brent such wonderful people. I appreciate them so much they genuinely care about people in general not just soldiers. During the holidays they host parties at their house for anyone who doesn't have family or for those who aren't able to go see their family for the holidays and they take it out of their own pocket, but you know we chip in we don't allow them to pay for it all but they cover everything up front by themselves just for us just amazing people with huge hearts I love being around them it is always smiles and to be lucky enough to be surrounded by genuine people like that is a reason why I am the way I am and why I have so much faith in humanity.

During my time with the EK Civic, I honestly didn't know how to race very well but it didn't matter because the car was so fast. In the racing community its known as you either have a fast car or you are a fast driver and I was not the latter. What did I do at first, I jumped in Baron's car he had a Honda S2000 and we would go out driving and I would watch what he did, how he shifted, why he shifted at certain RPMs or Revolutions Per Minute. I would learn everything I could then I would let him drive my car because it is very well known in the community if you want to see the potential of your car you let someone else drive it. He made me realize how fast that car actually was, because there is a difference in the potential of a car and what the car is actually capable of. I know that sounds stupid because you can reach the potential of a car by seeing what its capable of but with cars it's not. The car was capable of running the quarter mile in 12 seconds that is what the previous owner did, but the cars potential is much more than that. The car was capable of running the quarter mile in 11.5 seconds with race gas and the way the car was set up I was able to take corners at pretty high speeds but the previous owner never drove the car around corners he only drove it straight down the track and that was the difference. From being in cars and watching how Baron, Dontae, Adrien, Eugene and everyone that I knew who were exceptional drivers I took everything I learned from them and added my own techniques and we did fairly well we only lost 2 races. I lost to a Pontiac G8 and to Jake with his DSM AWD Talon. That night I cried myself to sleep lol Jake was a phenomenal driver and he knew every inch of his car and what his car had to offer. He brake boosted during the race and I lost by like 3 car lengths I won't explain that race because I don't know how many of you will understand it but Jake amazed me one of the best races I had till this day but I don't race anymore. I also feel I may be boring you with all this car talk so I will get back to the story in a bit.

Now being back at Fort Drum and training we started to get an influx of new guys I will not name them all I just won't its way too many. To name a few we had Eshawn, Lex, Prescott, Bartell, Cordell, Jerrick, Hansel, Big Country Curtis, and Old Country Curtis, and I forgot to mention previously good old Sgt Walton. Sgt Walton came to us in Afghanistan like a month before we came back home. Dude was a stud he had his Ranger tab, Sniper tab, Airborne, Air Assault, and not to mention I think he was just like fucking 22 years old. Guy was great he said "yo Rod, I'm a get a tattoo on the back of my left arm and it's going to say Wal-Da-Beast" lmfaoooooo. He was a great leader I miss him he is still in and doing very well but he is in a special unit now not doing dumb regular Army stuff he is where he should be. These guys were pretty much the guys I hung out with throughout the remaining years of my contract after I stopped racing which was around the time they came. What happened was 5 of us decided to go out and take a drive so it was Whitcomb, Baron, Hugo, Cortez and I. Whitcomb drove a Blue RX-8, Hugo drove a Blue Mini Cooper with Rota rims on it, Baron had the S2000, Cortez had a 2.5 liter turbo STI. We were taking a ride to St. Lawrence Harbor I believe and once we got to Route I81 South we were just speeding and I couldn't tell you how fast were going but at the time I looked down I was going 120mph and I was the third vehicle. We turned up on Exit 47 and took Route 12 and as we were driving someone caught wind that a State Trooper was following us and as we all do since we are men we all pulled over in this small lot and the Trooper followed us in and guess what happened, fucking Hugo decided he didn't want to get pulled over with us and left the lot and the Trooper called it in. He came out of his vehicle chewing us out. He told us that he got reports of cars speeding down the highway swerving in and out of traffic and the whole nine. He told us that if we wanted to go out and race to go do it in the back roads where there are no people around and when we crashed, he wouldn't mind scraping us up from the asphalt. Then proceeded to say that he was going to lock us all up and crush all our cars if he had the resources, but he was busy getting somewhere I forgot if he had a call or something. Then he let us go and well the man was completely right what can I say. We were acting like a bunch of idiots we weren't really swerving in and out of traffic we passed maybe 10 cars it was only 1 exit from 48 to 47 and on a Sunday but you know we got it and at the end of the day he was right. So, I stopped all the dumb shit and pretty much cut racing from there I mean every now and then when we went to Alexandria Bay, we would speed a bit and have fun but nothing to the extent of what we used to do. It was fun while it lasted though and the thing about that whole situation was that Whitcomb, was a Lieutenant. If we would have been arrested well there goes his job for street racing and fraternizing with lower enlisted personnel he would have had it the worst so he would only hang out with us in the parking lot when he came to visit the barracks for work or at the end of the day formations because we all knew we all fucked up lol and we didn't want him getting in trouble for us either. I told Baron and Dontae to keep Hugo away from me because I wanted to beat his face in for leaving us like the little bitch he did when the cops came. Anytime one of us gets pulled over we all stop nobody has ever ran we know what we were doing, and we accept the consequences as they come if they come so I made sure Hugo stayed as far away from me as possible. Later on, time passed, and we threw it behind us but never again trusted him to go out and ride with us, but he was a very cool guy aside from being a bitch when cops are around, and we still talk every now and then.

So before continuing to training and everything else I have to tell you this funny story because till this day it is just hilarious. Well it may not be funny, but it was fucking scary funny. Since this time everyone and their families are stabilizing back in Fort Drum and I am just pretty much alone not talking to anyone, and in all honesty I leave my phone in my room because I don't talk to anyone or have a girl my phone probably went a good 4 – 5 maybe pushing 6 months without a call or a text I am telling you man lonely nights but I spent most nights with my people from the platoon. Orian was at the barracks one day and we decided to go to the main PX which stands for Personal Exchange sort of like a Walmart but for the base. After we buy what we have to for the upcoming training program they will lay out for us, we start walking to the food court. Sooooo there was this girl right lol, and she was beautiful and so I said "Orian she's beautiful" he replied "yea she is bro." I wasn't going to go talk to her I just simply thought she was beautiful, and I wasn't really over Jaylene. We left and several weeks later we had an FRG or Family Readiness Group meeting at the Command Post (CP). The FRG meetings is where all the soldiers bring their families to work and our supervisors and bosses talk to them about up and coming training events, times, dates, and how it will effect time with the family which none of this matters to us single folk but we are required to go. When you enter the CP there are 3 rows of lockers immediately in front of you and two stair cases one to the left and one to the right leading to a balcony where we host classes and I won't go into more detail than that but the door is in the center of the room. Orian and I are coming from the back of the CP and our lockers at the time were located in the front row. After fixing some things we were making our way to the front door when, I saw this girl walking up the flight of steps to the left and Orian said "what's wrong bro." I simply stared at her and tapped hit him in the stomach and said "bro" and he looked up and saw her and said "bro" I said "bro" at this time she hugged her husband and Orian said "bro" and we said "brooooooo" then looked at each other and said "we never speak about this to anyone ever" and he said "no one ever finds out about this." That has been our secret for eternity lol it was bad, then I found out since no one ever told me. If you see a woman anywhere on a military base do not even look at her because she is married even if you want to help her because I have given women rides that I see walking across base because I used to feel bad but after that incident fuck that I won't be getting written up or nothing anytime a woman comes by my eyes went straight to the floor lmfaoooo.

Around this time, Jaylene had contacted me and apologized for what happened. So, I had asked her if everything was ok and well, she lost the baby. We started talking again but just stayed in contact and the issue was the love man. As fucked up as the entire situation was, I don't know man I really don't. She just genuinely cared about me and the love was there and we had a strong bond and I completely understood what happened and part of it was my fault, not taking away from the fact that it was her decision to cheat that is not what I am saying I am saying I know what she was going through and she truly needed me and I wasn't there for her. So her feeling of abandonment, loneliness, depression, was part my fault and all awhile she is there being strong for me and supporting me knowing I can't offer her the same thing in return for the moment I appreciated her presence that was my baby and you know till this day till this very day she is the only one who would ask me before we started talking everyday if I was ok mentally and physically. Like I miss her I truly do and she had a love for me that will never be imitated which is ok and I never take it or have taken it for granted and that is why I hold on to her so tight and so close to my heart despite everything that happened because she did genuinely and whole heartedly love me and that went without saying and it wasn't to be questioned. At times I feel as though I do have the right to miss her in which I do very much. That's why I will never release our conversations they were very special to me, just her choice of words the sincerity in her voice the love that was emitted you know you could feel it that heartfelt soul binding love, didn't matter the distance and I just miss her man I do very much so.

To reintroduce Amelia, she was a part of this family and household of many siblings. We were great friends; we had a good connection and she would talk to me about her issues and things of that manner and she had also lost a child with her ex. I wasn't very fond of him and what she told me about him and his personality and how he treated her, in which I had told her to take it slow with him but with the pregnancy and all what can you do. At the time I believe he saw me as a threat to their relationship which I wasn't, but any who he like every guy does back in the day called me and threatened me but hey cool I get it I just told him to fuck off anyway. After everything was said and done, he had already cheated on Amelia prior to him even knowing me and her were friends but of course I was the threat. They had parted ways and Amelia and I stayed in contact for a while then didn't speak for a period of time. I guess this may be a weird time to discuss this but since we are on the topic, I may dive into it. I am not sure how this will play out or fit here but I don't know it seems right so let's talk about it. Give me a minute because I have to think about how to word this, so you understand what I am telling you. So I just spent 30 minutes literally thinking about how to say this and I can't find a way to say it really, and I don't want people to find this as a way to cheat or anything because we haven't spoken about companionships versus a relationship and monogamy yet in-depth so I don't really know how to dive into this so bear with me. For a quick definition before you guys get to the discussion board after the story finishes let me explain a companionship and relationship. A companionship brings the center of focus and attention at depression, sex, loneliness, and voids. People often confuse this with a relationship due to the fact that they just want to find someone to fill a certain need or they feel as though they have been single for a certain amount of time or they feel so lonely they need to deflect their pain and suffering and the best way to do that is to be in what you the average person would call a relationship. When one or the other gets tired of being involved, they either find another person and cheat or simply break up because there is nothing left, or they cannot get anything out of said "relationship." There are no feelings, or they lost love or have no interest in the other person. I hope I didn't lose you there, so now in a relationship, the center of focus is growing together learning from each other being able to communicate as adults creating a foundation and an environment where positivity flourishes where mistakes are made and are taken as an opportunity to learn effective ways to assess a situation and understand your significant others thought process and why they made the decision they did. It does not always lead to marriage and it does not always lead to love and it does not always end well but as adults in a relationship sometimes life has its way and things do not work out but there will always be a line of communication because of how you both grew and learned from one another and the bond and trust will always be there.

Now with this information I have vested in you, we can discuss some things. When women come to me with their issues and concerns about a relationship, we talk about it. When they tell me certain things about this guy they are into and all a while she is talking I am thinking red flags several times so I openly tell them exactly the problem with said guy and if she gets into a relationship with him how it will go and how it will end. To say the least, it usually goes as I said but when a woman has been feeling alone, insecure, etc., and a man comes into her life and gives her attention they can't see past the attention. Attention is like the primary wall or boundary for a guy make his move and it's so simple to see past and view his agenda but I won't be getting into all that, anyway she will create all these excuses for him and void everything that I said about him because this is the first time in x amount of years that she has had this feeling of being wanted and that feeling of being loved and wanted opens doors for manipulation because now the guy is in her head. This guy that she is starting to speak so highly of does not want her he simply wants to use her for sex correct. Now as this companionship begins the guy starts to feel threatened about every guy that is her friend, so the controlling begins. You're not allowed to talk to any guy but me, I am your man, but on the flip side he has several female friends but they are not friends they are friends with benefits and he won't tell them he is in a "relationship" because then he would lose them so when his girlfriend doesn't want to have sex where does he go? Do I have to spell that out for you? Any who it is simple because now he has her manipulated she is giving him excuses already and he will not post any information about him being in a relationship and she is curious to know as to why and the response is "I like to keep my relationships private because when people get involved then arguments start." I am not sure if this is sounding familiar or not but I really don't care, next she receives a text message from a guy, old friend and her boyfriend is upset that she is getting texts from some random guy he doesn't know and why is she getting texts from a guy when she is in a relationship.

So why is this a major problem? Because her boyfriend knows what guys intentions are with a woman because of his intentions with her. Get it? He had no intention on actually being in a relationship with her, he just simply wanted to sleep with her, but the sex was good and consistent i.e. one of the main reasons for a companionship, so he decided to keep her around. So the consistent pattern is that he is a dick head and treats her bad but he knows she will not leave him because every now and then he makes sure to treat her right and buy her flowers every once in a while and that is to show her that he has some type of potential to be good and thus gets all the sex he wants all a meanwhile he is sleeping around with several women.

That is why he or men in general or the average man tries to control his woman and not allow her to have any male friends because on the foundation of the reason he wanted to be with her he understands that the average guy will try to sleep with his girl and he knows how men's minds work. This entire time she sees his potential because he gives her flowers and treats her right once in a while but as long as he keeps doing it once in a while she will continue to believe in his potential to be a good man and continue to give him sex and continue to be by his side and avoid all men in her life to make her cheating boyfriend feel secure. Got it? I believe that was pretty concise and frank lol maybe not I don't know nor care lol. We will discuss this more in-depth after the story finishes so a few more chapters but many more pages to go.

Some time went by and I honestly just I don't know I guess I was feeling lonely and didn't have anyone to talk to and simply called Amelia out of the blue and I didn't even know if that was her number anymore or anything and well she picked up and hung up right away it was the weirdest thing lmfaoo. So, I called back and we started talking and stayed talking for hours honestly just like picked up where we left off like nothing ever happened and that was pretty much how we started our relationship. This is a good time for some important information which I don't want to release but it is important to the story. Well Amelia such a beautiful woman, well spoken, great sense of humor, very, very genuine, and ummmm well she had breast cancer. We will pause the story for a moment. My brother just called, and he isn't doing so well.

This time of year, the Thanksgiving and Christmas time isn't a very good time for the platoon and I. We lost a couple good men and it was very rough to deal with. I can't say it was everyone's fault, but we all do feel like we all could have done something to help and maybe we could maybe we couldn't, but we will never know, and we lost really, really good friends. At this time when I receive phone calls like this and my brothers are so far away, I feel as if my hands are tied. I can't go and see them or spend time with them, it is a completely different scenario when someone admits to you they are having suicidal thoughts over the phone and actually being there physically next to them and they admit it I can't go in too depth into it because I have to finish this chapter but I will in the discussions I promise. When things like this occur and I am not able to be there physically, the best thing I can do is call as many people as I can and get them to call and check up on a brother who has been having thoughts. The more people that call the more the person feels wanted the less of a chance anything will actually manifest. In all honesty I can say with assurance that nothing will manifest from my brother he is a very strong guy mentally just this time of the year is rough on us and he doesn't really know how to ask for help so he calls me first then I start making phone calls and I have to call on a few people for this and we all come together and help out but the lurking emotion of loneliness will always hover because even though he may feel more wanted and loved after everyone checks up on him, at night when there's no one around he is left with his thoughts and no one is there to just give him a hug and tell him everything will be ok and that's a huge issue with isolation, depression, and suicide and its rough from 3 thousand miles away we are all in different states and trying to uphold and care for one another is very difficult from a distance you can only do so much.

Let me explain how my day goes, I managed to get out of work early great. In my mind going home I think to myself well I have so much extra time I am actually able to write today that's pretty good motivation for me. I get home I start cleaning a bit and my uncle comes downstairs and asks for matches to smoke his cigar ok cool. An hour later nowhere near done cleaning and I hear a knock then my uncle yells my name, so I knew it was sort of serious I open the door and he said he lost vision in his eye. He looked bad so I took his glucose level and whatever not important I take him to the hospital, and he had a stroke. At first thought it didn't appear as a stroke so I threw it out the window because he went up and down the flight of stairs 3 times to get his meds and identification cards to go to the hospital and he was perfectly fine, I mean a bit of unsteady gait but still had his strength and cognitive ability but it turned out to be a stroke after all the CAT scans confirmed it.

None of that information is important to you guys but I say that because as I said previously like I just feel like I can't take a day off because, I don't know man I really don't. I am just tired and its not to say it's my uncles fault but you guys have no idea how I have been there for him making sure he's taking the meds and when I check the meds are nowhere to be found and he's not taking them it's like only so much I can do and I am tired yall. Like I just want to take off for a while and focus on building a family and my career but as selfish as that seems like I don't want anyone to pass away because they needed me and I wasn't there because I was out focusing on myself. I know what you guys are thinking and what you guys are going to say and just please don't say it or think it we live two completely separate lives and the situations that happen to me on a day to day basis are situations that you will never encounter and I hope that you never have to deal with. I just don't even want to discuss this anymore I am going to get back to the story.

Back to Amelia I first met her in late 2009 an amazing woman. She was very beautiful, just like any woman she disliked some of her features. In her family pictures she was the one with the most weight, but she wasn't fat nor chubby nor anything like you would think when I say she had weight on her. She was just shaped she was beautiful with curves, but the way she grew up and the people she grew up around were relatively thin and from what she would tell me when she would go out with friends guys would approach her but not many like her friends would be approached.

So, question, have you ever met a woman who was so beautiful she resented it? She was so beautiful that her beauty made her insecure. Due to the fact, that in her life it came to a point in time where she would never be approached. She ended up resenting her beauty and the feeling of loneliness would envelope her and the thoughts would come that maybe just maybe if she wasn't that pretty she wouldn't be lonely, or for the simple fact of never being approached she didn't realize that she was beautiful and she would be easily manipulated by men that knew how to use women or the woman would fall in to a circle of mal habits and become bulimic or anorexic because she thought maybe if she was as skinny as her friends she would be approached more and this toxic unhealthy habit forms and this is what our society does to our women.

Then again you would never know if you never have actually spoken to these women or actually had a conversation because the underlying factor being people placing stigma on her because of her beauty. Because you're so insecure about yourself you relay that off of other people believing oh she is beautiful she probably is stuck up, or she is out of my league well my prideful friend you will never know because of your biased insecure selves will never allow yourself to see outside of your own prejudices. I understand that everyone wants to have sex

I understand that we love sex, but it is ok for a point in time to have a stimulating conversation with each other and truly find out what one another is about and what's important to them. I am not saying you have to fix everyone's issues like I do. All I am saying is that it is ok to have friends of the opposite sex, it is ok to have day to day interactions with people you don't know. Trust me you will learn and grow from hearing out other people's opinions and points of views. Maybe that woman who was too beautiful for you and out of your league had the same interests as you and maybe the connection was instantaneous but you will never know because you allow your pride and biased opinions get in the way and for that we have welcomed norms that should have never been allowed. We have lost a great many women to it and me personally have lost many women to it and all I want is for us to simply work together plain and simple. We can do very well for ourselves if you would just put the thought(s) of sex aside for one weekend trust me I been without it for 28 years you won't die lol but you can learn a lot from the other sex if you put your agendas to the side for a moment, one day, one weekend will not kill you. Go out and simply just socialize, get people's opinions and views that are different from your own you will mature as an individual that is guaranteed I promise.

For the women let me explain something here, all you ladies going through this and not in detail because I won't let all the secrets out but, I know you. I know you are beautiful even if you do not think it. You may have a bit of weight on you, you may have a lot of weight on you. You may want to lose all that weight because you truly believe that you are fat or obese and you want to feel beautiful, you may want to hear that guy you have a crush on tell you that you lost weight because if he tells you that you lost weight then it's not the weight loss it is the fact that he actually noticed you and that attention that addictive drug of attention will have you so encompassed in meeting your goal of losing weight that you will continue to do it until he asks you out. When he does and just uses you for your body and now you are left broken and depressed because you thought he would actually like you and stay with you just know I am here for you the words in this book will help you too but understand that when you decide to begin that weight loss journey it is for the betterment of your own health and life. Never do that for a person ever. I know you women very, very well I have been doing this for a very long time and I want you to understand even though you don't talk about it maybe you don't know how to articulate it but I know the pain you hide inside I know that even though you may lose the weight, you don't lose the insecurities. So, stay mentally strong yall and do what you believe is best to better yourself in your life and to be able to grow as a person. I love you all too.

At this point in time in the military training started up and the days were going by quick. We would spend weeks out at a time, and it would get to a point where the wives would go out and complain. We just recently returned a few months ago and weren't able to leave due to being a part of the GRF and now it is nonstop training so all throughout the year families literally spent maybe 2 to 3 months together out of the year. It didn't really bother me too much I didn't really have anyone other than Amelia and Jaylene and I were still in contact but even at that being out for 6 days out of the week there wasn't very much communication honestly. What actually happened was that pretty much First Sergeant Idiot didn't like being home too often and Captain America wanted a nice Officer Evaluation Report so they would put us up for every task or detail that came down from command it was very annoying and on top of that we had a drug test almost weekly for several months and a physical fitness test every few weeks. That unit became a horrible environment to work in real fast with those leaders.

We were getting new guys on the left and on the right the old guys were ending their contracts with the military and going home. It was difficult to maintain order at times even though for the most part we were adults and we wouldn't get in trouble, but the other units would ruin it for us with the DUIs and drug paraphernalia. It was a real headache, and if you ask anyone of my brothers, they will tell you they only saw me drink twice in all my years of being in the military. If you ask them what I would do on my spare time, they would tell you literally I would go to sleep. I would stay away from anything that I believed could bring me trouble. I would literally after work go and wash my clothes and go to sleep especially if Amelia was mad and didn't want to talk to me, I would just sleep.

Towards the end of the year we got this new kid his name was Miko. Real good kid man great attitude, work ethic, respectful, and funny as hell. Dude was really strong just and ran like the wind. He was added to our platoon and he fit right in but he was young so he couldn't really go out and drink with the platoon but he was so cool everyone adjusted to him they would just stay in the barracks and Big Country Curtis would bring his guitar out and play and Walther would come out of his room with a beer in his hand and yell FUCK CQ, then all of a sudden everyone that was in the barracks would open their doors and yell down the hall way FUCK CQ it was such sight to see and music to the ears lol. For those of you that don't know what CQ is, it is the soldiers on 24- hour desk duty to make sure the barracks are safe and clean pretty much the barracks security guards.

One weekend the guys decide to go and hang out and go bowling so yea they ask me to go and why not what's the worst that can happen out there. We go bowling we are having a good time and Roy good old Roy and Eshawn are getting beer and Jerrick goes to find them. When Jerrick doesn't come back I go to look for them and well as I am walking into the bar area Jerrick is in front of me and all we see is a chair flying across the room and in my head I am thinking "welp yea this is the reason I don't go out lol." Some guy called Eshawn a bitch and we in the platoon don't use nor appreciate the B word and Eshawn is the wrong person to say that to because that is instant retaliation but hey as men sometimes you need to punch people in the face to make them understand that no its not ok to talk shit to people you don't know drunk or not you will get beat the fuck up. At this point Cordell, Roy, Eshawn and Jerrick are in a brawl can't really tell who is trying to stop the fight or who is trying to stomp this guy out, so I go get the other guys we pay and leave and in that the cops weren't called and we pretty much never went back, well for a while lol.

    I just realized I am not allowed to talk about our training lol which pretty much sucks, but it'll help the chapter go by faster. So, from time to time Amelia does this thing where she just completely stops talking to me. Time would go by and I wouldn't really hear from her and I would just hope she would be ok. Throughout my time in the barracks I only had a roommate for probably 4 to 5 months out of 2 years total. It got pretty lonely, so my first roommate was Deegan but after Afghanistan he left and finished his contract fairly quickly. The time he left was roughly around the same time Amelia disappeared. It sucked honestly because it was just like fuck, I didn't know what to do or what to think. We weren't really on bad terms or anything, but she would just not answer phone calls, texts, or direct messages. It wasn't like I would send 30 or 40 messages like you people do which is nuts to me but I would just send texts like the good morning or good night, and several times throughout the week I would message her or call her just to check up and make sure she is still alive and I wouldn't get an answer. I really couldn't tell why I was so loyal and the thing about this is that sometimes it would just be days, sometimes weeks, sometimes months would go by and I wouldn't hear from her it was more worrisome than anything. She really didn't have a very good past and with her current health issues my heart ached man.

    There would be times when I knew she would just ignore me because she would just start up a Facebook account or Instagram or just completely ignore or delete my comments on her Instagram or twitter. Well come to find out there was a new guy in her life or another guy in her life. To give benefit of the doubt I asked about him importantly his name was Marcel but known as Marcellus, and she said he was her friend, best friend, more so over a brother. Which ok cool, but as time passed the more, I could clearly see that there was more to that friendship. When I confronted her about it, she denied it so vehemently. Now I don't really want to get into all the details of this situation because it is several tens of thousands upon thousands of texts, Facebook messages, Instagram messages, and twitter posts and I will not go through it so I will try and make this as concise as possible. When conversations arise about certain issues in relationships I have no problem discussing the issues Amelia and I had but in all honesty to lay out this relationship message by message in chronological order, I would have to write another book simply on what happened in these few years between her and I and I will not do that it is not that important.

It came to a point in time where Amelia just had so much hate in her blood for me and I didn't ever understand why. At this point in the relationship she would just ignore me when she felt mad at me and that could be any time throughout the day or week. She would just wake up hating me or curse me out I never understood it. She had started a Forums Spring account or the questionnaire website. People would just ask her random questions and when she felt like answering it, she would. The issue with this was that there would be times I would be trying to talk to her and see how she was doing and feeling and see if she was ok and she would ignore me. Simultaneously she would be on the website answering questions and just completely ignoring me. To test it I would ask a random question and she would simply answer it but ignore my texts. So cool if this is what we are doing I will ask all the questions I need to confirm my suspicions. This whole question thing was done anonymously, and it got to the point where someone asked her like what one thing is, she needs to have to be able to sleep at night, and her response was her stuffed animal which she named Marcelly. That was very important, to you guys that would confirm that she is cheating on me. The way I know people that stuffed animal isn't a stuffed animal. That stuffed animal is a resemblance of their relationship, that stuffed animal simply put if she can't sleep without it is because she feels protected by it because there was a situation that happened and he protected her from it and that is why her love for him is so strong, whatever happened between them sparked a bond that wasn't going to be easily broken.

Now things are coming into fruition, another question was asked because she had placed this note on her Twitter and all it said was 4 letters. I had already known what it meant when I saw it, so I asked her about it when I noticed it and she lied to me about it. On this questionnaire website someone had the same thought process as me and wanted to know what it meant and asked her, and she told them what it stood for and it was what I had thought it stood for. She didn't just lie to me, but the truth was there, and she laid it out for whoever asked. I didn't really know what to do this girl was simply amazing, but she turned into such a spiteful woman and the only thing that changed throughout the years was that this guy Marcellus came into her life other than that there was nothing absolutely nothing. The worst part about this whole situation was that I wasn't the only one who noticed the negative change. How she would talk to people and just overreact so fast it wasn't that sweet wholesome woman I met at first, I couldn't tell you who she was, but I knew that she was my woman and I had to fight for her.

Now I am seeing how much this man means to her and I have to find a way to get my woman back. I begin to see this pattern, at one point during the whole random question website, someone asks something on the lines of who is your baby and at the end of the sentence leaves 5 periods. She answers the question saying only you 5 periods, so to put this into perspective maybe some of you have done this maybe some of you haven't. In high school mainly so take that mainly lightly please, when you were talking with someone or flirting with someone or having sex with someone and didn't want people to know you guys came up with your own secret code. Sort of like inside jokes and you only you and the other person would know what you're talking about, and everyone else around would be thinking I never seen them two together or even talking so how all of a sudden do they have inside jokes and are laughing almost themselves and its real cute right. Well that is what this was, and I really could articulate that much better I just don't really feel like it right now just too much typing and I still have like 4 chapters left. Any who on her twitter she would put things like I love you and 5 periods after so I would put, I love you too baby but then she would delete it and it would annoy me. So, Marcellus never had that he was in a relationship the only thing that corresponded and connected them was the 5 periods and their names. So, her Instagram name was, well it's all deactivated but I won't actually give it out that's a bit crazy lol let's say her Instagram name was queen-grumpy-pants his was king-grumpy-pants. They would never say they were exclusive or anything to that manner but it was clear they were.

Amelia was just a completely different person now, and at this point it was hard just even trying to get her attention. In all honesty the only time she would pick up the phone and it was just so sad man. She would pick up the phone so disoriented and I think she only picked up the phone because she couldn't read who was calling her because if she knew it was me she wouldn't have answered but after her chemo treatments when she was so drained and out of energy she would pick up and her voice she just sounded so bad and it killed me inside that I couldn't do anything to actually help. She just sounded so weak, her voice would crack and it was the saddest thing ever man and I would pray for her I would pray for her everyday even till this day aside from how shitty she treated me aside from the lying and cheating

I just wished that she was physically well and she wasn't she wasn't doing so good man. I honestly don't even want to discuss this anymore I might just expedite this chapter.

Summer leave was coming and decided to catch a flight to LA to go and see her. At this point and time Jaylene and I were still in contact, she was just great to talk to and I still love her always did always will. So, my dumbass got on the plane and flew to LAX, man was I stupid lol. It was 3 in the morning and every fucking hotel on Century Boulevard was booked and had no vacancy. When I booked the ticket, I didn't think about a hotel lol I was so excited to just go to California. I ended up walking all night and finally found this small hotel called the Tivoli on West Century Boulevard. I booked it for a week, and that's where I was. In the morning I would wake up at 7 go out for a run shower eat then hit up Amelia. The first day she ignored me, so what did I do, well what the fuck I was in Cali man super stoked lol I was like a real tourist lmfaoooo it was great. I fucking went to In and Out Burger and it was as amazing as they said but the fries were absolute garbage lmfaoo. I would recommend it any day though the burger was fucking great. I simply just ventured out on my own, I didn't know anyone within a 3-thousand-mile radius but fuck it I had fun I just made sure to be back at the hotel by 8 at night. So, day 2 comes I go out for my run and the people were great they all waved and said hi super nice man, then I would go back to the hotel shower and hit up Amelia and no reply. I felt like venturing out more, so I google the nearest beach and it was Marina Del Rey and welp I walked my happy ass over there but man oh man was that shit far as fuck from the Hotel I think I walked 8 miles just one way up and down hills too I was freaking beat man. Let me tell you guys something though as I was walking up this big ass mother fucking hill, I got to the top and it was beautiful. It was on West Manchester at the peak of the hill I took a photo and it's still one of the most beautiful photos I have ever taken and to just be a top of that hill overlooking the Pacific I know why people love Cali the feeling was amazing. I walked down and I walked the path back and forth seeing the community just people watching seeing how everyone interacts and it is completely different from the East Coast. The conversations, the slang and vocabulary, the diversity of sports and people it was a good thing to see and absorb. Afterwards I walked to the water and just sat there all day it was so calming and relaxing and I didn't bring a beach towel or hat or anything just sat in the sand took off my shoes and socks and shirt and just sat there probably one of the most peaceful moments I ever had in life I will never regret it and I am forever grateful to have been able to have the purchasing power to simply just buy a ticket and fly somewhere and experience a new surrounding it meant a lot to me honestly. I am forever grateful for being as healthy as I am and being able to do whatever I want when I want to live a life so free it's a good feeling honestly.

Night falls and it's time to get back I have a lot of ground to cover before getting back to the hotel. I finally make it back I shower and go get some Del Taco across the street and it was amazing lol. Day 3 comes, and I do my morning run routine, get back shower hit her up, nothing again, then I go out. After everything is said and done, I wanted to venture out and more and further I was addicted to Cali I love that place that's where my soul lies. I couldn't possibly tell you how I managed to come across this lol, but somehow, I ran into a city bus terminal across the street from LAX and thus my adventures began. I went to Santa Monica first and it was beautiful. I fell in Love with Santa Monica I would love to purchase a house there and live there. I just did the tourist thing did a walk by, then went to 3rd Street Promenade it was great like an outdoor mall lol. This guy had his Monkey out doing backflips it was great I probably stayed there longer than I should have lol, but the Monkey was so cool. I walked the Boardwalk till the end and just relaxed sitting on the bench over watching the ocean it was pretty nice and calm there I loved it. It started to get dark and the last bus to LAX was almost arriving, so I had to make it to the bus stop fairly quickly I just didn't feel like walking that far back to the hotel that night especially not knowing anyone it sucked. I finally got back to the hotel showered and went to go eat at El Pollo Loco across the street that place was awesome too, then just watched movies until I fell asleep.

On Day 4 after my morning routine I messaged Amelia and went to go shower. As I was getting dressed a message popped up and upon my surprise it was her, I was so excited. It didn't go as expected. She gave me the run around and then told me she didn't know where I was and this and that and they were clear excuses, she didn't want to see me, I mean she had an I phone which come with Apple Maps but it was just clear she didn't want to see me so I just packed up and headed to the Hollywood Walk of fame and boy did I get off at the wrong bus stop lmfao. I know I fast forwarded that last part which is actually really important to the story as we come the end of our relationship later on but it just put me in a really sad state because you people will never know the depths I have gone for women and its not to be discussed but fuck man you guys really don't appreciate shit but at this point in my life I am past it so there is no need to discuss it because you guys will just simply think I am lying if I tell you what I have done for women and you guys will believe that there are not people like me that actually walk the Earth that do things like what I have done and never ask for anything in return or never had an agenda behind helping others than to see the person better themselves and to see them happy so I am not discussing any of it but this I can because she was my girl at the time and I flew 3 thousand miles to see her and it was apparent she ignored me and just didn't want to see me so I will never do it again. Any who back to the story, I got off at the wrong bus stop and I found myself walking on Melrose Ave I felt like Bobby Valentino but when I was walking down Melrose there were absolutely no women there that I could tell to slow down lol that's a great joke if anyone gets it lol.

I ended up passing Paramount Studio it was so nice I took a picture of it; you guys don't even know how lost I was lol. I kept on walking because I had the whole day, I also passed Raleigh Studios then somehow managed to walk into Santa Monica Boulevard and was so confused lol I was like isn't Santa Monica the complete opposite way from me why is the Boulevard all the way out here lol I was just hoping I was going in the right direction and try and remember where I got off on the bus but I kept that as a mental note and kept walking. I passed by Sunset Avenue or Boulevard or whichever one it was and just kept on walking. I got tired then stopped at a place to eat I couldn't tell you where I forgot. After eating I guess I was better lol and I saw the Hollywood sign lol I was so excited like a real tourist out there lmfaooo. I started walking towards it and ended up on the walk of fame I think or whatever lol it was Hollywood Boulevard, I was walking and saw everyone's name in the stars it was pretty cool not what I expected though, I guess because I don't really care about any of that stuff but it was definitely nice to see it and experience it. So I walked the complete opposite way and found myself at (and I don't want to sound disrespectful) but it was like this big Asian restaurant, well I am unsure what it was I didn't go inside but it looked like Rush Hour was filmed there and I couldn't tell you if that was true but for graphic purposes I think you can get the picture. I couldn't get to the Hollywood Sign, I was trying to and it was getting dark fast and I had to walk all the way back to that bus stop for my bus so I took a picture from this 7 Eleven that was nearby and the picture came out atrocious lmfaooo I was like damn I have to come back and try to get closer. On the way back to my bus stop I found this cool Guitar store and I was talking to the owner and he gave me a Guitar Pic for Big Country Curtis it was a great souvenir I hope he still has it actually. Then I made my way back to my bus stop just thinking ok I passed Sunset, where's next, oh yea Santa Monica I don't know why they named this one Santa Monica, that shit is far from here, or maybe this reaches actual Santa Monica, hmm I could walk it but nah its getting late, oh look Melrose lol and that's how I found my bus stop lol judge all you want but it worked lol.

I finally got back to LAX and walked back to the hotel. I took a shower and headed to Del Taco, fucking love that place. So, as I am cursing down the street in my 64 lol it was an appropriate time to say that since I am in the California part of the story lol. I am crossing the street and I see this Caravan and there are 6 people around the hood of the van but as I get closer I am able to see who they are and I am thinking, oh this is great, it was a swat team preparing for their mission and planning their entrance into a house. They had the whole blueprint of the house on the hood of the car lol. As I was walking to Del Taco I said be safe guys and they all looked at me with their angry faces like I'ma fuck you up and all I wanted to do was join them and help on their mission, man they picked up and got in the van so fast and left for mission lol I felt sad I couldn't go out with them I would have been great help honestly. Safe to say I got my Del Taco and went to my room and fell asleep.

As day 5 came I felt that I could venture out into LA the city more in depth. So, I found a bus route and went on my merry way after my morning run. I didn't know where I was, all I knew was that the Summer X Games were in town and I tried to go see it and got completely lost. As I was walking what it seemed to be Central LA, I couldn't be exact I don't remember any landmarks, I mean I could go find the bus routes and tell you exactly, but I don't really think that's important. It was just a nice experience, completely different from NY, NJ, PA, CT, and that whole metropolitan area of the East Coast. People on the bus were just working from their laptops, the conversations were interesting there was a lot of socializing going on which is the part of Public Transportation that I love. At this point I decided to just get off the bus and walk around. I found myself by this massive building and there was this little trolley I don't really know how to explain it, I guess it would be more of a Cable Car like the ones in San Francisco. So, this Cable Car I bumped into would take people directly to the building it was like mind blowing for me I have never seen something like it, it was pretty cool. I decided to keep walking and I passed this overhead and as I walked over the bridge it led me to the roof of a building and I know this sounds so weird because the whole thing was weird to me too. To try and explain it better the bridge continued to go on for traffic but the sidewalk curved to the left into a building and it was pretty much like the roof and I was worried I was going to get caught up in a trespassing violation but didn't really care because it was worth the experience. I found an exit and went through and all of a sudden, I found myself on another bridge a really long bridge that connected these two buildings and the bridge was pretty high and I was by myself walking into this unknown building.

The building I was walking into was a massive structure, it had to be well over 20 floors. The beauty of the building was that it had 5 sections that connected to the center part of the building. As I walked to the door because it wasn't an entrance of the building, it was more of an exit, I was just hoping that the door was opened. I got to the door and opened it and was very relieved. Now once in the building as I looked around for and exit, I had to admire it, it was beautiful. The 5 buildings surrounding it were connected to the center by a main elevator and walkway. The elevator was the center of all the buildings and sort of a spiraling staircase you could say it was but it was a simple marble floor circling down the whole building it was really, really nice and I didn't articulate that very well so I apologize but I don't really know how else to describe it. I entered at the 5th floor and walked all the way down until I found the exit. Upon finding the exit I found the bathroom and ran in real fast before I spent another 3 hours walking without a destination. I stepped out of the bathroom and walked around to the front entrance and left. I ended up going back to the hotel and got back pretty late because I was so lost, but needless to say it was a good experience.

Day 6 approached, and I decided to just go back to Santa Monica and relax. I spent the whole day there because other than San Diego, Santa Monica is where my heart lies. I actually ate there before going back to the hotel and decided to call it an early day because I had to pack to get back to Jersey.

Day 7 I woke up didn't run but I had to check out of the Tivoli at around 10am, my flight was at 9:30 pm. On this day it was pretty cloudy, but I wanted to take in the full benefits of being in California, so I went back to Marian Del Rey and I was talking to Jaylene at this time. Around noon my phone started dying, you know Galaxy S2 battery problems lol. I decided to call it early and get to LAX for my flight in 8 hours. I checked in and sat at a table near this restaurant while charging my phone.

Jaylene and I started talking again and she told me that if she would have known I was in LA she would have come to see me. It was just fluff talk because I was still in LA until 9 and she never offered to pick me up and hang out the whole day so after another 30 minutes we stopped talking for the day and I just got really sad. Moments later this beautiful young woman approached me and asked to sit with me. Of course, there isn't a problem with that and so we introduced our selves and her name was Alexia.

After some talk, we decided to grab some food and some drinks. Starting to get to know her she is from Australia and she is a Dancer / Dance Instructor. She was super funny and so genuine, which is usual when I meet women from different countries, I love it so much. Not to say anything about the lovely people here in the States but it's very rare that you get approached by women here and let alone just want to socialize and have a conversation and on top of that even approaching a woman here to simply have a stimulating conversation is difficult without them thinking you have some type of agenda. I do not feel like getting into that whole conversation now but any way, her flight was at 8pm so we literally talked and hung out and had drinks the whole day until her flight came. We stopped drinking around 6 I believe then went to her terminal and just sat and talked and she showed me pictures of Australia and man was it beautiful. She was feeling a bit under the weather, so I just gave her a hug and held her for a bit, but she was starting to go to sleep, so I just let her sleep for a few moments on me until her flight arrived. Her flight had touched down and we started talking again and she was just so nice, she told me when I go to Australia to let her know because she has a big house and has plenty of extra rooms so I could stay in it and wouldn't have to spend money on a hotel so she gave me her Facebook to keep in touch just a genuine soul that woman was. I walked her to the boarding line gave her a hug and left. Last time we spoke she had a beautiful son and was doing well. I was very happy for her I think she will be an exceptional and phenomenal mother she has an amazing heart. I flew back to Jersey and my mom was all upset that I didn't tell her I was going to California or that I was on vacation and I heard it from her, oh man did I lol.

Anyways I spent some time with the family and just mainly with Adrien and Daziel and Dennis. That is where most of my time went and I love them guys and I say it constantly how I appreciate them and how much they have done for me I could never repay them and I haven't placed in this story how much they have helped me which is a disservice to them but at the same time I can't explain everything it's just strictly between us but not once have they ever hesitated or asked for anything in return and I am always grateful and appreciative to them for it they know that very well. During this time back Jaylene and I spoke briefly but little did I know that, this short amount of time that we were speaking was going to be the last time I would ever hear from her. In June the month previous she had said some rude disrespectful things to me and I can tell you it honestly hurt and it was clear that she was fed up, but I didn't think that I deserved what she said to me she had never spoken to me in that manner ever and she was at her breaking point with me. She had made me promises so I had thought that she would always be around, she promised she would always be there for me when I needed her but things just got out of hand and she left, and it hurt it hurt immensely. Was I grateful for her coming into my life when she did? Absolutely, and like I have stated previously if it wasn't for her I wouldn't be able to tell you the type of person I would have become so you are allowed to have your opinion, or if you want to be ignorant and let out all the jokes because I had honestly never even met this young woman, and how I would allow someone from the internet to have such an impact on my life you can make all the jokes you want it doesn't bother me. For the fact being that whatever me and that girl went through had more of a meaning and we had more of a bond than most people do in their own relationships now, so if you were to ask me if I regret any part of it, I would tell you the only part I do regret is not allowing her to pay for my plane ticket to Cali when we first had met which was the most significant time in our relationship and I should have placed my pride aside and maybe things would have turned out different, but aside from that I would have to say no I don't regret any other part of it and I hold her in a special place in my heart and she will forever mean the world to me.

It's time for me to get back to base so I return back and for your information and story line it is July of 2012 going into August of 2012. Now once we have returned, we are pretty much packing and securing things because we have a training rotation in the National Training Center in California. This rotation in total length is 1 Month long, time comes, and we head out. Once we get there and unpack and acclimate to the climate it's time to begin training. I now find out that I will be placed in the Headquarters Platoon and the reason being was that because I was leaving the military in a few months. That was a total bullshit excuse from the seniors because they simply didn't like me and I know that you guys are thinking oh well you're just playing the victim, no that's not how it works in the military and First Sergeant Idiot and I never liked each other and never seen eye to eye so for the military personnel that are reading this will be able to understand and those that aren't military its ok think whatever you please it doesn't bother me at all and I am not going into detail will all the things that happened between my platoon, First Sergeant, or I it's just not happening. So, fuck it before we head out, I tell Amelia that I have to hand in my phone for the time being because we will be out in the field for 2 weeks training. I message her and tell her to just text me and call me leave messages everyday so when I get back, I have something to look forward to from my girl. She said she would, but we weren't at the best times in our relationship now and I was pretty sure she was relieved that she wouldn't have to worry about me texting her and calling her for 2 weeks.

Now the information comes down that these next two weeks are a trial for the best platoon. The platoon that does or outperforms the other platoons will be the ones to deploy next year when they go back to Afghanistan. Our platoon usually outperforms the rest of the platoons during squad and platoon training events we would honestly win like 70% of events either our squad or platoon as a whole. Our platoon was very family oriented we were all very close, for the most part our whole company was close, but we weren't all in the same platoon, so it changed things during events. There would be a lot of people out to show off and things of that sort but our platoon was never like that, if someone was struggling we would drop back and pick them up, if someone needed water we would refill with our water and not let them fall out of the event, we just wouldn't let anyone fail or ever allow one person to haul all the heavy weight we would split it up per mile or keep switching we just had a good thing going but with me out of the picture it was up to the young guys and they did an exceptional job I was very proud of them. During the whole training center I was getting my ass handed to me by some tough guy who failed out of Special Forces training but many things happened in those 2 weeks that aren't meant to be discussed but aside from that tough guy made a mistake and I was correct and from there no apologies were had and no apologies were given for the way I or the squad was treated but as men it was ok we knew what was going on behind closed doors. Later on, tough guy came out of his act and showed his true colors and turned out to be a good dude, but a straight dick head and we never had problems from there. Leadership was lacking in Alpha company from senior leadership all the way down the chain. It was very discouraging to see and for people to allow it was an eye opener. I was one of the guys who would not allow it.

Sergeant Niko who was now gone and went to Drill Sergeant School always said if you are better than someone else at their job take it from them doesn't matter their rank. We had some very complacent and lazy sergeants in Alpha Company it was disgraceful. The military doesn't care about you as a man, Morales, or leadership abilities all they care about is if you can run fast, or kiss up to the First Sergeant, or do things that give him and the commander good evaluation reports. I never once cared about all that bullshit, the military is pretty political, and I have no care in the world for it. For a small example it was night time and everyone was sleeping, I got up to use the bathroom quickly and I understand everyone is tired and all but still during training there are things you can do and things you can't, one thing you can't do is sleep on guard. I am walking to the bathroom and I see someone sleeping on guard, so clearly I give him the benefit of the doubt he is pretty tired this is the first day they can actually get a few straight hours of rest especially after climbing this mountain with all weapon systems and setting everything up ok I get it. My thought process is to simply wake up the kid and tell him to watch out for supervisors that are roaming because he will get smoked for sleeping on guard. As I was walking to the restroom the shed that housed the ammunition for the training was open, and I saw a leg sticking out and clearly noticed the guy was sleeping. As I turned into the shed to wake him up, I noticed it was Cordell. Cordell is a very hard-working kid and it takes a lot for him to get tired and sleep on guard he is my brother in my platoon, so I know him very well. I woke him up and asked him what happened because this isn't usual for him, he said that no one came to relieve him of his guard duties, and he was on guard for 3 to 4 hours. Now I was fucking heated because that meant that his sergeant didn't come to check up on him and do his job as a leader and no one in my platoon was getting fucked like that even if I wasn't in the platoon for training fuck them dumb ass sergeants. I asked him who was his sergeant or supervisor and he told me who it was. Right away I knew how much of a bitch this guy was, he was a lazy piece of shit sergeant that got his rank because the military needed E-5's which is a sergeant rank and they lowered points and he got his but by no means does that equate to him having leadership potential and being a sergeant so I fucking went over to him kicked his feet woke his bum ass up and yelled at him. I told him to go find the person that was supposed to relieve Cordell and he said he doesn't know that, that is supposed to be between the squad and I said no the fuck it isn't that is your duty to make sure your guys are rotating and not fucking eachother over and he said I don't know what to tell you and fell back asleep. Those are a majority of your leaders in the military its fucking astounding. I went to Cordell told him to go inside and get rest and I will cover his shift until the morning. I don't remember but I think I did a 3-hour shift then stayed up another 24 hours after that because of the mission we had but our platoon we don't do shit like that. There are a couple people in the platoon that try to do that and get away with it, but we stay away from those kids and immature fucks. There are plenty of scenarios like that throughout this year and last year of training but as I couldn't really discuss the training, I can't really go in detail of how everything transpired but its ok.

The training ends and it's time to wrap up, so we start the week by doing layouts and making sure we have everything that was issued to us, so we go back with everything that we came with. At this time, we received our phones back, opening it up and checking everything Amelia left me maybe like 3 messages and I was pretty sad. I thought I was going to open my phone up to such an abundance of messages and nothing to that sort. So I was just really down kind of realized how much I meant to this girl, it was at a point where she really didn't care about me and she would just talk to me when Marcellus was just over the top and didn't want to deal with him. So, coming to the last part of training, we had to turn our vehicles back in. At this point the higher ups gave everyone permission to call their significant others or family members from California to come to base or this little common lounge off base with a pool hall and things of that sort to hang out for a few hours before leaving tomorrow. I was at the truck line and saw Cordell and asked what he was doing there because he is from Cali and his family is there and he hasn't seen them in a while. He said he had to turn in his truck so he couldn't go, and I just told him to go and tell higher up that I am here with your truck and will turn it in for you and he got up and left. He deserved it he got fucked badly so a little peace before going back to 10th Mountain would really help him. I tell you what I sat in that truck line for hours I was one of the last trucks to get processed back in and during all that time in the truck I contemplated hitting Amelia up but, for what I knew she wasn't going to come and see me and let alone I didn't want to hear the 10 thousand excuses she was going to tell me so I just hit her up later that night and the next morning we gathered all our things up and left back to good old Fort Drum. You know thinking about its Cordell and I went through a lot lol. We almost got struck by lightning, witnessed an Earthquake lol that is an inside joke you woke get it but it's fairly funny lol, we worked like 8 days straight on 10 to 12 hours of sleep the whole week then I put him in my car and took a 10 hour drive straight to Maryland so he could see his family that was a fucking long day let me tell you fuck that shit, that shit sucked donkey dick. All in all, he was a good guy and deserved it so I did all I could for him. I wish you guys could meet everyone, honestly just a group of amazing men that I was more than happy to serve with just good men all in all. We get back to Fort Drum and it is time to start decompressing and getting ready to leave the Military but there was one hold back. When we returned, we found out that 1st Platoon our platoon had won the training event.

With that said we thought we had an understanding, which was that the platoon that won the event would be the ones to deploy. Of course, why would you believe anything higher ups said. Well they lied, they decided to switch up the company and break apart the platoon mix and match soldiers and deploy them. It was horrible, everyone one was upset to say the least. The guys in the platoon wanted me to deploy with them but there were a few things from stopping me from doing that. One being Amelia, I thought well if I were to get out of the military I would be able to maintain my focus and energy on her solely, if the guys were to find that out they'd kill me and rightfully so, two was that the chain of command I wasn't very fond of and I know how they operate and make decisions and I wasn't not agreeing with them at all, third was I didn't feel like they needed me anymore. I trained with them for two years they know how I make my decisions and why I make the decisions I make, and I believe I articulated that to them very well during training. They know what happened to us and me in Afghanistan they know I don't ever hesitate or get scared or get anxious when it comes to making decisions under stressful environments and I believed I instilled that in them very well. They were a very strong intelligent group of young men and I believed in them and I also didn't plan on being in the military for that long, I believed this group of men would be able to handle any situation that came to them, except for one that we didn't account for. It was a situation that is not spoken about amongst us, we didn't prepare them for this certain situation because we had placed the thought in the back of our minds and forgot about it and that was a grave mistake. Nonetheless the guys handled it very well and mature and it just breaks my heart that they had to endure that pain and now walk around with it but as I said before they are a group of very strong men and they handled it better than expected.

Moving forward with that I had spoken to Lionel about the whole situation except for the situation with Amelia and I and he made it very clear to me. If I didn't plan on making a career out of the military there is absolutely no reason for me to stay in. He said he was going with them and Tiago and everything was going to be ok and just reassured me which I believe is what I needed, and they went on their way. Now with all this going on simultaneously I had found out that they didn't want Lex to deploy. I found out that the reason for it was because he had glass ankles which was a complete lie because he never had an ankle injury at all while in. I can see through their bullshit and I spoke with the First Sergeant to see if I could change his mind to deploy and that was not happening, I did the best I could and I fought for him man I fought for his spot on deployment and it was so disrespectful how they broke up the platoon like that. They even allowed this new kid who didn't even come with us to the NTC event to deploy over Lex and that's when I had enough and made my decision to leave. I couldn't be around these ignorant leaders' man. Lex fought, trained, lost sleep, all for what so some new kid could come in and just get the right to deploy over him that was really fucked up. Higher ups were a bunch of bitches I just couldn't be around them anymore.

The only person Lex really had while everyone was gone was Hansel. Hansel was our little brother; he was a small kid, but we took care of him very well. He had some issues that aren't to be discussed but people didn't like him very much. He was a good kid with a good heart the issue was that he would out PT everyone didn't matter who you were. He would do more pushups than you, more sit-ups than you, and run faster than you. He also read a lot, so all the military standard books he would read and learn them, and he was smart man. Simply put because he was small, he needed a bit more help than others. He had some issues with other platoons then came to us, then had issues with some team leaders so he was put under me as my soldier. My platoon knew I was patient I didn't get mad and I smoked people for reasons, not just because I felt like it. The whole time that he was under me, I didn't get a complaint about him, I couldn't complain about anything other than the fact that he overslept a lot but it wasn't a problem I would just run back to his room wake him up and get to formation.

I remember we were training for squad tactics and it was our squads turn. Sergeant Walton didn't feel like doing anything that day it was fucking great and they gave us ten minutes to devise a plan of attack and said, "Rodriguez just make up a plan I don't feel like doing shit today lol." So, I said "ok what do we got," he told us "we just pretty much have to attack this village with x number of complexes, and they have heavy weapons and an immense amount of guards and no one has conquered it yet." I said, "ok let's do this" and he said, "fucking A, I love it lets do it." We make our way through the woods and it was fucking great we were so quick and so patient just great teamwork the opposing force didn't even see us coming and we crept up on the village they didn't know we were there. They started getting anxious and radioed in to higher ups and asked if we had left yet and higher ups said yes they left 30 minutes ago they aren't there yet and the opposing force said no, and it was a few more radio transmissions then we gave them 5 more minutes of silence then attacked the village. Infiltrating the first building we got mixed up and Sergeant Walton went up to the second level with only 1 person and got killed in the first building so that made me senior and now I was in charge of everyone I split the teams up again and we went with two man buddy teams to every building. We cleared 2 buildings and Hansel was taking point to the next building and we hit an alley way and I picked up the Squad Automatic Weapon from one of my soldiers who died in another building. As Hansel was walking by a small alley way, one of the opposing force members was no other than the man Santino himself and he fired at Hansel and his weapon jammed and I just yelled at Hansel and unloaded as many rounds I could at Santino and he was taken out of the training now because I killed him and Hansel turned around and said "thanks g" and I said "no problem just get us into the last complex." We breached in took out the guy on the first level and Hansel went to the roof and got taken out by a sniper, I dragged him down reloaded and took out the sniper and our squad was the only squad to complete the mission. I was very good with tactics and planning because of Sergeant Niko, Lionel, Orian, Tiago, Sergeant Curtis, and Sergeant Walton. They just knew what it was man they were very intelligent. After everything settled down Hansel turned around and told me I was the best Team Leader he ever had. At work all it takes is patience and some humility all you have to do is place your pride aside, but some people simply can't just do that. I didn't allow anyone to disrespect Hansel he was our little brother and people had a lot of respect for us, our platoon and just me in general. Man I was doing a 24 hour shift and I didn't have any one it is supposed to be x amount of people but my soldier was taken which was a very long story to discuss but I don't bother people so I was doing the shift by myself until Eshawn, and Lex found out and they called the guys and they all stayed up with me the whole shift they gave up their weekend to help me out man I love them guys, Eshawn, Cordell, Lex, Prescott, Walther, Hansel, Santino, and Seymore, Asher I appreciate everything they have done for me man.

It's almost 7pm now and I haven't eaten all day which is usual I really only eat one meal a day but anyway, I am not going to start writing the next part of the story because it's pretty fucking sad and depressing so today is January 1, 2019 so Happy Fucking New Year's lol and I hope you guys have a blessed day I will write later on this week I have a lot of shit I need to do still before I start work so have a blessed evening and sleep tight yall.

Chapter 16

The Unforeseen Difficult Transition

So, I am back, and I hope that you are ready because I am not and it's going to kill me writing about this. Well this time of the year towards December of 2012 everyone goes on leave to visit and be with family for the holidays. At this moment in time I am supposed to be leaving the military but since I am Mike, I got fucked lol. I had to start the out-process part of leaving the military and well how am I supposed to out process if no one is on base, fucking outstanding right. So, I had to wait until everyone came back from leave to start out processing.

With this spare time, I had, I looked into school because I had absolutely no plan after the military. So, I found a school which was Sanford Brown in Idanre, it was a school that trained and educated students to become a Medical Assistant. I went I took the exam I spoke with the VA Liaison and well we had our start date lol. Leave is over and now it is January 2013, everyone is back at base and I begin the out-processing phase and it went smooth which is weird to say the least, but I was not about to complain lol. I left the military on terminal leave, which meant I was still a soldier until March 2013. This meant that I was not allowed to get into any trouble at all or terminal leave would be canceled, and I would have to finish my contract in the military.

I finally sign out of base and start my long lonely but very happy drive home. I left Friday around noon and I made it to Adrien's house around 7 or 8pm. As I stated previously Adrien was always my first stop when I made it back home, he would always be the first to know. I slept over his house the whole weekend and he actually set up a dinner with our friends for my welcoming back party, I'll never forget it, it truly meant a lot to me he is a great guy a lot nicer than I am and I just simply appreciate all he's done for me and continues to do for me it never goes unnoticed or underappreciated. I finally arrived at my house on Sunday afternoon and spent time with the family and prepared my things for tomorrow. I did something really unintelligent at this point in my life and I had absolutely no guidance on what I was doing or how I should go about following and planning my life out after the military. You really don't have anyone to explain to you how you should navigate life after the military and I believe there should be a type of support group or something similar that has people experienced in the military and civilian life after the military and no I am not going to start it. I did fairly well for myself due to the fact that I adapt to situations extremely fast and I know who I am as a person, so I know what I am able to handle and as difficult as it was I did well.

From the previous paragraphs to place it all together I left the military on Friday and started school the following Monday. I gave myself 3 days of recuperation before starting school and that was one of the worst things I could have ever done. I will not be able to tell you how long this explanation is going to be that I am about to give so if I go on a rant or it carries on for too long, I apologize. Ummm well where do I start, I guess we will begin by explaining reintegration. So I explain this as an Infantryman, for those that do not know what an Infantryman is, an Infantryman is a soldier trained in the Art of War which is the most basic and simplistic definition I could possibly give you, we are the men on the front line. With that definition this will be one of the only times in this story that I will allow you to infer and do as your mind wishes with thoughts of what we did in Afghanistan even though I have explained it previously but for better or worse that was my job. When we go out to train, we train to for lack of better words we train to hunt, infiltrate, and subdue the enemy is as nicely as I could put it. This is your life day in and day out of the military, you eat, breath, and live training. You are always out training and everything you do focuses on maneuvering and subduing the enemy. You never truly learn anything else and when you do it is more in-depth training on how to better maneuver on the enemy, survival tactics, and higher levels of infiltration techniques. For those that are starting to piece the puzzle together you pretty much trained as you will be a soldier for the rest of your life, as if everyone will make a career out of the military. So when you are released out to the civilian world you forget how to navigate through it, you forget that you aren't allowed to talk to everyone in a demeaning manner, you forget that everyone else around you has feelings and some are more sensitive than others. You tend to lose your patience extremely quicker because you are taught that violence of action wins the fight which in fact is very true but as 18 to 23 year old's and I place myself in that category to because that is when I was in the military, no one trains you on how to decompress. No one is there for you when you leave the military once you're gone you aren't the military's problem they don't care about you nor how you are doing outside and if you're doing well for yourself or if you need help or advice or just someone to talk to because you need to vent because civilians just simply don't understand you and the issue is you, you forgot how to talk to people and it takes time to relearn that but they don't tell you that they give you a certificate of completion of contract and say good luck fuck face.

The issue with me is that I was very fortunate, due to the fact of how I was brought up. By that I mean my friends, people believe that you raise your kids and sorry to break it to you, you don't point blank period. We will discuss that later though don't mind that sentence now. I was very fortunate to be able to venture out in the world and make the decisions I made and make the mistakes I made to be able to learn from them so when I came to this point in my life I knew what to do. Many times I wasn't able to talk to Adrien, Daziel, Jeremiah, or Dennis, which was no fault of their own it was the simple fact that they wouldn't have understood what I was going through not simply because they weren't in the military but because they would give just generic advice and they know as we are brothers we don't care for generic advice but when there comes a situation that they don't know how to give advice to which is extremely rare because we all were in the street and we all are well rounded in the cycle of life, they wouldn't know what to say and when they give generic advice and they know I just end the conversation and change the subject because I don't deal with generic bullshit it just shows you don't care what I am talking about and it's tough to deal with. So being blessed at such a young age to make mistakes and take accountability for them as a man it taught me a lot and as a man it helped be become who I am today and how I analyze situations and adapt to them stemmed from my thought processes and how I developed them throughout my time on this planet.

    I say all this because the age group of 18 to 23-year old's many of these soldiers are kids. They have never ventured out in the world and don't have the experience needed to transition back into civilian life. Many of these kids come from small towns or small cities and never left that little 3 to 5 mile radius so they don't know what the world has to offer, they don't know how evil people could be, they don't know how life will take advantage of them until they reintegrate into society and get lost because all they know is war and previous to that they have never even been on a plane or ever traveled and socialized with other people so this difficult transition hits them hard. Above that they have no one to talk to, their brothers are from all 50 states and the closest one lives 3 states away which is 15 to 24 hour drive but they don't have a car because they spent all their money because they never received financial advice on how to control and invest 20 to 35 thousand dollars because school doesn't teach you that.

They simply like to teach you about the circumference of a circle and the area of rectangle like that is necessary to being successful in life. For many people it is I am a car guy so it's important to us lol I'm just throwing things up in the air so relax there are many things school teaches you that I have never once used in life so just meaningless knowledge is what I am getting at, so calm your titties.

Now these kids have to navigate through the civilian world, empty, depressed, alone, drunk, high, homeless, and no one cares about them or us. They are used to the point where you almost forget who you are as a person and many kids have not even found themselves before joining the military and they get so lost in the system and it fucking worries me. What you need to understand from all this is that, military recruiters shouldn't accept anyone into the military. Partly it is the military's fault because we get so low on soldiers they do this mass hire and the basic training Drill Instructors just pass them through and it shouldn't be like that, because if you lower the standard you lower the quality of the soldier and that goes for everything not just military personnel. The second thing to take from this rant is that I know plenty of people in the military and with various jobs. Some people have jobs that are literally 10 to 12 hours and their day is over, for Infantryman that is never the case we could go a whole month without a day off or go live out in the field for 3 weeks and that is how it's supposed to be. The factor is that when we leave the military our skill set is limited to a security guard. When everyone else leaves the military, they are able to find careers in their skill and more. All I am saying is that someone has to come forward and reallocate some resources to help these kids transition and reintegrate into society as a functioning adult and we all play apart in this, everyone helps every talk every hug it all helps, you may believe that it takes a village to raise a child and it does but it also takes all of society to help one person find themselves and that is where we lack because everyone is so preoccupied with themselves and finding escapes to run from their problems we don't want to be bothered with everyone else's problems and that is where I come in but we can't discuss that just know a simple talk, hug, even just letting someone sleep on your shoulder on the train it all helps you simply couldn't imagine how much it helps even a simple smile heals someone for a second.

School was an extremely difficult transition, not only did I not open a book for 4 years but this profession I chose was dominated by women. I was nowhere near any woman in 4 years, I damn near had to relearn how to communicate with them it was fucking crazy. As I am who I am I adapted very quickly it took maybe a few hours and I met some very amazing women and they have become very good friends of mine. I was only one of 2 men in the class and me and him got along very well except for a minor hiccup which is neither here nor there. These women were very warm, and genuine, and funny so we had a great class. The teachers were phenomenal they loved to go in and teach and have fun doing it and I learned a lot but studying was very difficult for me so many times I just didn't open the book I relied on my memory which was pretty good and I would pass my exams with high grades. The main courses that I definitely needed to open the book for were, Hematology, Anatomy and Physiology, and Microbiology other than that I barely studied honestly, but throughout the courses we had study groups during some class times and that helped greatly.

During lunch hours we would go to the Pizzeria or Chinese spot across the parking lot and eat. We became very close, it was to name some girls, Janet (had an amazing sense of humor), Norathania (was the homegirl she was great to be around), Vera (class would be less rowdy without her she was funny and called me out on all my shit it was so funny), Yvette (was the strong Hispanic woman she had spice in her lol), Cecelia, Ileana, Melinda, Nayana, Destiny (was my homegirl she was an amazing girl), and Railey (was such an adult very organized and strong demeanor her husband owned a boxing gym near school and I would tell her all the time I was going to visit and spar with him and beat him up lol good thing I never went he would have knocked me the fuck out lol) Sonia (had a great sense of humor from day one we meshed well she had no shame just like me). There were several other girls, well honestly the whole class got along well I would just make the class laugh all the time and the teachers couldn't do anything about it, but I was respectful about it. Just in between lectures I would just start joking with every one or playing with girls hair and the teachers would get mad because the girls would be falling asleep while I played with their hair and the teacher would just laugh and yell at me and tell me to go to the back of the class. Little did they know I was cool with the kids in the back of the class too lmfaoooo it was a good time in that school great memories. We also had 2 sets of twins in the class which was super rare I never experienced such a thing and they were both funny lol. One set of twins were more social than the other, but man did we have fun.

So, throughout my time in school every so often I would go back and visit my brothers in Fort Drum. I visited them so much they said they saw me more outside of the military than when I was in the military lol. That is because I would just go to my room and sleep all day if you don't remember. At this point the fellas had deployed back to Afghanistan and I would go every so often and check up on their wives. There were some that were moving, others just needed some help watching the kids so they could run errands and things and others were simply alone and they had moved there from various states across the country and couldn't really move back since they spent their income on purchasing a home. So, I would go, and visit make sure things were ok and help run some errands for them. Aside from this I had to check up on the guys at the barracks. Mainly Lex, Asher, and Hansel, Asher was always doing well he was a great guy I didn't have to check up on him much, but he was a very, very good friend of mine even till this day. Lex was a fucking phenomenal dude, I had to check up on him frequently because I know how bothered he was when our higher ups fucked him over it was very disrespectful. Lex just has a big heart I am unsure if I told you the time when I went to go eat but went to his room and asked if he was hungry. He told me he was but didn't have any money or funds, which was weird because we always cover each other when we go out to eat so when he said that it didn't make sense. When I had asked him about it, he said his friend in California was involved in a car accident and totaled his car and lost his job due to transportation issues. I asked him if his friend was ok, but what did that have to do with him no having funds to eat. He explained that he offered his friend all of his paychecks for the next 2 months so he could find a job and get back on his feet because he has a wife and a child and that broke my heart man. Like I said previously these are just genuine people I meet man I will forever be proud to say they are all my brothers. So, throughout that time we all chipped in and bought groceries and helped him out until he started getting his pay checks back. So, I always went to check up and made sure he was doing well other than feeling left out and abandoned by the unit which fucking sucks, but he did very well.

    Moving forward, well Hansel I needed to check up on. He was our little brother and had some issues here and there. I went to his room and he was always happy to see me, but when I opened his door, I saw about 6 medication bottles. So, I asked him what that was about, and he told me that he had another TBI in training and he was told to take the medications. He hit his head while training and his helmet came off and he hit the ground and was knocked unconscious. He began to tell me that he had problems with his short-term memory and couldn't even remember where he put the remote to the television and small things or that sort. This meant I had to check up on him closely now after finding all this out. After visiting everyone I went on my way back home.

During this time Amelia and I weren't doing so well, she became extremely depressed because of the cancer. At this point she kept on telling me that she was tired and simply just wanted to go on vacation or just sleep for 2 weeks. Simultaneously there was a picture and story floating around the internet about this beautiful young girl who was battling cancer and I do not remember how the story went if the parents were not able to pay for the medical bills or not but the girl was fighting and kept this huge smile on her face and it just attracted everyone because she was so strong for her age. Amelia became very attached to this girl and her story. So, we spoke about it and it was a very depressing conversation to say the least, but she was ok after the talk. After a few weeks she went back to being her moody self, hating me then loving me and arguing and defending Marcellus and I just continued to be there and support her and try my best to be the best man I could for her, but it was just rough.

After a few weeks and exams pass by in school we are getting into late February Hansel texts me and I don't want to go look at that text. I was just not in the right state of mind because of what was going on with Amelia and I. I thought to myself I will text him back later and if I don't it doesn't matter; I will be up there in 2 weeks I will check up on him when I go to the barracks. It's now March 13, 2013 and I receive a phone call while in class from Lex which was weird. I step out and pick up, and well Lex tells me Hansel passed away. Hansel took his own life. After all the years of helping people, not allowing anyone to commit suicide, giving people a reason to live, giving people meaning in their life again and seeing them change and grow as a person and almost never have a suicidal thought in their mind again. The person I fail is my own brother, I could help everyone at any time, but

I couldn't help my own brother. That shit hurts man. As much as I hurt and cry about it, it doesn't bring him back and it doesn't change the fact that I fucked up and all I have left is this text message that I never responded to or returned a call to because I thought I had time. I thought its ok I will see him in a couple weeks, he will be alright if I don't answer this one time he was doing well. The truth and matter of the fact was that he wasn't, and deep down I knew that because I knew his history, I knew what he was battling inside that he never spoke to anyone about and he needed me and I wasn't there for him. All I had was a simple task to take care of everyone and everyone's families that were still state side while everyone was out fighting a war that wasn't theirs to fight and I couldn't do it, as a man I acknowledge that I fucked up and we lost a genuine soul and that, that will forever be on me.

Soon after Hansel passed, Amelia was acting weird. A bit more moody but leaning towards the depressed side again. Then the girl that was battling cancer, she had passed away and Amelia took it to heart and broke down and cried it was sad. I didn't know what to do, I couldn't do anything I wasn't there next to her, I couldn't console her, I couldn't hug her and tell her that I loved her and tell her that everything was going to be ok. The months leading into this weren't the best in our relationship and Amelia's health was declining, she was vomiting blood several times a week throughout the month of February and her physician told her it could be due to the Chemotherapy, so they kept a close eye on her. On April 25, 2013 I spoke with Amelia because when she goes to work in San Francisco she usually turns off her phone for the weekend. On April 30, 2013 I received a message from a lady named Melody she had explained to me that she was Amelia's aunt. She had informed me that Amelia had passed away due to the cancer.

I'm done crying and writing for today, giving you my all and the pain from reliving this again is excruciating I'm done for today.

After talking to Melody, she explained that Amelia was actually in a coma and not deceased. As you could imagine this was pretty difficult to understand, because I wasn't sure why she told me that she had passed away. Also knowing that Amelia and her family did not get along very well I was worried that they would pull her support and I had no say in it because they didn't know me. They knew of me because Amelia had told them she was going to visit me this year and told them who I was in which she stated I was her boyfriend. We did come to a middle ground about her visiting and when would be the best time due to her job and that is how they knew of me and that is why Melody messaged me. Continuing the conversation Amelia had started responding and awakening from the coma very slowly. They still hadn't allowed me to go and visit her, but they were doing their job and I appreciated it. She had started breathing on her own later within the week, but the physicians had stated that she may have subtle to moderate amnesia.

 Amelia had finally come to and woke up from the coma, she had awakened with moderate amnesia. Melody said they had to explain everything back to her and the whole time I was thinking that she wasn't going to remember me. At this point as I have never met her, and we barely even spoke over the phone I was pretty fucking sad man. I couldn't articulate how happy I was that she woke up and started eating and she was ok but how can I even explain the good parts of our relationship to her when there was never anything tangible to go by that would make her remember me. It was a very difficult situation to deal with. Later on, within the week her family had given her, her phone back and we started talking again. It was just not the same, far from it. At this point it was nothing to be discussed because her health was priority, but we did talk about certain things here and there.

 She had finally started coming back into her own personality and it was difficult to say the least. Amelia said she didn't really remember me but was explained by her family that I was her boyfriend and her and Marcellus were not together. Throughout the years of knowing and being with Amelia she had created a notebook about me, which she confessed to me about. The contents of said book were a variety of feelings she had for me. Days when she felt that she was unable to express herself or felt that I wasn't treating her right she would write about it in this notebook of hers and when she was discharged from the hospital she found it and read it and started to distance herself from me. It was very difficult to talk to her and I wasn't sure what I had did wrong or what exactly or how exactly she felt about me at this time. I knew one thing for certain, that no matter what happened her health was priority, and it was to be taken more seriously than ever, I couldn't lose her again. Even if she just truly didn't want to be with me, that would be ok as long as she was healthy. The weeks begin to progress, and she begins to turn back into her old self. It was very difficult to watch and there was absolutely nothing I could do about it.

Around this time of June 2013 there was this one girl who was always involved with Amelia come to find out she was a part of the family. I had gone into her Instagram account to befriend her when I saw something. On her Bio text she had the names of her kids which were Mikey and Jess obviously as stated previously we won't place the kid's names in here out of respect. If you have been paying attention I haven't lol because it took some time for it to click that she was one of the sisters and her name was Nadine. Once I finally put 2 and 2 together things finally started equaling up. Nadine and I had spoken several times and she did mention to me the important things about Amelia and Marcellus. Come to find out they were going out and had actually lived together for a while before breaking up. Nadine had moved out and Amelia moved in with her and was taking care of her for a while.

Learning about all this information it pained me, as honest and faithful as I was and probably very naïve as well, the fact of the matter was that my heart still yearned for her. That is something I cannot change, the only thing I can do is decide whether I want to pursue this quote on quote relationship or not and my decision was to pursue it. I knew I was a better man than Marcellus and I knew how pure my love for this woman was. Simultaneously thinking and understanding was that I am not sure what the actual history of Marcellus and Amelia are. This was difficult for me to understand. There was more to that relationship, that bond they had was so surreal, the way she would defend him and the way he would just brush her off, she was attached to him whole heartedly. I have only seen this in such rare cases, where the man could do absolutely nothing wrong in the woman's eyes. He could cheat on her right in front of her and she would turn a blind eye or deny it or make an excuse for him. For the guy it didn't matter because he knew he had her tied around his finger and he had all the free will he wanted and knew when he gets home, she will always be there.

Usually these types of bonds are formed over some traumatic experience that happened. The traumatic experiences vary or something sexual in nature as in she lost her virginity to him and I wasn't able to gauge what direction was the situation that led her have such a bond and attachment to him. After years I still wasn't able to find out and I was able to narrow it down to something physical, maybe something happened while they were together and he protected her and she kept it a secret and held on to that moment for way to long and damaged herself from it. At the same time there was the instance of when they met and how they met. This will fast forward the story a bit so I apologize but we will get back to this so just let me explain.

Amelia had explained to me that they had met back in 2009 or well that was the last time they had sex. This was all a lie, so throwing this out there for anyone that needs to confirm that they are not crazy. I am not tech savvy when it comes to social media, I do not know how to navigate nor hide nor look for things on social media.

All I know is that when they officially broke up Marcellus had deleted all their pictures together and made his profile public. So, on twitter if you simply place in the Twitter name of a person, every post they are tagged in or have made will show up. Since Marcellus had made his profile public it showed all the posts where he tagged her and their conversations, and man was I so regretful to even place her name in that search box. There was a lot of pain there and things I should not have known and wish I would have just left it at that. Come to find out they had actually met on twitter in like 2010, and when they met Marcellus had a girl. He had tagged her and given her a cute little nickname and thus they became friends and that's how the relationship started. As the relationship went on it was clear that she loved the attention she was receiving from him. Which was understandable due to the fact when I had stated earlier Amelia was the one with the most weight on her from her family but was far from fat or obese she was beautiful and the curves on her were dangerous but she just did not know what she had to offer physically because she was very insecure at one time. It was understood that their relationship started as something sexual and that is what sparked the relationship. Moving forward it was brought to my attention by Coralyn her sister that she had Marcellus' name tattooed on her arm. If you guys know anything, placement of said tattoo was very important. The tattoo was on her left bicep, not just that it was the full government on there. This tore me apart man as funny as it sounds when she put that pic on her Instagram, I liked it and just thought ok she is showing off her tattoo but the picture was never clear so you couldn't understand it.

Someone had commented, asking what it said, and she just replied look closer. After finding out about this I fucking went back and looked, and it was his full name right on her bicep. To the understanding that this man meant more to her than any other human on this planet. If you haven't figured it out yet, when someone has the name of another person on their arm it symbolizes not love but strength. It symbolizes that, said person is their foundation, their rock, their support in life and no matter what happens nothing will ever separate them. This was all confirmed by Amelia and she did confess all this to me, and it pained me, and I still went after her. I knew who she was before this man entered her life and I knew how wholesome and genuine and filled with love this woman was. Whatever bond they had; I just wasn't able to break it honestly.

Coming back to the story July comes around and well Amelia was supposed to come and visit for Independence Day but chose not to. It just turned into a weird week; I couldn't understand it. July 4, 2013 was such a weird day, I couldn't control my feelings, nothing at all felt right and Amelia was just not answering the phone. I just didn't hear from her at all, but this just felt different. The next week comes and I see she starts Tweeting and I didn't understand why she wasn't answering me back. Well Amelia went to her Aunt's house on Independence Day and while walking back to the house with her Aunt, nephew, niece, and herself, they were robbed at gunpoint. The thieves had taken everything from them and held them at gunpoint with a shotgun pointed at Amelia's head. She was simply releasing her feelings on Twitter, where she claimed that he didn't call her or checkup on her at all after being robbed and obviously I had thought it was about me but clearly it was about her actual boyfriend Marcellus. As I said before that man did not care about her at all, when I just felt things were wrong, I began calling and texting and got no response and come to find out well she didn't have a phone because she was robbed at gunpoint. This was a trying time for me because this is when it hit me like, let's just say she did claim me as her boyfriend which supposedly she did to her family ok cool I'll take it.

In all honesty what could I do for her from 3 thousand miles away I really couldn't do anything. Let's take away the infidelity and let's be honest if we actually were in a working stable relationship what did I actually have to offer Amelia as an adult other than some support and integrity when it comes to being faithful and loyal in a relationship I couldn't really offer her anything.

Simultaneously during these times Amelia had a Forums Spring which was another ask / answer website. Well the truth was finally set free; Amelia had a child with Marcellus. Coralyn had explained to me that is the reason behind the tattoo, which was part of the reason, but it was a very small piece to their relationship. Backdate 2 years to October 2011, Amelia had a Tumblr page. That was the page where she released a lot of her anger and emotional pain. On Halloween of 2011 she had posted pictures of a woman whom was pregnant and had a skeletal face paint and her belly was painted Orange like a Pumpkin, and the guy or baby father had skeletal face paint as well, and none of this meant anything to me at the time. Backdating all this, back to Twitter around July 4, 2012 Marcellus had posted a comment saying we are planning our future together and that includes a bear and posted a picture which was deleted. If anyone is piecing this together if I haven't lost you in all this back and forth mess, where was I during the first week of July 2012.

Well you guessed correct; I was in Los Angeles trying to visit Amelia. If you are piecing it all together correctly, she was pregnant, while I was there and that would play a huge factor in her not wanting to see me while I was in her area. If she was pregnant in which we do know that is correct because she was pregnant since October of 2011 which she confirmed that was her and Marcellus in the picture she posted. Aside from that when she gave birth she was putting all the pictures of the baby and her in the doctor's office at their routine visits and the child was handsome and aside from all the things that happened I was happy that she gave birth to a healthy child.

Now that all the secrets were aired out it was time for me to make a decision and I had decided I would fight for her heart one more time. During school, the year was coming to an end and it was time for my externship. This was a 9-month course and my externship was due to begin the last week of August. I wanted to push it back so I could take a break from all this stress, well not really stress I don't know how to explain it but more so over all the things that were going on in my life I just needed some time away to reevaluate, regroup, and refresh. I was dealing with a lot and I was not noticing how badly I was treating my mother. I was taking out all my frustration on her and I didn't even notice how much I was stressing her out and making her cry. She in turn would take out her anger on just innocent people at grocery stores or people simply doing their job when they are speaking over the phone and I tried to explain to my mother that she couldn't talk to people like that but it wasn't her fault she was just releasing her anger out and displacing it because she couldn't talk to me because I was so unapproachable because of what I was going through. Aside from that rant I wasn't sure if I was able to push back my extern to start a week later, so I waited until school gave me the ok from the office. Friday came and I got the ok from school and when I returned home that day, I bought my plane ticket to Cali so I could go and relax, try and see and talk to Amelia, as well as see my sister.

Well first things first, I hope after all these chapters you guys have begun to realize that only certain things happen to me Michael and I just don't know why I attract such weird and unnormal situations lol. I went to Greenville Airport and happily got on my flight to California. First, we had to take a Hopper Plane to Maryland, then fly to California so ok cool. I arrived in San Diego Airport around Noon time. Anytime I fly I only carry 2 bags to make traveling easier this way I don't have to check in any luggage. The plane landed, I walked out crossed the baggage claim area received a text from my sister that she was outside, went down the escalator and realized how small this got dang airport was. I saw the main entrance and exit from the airport; I was a few steps away the automatic doors opened and all I heard was "Hey are you Michael Rodriguez?" Just like that in a split second that instant my mind jumped back into military mode, my thought process jumped so fast through the past several months and it was very clear that I knew absolutely no one in San Diego except for my sister and if not one person has ever called me by my full government name and my mind wondered. I was thinking Marshalls, CIA, FBI, ATF the whole nine but I couldn't justify any of the task forces searching for me. I never sold drugs or trafficked drugs; I have never been arrested so the curiosity had intrigued me. I stared at the door till it closed took a deep breath and turned around. As I watched these 2 men approach me, I said, "yes, I am Michael Rodriguez, how can I help you?" Watching them and evaluating them was fucking great man. Their posture, their tactics, their distance management between each other and the lead man's distance from my self-man, their hand placement and focus, it was great to see such trained individuals I saw where my tax money was going. They did a good job, aside from the fact that they actually never introduced themselves. I asked them what this was about, the lead man replied nothing serious just wanted to ask you a few questions and he pulled aside his blue jean jacket and showed his silver badge and side arm like ok cool I know you are cops that was clear when you called me by my full name in a state where I know no one but we will play the game. He had asked me what I was doing in California, and how long I was going to stay, how much cash did I have on me, and if he could search my bag. But just because he asked so nicely, I told him. I explained to him I was on vacation from school and came to visit my sister who was going to USC at the time and I was only going to be here for a week. I also said he could search my bag and that I had 500 dollars cash on me, then I proceeded to ask what was this questioning in concern to. He replied, "you bought your plane ticket to California last night." I said, "yea I didn't know if I was able to take time off from school until yesterday, what is wrong with that?" He replied "the only people who purchase plane tickets to California 24 hours before their flight are usually high profile individuals from the Mexican Cartel and sneak their way into the country for meetings, are you or do you have any plans on going to Mexico?" I replied "what, no what the fuck, if I wanted to go to Mexico I would just buy a ticket to Mexico, I have a valid passport and I didn't even bring it because I have no reason to go to Mexico." He replied "ok, you're all good you're free to go." So, I packed up my bag and left, then the coincidences had begun.

I stepped outside in search for my sister she had a fourth generation 2006-2012 Nissan Altima. So, I step outside in search for it and it is nowhere to be found. I call her and she is the first car there and pulls up and puts the window down and says get in bro. All I could do is just simply laugh because now I know how this entire week is going to go. Knowing how everything works I know they have a profile on my sister, and they know what car she drives correct? While I am in her car, she is taking us to some restaurant to go and eat and says, "why are you laughing?" I tell her because I just got stopped at the airport and you are not driving your regular car and now this looks mad suspicious lol. She says, "what do you mean you got stopped at the airport?" I told her "I will explain that when we get food." For you regular folk this may mean ab-so-fucking-lutely nothing to you, but for me and us and people that know how investigations work, you create a profile on every fucking person associated to the person you are investigating. So, we get to this restaurant and once we get the food, I begin to explain to my sister about what happened at the airport and she's just in awe. Of course, not too surprised because I just have a track history of just weird outlandish shit happening to me that you would only see in movies lol.

Then she looks down and I ask, "what happened?" She replies "well I guess Mexico is out of the picture," I said "fucking damn right Mexico is out of the picture, lol I just told these fools I wasn't going, come to find out you want to go border hopping for some cute ass Lobsters fuck that I'm not getting hitched at the border because you want to eat some big ass Lobsters lol the government now thinks I traffic drugs for the Mexican Cartel lmfaooo dumb fucks lol." So, we laugh and make way to her apartment where I meet my brother from another mother Cormack. Cormack is Liv's boyfriend and Liv is my sister's roommate.

Cormack is awesome man such a good guy, this guy had the fucking absolute best job in the fucking world and I wish I could tell you guys what it was but I guess it is pretty confidential so it's all cool I know what it was and I wanted to do it lol, night time came and we all fell asleep.

Morning came but it wasn't the bright beautiful Sun that had awoken me from my beautiful dreams, it was this pounding knock at the door. I thought to myself what the fuck, who is knocking on the door like that we are all home already let me see who it is. Man, oh man, it was this tall dude asking me some weird ass questions that I had no answer to. I was still groggy from getting woken up like that, I wasn't in the military anymore I wasn't used to getting woke up like that, complacency kicked in real fast. This guy had asked me if I was leaving the apartment. I said, "I am not sure why?" he replied, "we are going to do some Mason work on the steps they are cracked." I looked and saw two guys down the steps and said let me ask my sister. When I had closed the door, my brain kicked in to overdrive real fast, I may have been complacent but when things start clicking and the math tends to not add up I get into detail mode and watch everything, every movement, every word, every stutter, choice of words, vocal patterns, hand placement and neuronal excitability I start catching everything and I usually do this voluntarily but when I get caught off guard like this I start pinpointing weird shit that doesn't make sense. So, my sister had a balcony and the shutters were closed because I was sleeping in the living room, so I opened the shutter momentarily to see who else was out there and what else I can catch from these guys. Damn I guess I have to explain the layout of her complex huh?

There were 2 complexes of apartments divided by a center walkway, on both sides of the walkway were bushes and mulch. The walkway was in the direction of East and West, to the North and South were the apartments. Each apartment had a balcony facing the walkway, if you stepped on to the balcony you were able to see your neighbors across from you and their staircase going up to their apartment as well as they are able to see you and your staircase. If you walked East on the walkway it led to a parking lot, if you walked West it would lead you to the sidewalk on the main street. With this basic layout I can finish this part of the story, I peeked out the balcony through the shutters and saw more Masons on the other staircase which what was supposed to happen if they were truly there to fix the steps they had to look the part. The issue was they were all looking at me and into the apartment. If you don't understand, when you are doing reconnaissance or surveillance you try to get someone to get as close in as possible which was said guy who knocked on the door and peeked into the apartment and tried to gauge the layout and you use guys on different levels and try to get as many vantage points and information about the place you are trying to get into. It may sound a bit crazy to you guys but if you have never done it and recon work you wouldn't understand and this isn't some conspiracy theory lol the people that understand what I am talking about know how straight forward I am being. With all this information I have gathered now I have enough to go and ask my sister some questions. This thought process took maybe a minute, minute and a half but for the story it seems I made them wait outside for 15 minutes lol I didn't do that. I went to my sisters' room and my mind had everything calculated I was awake now. The first thing I asked her was "hey Daphnie, question when people come and do work on the building does your landlord usually tell you?" She replied, "yea he usually tells us a week in advanced why?" That response itself answered and confirmed all my questions, just so you guys know when I peeked out the shutter I looked to the East towards the parking lot and they had some work trucks there, and the ladders and paint buckets the whole nine but there were things in that truck that you didn't need to strip some concrete any who. I explained to my sister that there were some men outside that said they wanted to know if we were leaving because they have to strip the concrete and place some new steps so they needed to know if we were leaving because they were going to start to work at 8. My sister said, "yea we will be out by then." I went to the door and told them yes and evaluated all them muthafuckers lol they all fit the cop profile. Now I knew they were trying to tap the apartment but fuck it we weren't going to be there anyway and I haven't done anything wrong lol but I know I know they have to follow through but like dam if they would have just asked me I would have let them tag along the more people the more conversations lol.

We head out and they all walked down the stairs ahead of me annnnnndddddd, I start looking and counting heads. As I was doing that, I noticed that they all stopped what they were doing and watched my sister and her roommates, and I leave. All eyes were on us and I counted about 12 people and 3 Ford Trucks with no tags, no decals, nada showing their company or who they worked for, bravo guys real fucking discreet my man lol.

We headed out and I don't recall where we went but I had an iPhone 4 thanks to Adrien and his girlfriend at the time. When we got to breakfast after ordering our food, I looked at my phone then looked at my sister and she said while laughing "What?" I said "welpt my phone just shut off and reset itself lol." She said, "but what does it matter you're not doing anything wrong." I replied, "yea you're right I will just leave it on." After the day ended, we went back to the apartment and they were still there. As we started walking to the car the vibe was still there. As I looked around everyone stopped and we were all just there watching each other and I started assessing the work they did, and nothing it looked like they didn't do anything to the steps. We just went upstairs and relaxed for the day until we went out at night.

The next day we went to the San Diego Zoo it was a great experience. During the time spent at the zoo I was talking to Amelia the whole day. It was difficult, I was trying to go see her, but she just wasn't allowing it. When it came down to it, she chose Marcellus and that was the beginning of the end of us. Aside from everything that happened we had a conversation and she would just not let go of him and it hurt. When we spoke, I was on the bus taking a tour and it took so much strength to not cry and I did either way. After the day ended, I just felt like I needed to vent, and I texted Nadine and she said she may be available to hang out tomorrow. After that I just spent the night by myself just not really wanting to talk to anyone it was just a difficult day. You try to be the best you can support, care, and love unconditionally and just for some reason it will just never be enough.

The next day comes and I drop my sister off to work and head out to Los Angeles. My first stop was obviously Runyon Canyon, it was great actually. There are just certain things that you can't do in the East Coast that you can do in Cali and it was a great experience. I just went out driving around and just trying to experience as much as I could because Nadine couldn't hang out because something came up. That was perfectly fine, on the way back down to San Diego I stopped at the Long Beach Aquarium, or I think Aquarium of the Pacific I have the booklet somewhere, but it was super nice. I think my favorite animal there was the Zebra Shark, that shark was beautiful, I wanted to jump in the tank and hug it but I was like ehhh nah it'll eat me lol but that would be nice to see outside the Aquarium like scuba diving and seeing it in its own natural environment.

Driving back down to my sister's apartment I was just enjoying the ride. It was nice we don't have roads like California roads in New York. How wide the highways are, the overlapping highways one above another above another it was amazing. I love driving so things like that I enjoy very much, then passing and riding alongside the Pacific it was a great experience I loved it. I loved Sunset cliffs, I loved La Ojlla Cove, La Mesa, Mission Beach, everything I loved it all, but my heart just lies in Santa Monica. I finally returned to San Diego and picked up my sister from work and went home.

The weekend comes and its almost time to leave and we decided to go out for dinner. It was a nice BBQ restaurant with pretty good food. At the end of the night Liv and Cormack left and my sister and I went to meet up with some of her friend's for a Bond Fire at a beach I believe it was my first Bond Fire and it was cool as fuck in all honesty. Just relaxing at a beach watching the waves and fire it was just dope it was peaceful and you know I understand why everyone loves California so much. I mean aside from all of the dam vehicle regulations, forest fires, and earthquakes, if I did live there I would never want to move out.

The next day came and it was time for my flight. I took my flight from San Diego to Maryland and there was a delay in my flight to New York. After one hour passes from the delay, they start releasing more information because people are getting anxious and asking what is going on. Usually I don't care very much I am very patient and let people do their jobs so when the flight is ready, they will tell us. Today was thee exception to that rule lol, information was released that the aircraft this small hopper plane could not keep an engine on while the air conditioner was on. In my head I was thinking welpt this is the day I am going to die, and it will be from a free fall in an airplane lmfao. I texted my sister and Adrien and my sister said good luck lol. Adrien said something along the lines of well at least you'll die from a heat stroke before the plane hits the ground lol his sarcastic ass lol, I love that kid. I didn't and still do not know much about planes but in a car the engine and air conditioner aside from being 2 completely different systems the wire harnesses intersect at only so many places so I was beginning to think it was a short but definitely a wiring issue and if that is a wiring issue I don't want to be anywhere near that plane lol. After 2 and a half hours they "fixed the issue" and on to New York we went. It was horrible, that plane was so small shaking from all the turbulence it was the worst ride I have ever taken in an airplane, but we made it safely thank God.

I took the rest of Sunday to relax and get ready to start my internship at the office. Aside from that I spent most of the day talking to Nadine about everything, she was very good to talk to and she was very nice. She helped me a lot throughout the years and I was very appreciative of her.

Monday comes and I start my internship at the Cardiologist office. There were some wonderful women there which were Melevna, Tessa, and the office manager Amaya. They were a strong very intelligent group of women and I must say I am glad I was with them. The school had a very good system with intern and externships I must say the school was very helpful from the ladies at the financial office all the way to the front desk I love them all they all got flowers lol. Aside from all of that I will not go into the day to day interactions or month to month events, but those ladies helped me very much. I fucked up a lot and sometimes you just need strong women around to tell you to man up and that's what they all were to me we were a good family. Towards the end of the externship they decided that they wanted to keep me, and I officially started working there October of 2013 and pretty much never left. They took care of me very well and they will forever be a part of me.

After the externship we returned back to school for our assessments and it seemed everyone did very well. As much as people like to look down on I guess institutions and technical schools per say, I can't lie that school was pretty fucking organized and the people who worked there loved us and they loved their jobs they did a lot for us and they went above and beyond and it helped many people to this day. People branched out to start working in New York, working in Greenville Airport, getting their Nursing degrees, or becoming Radiologist and Anesthesiologist like in all honesty can't really say anything bad about the school it was sad that it shut down but they did a lot for us and I made sure I articulated that very well to them. I would go and visit and talk to the staff and thank them bring them some donuts and talk to the new students like I appreciated it they didn't have to do all they did for us especially knowing the school was going to close so I thank them for it.

School finally came to an end and I started working at the office full time. Amelia and I were still talking but there was just very minimal effort coming from her side as usual. I was just simply attached to her I just couldn't let her go as much as I wanted to. I guess I was just holding on to the memory of how she was when we first me, how nice, caring, genuine, loving, it all meant the world to me but post Marcellus she was just a totally different person and I tried I fought for her back and there was just nothing I could do.

During the first weeks of November things were just different with her. It just became really sad and depressing to talk to her. She was just talking about death a lot and again she just wanted to go on vacation and just take a break. After all these discussions her pet rabbit had passed away and everything just hit her at once and she was just not ok. She simply just wanted to live her life without the thought of dying and all these issues she had going on she didn't want to let go of. So, well in mid- November she had fallen into another coma. This girl just spent the entire year fighting for her life and to think she was getting better things just got worse. No one really knew what was going on and after several days she came to but stayed in the hospital for 2 weeks. As usual I just couldn't do anything about it, but I tried, I was there as much as she would let me be. When she left the hospital, it was different she was different. She seemed exhausted from life and she had said she was tired of fighting she just didn't want to do it anymore and there was just nothing I could do. She just started being more distant, she just wasn't happy anymore, but she said she was completely over Marcellus and the drama and arguing and come to find out she was truly tired of it all. He made all his pages public, erased all their pictures, comments everything and she just deleted all her social media. I just didn't know how serious she was because she was acting the same towards me just distant and not talkative at all and there was just nothing I could do other than give her the space she needed after the rough year she just had and being in the hospital. The new year approached and so I just messaged her to check up see how she was doing she said she was doing fine and going to her doctor's appointments. I didn't text her for a week or two, then I would just randomly check up on her to make sure she was alive and healthy not to really discuss anything about us because it was clear she didn't want to be with me there was no effort I was the only one who would initiate conversations and they were stale and stagnant she just wouldn't respond. In March of 2014 I messaged her, and I got an automated response which I knew then she blocked me. I messaged her using my mom's phone I just needed to know that she was ok and we spoke for a while and she said that the cancer was in remission and she was on close observation and follow up, so as you can imagine I was pretty happy to hear that even though we both know it doesn't mean all cancer cells are gone but after the last few years she had, remission was a relief. She said she was doing well and for the moment was ok and pretty healthy. After that conversation a week passed by and I had texted her from my mom's phone and she blocked that number as well. That was the last time I heard from her, I chose not to make another effort because it was clear she didn't want me in her life anymore and we may not have left on good terms but simply knowing the cancer was in remission, as much as I cried myself to sleep I was happy knowing she was healthy and that was the end of Amelia and I. I have never heard from her since and that is just the M.O with the women that leave my life there just hasn't been one that stayed or cared to check up but that isn't something you can force you know if someone wants to leave you have to let them walk out, my story was a bit different because I just needed to know that these women were still alive and healthy. I may have gone over and above for women that never cared for me, but their health and well-being is more important than my feelings or wants or needs and that was the end of Amelia and I.

So, to say, at the end of the day it truly wasn't my fight, but did I stay to fight? Yes, did I have to, well no. Due to the fact that I was overlooked in the battle, did I really get anything out of trying to save her? No, but I did try, I gave it my all for her to see that there are still genuine people walking this planet that truly care. When she made her decision to choose him over me, was I upset, yea of course I was. Did I fight her over her decision? No, because I lost it all fighting for her, being by her side when I was never seen as a respected individual in her life. I gave it 1000 percent all hours of the day, all days of the week, all weeks of the month, all months of the year. I honestly don't regret it but that pain still runs deep through me and I will never forget the pain or the pleasure of having her in my life, at one point everything was perfect and she helped me through some tough times and I will forever be grateful and appreciative of her for that.

On another note, I do see now that Marcellus was never in the wrong, he was doing what anyone would, just protecting his woman. In all reality Amelia was never my girl and it was hard to accept that and I gave every excuse I could to myself to stay and I shouldn't have I was loyal and faithful to someone who didn't care about me and it's not that she was playing me it was the fact that she could have just been honest, in this society we are far from honest and it's something we just have to work on but to do that people have to be honest with themselves and people simply just have to much pride for that. I truly hope that one day we can communicate a bit better, it will be beneficial to everyone as a whole. I will leave it at that, I think it is time to wrap up this story we don't have much left to talk about but we kind of do, so it's a good time to take a break if you choose go get a cup of coffee kiss your spouse and give your kids a hug and lay this book down for another day. Stay blessed yall its always Love.

Chapter 17

The Distraction

So, ladies and gentlemen, I will start off by saying I love you all and appreciate that you even read this far.

There were going to be 2 chapters left but I will condense them because not many situations of importance happened between 2014 and now but there were few. This chapter is not going to be like previous chapters either so please bear with me.

I have to go back a few months into 2013 I wasn't able to add this small piece due to the explanation of the ending of Amelia and I. In December of 2013 I was contacted by my old Squad Leader Sergeant Niko. A lot of back and forth so I apologize for that, but it is needed. When I had left the military, I had kept contact with everyone I could. I just have an extremely high level of interpersonal skills and I just couldn't tell you where it came from but due to several women that were in my life it has manifested into an amazing characteristic of mine that I am proud to have attained. People understand that I am very genuine, and I care very much about everyone's health and well-being. Whenever someone would retire or leave the Army, I would always stay in contact to be able to have a form of communication. I know how we work in the military and I know that civilians have trouble communicating with us. It shows daily, thus if anyone ever needed to vent, I was always around. The things that we went through were rough and I know everyone in my company, I know their thought process, what makes them tick, what makes them smile, what irritates them and how they react to certain stressors. With this knowledge I knew it would be difficult for my brothers having their freedom again.

As I thought it has taken a toll on many of my brothers and I wish I could do more. So, in 2013 when Sergeant Niko contacted me things just weren't ok, and it was clear. We all make mistakes and sometimes the consequences are more than we had burdened for. All of this is ok because we are all human and we are allowed to make mistakes and just the weight that was on his shoulders got too heavy and as a man it is ok to ask for help. I did my best to help from a distance because he was just too far for me to help, I couldn't pack up and go help and he knew that and understood. As physically and mentally strong as you believe you are there will always be a situation that can break you if you don't keep your health on track. He hit that point, many of us from that unit hit that point, and to see my leader struggling like he was it hurt. As a man, as a brother, and as a subordinate it hurt honestly. He expressed his concern about falling to the bottom of a pit he never thought was possible. The issue was that he was keeping all his struggles inside, he was just bottling it in and not talking to anyone until he contacted me. You guys have to understand that just because you express feelings doesn't mean you lose your man hood, just because you allow yourself to be vulnerable doesn't change the fact that you are still very much a dangerous individual not to be fucked with. We came from an era where if someone looked at you disrespectful it was ok to punch them in the face, if someone sounded like they were talking to you disrespectful it was ok to punch them in the face and allow them to rethink their statements. Even though we don't live in those times anymore and everyone gets away with being disrespectful it doesn't change the fact that if the line does get crossed because they see you being vulnerable a physical altercation will take place and people will feel pain because people change when they feel pain, pain forces people to rethink their decisions. With all this being said he pretty much had to start life from square one. Aside from all his accomplishments, aside from all his accolades, aside from doing everything he did for us he had to start from square one and it was difficult to see him go through that. As the man that he is, he acknowledged his faults like a man accepted the consequences and began fighting a losing battle. As we do, he improvised, he adapted, and he overcame all his struggles and he is now doing very well for himself and I am proud of him.

Your position, your stature, your power none of that matters to mental health. Depression, grief, all the emotions one feels, if you don't air it out if you don't have someone to vent to and to talk to, your time is limited I am sorry to be the one to tell you that. It will encompass you; it will leave you with a void that nothing can fill. You can run as far as you want from it, you can work all the hours you want to escape from the pain of feeling that void but at the end of the day no matter where you run to, that void will always be with you. Until you acknowledge it, until you say I have to fix this everything you do to avoid it will be in vain. You will hurt a lot of people that care about you when you do that. They will leave you when you push them away, because they have tried to help but many of them couldn't stay and bare to see you the way you are. Don't think they left because they are tired of you, they left because they tried to help you and because they couldn't help you they left, they couldn't keep seeing you running away and hurting and not being honest with them when they ask you what is wrong. It takes a toll on them as well and that is what many of us fail to see. Depression doesn't only effect you, it effects everyone around you and you have to stop pushing everyone away trust in me when I tell you there are people that care, trust in me when I tell you that as lonely as you feel you are not alone, trust in me when I tell you that people see how hollow you are, we can see the void from the outside and trust in me when I tell you we tried to fix you but you have to make the decision to allow us to help you. You are not inferior to us if you ask for help, we are all here together we are here to help one another. The only way to rid it, is to resolve it, to tackle it headfirst. You are not less of a person because you are depressed, you are not less of a person because you have suicidal thoughts, you are not less of a person if it manifest and you hurt yourself. You have to, you have to ask for help. We are here to help you, don't think because you suffer from depression that people will view you differently or will think less of you and try and take advantage of you that is just simply not true.

I need you guys to be more honest with yourselves, I need you guys to start communicating more effectively. Even if you truly don't know how to, just acknowledging the problem to a friend is a significant starting point. That is where the help begins but it starts with you. I know how difficult it can be, but you can heal from it, at times I understand what most people don't. I know that it is uncontrollable and comes at the most inconvenient times, and I know it confuses you. There are ignorant people out there that will be hard on you and tell you oh that's what your depressed about man you better man up or they will tell you they been through worse and you got it easy. Yes those people are floating around but they don't understand that if it is a big deal to you it will eat at your soul no matter how insignificant it is to someone to you it is very significant and causes distress and we have to fix that so you may be able to live your life freely as you deserve be. You also have to understand this, depression sometimes is not about certain past traumas, depressions is not always about some things that bother you that make you over think life on an hourly basis and think people hate you and think you are useless. Sometimes depression is something so simple as a chemical imbalance and sometimes medicine helps and honestly sometimes it doesn't, I have seen both. The issue is if you don't talk or communicate you will never know if it is just a situation that you need closure for or an actual chemical imbalance either way you have to open up to someone about it. Talking about it will set your pain free even for a moment it will, and when you feel that release you will yearn for more of it. You will want to keep talking it out and freeing your pain and you will start to be more positive, you will begin to actually feel alive again, you will start to find peace and you will be able to feel love again. It all begins with you though, trust in me when I tell you that there are people out there that care, there are people out there that want to hear your concerns, there are people out there that will take time out of their day to help you feel better about yourself and help you become a better person and help you progress in life without wanting anything in return expect that you continue to do well for yourself. We are out there, and we care about you.

Moving forward in July of 2014 I started a second job at the emergency room. It was one of the best decisions I have made in my life and thanks to the day and night managers my second mothers they guided me and trained me very well. I consider all the nurses there my second mothers they are all filled with just genuine love and support and I love them very much. Very soon after I started many people began to leave and retire. I was the only one who spoke Spanish and I was on the night shift, so they needed me a lot and it was rough.

They are family to me so there was a time where I was the only person working night shift, and I would feel bad so I would literally be at work all 7 days a week. It got so crazy my boss that did the schedule told me she didn't put me on the schedule because I go to work every day, and she just wanted me to do a four hour shift during the weekday so it counts towards my actual schedule and I told her that's not a problem. I was never late, and it was a great experience they trusted me treated me like an adult and we worked perfectly fine together never any issues.

The issue was I still had time to myself, and the thoughts started running through my head about Jaylene, and Amelia and I would just get so sad. To combat all these feeling what did I do, I started going to school and I started going to street races again. I started going to Mableton County College with really no agenda other than to get away. I wasn't really focused on gaining a degree I was just running honestly. It wasn't a bad decision at all because at the end of the day I met many genuine people they made the time pass and it was a great experience and I did learn a lot, many things I don't care about but I guess that's college for you. Man, so I met this girl she was the most beautiful girl in the class and honestly that's pretty usual I couldn't tell you why I was always cool with the best-looking girl in the class. I never did anything except argue with the instructors and make the class laugh. So, this girl was Mediterranean she was like 5 foot 2 about 110 to 115 pounds and she was super funny. We would laugh all day long so this one day in class we were doing a group project and she found out how old I was which I was 24 at the time and she said "wait what you're 24 holy shit you're older than dinosaurs you're going to die tomorrow when you wake up." The group busted out laughing while I was just in shock like damn the disrespect is real around here, I had no comeback for that she got me good, that semester flew by it was great such a good group of kids. Honestly this wasn't even cutting it either I still had enough time on my hands, so I got back into cars and street racing in which I didn't really race at this time I was well past that but just going to car meets socializing and spectating was as far as it went. The people I met there were amazing Klaire, Alexander and his girl Donna, Fern and his girl Bridget, Reynaldo and his brother Smedly, Duncan, Monty, Dionte everyone I can't name them all but fuck it was a lot of people in those years.

 January of 2015 comes by and back to school I went. This was a pretty tough time I honestly felt like lost in which I was, but I wasn't focused at all on anything. I met 4 women 2 of which were such amazing women man I just can't speak more highly about them so we will cover them one by one. The first and this is not in order and this will not be very in-depth, the first one well will speak about is Regina. This girl was in my English class and I couldn't tell you how we began talking honestly but she was amazing. She was from Egypt, beautiful, genuine, honest, and so caring and sincere. I was just spiraling downward and when this girl would just see me in my own world, she would just come over snap me out of it and make me smile. She could tell I was struggling and after class she would walk and talk with me and days where things would just be overwhelming, she would be able to see it because I don't show it. I don't ever stress about things and you will never know I was ever going through struggles I am just very in tuned with myself and I maintain composure extremely well its extremely rare when I slip. Somehow she would be able to see through it and when we would be walking after class she would just stop me and grab my face and make me look at her and she would tell me to relax take a deep breath everything will be ok we will get through this, then she would give me a hug and we would go to our other classes and I honestly never realized how much I just needed that, something so simple as that to make me feel better. I fucked it up she definitely should have been my girl but I was just down man and I completely overlooked her because I just couldn't concentrate I couldn't re-center my attention and I can tell you now, how much I need that hug and need someone to grab me and tell me everything will be ok and the thing about it was that it was so genuine she truly did care and because I was just all fucked up I lost her and that one was on me and fuck do I need that, a woman's presence, a woman's touch, a genuine caring soul a hug and I lost it and I have to take accountability for that, and that shit hurts.

Ummm well the next woman I can't speak too much about so I will try to articulate this as best as I can. Her name was Livia, she was in my Algebra class. In all my life, all the women I have met and helped I could tell you without doubt that this young woman had one of thee most purest of hearts I have ever encountered, one of the most purest souls I have ever felt, one of the most genuine, honest, caring persona

I have had the privilege to spend time with. So, I had made a variety of observations about this girl from the first day of class. To explain things because I am weird, when I walk into class, I evaluate everyone before I even sit down, everyone in the class their body language, clothes, tone of voice, facial expressions its very quick. So, the observations about this girl I quickly didn't like, it was very clear that something was wrong. I had to be very careful in my approach to her, so throughout days in class I would hear her talk to herself while we were doing problems and equations. I guess to elaborate so you guys could understand, you know when you're taking an exam and you think to yourself "fuck was I sleeping or did we actually learn this in class, or fuck this is a hard problem." Well with Livia she would say it out loud not noticing she was thinking out loud, but it wasn't anywhere near what I just gave an example to. She would say things like "I don't understand this, I am so stupid." What she was saying to herself would raise huge flags, and for your understanding I sat in the last row to the left of the classroom and I sat on the far right of the table so next to me was the center isle you can walk through and gain entrance to the back of the class and she sat on the table to the right of me in the middle and in-between us was on kid who never came to class.

That is how I was able to hear her talk to herself we sat very close to each other. One day we had to do a group project in class and our teacher wanted us to get into groups of 2 which was perfect, so I found my way to approach her. The table in front of me had 3 people and there was a guy to the left of me and a guy in front of me. I told dude in front of me I forgot his name that dude was really cool, I told him to get with the guy next to me I was going to help out Livia he said yea no problem. I turned and told Livia to come to our table and man let me tell you my teacher gave me this look and I knew the look I get it from everyone all the time when I am dealing with women. I didn't give a fuck either, so we began doing the work and I sort of knew what I was doing, well I was ahead of the group so I just let her do it alone to observe her some more and she was just beating herself up about not knowing anything and I had already got all the information I needed to start talking to her about her. I didn't care about the math class anymore honestly. Class ended and the professor told us to just hand it in tomorrow, so I just asked her if she wanted to meet at the library after we finished our classes for the day, and she said yea. That is how our friendship started, we met after school and I just let her do all the work and told her I would just check it after she was done. She did the work and it was wrong all wrong, I started to explain how to do the problems in a different way and she said, "oh my god I'm so stupid how did I not know that." Well what was my first question if you can guess, I said wait who is telling you that you're stupid. She said everyone had called her dumb and stupid from a young age and well what happened she started to believe it. I can tell that I still had some time left to change that part of her mentality but boy was it going to take time so I committed myself to changing her thought process but there was something else very wrong I couldn't pinpoint but I had to find out what it was because the feeling that generated was that it was pretty significant and bad and if this girl was told from a young age that she was dumb the doors of what ifs and what she has experienced in life is way too vast for me to narrow down in a day. I cannot explain the thought process on that but to you guys it may just seem ok someone called her stupid and she believed it what does that have to do with other life experiences and I hope you guys never have to find out how I did at such a young age but it's not the simple fact of being called dumb or stupid but you have to broaden the mindset to her environment, how she was raised, their persona, traits, and characteristics of the people that raised her, did they call her stupid and displace their hate on her or was she a burden to the people raising her and they took it out on her or what about her friends if she ever had any true friends, any support system she had are they still around what happened to them did it affect her, just it's just too much to explain honestly but just broaden your mindset.

So moving forward we began to hangout a lot mainly at the library because this Math class and helping her took a tremendous amount of time and I was usually out of the area hanging out with a girl that I met and we won't speak about her but it ended pretty fast. We had a lot of work, Livia and I would stay at the library till it closed at 10 and times we would just go and get something to eat and hangout in the parking lot talking until 2, 3, or 4 in the morning she was just a whole hearted person. Well Valentine's day was coming up, so I had to buy flowers for 4 freaking class loads of women and my jobs lol. I don't know it was always nice to do something like that everyone enjoyed it. I gave flowers to the women in my Psychology class and man I don't know what it was they were all scared. Some girl said but I have a boyfriend and I told her listen girl I am not trying to get with you it's just a nice gesture because I know women like this time of the year and appreciate it and I don't know what people are going through and I don't want any girl to feel alone also I am not forcing you to accept the rose if you do you do if you don't you don't but if you do tell your boyfriend my name is Nate lmfaoooooo and well she laughed and accepted it. Other girls wait because this is my favorite, so I always get three different color rose bundles which are usually the common red which is corny and so generic but the girls love it I also get cream or white and either yellow or pink depending on what my flower shop has. So I go around the whole classroom with the 3 bouquets of roses and they choose whatever color they like and the girl says "wait is this real" lmfaooooo I say "no its kind of fake the roses are plastic" and when they grab it they're like "omg this is soo nice thank you" but that's not the point like you can tell who really appreciated it you can tell who was alone and appreciated the rose and sometimes some girls cry so I have to give them a hug because I feel really bad I can't stand it when women cry and I don't do it to make anyone cry I do it because

I don't want any girl to feel alone on Valentine's day I kind of feel like its wrong man honestly. There are times when I am walking inside of the school and obviously I would get a million looks from people and I don't care and you have the girls that say as I'm walking by them omg I wish my boyfriend did that for me so sometimes if I have spare roses I would give them one and tell them to tell their boyfriend I said he a chump lol and the girls laugh and take the flower, I'm like oh shit he really is a chump lmfaooooo. I try telling you guys I have never spent a holiday or birthday with a girlfriend so I know how lonely it gets but I do the best I can to make everyone feel good and special because I know what it feels like to feel alone, unwanted, depressed but I am a lot better now I have healed from it and I am moving forward with life, it just took me many years but that's beside the point that was a little rant my bad lol.

So, I can see from the get-go Livia was extremely special, so I did something a bit different for her. I got her a rose separate for herself not apart from the bouquets I bought for the class this was an individual rose individually wrapped specifically for her. It was very evident that no one has done anything nice for her in a very long time or actually never has, so I took it upon myself to teach her how she should be treated and to try and change her mentality to make her believe she was intelligent and she was beautiful and she was worth more than what she was allowing herself to be treated. I got to class and put my things down and started handing out the roses and I got to this one girl and when I showed her the flowers man did, I feel bad. The tears came running down man I was like oh shit what happened with her boyfriend. Her chump ass boyfriend broke up with her yesterday the day before Valentines, so she thought she wasn't going to get anything for Valentines, and she was so heartbroken from the breakup she gave me a big ass hug. I told her that there were extra roses and she could take them home, but she had to stop crying because she was going to make me cry too. She accepted and she tried to stop crying in which eventually she did then the professor was just like in awe and he was like "dude can I record this" lol. I said "yea sure just don't record my face and its ok" and he said "yea no problem" and he went around the room recording it and he was like "I have never seen anyone do anything like this that's pretty nice of you." I went to my desk and gave Livia her individual rose and she said "that's for me," I said "yea" and she just looked at the rose and looked at me and that look I'll never forget it, I knew I did good. With that look it was confirmed no one has ever done anything nice for her nor anything like that and it's not even such a big gesture, all it took was a simple rose and how the mood of the whole class changed was amazing and Livia was just in shock like she didn't even pay attention to the lecture she was just looking at the rose the whole time in class. When class ended that girl that cried gave me another hug and said thank you it means a lot to her, another girl actually drew out a rose she was like a little artist it was real nice and I actually still have the drawing in my math binder I kept it there because that meant a lot lol I never received anything from any girl like ever so I held on to that picture it was really nice. Livia had stopped me and asked me why did I do that why did I give her that rose, and I explained to her I knew that no one's ever done anything like that for her and I thought she deserved it because she was very smart and beautiful and genuine so I thought it would be a nice gesture and her eyes got real watery and she gave me this big ass hug I'll never forget it and she held on tight but she truly deserved it.

As the months pass, we hang out more and more and well Livia to put it simply, Livia been through it man. She has a very, very sad story behind her and how she's not broken, how life beat her up and she kept on trucking and kept herself up and mentally stable I just don't know how she did it, well I do because she told me but fuck man just thinking about it makes me want to cry. I did the best I could to teach her and show her genuine people still exist and she was very happy to be around me and we would still go to the library and during finals week we spent every day after school in the library until midnight studying simply for math alone just to help her pass the final and me as well because helping her helped me tremendously. Finals comes by and we get into the room and I wish her good luck I tell her not to worry because she is smart and she will do well, I had finished before her and I had to go to work so I waited for her to finish since we couldn't hang out because I had work. So, we went our separate ways and I totally forgot to call her after work, and I fell asleep I was tired man. At like 1 or 2 o'clock in the morning my phone rings and I'm like oh fuck who needs me and it was Livia, I picked up I was like "hey is everything alright," man the joy in her voice she was so excited she said, "I passed I passed I got a C plus but I didn't even think I was going to pass thank you sooooooooo much if it wasn't for you I wouldn't have passed thank you thank you so much." Can I tell you guys she is one of 2 women that have ever thanked me for helping them, that phone call alone meant so much to me and it still does I'll never forget that day just those small things to make me understand that I was doing the right thing by staying all those long hours and keeping her positive that thank you just brought everything together and it helped it really did just knowing how happy she was and I was able to be a part of putting a genuine smile on her face and helping her pass a class she didn't think she was able to it felt good knowing I was doing the right thing man it really did.

As the year progresses and everything, I learned about Livia I thought it would be a good time to take her out. So, we have to back track a bit to the first day of class, when I was observing the class and noticed Livia, I saw this ring on her finger. She always wore it every day never missed, and at times she would just look at it but would rarely touch it. This doesn't mean very much to you guys so let me explain so you could understand it. My first year at college in Mableton I was in stupid ass Student Success class where I met the Mediterranean girl, not important but just to remind you. My teacher was just different, and I didn't explain this because there was no need to until now. The teacher was just very uncomfortable it seemed to me. So, as I observed her, she kept touching her wedding ring or band or whatever it was. So, it was very telling how close she was to her husband I had no knowledge if he was alive or deceased, but it was clear he was very important to her. Aside from this it was very clear that she has been through many years of therapy by her body movement tone of voice choice of words that lady suffered man let me tell you. I knew it was going to be a long 4 months. So, what happened was I hated school still do because these teachers talk to you in such a demeaning condescending tone because they think you're all idiots and never been through anything in life and that is when teachers and I clash. I don't put up with that and I call every teacher out that begins talking in that manner. She began to explain that college is important because this and that bullshit whatever I didn't care I usually just get up and go to the bathroom to stop myself from talking shit. But this time I stayed because there was something more to this lady.

She had 3 or 4 degrees and was very proud of it and this and that in which she should be aside from how I feel about school I don't ever take away anyone's hard work or ethic away from them I know how much she sacrificed for those degrees I know it's not easy so granted keep that its yours. What happened was that she almost lost her husband I don't recall if it was cancer or something else. The issue was they didn't have insurance she had to refinance the house a couple of times and they almost lost it they couldn't pay the medical bills her husband was on his death bed and he was all she had and now that's important to me now that tells me why you act the way you act that explains why you went to therapy and that explains why she kept touching her ring during class. She was not comfortable talking in front of people I have seen this many times many, many times and for your understanding shrinks and anyone that knows public speaking they tell you when you are in a stressful environment you have to picture something or think about something that calms you something that helps alleviate the anxiety but when you are in front of people your options are limited. Now with the understanding that you have to think about something before you speak you have to be careful you don't forget what you want to say and what do most people do they take a deep breath before they begin talking, pause then begin. So, this teacher would take a deep breath touch her wedding ring turn it then begin to talk to the class. When she would explain what she was going through with her husband she would always touch her ring and turn it and twist it because she attached memories to her ring and her husband is what is able to calm and relax her during trying times and that bond that they share is attached to that ring of hers so she uses it for comfort because even though its attached to many depressing moments she has attached the best moments to it as well and that is what she searches for when she needs to relax and calm her anxiety it's a pretty nice method but takes a long time to develop so it was clear she has been through years of counseling those kids in the class didn't notice any of that but things like that are very clear to me no matter how clean kept your composure is I see it. This understanding I have of people it's my life it's what I do it's what I'm good at and I don't know why but for better or worse its who I am.

Back to Livia I hope you guys understood that story, so I had never asked Livia out because of the ring. I knew what it was when I saw it and I knew what it meant to her by the way she looked at it but there was more to it. I took Livia out to an extremely nice restaurant and let me tell you that shit was by no means cheap lol. I thought that she deserved it and after coming to an understanding of what she had been through and knowing that no one has ever done anything nice for her I thought it was up to me to show her how she should be treated. We get to this restaurant and the restaurant was by the water and it was flooded so there goes our reservations lmfaooo, so I took her to anther nice restaurant super fucking nice and she had always wanted to go there, and it was perfect man.

There is a really funny story behind this night but man I can even say it because you guys just won't understand and there's no point in me saying that, but it was just a reminder lol. Anyways we get there and we get to our table and I pull out her chair and push it in when she sits down and then we ordered the wine and meal and while waiting for the food we were talking and man you know what I love about this girl I completely forgot. So while hanging out with her the girl doesn't bring her phone she's super respectful and it's just me like I don't care lol we aren't together or anything but I loved that about her and her phone went off before we started talking and she was like "oh shit I'm sorry I thought I left it in the car." I had told her it was ok no worries and she said no I think its disrespectful I don't like bringing my phone when we hang out, man I told you she is just genuine. The thing is we talk the night away I love that we just simply talk, not a minute goes by that we don't she's just great honestly. So, I asked her what the story behind the ring was. She had told me her ex had given it to her which was clear and confirmed I just wanted to hear it coming from her. Then I clearly asked what happened and he was her first boyfriend and he had moved in with her well aside from all the years we go to what's recent. He was living with her and she came home early from work and found him fucking a girl. So, if anyone takes that in, let it sink in that he lived with her, so her house, another woman he was having sex with, on her bed, that's pretty fucking bad well beyond that but any who it gets better. So, I asked what did you do, she said she dragged the girl off the bed down the stairs and threw her ass outside oh man was that fucking great my homegirl did a good job she's a fucking fighter I love it. Clearly they broke up but stayed in communication, which was the fact that she did love him and that is why she kept the ring on so I told her just be careful because if someone is truly into you and they notice the ring it could push them away.

She began to explain she didn't really like relationships or anything of that nature because she doesn't like emotion, and she runs from it, it's very uncomfortable for her because you know, well fuck I can't even tell you that ummmm I will get into a discussion about it after the story I will tell you guys everything I just can't tell you her story it's just wrong this one thing about her ex it's a common happenstance so I could give you that but I won't go deeper into her life she means a lot to me and I wouldn't ever do that that is her story to tell. So, she seemed a bit uncomfortable, so I asked her what was wrong, and she asked why did I do that. I was a bit confused, so I asked her did what, she replied "like pull my chair out and push it in." I told her because that is how you are supposed to get treated I don't ever want you settling for anything less, you are very beautiful and very honest and genuine you deserve more than what that chump has done for you and to you it's really fucked up. To make things worse he never told her she was beautiful and let me tell you Liv is a solid 20 man she is super fly but just people walking all over her and not appreciating who she is as a person man it pretty much ruined her and she just didn't and doesn't deserve that and she said that it felt weird but it was a very nice gesture and I told her she should raise her standard she will be well off with more positive people in her life and it was fight man to get her to believe that she deserved better it was a fight man. She told me I was the best and realest friend she has ever had, she never had anyone care about her the way I did. I told her I would always be around when she needed me all she had to do was call. We had an amazing night and I gave her another flower and we went home.

 Some months passed by and it's just sad man. Life really hit that girl hard, something had happened to her extremely sad and my job as her friend was to make sure that she was ok. I would check up on her and see how she was doing and make sure she was going to her doctor's appointments. One day we had crossed paths and she had a lot of questions so we sat down and I spoke to her about what was going on telling her not to worry and reassure her everything was going to be ok and I was there for her and as we were talking I said everything will be ok I love you girl. Man, when that shit slipped out it was over for our friendship man. I had never had that happen, I tell you she was the first girl that I fell in love with and during the discussions I will explain the types of love and all that but listen it was mutual. That was the oh fuck moment because I saw her eyes and I was just thinking dam Mike good job fucking that up. We finished talking and let me tell you I didn't hear from that girl until I bumped into her at school. I was ok though, I knew, well we both knew you know she just isn't emotional and she told me she runs from it but fuck man I do I love that girl very much and I keep her in a special place in my heart but 1 slip up man and I lose someone important to me. You guys have all the chances in the world me all I ever get is one and I'll never hear from a girl again its really fucked up but man whatever. When I saw her I asked her how she was doing and she said she was well and she was going to her appointments which got changed to yearly and that meant really good news to me so I was very happy to hear that and to know she was doing well with a smile on her face. That was the end of Livia and I, it was nice crossing paths with such an exceptional soul man I'll never forget that girl she means the world to me she's always in my prayers.

Well in December of 2015 I well, we lost another brother to suicide. It was tough honestly, you try to take care of everyone and you're stretched so thin and you're so tired it's not about complacency, some days you just miss the signs and I wasn't around and we didn't speak very much after I left the military but my brothers were always around and everyone missed the signs and now he's survived by his wife and children. I had only met them a few times and we may not have seen eye to eye at work but outside of work I saw him be an amazing father to his kids and a great husband to his wife and that is what I respected about him, and now he's gone. I keep his family in my prayers always but it's tough I tell ya. Then to have other brothers tell you they are having suicidal thoughts and aren't doing well I just don't know how to help everyone anymore especially being thousands of miles away, how do I help someone feel wanted, how do I help someone to recover from alcoholism, how do I help someone free themselves of drug abuse from 2 thousand plus miles away I just don't know. Talking and calling only does so much, I need to be physically there the presence the physical presence means more and has more power than just a phone call. People need to see that you are there for them, they can't just hear you say that shit over the phone it's too generic, it can be played and taken anyway they feel like interpreting it. You can be on the phone and working and telling them to stay strong to be positive but that doesn't meant shit because you aren't giving them your full undivided attention which is what they need and when they feel like it's not genuine and they feel like you don't care they will create an excuse to hang up because they feel like they are a burden on you and you will never hear from them again and that feeling fucking sucks. You do your best to take care of everyone but there is only so much you or I can do from such a distance man and I try I love my people but I have to admit I am at a loss I just don't know what to do to help everyone and I don't want to lose anyone man, we, together have been through a lot and I as an individual have been through a lot and lost a lot so many people count on me to be there for them because of my experience and how I care for them but at this point I just don't know how I can help everyone and I don't know how to ask for help because there isn't much anyone can do anyway. I try my hardest to make everyone feel wanted and needed and important but fuck man a phone call only goes so far these days it's tough its fucking tough, and I don't want to I can't I can't lose anyone else and its killing me inside trying my hardest to keep everyone mentally stable man. I fucking love my dudes they are some an amazing gentlemen but I just don't know what to do anymore I am honestly at a loss and I am trying to figure out how I can help everyone, its taking time and time is something I realize I don't have much of anymore. This past year took a toll on me and I feel like a little part of me is dying everyday trying to help everyone giving myself to everyone, so I don't lose them, and I am losing the battle. Every call every text that comes seems to be worse and worse and people need me but I feel like it's a losing battle which bothers me because I don't want to lose anyone and with everything I am dealing with on my end its tough checking up on everyone and honestly I try my best but it's just not enough man it's not and that's the honest truth. So, I do my best and keep everyone in my prayers but sometimes I don't even feel like that's enough honestly.

Back to 2015 I met this girl or well she met me she helped me with some things with school and we became pretty good friends. The girl had a rough past but not to the extreme of Livia which is not really to compare lives nor life experiences, but I haven't met many people with a more extreme life path than Livia but this girl she had it rough man. So, I took it upon myself to help her and show her people with honest and good intentions and genuine hearts still are around. Well that completely backfired, I gave her 3 years of my life trying to show her that not everyone was after her, that there are still people that want to see others succeed and elevate others to a position where they can succeed. When I saw I wasn't getting through I stepped it up, I created an environment where she would never be physically nor mentally abused and I took her in. She didn't have to do anything or pay for anything all she had to do was graduate and receive her degree and we would be equal that was her only objective. I didn't receive anything in return but being degraded and belittled, and it was ok I allowed it because I know what she was going through and sometimes she just needed to air it out but it got to a point where it was just too much the disrespect was just too much she was so destroyed she couldn't see past her clouded judgment from previous life traumas and I took a hit emotionally, physically and financially for her just to show her that there are good people that truly do care about others and don't want anything in return and it was just too much.

    She never grew mentally which saddened me a lot, and I write this because I want you guys to understand that one day you are going to have to be alone and when you are left with your thoughts and you think and truly believe no one was there for you, well we were there people like me were there and we cared and we tried to show you and it was on you to accept the fruits of what we offered and if you decided otherwise then that is something you are going to have to take accountability for as an adult. One day you're going to have to answer for your decisions and I truly hope the consequences aren't negative I hope you do very well for yourself in life. I can't see people struggling, I can't see people down and when I see it I have to acknowledge it and I have to help because if I acknowledge it and I have the ability to help then I have the responsibility to help and I will give you my life to help you see that there are people out there that care about your safety, mental health, and well-being. In doing so I damn near almost lost myself taking care of everyone and I have to take accountability of that too because it was my decision it was my choice to help because I know myself and I know people I know how people think, I know why people do what they do, I know why people make the decision they make, I know why you run, I know why you displace, I know why you hurt I know your pain I see it and I know I can help these past two instances with Livia and the girl I took in were just 2 of many and I have given years to helping people mainly women see that their viewpoints were wrong and they needed to change and some take years some months some days it is all dependent on the person's life experiences and level of mentality and some like the girl I took in simply don't change and all those years I gave are lost and that's ok because at the end of the day I tried I know I did the right thing despite being shit on and disrespected for years I know I helped and you guys need to acknowledge who in your life is trying to help you. Not everyone is like me, I know when you are trying to push me away because you don't want to feel like a burden and I see it and I welcome it and I welcome you and that moment people actually see that you are truly trying to help them is the first step they take in beginning to change themselves and their mentality and viewpoint on life so when you ask for help ask for it directly as hard as it may be. You have to be upfront because there aren't people like me I'm just Mike and I'm weird and I just simply care about everyone and I see every detail in your eyes and I walk up to you and ask if you're ok, you couldn't believe the amount of people I have just talked to in Walmart alone because I can tell they were crying but all you have to do is approach them and tell them you know they are struggling tell them to stay positive and you will see them quickly change because they believe people can't see that and some people, well actually many people will vent to you because they just need an ear to confide in and after that release they will thank you and they will feel better and all it took was an acknowledgement and 5 minutes of your time.

After the 3 years with said woman, ummm well Nameless came into my life. That girl set a spark in me that will never be put out. Things shouldn't have ended the way they did, and I will never forgive myself for losing that girl. Shit hurt man, and I won't talk about it and all in all I have to thank her because if it wasn't for her this story would have never been finished. I met her and was on like page 10 and this is page 225, and we still have a lot to talk about after this story is finished.

Honestly it should have ended with her, the girl was perfect and it just is what it is, if I could just go up to someone and ask for their hand in marriage I would but we don't live in those times so in my pursuit of her to have her by my side as my woman long story short she fell into another man's arms. That completely shattered me, who would have thought it was going to be a beautiful, genuine, small time girl from New York that was going to break me, she broke my soul honestly. What that girl did for me I will forever be thankful for and I will forever be grateful for crossing paths with her no matter how things ended. I pray for her and hope she finishes school and I hope things are going well in her relationship she deserves the best life has to offer she truly does and I hope she receives all she wishes for, a soul like hers you don't come across with twice in life and I am well as heartbroken as I am she isn't one in a million I tell you her presence her aura I never felt anything like that aside from all the people I have met and when I told you there are a group of special women she isn't a part of that group she is tiers above it and to have experienced it and shared time with her I will always be appreciative of her and to her for allowing me to spend time with her. So, this is where the story will end, just remember that, It is always Love.

> **The answer to everything, will always be Love.**

The Farewell

This is my farewell, I thought it would be rude of me to end the story how I did without thanking all of you for taking time out of your day to read my story. First, I will be the one to tell you that I wasn't always a good person. I have made many mistakes in life and have hurt many people and there is no apology for that. I take accountability of all my actions and if I could change somethings I would because I don't like to leave things in the air I know things need closure which I was never privileged to have so I know how it feels to be left out to dry alone.

So, I am leaving, but before I do, I need something from you guys. Listen after 16 plus years I finally broke, I realize I am in no position to help anymore so someone is going to have to take my place. All I ask is that you talk to each other, I need you guys to communicate more and simply not just more but more effectively. I need you guys to put your pride aside, winning an argument is not worth losing the person you love. If you see your significant other struggling and they are trying to talk to you please don't dismiss them, sit, listen, talk, find solutions and if you can't then as adults it's time to go your separate ways and that's ok. There is nothing wrong with growing apart, what is wrong is keeping each other in arm's length because you don't like to be or feel alone. You're just creating a cycle of negativity that will encompass you and it will get to a point where there will be no coming back from it. All you have to do is verbalize your feelings, emotions thoughts everything that is on your mind let it out because I don't have much left in me to help anymore.

    I lost it all fighting for people, I gave up my life to society. I was hoping I could change the world when I realized I was wrong. This world, this society we live in will not change and it's me, I, that has to adapt to it and that is what I am doing after all these years and after this past recent heartache in which I will never allow myself to be so vulnerable ever again it was a mistake and a grave one. So it is time for me to move on and I honestly don't want to be around people anymore man, I love you all but I have a dream myself that I have delayed for too long in search for Love when after what just happened I realized love is not meant for us all and I have to come to accept that. I don't even have much love left to offer women either this love I have left I am giving it to my kids, all I have left to offer a woman is honesty, integrity, genuine support, respect, affection, attention, trust, and a great sense of humor but all that plus love wasn't even close to enough so I don't think all that minus love would change anything now. So, in accepting that I had to take action and I had to finish this for you guys because I won't be approachable anymore. I have refocused my attention on trying to gain financial independence to raise a family. To do that I have to let you guys go. As nice as I am, I cannot let you go without giving you as much advice as possible to help you navigate through your troubles and mishaps and struggles. So, I will give you everything left in me, and after that I am gone. I was going to open a business where people could just come in and vent and talk and spend time away from their issues and have like movie night and poetry night and just be in a comforting environment free from verbal, emotional, and physical abuse but I just can't at the moment and I am in the process of writing a story very sad but based on true events and I also began writing a movie which will be a change from the norm and it will be based off the story but you need to read the story screenplay and watch the film in order to comprehend what is going on and I will let you know now you are not emotionally ready to read that story and watch that movie but it's something I must show you all before I leave and I don't know how I will make this come to life honestly but will do my best because you all need it. You guys have to see what happens behind closed doors. Reading it is just not enough you have to feel the emotional burden people go through and when you see it, you'll feel the pain and you will understand it. I will also leave an email for any questions, comments or concerns, but as previously stated I won't make any promises that I will even check it. Let me tell you I was broken, I was depressed, you know I am a man and I am human, it took me over 16 years to finally lose my patience and for me to finally break but I have found my peace and you guys don't have to worry about me I am ok now. I mean the whole situation with Nameless is still fresh because it is so recent but as much as it hurts I am at peace with it and I hope he truly does treat her well and that is all I have to say about it I pray for her happiness and success and wish her well in all her future endeavors from the bottom of my heart.

So now I will give you all I got left, after the farewell I will give you all the poetry I wrote, then I will leave you with advice that will help you in your life, I won't just leave you alone, hurt, and crying like I have been left. I will always be here, but I found motivation which took me a while to find. To me motivation has to be tangible, I studied people and I never understood how people could be motivated by something that wasn't there and I always admired that about everyone. People would fight hard to be successful because they want a certain car, or house or just something they didn't have, and it was always weird to me. I just recently learned how to do it myself and it was tough. I am leaning towards adoption and that has been my motivating factor, being able to provide for my kids and being able to give those children a life they never thought they deserved is what is motivating me now, to see them smile and enjoy a life of bliss that would truly make me happy. I will adopt and give my kids all my undivided attention and that is what I am working towards. So, I would like to thank you all for taking the time out to read my story and I hope I have helped some of you. I love you all and I will keep you all in my prayers. Thank you again and stay blessed. Also from my favorite rapper Joe Budden "Sometimes I just need a hug, real shit pain shared is pain lessened." I have shared my pain with you and I hope it helps some of you in all honesty I love you all.

So, my people if you haven't noticed I am at a precipice and if I have to make a decision between you or my kids then I hope you know the decision is clear. I have given you guys the best years of my life and my kids are well deserving of 100% of my time and attention. If I were able to help you and raise my kids I would but that isn't possible. So, I hope you guys gather all the information here and maneuver through life making the best decisions possible with the information I have given you to live a life of bliss. I pray it works out well for all of you because I love you all, take care, be safe, communicate more effectively, Love genuinely, and spend more time with your family and children because they need you. Stay Blessed. Remember the answer to everything will always be Love.

It is always Love.

Poetry & Thoughts

Memories

Memories and scars remind us the past is real
Every moment nothing to fear
Moments and memories continue to be real
Other events cause us to shed tears
Ruthless memories are my imperfections
It was never easy to reminisce
Effortless but destructive causing disaffection
Shoving me and pushing me into an abyss

Birth

Allow me to ignite that fire of imagination and creativity that burns inside your soul, by telling you how the Pen made Love to the Paper and thus, a story was Born.

The Question Remains

They say, "it is better to have Loved and Lost than to not have ever Loved at all," but if every woman I have ever Loved, I have Lost, what does that say about me, as a man?

Love is Never Lost

Chemically speaking you can break a bond, but emotionally speaking you cannot, because the Heart remembers what the Mind forgets.

Time

Time is a band aid, a simple illusion to make you believe that you have healed, because you have forgotten.

Solace

I was sitting on the beach listening to the waves crashing against the cliffs, when I heard your voice whisper "I Love you," I replied, "I Love you too."

Her Love Outlived Her Place In My Life

She came into my Life and placed her hand on my heart. She walked away with it, forgetting that I needed it to Live.

Mirrors

"Objects in the mirror are closer than they appear," but it appears that, her fading face in the distance is no closer today, than it was Yesterday.

Diverging Paths

Whatever you choose to do in life, whatever path you choose to walk, make sure it's the Scenic Route.

Departed

She not only faded away, but I could not feel her anymore, I could not feel her thoughts, I could not feel her emotions, I didn't know who she was anymore, she became intangible, and that is when I realized, I had lost her.

Perspective

There is a saying that states "you go through life without ever seeing yourself." I came to an understanding about this very late. This saying, quote, or statement is true. It took me a while to realize that we all understand it, but in different ways, yet we all view it all the same. So, the blatant truth is, yes, You never have actually seen yourself. Speaking in a literal manner, you go through life being able to only see yourself through mirrors, reflections, other people's eyes, so it is completely understandable why people's opinions of you, are important to you. That is why we have to be careful how we treat each-other, how we view each-other, and how we talk about each-other, because the most minute opinion could take a heavy toll on a person. This is why we have to watch how we talk to our women and how we view them, in respect to how they view themselves and their own insecurities and how we can combat those insecurities and up lift our women. If you never get the chance to see yourself, how is it possible to form an opinion about yourself? You do it by accepting the opinions of others about you, usually these people tend to be the ones closest to you, whom you give weight to their opinions of you, and what they see in you and what they think about you as a person.

Pain is Addicting

So, when a person stays in an unhealthy relationship, if all they have ever known was pain in their life, they will continue to pursue pain. Simply put, because they are addicted to it and cannot break that cycle under the belief that they will never encounter happiness. They do not know how to separate themselves from this grey cloud that hovers over them. Even if said person does not want to be engulfed or surrounded by pain anymore, they simply cannot divorce the addiction.

Education

If you are spending years learning how to love someone, you are only educating yourself on why you don't love them.

We Ask

We, as men have lost the essence of the importance of our women. We, ask a lot from our women. We, ask that they leave their families to begin a new family for us, We, ask they change their name for us. We, ask that they change their bodies for us, by asking them to nurse our children for 9 months, knowing the pain and agony that comes with that miracle. We, ask our women to raise our children for us. We, ask for much more, but with all these deeds We ask from our women We, have lost value in our women, and it is time we have to take a look at all that We ask from them and give back to our women and take care of our women like we once used to.

Abandonment

    She didn't realize that, when she left, she took apart of my soul with her, and I still love her and adore her. It is a part of me that I will never get back and I am ok with that, because my heart still yearns for her.

A Lost Soul

A lost soul is one that continues to be by another's side because it is blinded by the unknown and fears it. A lost soul continues to work through a relationship because the fear of starting over is more intense than seeking the potential their companion will never exhibit.

Acceptance

This is not a type of love, though many confuse it as so. Accepting another individual for who they are and continuing to be by their side, is known as maturity, coexisting, and cohabitating.

Sexually Desired Love

A feeble love, it is brittle and easily broken; this type of love is a fallacy, one must be careful due to the power of lust which clouds and manipulates the soul into believing it has found another genuine soul, but has not.

Learned Love

Many times, being confused with Spontaneous Love, the time spent with another individual; the moments, the memories, the lessons; gives the soul an attachment an ear to confide in, a shoulder to lean on, but not Moirallegiance. This is a strong devoted love.

Spontaneous Love

A mutual Love ignited by the Soul. The strongest Love there is, it is not manipulated by one's physical appearance, monetary value, popularity, or resources; This is True Love.

Depth

How do you think I know myself and others so well? It is because I have explored the depths of the darkest places, never known to exist to man.

Runaway Love

When I gave you my heart, you ran away with it and gave your heart to someone else.

Stagnation is Death

Do not ever hesitate to do something, because if you hesitate you stall, and if you stall the mission never gets accomplished. Stagnation is death.

Remorse

Don't ever apologize for taking care of your needs, no matter if it was selfish or not, because at the time you thought your needs were more important than anyone or anyone's feelings and if something is that important to you there is no need to apologize for your actions.

Progression

I can't change the past, but I can try and help someone better themselves and their future. That is what gets me off my bed every day, being fortunate enough to help someone progress in being a better person for themselves and their families.

Irony

Irony states, Love is priceless, but may cost you everything.

Indignation

One of the greatest and highest emotions I have ever felt, lead me to the worst pain I had ever felt. No matter how negative her positive influence is, it's her happiness and she deserves to be happy despite how much she hurt me, I have no animosity towards her. It would be wrong of me to take away her happiness, it would be selfish and not many people find or know what true love is. Whether you call her love an infatuation or real, she found it and if it makes her happy, who am I to take that from her?

Destiny

When you walk a path with no purpose, where does the road lead?

Unavailing

I had the suture kit and was piecing her heart together one suture at a time. It was working, you could begin to see a genuine smile again that radiated from her heart. An understanding that there was more to life than that of the pains and downfalls of her past. That in this world there are people whom genuinely still care, but I couldn't overpower that seed of manipulation and despair and hate that blinded her. I just didn't have enough time to finish piecing her heart back together. I underestimated the power of sex and manipulation and never again will I make that mistake. This time it cost me a great woman who could have potentially had my last name a newfound respect for life no one has ever taken the time out to show her. Simply because she never met someone who genuinely cared about her, and by this time sadly, it was just too late.

Sacred

I don't ever try to find you in anyone else, the way you cared the way you spoke, and the power of your presence is unparalleled, and I miss you so very much.

The Paradox of Alcohol

Alcohol does in fact solve people's problems, but at the end of the day when all your problems are solved, Alcohol then, becomes your problem.

Void

That was just it, I loved her for who she was, but when she changed, all that she was, was left behind, and I searched for it long and hard, and I fought for years looking for the person she was, that person she used to be, that Beautiful Soul, with that genuine caring personality, that is why I held on for so long, because I knew exactly who she was, despite who she became, I knew her core values and beliefs they were genuine and filled with Love but seemingly so, her soul was overtaken by a fallacy of false love and there was no getting that old soul back no matter how much energy I spent fighting for it, it was gone.

Her

It's not because of her, it is because of her; only certain people will understand the meaning of those words.

A Dissolved Relationship

If sex ruined your relationship, whether it be a lack of sex or mediocre sex, it is only because sex was the foundation of your relationship that is, because that is what it was built on.

The Remedy

You're not supposed to nurse the illness, You're supposed to cure it.

Transparency

I know you believe your wounds are invisible, but they are transparent to someone that cares. I'm here to help you. I have your Cure.

The Storm

When your judgments are cloudy, whether it be because of Love or good intentions, you tend to believe all your irrational thoughts are justified.

Crossroads

You know, so I meet these innocent women and simply fall in Love with them. Their beliefs are so strong but yet so misguided. That these women are so pure of heart they don't realize what they do and believe is wrong. So I help them get back on the right path they derailed from and once they come to an understanding of what is right and what is true, I never hear from them again, and it completely breaks my heart, but I understand that it comes with the territory. The pros and cons of life and being able to meet such exemplary women with such a Genuine Soul, so I am always grateful for crossing paths with them no matter the heart ache.

What If

What if, everything I did to help others actually didn't matter, what if I actually never did help anyone and that is why they all left? Because I will never have the answer, all I can ever think, is that I guided them in the right direction with the correct knowledge that, if there were ever a serious problem again in their life, I was able to give them the tools and knowledge to correct their thought process, to be able to make the best decision for them in their life that would eventually lead to their happiness.

In Search of Confidence

Women, the internet is not a building block of self-esteem nor self-image, please stop comparing yourselves to other people whom do not value themselves nor care about you. You are above that, you have substance you have your dignity and self-respect and that goes a long way on the path of finding yourself.

Expired

In all honesty, there are just some situations in life that a person goes through, that they never come back from and some people never recover from this situation and it is the source of their downward spiral but, For better or worse, it is the way it has to be for their own personal development that is why the time-frame to intervene and help these people is so crucial and important, because even when all hope is lost, there is always a chance that, We may save one.

The Soul In Distress

The issue with emotional pain is that, emotional pain is more intense than physical pain. At its worse, physical pain can be felt throughout life, but may be treated with medication. The chronic aches and pains do subside and potentially for days. Now with emotional pain, there is no medication that can stop it, no heroin, no cocaine, no alcohol can relieve the pain even temporarily. The void the emptiness simply gets deeper and deeper without resolve. No matter what you do, nothing absolutely nothing can fill that emptiness, the only thing that has the power to heal emotional pain is Love, and many of us search our lives for it and not many of us find it, at that not many find it in its purest form. For a certain people who do find it, run from it, because they fear it, some don't understand it, and some simply don't want to acknowledge it because its power is not understood by the masses. So, we revert back to this life of vices that allow us to momentarily forget the void, but it's there forever, we must do better for each-other, and more importantly we must do better for our children. When the Soul is tired, drained, and exhausted the only thing that has the power to heal it, is Love.

Undying Love

Every day I miss you. I can never repay you for all the times that you have been there for me and supported me. I deeply and sincerely apologize for all the times that you needed me, and I couldn't be there for you because of work and that is no excuse. I look down upon myself for not being able to be there for you when you needed me most. I continue to help these women for you. It is not redemption, I can never right my wrongs but to be able to put a smile on someone's face and allow them to be free of their pain if even for a few moments, it helps them and reminds them that there continue to be good genuine people walking on this planet. I Love you and miss you dearly. Your fire still burns in my soul; the Love is always there. I hope you're doing well and are continuing to progress like I knew you would. Love always.

Untitled

Days go by and I just miss you, I'd like to tell the world about you but I hold you so dear and close to my heart on this high pedestal that I don't want anyone to know about you because you are just that important to me.

Manifestation

    I met a woman very Beautiful, Vibrant, Loving, Caring, just a Pure Genuine Soul. She was the Human Manifestation of Love in all senses of the word. She came into my life during some trying times, she supported me and Loved me in a way I can never repay back to her. Simply put she was just different. Just an Amazing Wholehearted Genuine Soul. I was fortunate to cross paths with. She will forever hold the keys to my heart.

The Prescription of Life

Do not be fooled by the Prescription of Life, because attention is the Placebo and Love, Love is thee actual Drug.

The Sacrifice

My Love, I was the umbrella that you needed, I was the one, you used to shelter yourself from the bad weather, then you took advantage of me and mistreated me, so I had no choice but to close myself and let the rain touch your sensitive skin. To watch you suffer was the worst pain I have ever endured, but that pain changed you for the better, it molded you into an amazing woman, in a way I couldn't as much as I tried seemingly so, I was your sacrifice.

She is Thee Exception

I never thought it was possible to meet a woman who challenged her place in my heart, I was sold on the idea, that it was her alone.

November 6, 2017

The issue is, I did not lose you, and you did not lose me,
we, We Lost Each Other.

Discussion Board

The Discussion Boards

This is a part of the book a few people were waiting on. To explain, this final portion of the book will be just general advice. By general I don't mean cliché thoughts, I mean it will be a broader perspective to help the most amount of people get through their struggles because I would personally need to know every detail about you and your situation to be able to help you. Since I cannot do that, I will do the best I can to write this out in a general perspective for everyone. If it actually is able to help you then I wish you well, and if not then I apologize and try and use the information here to do the best you can to navigate through your thought process to be able to make the best decision possible for your own personal growth and development and I hope all goes well. So, I will keep you all in my prayers. Let us begin I suppose.

Relationships

Relationships will be the first discussion because it is thee most important. We as I guess a society do not place a heavy importance on relationships as we should. Relationships are thee single most important event in people's lives and we get into and out of them so leisurely. This is because we have devalued relationships. Relationships do a lot for us as individuals, it keeps us mentally focused on objectives that are important to us as we grow as individuals and progress through life. It allows us to have a certain motivation, it gives us reason and meaning. On the contrary it also does the complete opposite if things go wrong or do not end well with our significant other. We lose our focus, our train of thought, our judgments are clouded, we become depressed and dysfunctional. This is not news to anyone, but people refuse to give power to a relationship and what it does for us in our lives. Just because you do not acknowledge how a relationship changes you and your thoughts does not invalidate the change of your character and person you have become due to the relationship. You can deny it all you want, but when you are working overtime to try and take your mind off how horrible the relationship ended, well that's a way of recognizing it because you don't want to be alone with your thoughts and the best way to do that is to run and spend as much time away from home as you can. While I am talking about relationships I don't solely mean actual relationships when you are trying to find a significant other I mean any type, a relationship with your parents, your best friend, a sibling anything involving people that changes and alters your mindset and discourages you to the point that you don't want to think about that situation well that is what I am talking about.

We have to place more of an importance to relationships is what I am saying. Basic example high school kids calling everyone a friend is pretty absurd. Just because some kid likes to smoke marijuana and is funny does not categorize them as a friend. Especially when the only time you spend around each other is when you smoke bud.

You don't know anything about each other aside from the fact that they are funny, then when you actually need an ear to confide in, they are not around so ask yourself are they really your friend or just an acquaintance? I am not going to get into that discussion you guys could figure that out, but we have to talk about finding a significant other before I go to sleep and forget what I need to tell you guys, but you get the picture.

Now we have to discuss relationships on the basis of finding a significant other. So, you guys are very quick to jump into "relationships" and this is such a common misconception you all don't want to acknowledge either, so I have to bring it up. There is a difference in a companionship and a relationship, when you guys talk to your friends about getting into a "relationship" you are pretty much explaining a companionship and you need to understand the difference if you truly want to be happy so I will help. A companionship brings the center of focus and attention at depression, sex, loneliness and filling a void. People often confuse this with a relationship due to the fact that they just want to find someone to fill a certain need. Or they feel that they have been single for a certain amount of time, or they feel so lonely they need someone around to fill the empty space and they need to deflect their pain and suffering and the best way to do that is to be in a "relationship." When one or the other gets tired of being involved with them they either find another person and cheat or simply break up because there is nothing there. There are no feelings, or they lost Love and you can never lose Love for someone the Love will always remain with you. A relationship, the center of focus is growing together and learning from one another. Being able to communicate as adults, creating a foundation and an environment where positivity flourishes, where mistakes are taken as an opportunity to learn effective ways to assess a situation and understand your significant others thought processes and why they made the decision they did. It does not always lead to marriage, it does not always lead to Love, and it does not always end well, but as adults in a working relationship sometimes life has its way and things do not workout. In the end there will always be a line of communications because of how you both grew and learned from one another and the bond and trust will always be there. It is tough I will never lie to you guys, its tough man. To be in a relationship it takes two people who are able to compromise, who are able to admit faults, who are able to place their pride aside and see a situation from your partners point of view and people don't like doing that, that is why the average person is comfortable in a companionship. Once the arguing starts one of them realizes the arguments aren't worth the sex, and why should they put up with it when they don't Love you, you are just convenient and that is the truth man sorry to be the bearer of bad new but if you didn't like to hear that well the worst is yet to come in the other topics we have to discuss. I am sorry that you are being used, I can't go into that right now and I will end this discussion here and let you guys talk this out, but man listen I don't like seeing people get hurt. It's simple honestly, end the relationship, reevaluate yourself take the bad parts of the relationship and grow and learn from it, the good parts of the relationship hold on to them, hold on to them dearly because sharing experiences with people is such an important part of life because your memories are what you will have when you are on your death bed and you don't want to be laying there depressed and regretful, lay there with pride and strength and with a smile knowing you did your best and shared some great experiences with people, that you won't regret I promise you.

Infidelity / Infertility

This topic has many paths and areas we need to cover. I am hoping to not actually cover all of them and letting you guys talk about them because it's a lot and I just can't cover it all honestly so I will cover some important parts and then go from there. I am not even sure where to start because it is just a heavy topic and I don't want anyone getting the wrong impression or ideas, but I don't know but we are just going to have to dive in it.

I guess we will begin with infidelity. Aside from everything that was spoken and said in this book just forget it for a moment. We are going to talk about infidelity in the average relationship for the average couple. Without knowing who is reading this it has to be a bit generic because I don't know anything about any of you so just follow me through this and if it helps you then I am happy for you. To begin you have to dig deep and try to recoup and find the basis and foundation of your relationship. It may be hard it may take some time, but this is a must. This is a difficult task because most people are not honest with themselves about why they chose to be in the relationship and that's ok, but this is where you grow so mistakes are ok and it is ok to admit your wrongs. This is a bit difficult without having someone in front of me to talk to because just trying to put this in perspective for you is difficult, so I am thinking who do I start with? The person approaching or the person being approached because the thought processes that go with it are what make or break a relationship. Damn this may be longer than I would like it to be but fuck it.

We will start with the person approaching someone who they see as a possible significant other. I am saying this in the form that they actually want to be in a relationship and not going after someone for casual sex ok so let us establish that right now. The issue is why they approached this person. What were they appealed by, looks, body language and posture, they liked the way they carried themselves and thought well I like that they are very confident, their posture, the way they speak, and they feel that they admired those characteristics. What was that defining factor that appealed you to them because that was the sole purpose of your pursuit of them and that is why the thought of a relationship took place and this is very important. People tend to lose sight of this and after many years they forget why they wanted to be in a relationship with this person when times get hard.

Complacency is a huge factor in the death of a relationship, you need time to think, you need time when things get rough because this is not just a relationship. This is someone you care about, shared experiences with, and gave yourself too. When times get rough in a relationship arguing does not help anyone at all. The yelling, the screaming, the blaming it does not help anyone. The one thing you cannot do is bring up a past event. We will get into a tangent but it's important.

When you and your significant other get into a discussion, I say discussion because I don't like to argue so I won't use that so let us be adults and communicate. When you and your significant other get into a discussion about something that bothers you and after you talk it out, if one of you still feels bothered by the situation, then you need to have a new discussion about it. When things get rough and when people get mad and it becomes a heated debate, that one thing that bothered you that you didn't bring back up after you discussed it you throw it in their face after many years let me tell you, you are wrong for that. If the discussion was over and you still felt a certain way about it and didn't verbalize it and you bring it up months, years later during a heated conversation you're a piece of shit, I will be the first to tell you. Just because you're annoyed because the discussion was taking way too long and you didn't want to talk about it anymore, so you adhere to the other person just to close the conversation man you are a fucked-up person. You are making the other person believe that they found resolve to an issue in the relationship and you sit there and hold it in because you want to leave or go to sleep and don't want to talk about it anymore you're a piece of shit man for real. That is where the complacency comes in, because you know how your partner feels and thinks and you just don't want to hear their voice anymore, so you just adhere to what they are saying to end the conversation, it's wrong. When this begins to happen, the thoughts and temptations begin to creep into your mind, and it begins to take a turn for the worse. I tell you don't do it, don't break your partner's heart. Once you begin to cheat and you find what you believe it to be a new spark a new feeling, trust in me when I say that your partner sees it.

    The cycle begins the denying, the staying out late, I'm not going to get into all of that, but you know what I am talking about. If you are ok with cheating and leaving your significant other in the house crying, alone, depressed and making them believe that they are the one that was wrong and making them apologize for you cheating on them, you are the biggest piece of shit walking honestly.

    So, listen when you feel this way, listen man take a fucking step back and reevaluate your position in the relationship. Evaluate what You have done wrong, you have to look past the infidelity. What if You were the problem and you were too prideful to realize how much of a shitty person you turned into in the relationship because you got comfortable. Your significant other saw or felt that they turned into a burden on you and they tried harder and harder to make you happy but in doing so, all they were doing was just annoying you more because you honestly didn't want to be around them and they were just convenient for you. Listen man I am not saying people don't make mistakes, we do we are human, but does that mean everyone deserves a second chance? Well fuck no, everything is individually based that is why I have to write so general because I can tell you about people that do deserve a second chance but it is very complicated to explain and it would need a book on its own and I am not doing all that so you guys have to make the determination about who needs or deserves a second chance. I say second chance very stringently if that's even a word.

Don't give someone a second chance because they just simply been around for 3 years and you don't feel like starting over so you let them cheat no fuck that if you do that then I don't feel bad for you because you are making the clear decision to allow them to cheat and stay and allow yourself to get hurt so that is on you my dear friend and I love you but you're wrong for it stop hurting yourself. Take a step back and reevaluate yourself, your relationship, your goals, your needs, your wants, everything and factor that into your decision-making process and everything will work out for you I promise you, but this has to be genuine. It has to be from the heart, it has to be a true feeling because if you're just doing it because you want to be in another relationship so you're not alone you will find yourself in another all- encompassing circle of pain and depression because you are not thinking about yourself you're just thinking about how to get out of a shitty relationship and that is not right, it's just not how things work. I guess we will leave that there, I didn't cover all that I wanted but if anyone has real questions, I will just discuss it then because it's just way too much.

Infertility, this is extremely important and if you guys are wondering why I mated it with infidelity well it is story time, so gather around the campfire. This one hurts because anything involving children is a very sensitive subject for me. Man, I really don't want to talk about this shit, you guys are fucking lucky I love you and I am giving myself to you because these are things I don't speak about. This section will only be written towards women, due to the fact I have absolutely no experience with infertility with men. We will jump right into it, so ladies many, many issues can occur with your reproductive system. So, we state ovulation disorders, issues with the fallopian tubes, and cervical issues and uterine issues right that should cover it. If you ladies are thinking well ahead of what I am writing and thinking surrogacy I am not going that far because I have had people tell me things about surrogacy which I guess is just common knowledge but it was their experience and I won't disclose all that, but I am more leaning towards the relationship issues that come with infertility.

First things first, if you have infertility issues do not please do not hide it from your significant other. If you have any doubts or fears that they will leave you because you are not able to give them a child, well sorry to tell you it is time to leave the relationship. If your significant other talks down to you, belittles you, degrades you because you aren't able to give them a healthy child, leave them. This is no questions asked, so don't be giving them an excuse, just leave, end the relationship and go your separate ways. If you do get pregnant it will most likely be a high risk pregnancy and there are some risk factors as in age and I don't get that deep into the conversation but it will be difficult so the best thing to do is cut the stress out of your life. So back to this, because you women kill me. If you have infertility issues, and you are in a relationship, the person has cheated on you previously please, please leave the relationship. Do not I repeat do not justify your reason to stay by getting pregnant. Please do not do that. Do not think that if you leave that man your chances of finding a partner and having a child are gone so that is your justification for staying and allowing yourself to be mistreated because you know what, during your high risk pregnancy while your man is belittling you guess what he's doing while you're at your doctor's appointments alone, well you guessed it cheating on you. You have to change your mindset, yes as every year that passes your chances of getting pregnant decrease yes that is true, but do not think that is the end of your life and it pains me seeing you guys go through that because you know you're wrong but you keep justifying it and allowing yourself to get hurt. I know you want children of your own I know you don't want to adopt trust me I know. I know that you want the experience of nursing and bonding with your child and the possibility is there but do not be with a man who has been in your life simply causing you problems. Choosing him to be the father of your child and we need to speak about that too so don't let me forget that because that's important. Do not rush into the decision of choosing a father simply because he is the only man in your life, do not allow these physicians to place this burden on you because of the age risk factor, you have to take a step back and think is this the right decision because if you do that you will see that it is absolutely the wrong decision.

Trust in me I know how you feel whole heartedly but you just can't do that and I feel bad when I see it and then you are just suffering for the rest of your life because you have to live and parent or co-parent with said person and that person never changes and it's you and your feelings and emotions that are broken at the end of the day and I don't want to see you ladies go through it, I don't honestly it's not right. I will leave this discussion here and let you ladies talk about the rest of the events and situations that are attached to this subject because you people need to discuss more and communicate more so as much as it pains me I pray for you all because I know it's difficult and I see my ladies going through it and it hurts because I can't really help, and I feel useless but I try I truly do so I keep you all in my prayers. It's always Love.

Dating

Hey ladies, lol well I am laughing because this is kind of funny to me, due to the fact that this is such a common occurrence and seemingly, so no one has caught on to it. So, listen when you go out on a date, please avoid asking or answering the question of, what do you like in your significant other? If someone is simply trying to have sex with you or are genuinely interested in you, you telling them the answer to that question changes things.

They will change themselves and create that or those qualities you have verbalized that attract you to a person. They will do this and create these qualities for a short amount of time to get what they want from you and ultimately leave you. It's not your fault, you were genuine in your thoughts and answers but please avoid the question and answers.

If they were interested in, you and they created this false persona to be with you the relationship wouldn't work because they weren't true to themselves. Even if they did have true intentions to be in a relationship with you it's just not going to work because they are going to have to be themselves one day and if you don't like them, as in their real qualities or characteristics and traits they are going to lose you and to prevent that they create the false persona to keep you then the problems start and god just too much to write or discuss so just don't it, but I am sure you catch and understand what I am saying. So, be careful and much luck to you all. It Is Always Love.

Promiscuity & Labeling

Man, I guess we have to talk about this, I guess we will get it over with early I will try to keep it concise. Ok we will jump straight into it; everyone loves sex right.

Got that out of the way, now we have to actually talk about it. As adults no one cares who you slept with or how many people you have slept with, it's none of our business and in reality, no one tells the truth about it anyway. One thing we have to be careful doing though is labeling each other. You people start throwing labels at everyone having sex which is just something you can't do. To elaborate, we will start off with the girl who tries to find love through sex, and I will not talk about women who believe sex is the way to a man's heart we will have another section about that as much as that hurts me but we will do it later.

The women that try to find love through sex are a very different breed. These women I am talking about, well they are very misguided. What is sad about the whole situation is seeing them just get used over and over again and then watch everyone clown them and degrade them and label them it's pretty fucking sad. So, you have to understand that you can't label them without having an understanding of the reason of why they are doing what they are doing. You have to approach them and talk to them and gain their train of thought, because it's the thought process that deserves the label not the actions. I don't even want to place any personal experiences here so I will describe this another way. Alright so you are in high school and you know the girl who was labeled a hoe, and seemingly so a few times a year you see her with a new boyfriend right? As time goes by you meet some of them and realize they are some douches when it comes to women, they may be very good people but their intentions with women void their good persona. They tell you that you should go out with her and after a week just tell her you love her, and she will give up sex then they tell you wait another month then break up with her. So now interest is gained because she seems easy which is what everyone is telling you. You approach her and talk to her and now you guys have a date set for the weekend. As you are out with her, you gain more of an interest because she does actually seem sweet and genuine, so you wonder why all these dudes just use her. You don't get the feeling that she is easy, so you begin to question why these guys just use her. So, you question it, when you confront her about it, she tells you that she doesn't know because she just thought that if she offered sex that guys would stay in her life. At this point with that answer can you label her? Well no, because her conscious and thought process is that if she offers sex, she will find love so that does not make her a hoe not even close.

Now things change when you find a girl who just genuinely likes sex and wants to enjoy as much sex as possible. She is not in the prerequisites to be labeled a hoe either. The women who enjoy sex and want to experience it usually have a standard that they work with and if you do not fit that standard there is no game you can play with them, no word play nothing you are not for them and they will shut you down they don't care. Now there are a group of women, a group that just genuinely want to have sex and they target people. They will target people in relationships and married people just to ruin them and that my friends is fucked up they know when you are vulnerable and they will take advantage of the situation and break your relationship and enjoy it and that's a hoe straight up. We are all human we all have issues and we all make mistakes but when someone knows you're down and takes advantage of you and your situation man that's some fucked up shit. Just some horrible people in this world but whatever man.

Ok and now we have to come to this part of the discussion because this is fucked up. So if you are with a woman and the relationship is going well and you have feelings for her, then find out she has a history with many men or had sex with many men and it bothers you to the point you chose to end the relationship, well you're wrong for that. You cannot judge someone for what they did in their past, for one its none of your business and two they are a different person, they have moved on from their past so how can you judge them and make them take accountability for something they did when you weren't around? You can't, and for those of you that do you're wrong man you're fucking wrong and you're just ruining these women and its fucking hard to heal them and its fucking hard to make them understand that its ok to make mistakes and learn and grow from it, like fuck man, yall need to grow up and be adults honestly I won't cover this anymore in depth just end the relationship if he starts judging you for your past just end it.

Anyway, we have to talk about these other girls, your common friends that get into a relationship every few months and you don't understand why. So, let me explain this to you. All these labels that hover over women, no one likes to be labeled, so they find loopholes to get around it, so their friends don't see them any differently. This common group of women are genuinely some nice women so let me tell you what they do. They are different from the women previously spoken about in this discussion. These women you will see them in a relationship several times a year and wonder why she can't keep a man. Well let me tell you, it's because she doesn't want to, and she is the one ending the relationship. Why you ask, well let me learn you something you have overlooked. Your home girl loves sex, and who doesn't? She gets into multiple relationships a year because the meaning behind it. If she just goes out and is promiscuous every weekend, you'll call her a hoe, but if she only has sex while in a relationship, she is not a hoe and just has bad luck with men. Get it, got it, good, now stop being such judgmental friends and let people have sex with whoever appeals to them and stop labeling them. Well finish this section here.

Oh, yea I won't talk about this much. Just to let you know there are a group of women out there that are fucking great man. They love sex, and they will offer it, but they don't want to feel like they are being used right. So, all they ask for is dinner and a good conversation to gain a bit of a connection so they feel close to you and they will offer you sex at the end of the night. Man, and these women are great, many of them are exceptionally funny as well they are great. I guess we don't really have to talk about soul ties here, I don't know but I feel like I have left you with enough to talk about this topic with your friends and significant others. Just know, It's Always Love.

Depression / Ante & Post Partum

Man, aint this a very broad-spectrum topic we have to discuss. Honestly speaking I don't really want to discuss it because it will take a toll on me and I just simply can't allow that. I believe I may have to add in suicide into this topic of discussion, but I am unsure of that, but we will see how this plays out.

In a broad-spectrum view of depression so we can try and help as many people as we can. First things first, when you acknowledge that you are feeling down, sad, depressed and aren't able to control your thoughts you have to have to seek help. In all honesty I am against shrinks, therapist, counselors I am completely against all that shit, but when you feel alone and feel that you have no one to go to and feel that if you did and verbalized your feelings you believe they will not understand what you are going through please seek help. I don't care how old you are if you're 10, 13, 27, or 45 please go find someone to talk to. I need you to go talk to someone for the fact that no one tells you guys this. Clearly depression can be caused by many things. I say things because it is not always a stressor or trauma that births depression. At times when you feel like you have made peace with certain situations of your past and still feel as if you have depression and don't understand the reason well that could be because it may be a chemical imbalance within you, and I nor anyone of your friends can help you with that, and that hurts me to say but it's the truth and I need you guys to understand that. So, it is possible that you may need medication to balance out the chemicals in your brain to control the depression. This kind of sucks because people also won't tell you that this can take a while and there is the possibility that trying different medications to find one that works well with you can cause your depression to worsen that is why you need to seek an ear to confide in so they can watch over you and help you and support you while you are in the process of finding the medication that works for you. It is a tough road to traverse and you need all the help you can get and trust me we want to help but before we can help you, you have to tell us that you are having issues.

For the people that are depressed because of life, or a relationship, or work, you also need someone to talk to. If your depression stems from some sort of life stressor, and you understand it, it is very simple to overcome. At the moment to you in your mind it seems that you don't understand it because you wanted the situation to pan out differently or you believed that you deserved more and the explanations can go on for eons because everyone is different and thinks different so I will explain it simply. For all you that are depressed due to some sort of life stressor and are able to pinpoint the stressor, to break the depression you have to learn how to be at peace with the outcome of that stressor even if it is an ongoing issue. So first you have to take time off, I don't care about your job there are a million jobs out there you will find another one if you get fired for taking a personal day. Yea yea easy for me to say from this book I get it I got it and well I don't understand I have to pay bills; I have kids that depend on me yea yea all excuses I don't care. I have been dealing with this for many years you have to detach yourself for a moment if you want to heal yourself and begin to have a happy more productive life your mental health is what's most important and that goes for your children and your job as well. Your children will begin to see a change in you and will be able to support you and listen to you more when they see you happier, your productivity at your job will increase and your supervisors will be able to pat you on the back and say that you're doing well and they see that you are beginning to care about your job more and the promotions will come in due time, but first things first my people you need to take time out for yourself. So, take a day out for yourself, when I say that I mean either a Friday or a Monday so you can have yourself a 3-day weekend.

Leave your fucking phone at home and isolate yourself, if you have kids, have insurance and a contingency. So that means leave them with your parents, and if they have issues tell them to call a best friend or family friend as contingency. YOU NEED TIME FOR YOURSELF. Sorry for making that all caps I am not yelling I just need you to understand how important it is to be by yourself during this time of healing. For the people with anxiety well yall are going to have to deal with that and its time that you learn patience and distance. So, after you have separated and isolated yourself, you need to go to a location that calls to you where you are able to find peace. That can be a spa, the beach, a drive whatever place or whatever you do that gives you peace you need to go there or do that activity. By peace I actually mean peace, I don't mean do an activity that you usually do when you need to run away from your problems that is not peace.

Once you are in your place of peace you have to relax. Do the best you can to relax, ease your body physically, if at any moment you feel tense you are still in a state of stress so believe that you want to be in a state of peace and just relax. Do the best you can because this is important, so if you need some aroma therapy light some candles do whatever you need to do to relax but it's important that there is no music, television no background noise at all. The background noise could trigger some memories and lose your train of though and focus. Once you have relaxed you have to understand that this is the peace that you want. You want to be a better husband, you want to be a better wife, you want to be a better father, you want to be a better mother, you want to do better at your job, and you have to understand that you made mistakes. You have to acknowledge that you have been treating others horribly, you haven't been paying too much attention to your children, and you have been making mistakes and errors at work. Each one of these situations have to be isolated individually, you can't bring work stressors home and you can't bring home stressors to work, because your start to treat people bad that don't deserve it and we are human and at times we don't understand that we are doing this until someone we love pulls us aside and tells us that we are fucking up and when that happens you have to think about your interactions with people throughout the past several months backdating to when that stressor in your life began and how that changed you and how you interacted with others because subliminally you were taking it out on everyone and didn't notice so you have to acknowledge that fault.

You must take accountability of all your actions and admit to yourself that you made mistakes and that you want to truly change for the better. The issue is to resolve this stressor that has dramatically changed your train of thought and brought you to depression you need resolve, and sometimes we don't get closure for certain situations we go through in life especially when things ended unfavorable for us. That is a killer in itself, because the thoughts of what if, and I could have done better, or why wasn't I good enough they will destroy you from the inside out. Once you pinpoint the situation that became your life stressor you have to make peace with it.

Whatever the situation was, you have to make peace. If you were the one that was wrong, it is time you make things right. We are adults, it is ok to say that you were wrong, it is ok to give that person a call and admit you were in a different state of mind and ask for forgiveness. Even if you did something so horribly wrong and they did not want to accept your apology, it is ok because now you are a changed person and are trying to do better in life and are trying to become a better person. The mere fact that you placed your own pride aside acknowledged your faults and asked for forgiveness and truly understood that you were wrong it's the first step in becoming a better person for you, your family, and your job. If you were at the receiving end of a horrible situation, you have to make peace with that situation and or person. You are able to seek closure if possible but most likely the person will deny you of it. That is ok, you understand what happened to you, you may not understand why it happened and that will kill you inside, but you have to stop guessing and that is what is important to begin healing yourself. It wasn't your fault that someone took advantage of you, manipulation is something evil and its ok we all go through it. Understand that you were the bigger person, stop giving the satisfaction of them knowing they have power over you by having them in your thoughts. To be at peace with it you have to understand that whatever situation happened it is over. You have to learn from the situation take all the good that you learned from it and begin a new path to understand who you are as a person and once you have found yourself you will find resolve in your past and you will never feel the pain from it again even when you think about it now and then and that will be your strength. It takes time it truly takes time, so when I say you need to take a day off for yourself this doesn't mean just once. You have to do this several times a year and once you learn to control your thoughts and the depression, you and everyone around you will be able to see a change in you and when they verbalize that they see you doing better that is when you are allowed to start taking time off and taking your children with you because you are going to have to teach them what you learned.

You will have to teach them how to love themselves, so people don't take advantage of them. You are going to have to teach them that they are blessed even if they have nothing, you all have each other.

You are going to have to teach them how to find resolve you are going to have to teach them how to communicate effectively and be a family and talk about your issues, it is all a learning experience. Trust me you will feel better about yourself, you will be healed of your traumas and you will be a better parent and significant other, for some people this is not going to work because they will make excuses to not take time for themselves and that is ok I will pray for all you but the simple fact is if you don't come to terms with whatever weighs on your mind, you will be walking around with a chip on your shoulder forever and that is something you don't want to do because everyone around you will take the hit and you won't even realize what you are doing to them, so I will forever keep you in my thoughts and prayers.

For a difficult discussion to become more difficult, the group of people, well there are many groups of people that I didn't list and cant but well for those that have extremely intense traumas for those that have been molested, raped, physically and mentally abused the support most of you need is more than one person can carry. You need the support from a team of people, I know how difficult it is for you to actually verbalize the horrible situations that you have been through so this support group that you need are from both perspectives.

You need the support from people that have been in the same situations you have been in, and you need the support from a group of people who never been in the situations that you have been in. Some people are just evil, and they start to compare situations and I won't get into that just stay away from those people, the outside source you need for balance. It is not a sympathy group, it is a group of people that will genuinely do their best to treat you well and make you feel wanted and loved and cared for which is important, that need to feel wanted and loved after experiencing such horrors it will help you heal fairly quickly and when you need the support from one of them in the early hours of the morning when something sparked your thoughts and need a shoulder to cry on they will be there for you, trust me they will they are there to help and support you and they want to see you doing better so just trust in them not everyone is out to hurt you, you have to learn to build relationships again and you will and we will support you in every way possible.

Antepartum and Postpartum depression, well this is a tough one. We will begin with your thoughts. The common factor here being the thought that you have this belief that you will not be a good mother. The feeling that consumes you that makes you believe you don't have the best traits or characteristics that your child needs in a mother and let me be the first to tell you that you do. So do not let whatever situations surrounding your pregnancy make you believe you are not worth being a mother to your child because you are and you are the best person to raise that child and teach them about life, no one is more equipped than you are so change that mindset because you are the strength and the parent that your child needs. Next don't give any thought into the environment that your child is coming into. You are the adult, you have to manage the environment even though it may not be the most positive, you have to create distance between the negative aspects of your life and your child because your child comes first. By negative aspects I mean anyone that discourages you and your pregnancy because you allowed a man that cheated on you another chance and then you became pregnant with his child and he left, all those people that are belittling you and stressing you, its time you create a distance between you and them because that negativity they bring around you, will depress you.

You're an adult you know you made a mistake giving him another chance and he proved you right by cheating on you again but now you're pregnant and he is gone. Its ok you took accountability of your actions but now it's time to move on because your child needs you, and if you are under any type of stress it can compromise the pregnancy and you can develop issues, aside from depression and that will take a toll on your child so as difficult as it is to move forward without closure and without a father for your child you have to learn to be at peace with the situation as quickly as possible to have a healthy pregnancy and delivery, your child depends on it. Listen you need to understand as depressed as you are, pregnancy is still very much a beautiful thing and you have to learn how to appreciate it. You may be blinded now, but after you give birth you will reminisce on the past year and how you have grown and changed from the pregnancy, so it's time to get up grab a hold of yourself, stop feeling bad for yourself, appreciate the life in you and appreciate the journey you are in to be able to give life. It's not to say appreciate it because there are women that will never be able to have the experience, I have had several women express their concerns to me and it is a very sad conversation but you do have the opportunity to experience it and you are experiencing it so bathe in the experience, appreciate it, enjoy it, and grow from it, it will change you and you are stronger than your depression and you are not alone. It is always Love.

Post-Partum depression, well don't quote me on this part but for those of you that are mentally strong and catch yourself in Post-Partum depression I believe a cause for that may be hormonal imbalance due to the decrease of certain hormones after pregnancy so research that and get back to me because I am not too sure about that one but I do believe that happens and often but I don't think it is discussed very much, so if you like we can talk. Now for those that do catch yourself in this depressive state after you have given birth, I need you ladies to relax. There is a giant Elephant that is kept quiet in the room very, very, quiet and we will get to that. So aside from healing after the pregnancy you have a lot to deal with. You know you have that stress of going back to work hovering over you, keep that shit there as in hovered so don't think about it. You have absolutely no need to worry about work fuck that shit, they will be good without you for a while you do enough and more for them, so let them take care of your job while you bond with your child. You have to heal and get your body working back to normal pre-pregnancy. You have to start eating right, intaking all your essential and non-essential vitamins and minerals and get back to a good diet for your child if you are breast feeding, and breast feeding is an interesting topic, ok pause stop being weird but if you ever studied it and came to an understanding of how it changes due to a babies needs and dig into that literature it's pretty awesome honestly it was a good conversation in class I never knew these things but it was good to learn how our bodies are constantly adapting like that or I don't know maybe I am just weird, but it was interesting. On top of all of this you take the burden of cleaning the house, cooking, doing the dishes, doing the laundry, the sleepless nights and the days and weeks pass by and when you have that hour to yourself of just undisturbed peace when the baby is finally asleep and your man is at work and you can sit and just relax. That is usually when it hits you about all that you have been doing and not one person has called to check up on you, and your man has not actually helped but you don't want to bother him or feel like a burden on him because you give him excuses because he is taking care of all the bills and that is wrong baby girl. This experience is for the both of you to share, your child is not a burden, but the toll, the mental, and physical stress, you have on yourself it's not for you to carry alone oh no, no, no sweetheart that is why there are two of you. So, you need to talk and communicate and express your feelings you can't let this get you down.

    I guess we have to talk about this too while the Elephant is knocking on the door. It has been some time since you and your husband had sex or made love per say. Then he starts coming home late and your insecurities start to run through your mind because you are home alone all day long and there is almost no communication between you and him at all, all day long. The tension begins to build up and then you think of how everything was prior to the baby being in your lives oh and that is when you have to stop. It is not your child's fault and I know that you just think that because the time frame of when things started to change but you must stop. Then you start weighing yourself down with more thoughts, how you have to lose weight because you feel ugly and disgusting, how you think your man, boyfriend, or husband doesn't want to come home to you because you're not taking care of yourself, and baby girl you have to control those thoughts and stop them because if that is how you truly feel then you knew that from the beginning of the relationship and if that is true then why did you even give him a chance. You get into an argument and your husband or whatever says he doesn't feel important because all of the time and attention you give the baby, well sorry to break it to you but your mans a bitch, sorry just had to throw that out there. Anyway, if he makes you feel bad for spending time with your child when in all actuality he is not even helping out, well yea ya gots to drop him sis that man is no good for you.

So, let us open the door to this Elephant in the room. Not a long discussion but I have to admit since I am a man, we are some pieces of shit. So, sex after pregnancy, so after all that you women do, you have the burden to satisfy your man after such a life changing experience. People are going to hate me for this but hey listen what's fucked up is fucked up and we have to discuss it that is what this portion of the book is for. You are hurt, you are healing, and you are taking care of literally everything under the sun and placing everything and everyone ahead of yourself. You are tired, exhausted physically and mentally and on top of not having time to actually take care of yourself, you have to hear how sexually deprived your husband is and how you're not doing your duty as a wife to take care of his needs, yo us men are fucking horrible I have to admit its fucking nuts. The conversations I have had with people are so wild, but this is life. You know what too, many people will just dismiss what I say and ridicule me because I'm a virgin but man ya just don't know how to be adults and communicate, it's insane and I try to do the best I can to repair your relationships because I know how much your women love you but fuck, you all just keep messing shit up and they can't talk to you so they come and talk to me and fuck dude I tried man and you are out there just ruining the woman that loves you to death I hope you all come to your senses before she truly ups and leaves I really do because these are some amazing women you are all emotionally killing. So, listen you just simply have to take care of yourself and your child, us men should be last on the list. If a man starts belittling you about putting weight on after pregnancy or tells you that you aren't spending enough time with him, you ladies have to make a decision. I have been on a rant too long and I am going to have to cut this discussion short but, it is time to grow up and be an adult and put your children and yourself ahead of everything else, no matter how strong your feelings are, no matter how dependent you believe you are on a person you have to make a decision to leave for the betterment of your mental and physical health and well- being of your child. I am not going to get into the discussion of staying with a "significant other" for the kids, simply put just don't do it and that is all I will say about that.

Two final things I will say is one, in a marriage and being Post-Partum, you will feel the weight of doing your best to satisfy your husband. You will feel the weight of taking care of the house, the laundry, you will feel a bit insecure about yourself and you will notice that you are losing a part of yourself trying to regain control of your life. Listen it is ok, you have to express these concerns to your significant other so you can learn to fix these issues when they surface but you, alone cannot, and just because you run away from your problems just because you care for your child all day long then run to clean when the baby finally falls asleep doesn't mean you fixed your issues all you're doing is suppressing them and that is the worst thing you can do so please don't do it.

You need the help of your significant other, you both need to communicate and create a plan to combat these issues and there's a lot more on the list, but just talk to other women going through Post-Partum Depression they will tell you all the things that go on, all I listed were the problems that simply surface easily the rest many people are not willing to discuss because they believe that they are the only ones going through it. Just talk please it is not that difficult and if your significant other simply dismisses your concerns then its time you look for another significant other. Next come the men, so after you guys have a baby there comes a time of abstinence, mmmmmm well I guess that's a poor choice of wording because abstinence is a choice and after birth a woman isn't supposed to have sex for like 6 weeks or something like that but you guys get the drift. Well I guess we could put it like this, sex shouldn't be a priority after your woman gives birth, and it really shouldn't be on your list honestly. What is important is her recovery physically and mentally after giving birth, you really shouldn't be placing any pressure on her to have sex at all. You should be able to control yourself and wait and help her care for your child while she is still recovering. There is no excuse. I understand what it is like to be with someone you love and not be able to be intimate with them, as much as you hate to admit it I understand that it does, it does something to your self-esteem and ego and makes you feel insecure but you know what's not the answer to that? Cheating, so don't do it, and if it is really that important to you guess what? Talk about it, see a trend here, it's called Communication and it works all you have to do is verbalize and express your thoughts and feelings because at times it is not you, and it is not her, at times after pregnancy after your wife has healed and still doesn't want to have sex, it may be that her libido decreased dramatically after the pregnancy because that does happen so she will have to go for a follow up visit with you to check on that. So, what have we learned in this discussion, that Communication helps relationships and if you learn to communicate and verbalize your feelings, we will all be in a better place.

As much as I would like to continue this discussion, I believe it's enough for you all to begin talking about these topics with each other and I hope you do. It is always Love.

Suicide

Man, aint this a very broad-spectrum topic we have to discuss. Honestly speaking I don't really want to discuss it because it will take a toll on me and I just simply can't allow that. I believe I may have to add in suicide into this topic of discussion, but I am unsure of that, but we will see how this plays out.

In a broad-spectrum view of depression so we can try and help as many people as we can. First things first, when you acknowledge that you are feeling down, sad, depressed and aren't able to control your thoughts you have to have to seek help. In all honesty I am against shrinks, therapist, counselors I am completely against all that shit, but when you feel alone and feel that you have no one to go to and feel that if you did and verbalized your feelings you believe they will not understand what you are going through please seek help. I don't care how old you are if you're 10, 13, 27, or 45 please go find someone to talk to. I need you to go talk to someone for the fact that no one tells you guys this. Clearly depression can be caused by many things. I say things because it is not always a stressor or trauma that births depression. At times when you feel like you have made peace with certain situations of your past and still feel as if you have depression and don't understand the reason well that could be because it may be a chemical imbalance within you, and I nor anyone of your friends can help you with that, and that hurts me to say but it's the truth and I need you guys to understand that. So, it is possible that you may need medication to balance out the chemicals in your brain to control the depression. This kind of sucks because people also won't tell you that this can take a while and there is the possibility that trying different medications to find one that works well with you can cause your depression to worsen that is why you need to seek an ear to confide in so they can watch over you and help you and support you while you are in the process of finding the medication that works for you. It is a tough road to traverse and you need all the help you can get and trust me we want to help but before we can help you, you have to tell us that you are having issues.

For the people that are depressed because of life, or a relationship, or work, you also need someone to talk to. If your depression stems from some sort of life stressor, and you understand it, it is very simple to overcome. At the moment to you in your mind it seems that you don't understand it because you wanted the situation to pan out differently or you believed that you deserved more and the explanations can go on for eons because everyone is different and thinks different so I will explain it simply. For all you that are depressed due to some sort of life stressor and are able to pinpoint the stressor, to break the depression you have to learn how to be at peace with the outcome of that stressor even if it is an ongoing issue. So first you have to take time off, I don't care about your job there are a million jobs out there you will find another one if you get fired for taking a personal day. Yea yea easy for me to say from this book I get it I got it and well I don't understand I have to pay bills; I have kids that depend on me yea yea all excuses I don't care. I have been dealing with this for many years you have to detach yourself for a moment if you want to heal yourself and begin to have a happy more productive life your mental health is what's most important and that goes for your children and your job as well. Your children will begin to see a change in you and will be able to support you and listen to you more when they see you happier, your productivity at your job will increase and your supervisors will be able to pat you on the back and say that you're doing well and they see that you are beginning to care about your job more and the promotions will come in due time, but first things first my people you need to take time out for yourself. So, take a day out for yourself, when I say that I mean either a Friday or a Monday so you can have yourself a 3-day weekend.

Leave your fucking phone at home and isolate yourself, if you have kids, have insurance and a contingency. So that means leave them with your parents, and if they have issues tell them to call a best friend or family friend as contingency. YOU NEED TIME FOR YOURSELF. Sorry for making that all caps I am not yelling I just need you to understand how important it is to be by yourself during this time of healing. For the people with anxiety well yall are going to have to deal with that and its time that you learn patience and distance. So, after you have separated and isolated yourself, you need to go to a location that calls to you where you are able to find peace. That can be a spa, the beach, a drive whatever place or whatever you do that gives you peace you need to go there or do that activity. By peace I actually mean peace, I don't mean do an activity that you usually do when you need to run away from your problems that is not peace.

Once you are in your place of peace you have to relax. Do the best you can to relax, ease your body physically, if at any moment you feel tense you are still in a state of stress so believe that you want to be in a state of peace and just relax. Do the best you can because this is important, so if you need some aroma therapy light some candles do whatever you need to do to relax but it's important that there is no music, television no background noise at all. The background noise could trigger some memories and lose your train of though and focus. Once you have relaxed you have to understand that this is the peace that you want. You want to be a better husband, you want to be a better wife, you want to be a better father, you want to be a better mother, you want to do better at your job, and you have to understand that you made mistakes. You have to acknowledge that you have been treating others horribly, you haven't been paying too much attention to your children, and you have been making mistakes and errors at work. Each one of these situations have to be isolated individually, you can't bring work stressors home and you can't bring home stressors to work, because your start to treat people bad that don't deserve it and we are human and at times we don't understand that we are doing this until someone we love pulls us aside and tells us that we are fucking up and when that happens you have to think about your interactions with people throughout the past several months backdating to when that stressor in your life began and how that changed you and how you interacted with others because subliminally you were taking it out on everyone and didn't notice so you have to acknowledge that fault.

You must take accountability of all your actions and admit to yourself that you made mistakes and that you want to truly change for the better. The issue is to resolve this stressor that has dramatically changed your train of thought and brought you to depression you need resolve, and sometimes we don't get closure for certain situations we go through in life especially when things ended unfavorable for us. That is a killer in itself, because the thoughts of what if, and I could have done better, or why wasn't I good enough they will destroy you from the inside out. Once you pinpoint the situation that became your life stressor you have to make peace with it.

Whatever the situation was, you have to make peace. If you were the one that was wrong, it is time you make things right. We are adults, it is ok to say that you were wrong, it is ok to give that person a call and admit you were in a different state of mind and ask for forgiveness. Even if you did something so horribly wrong and they did not want to accept your apology, it is ok because now you are a changed person and are trying to do better in life and are trying to become a better person. The mere fact that you placed your own pride aside acknowledged your faults and asked for forgiveness and truly understood that you were wrong it's the first step in becoming a better person for you, your family, and your job. If you were at the receiving end of a horrible situation, you have to make peace with that situation and or person. You are able to seek closure if possible but most likely the person will deny you of it. That is ok, you understand what happened to you, you may not understand why it happened and that will kill you inside, but you have to stop guessing and that is what is important to begin healing yourself. It wasn't your fault that someone took advantage of you, manipulation is something evil and its ok we all go through it. Understand that you were the bigger person, stop giving the satisfaction of them knowing they have power over you by having them in your thoughts. To be at peace with it you have to understand that whatever situation happened it is over. You have to learn from the situation take all the good that you learned from it and begin a new path to understand who you are as a person and once you have found yourself you will find resolve in your past and you will never feel the pain from it again even when you think about it now and then and that will be your strength. It takes time it truly takes time, so when I say you need to take a day off for yourself this doesn't mean just once. You have to do this several times a year and once you learn to control your thoughts and the depression, you and everyone around you will be able to see a change in you and when they verbalize that they see you doing better that is when you are allowed to start taking time off and taking your children with you because you are going to have to teach them what you learned.

You will have to teach them how to love themselves, so people don't take advantage of them. You are going to have to teach them that they are blessed even if they have nothing, you all have each other. You are going to have to teach them how to find resolve you are going to have to teach them how to communicate effectively and be a family and talk about your issues, it is all a learning experience. Trust me you will feel better about yourself, you will be healed of your traumas and you will be a better parent and significant other, for some people this is not going to work because they will make excuses to not take time for themselves and that is ok I will pray for all you but the simple fact is if you don't come to terms with whatever weighs on your mind, you will be walking around with a chip on your shoulder forever and that is something you don't want to do because everyone around you will take the hit and you won't even realize what you are doing to them, so I will forever keep you in my thoughts and prayers.

For a difficult discussion to become more difficult, the group of people, well there are many groups of people that I didn't list and cant but well for those that have extremely intense traumas for those that have been molested, raped, physically and mentally abused the support most of you need is more than one person can carry. You need the support from a team of people, I know how difficult it is for you to actually verbalize the horrible situations that you have been through so this support group that you need are from both perspectives.

You need the support from people that have been in the same situations you have been in, and you need the support from a group of people who never been in the situations that you have been in. Some people are just evil, and they start to compare situations and I won't get into that just stay away from those people, the outside source you need for balance. It is not a sympathy group, it is a group of people that will genuinely do their best to treat you well and make you feel wanted and loved and cared for which is important, that need to feel wanted and loved after experiencing such horrors it will help you heal fairly quickly and when you need the support from one of them in the early hours of the morning when something sparked your thoughts and need a shoulder to cry on they will be there for you, trust me they will they are there to help and support you and they want to see you doing better so just trust in them not everyone is out to hurt you, you have to learn to build relationships again and you will and we will support you in every way possible.

Antepartum and Postpartum depression, well this is a tough one. We will begin with your thoughts. The common factor here being the thought that you have this belief that you will not be a good mother. The feeling that consumes you that makes you believe you don't have the best traits or characteristics that your child needs in a mother and let me be the first to tell you that you do. So do not let whatever situations surrounding your pregnancy make you believe you are not worth being a mother to your child because you are and you are the best person to raise that child and teach them about life, no one is more equipped than you are so change that mindset because you are the strength and the parent that your child needs. Next don't give any thought into the environment that your child is coming into. You are the adult, you have to manage the environment even though it may not be the most positive, you have to create distance between the negative aspects of your life and your child because your child comes first. By negative aspects I mean anyone that discourages you and your pregnancy because you allowed a man that cheated on you another chance and then you became pregnant with his child and he left, all those people that are belittling you and stressing you, its time you create a distance between you and them because that negativity they bring around you, will depress you.

You're an adult you know you made a mistake giving him another chance and he proved you right by cheating on you again but now you're pregnant and he is gone. Its ok you took accountability of your actions but now it's time to move on because your child needs you, and if you are under any type of stress it can compromise the pregnancy and you can develop issues, aside from depression and that will take a toll on your child so as difficult as it is to move forward without closure and without a father for your child you have to learn to be at peace with the situation as quickly as possible to have a healthy pregnancy and delivery, your child depends on it. Listen you need to understand as depressed as you are, pregnancy is still very much a beautiful thing and you have to learn how to appreciate it. You may be blinded now, but after you give birth you will reminisce on the past year and how you have grown and changed from the pregnancy, so it's time to get up grab a hold of yourself, stop feeling bad for yourself, appreciate the life in you and appreciate the journey you are in to be able to give life. It's not to say appreciate it because there are women that will never be able to have the experience, I have had several women express their concerns to me and it is a very sad conversation but you do have the opportunity to experience it and you are experiencing it so bathe in the experience, appreciate it, enjoy it, and grow from it, it will change you and you are stronger than your depression and you are not alone. It is always Love.

Post-Partum depression, well don't quote me on this part but for those of you that are mentally strong and catch yourself in Post-Partum depression I believe a cause for that may be hormonal imbalance due to the decrease of certain hormones after pregnancy so research that and get back to me because I am not too sure about that one but I do believe that happens and often but I don't think it is discussed very much, so if you like we can talk. Now for those that do catch yourself in this depressive state after you have given birth, I need you ladies to relax. There is a giant Elephant that is kept quiet in the room very, very, quiet and we will get to that. So aside from healing after the pregnancy you have a lot to deal with. You know you have that stress of going back to work hovering over you, keep that shit there as in hovered so don't think about it. You have absolutely no need to worry about work fuck that shit, they will be good without you for a while you do enough and more for them, so let them take care of your job while you bond with your child. You have to heal and get your body working back to normal pre-pregnancy. You have to start eating right, intaking all your essential and non-essential vitamins and minerals and get back to a good diet for your child if you are breast feeding, and breast feeding is an interesting topic, ok pause stop being weird but if you ever studied it and came to an understanding of how it changes due to a babies needs and dig into that literature it's pretty awesome honestly it was a good conversation in class I never knew these things but it was good to learn how our bodies are constantly adapting like that or I don't know maybe I am just weird, but it was interesting. On top of all of this you take the burden of cleaning the house, cooking, doing the dishes, doing the laundry, the sleepless nights and the days and weeks pass by and when you have that hour to yourself of just undisturbed peace when the baby is finally asleep and your man is at work and you can sit and just relax. That is usually when it hits you about all that you have been doing and not one person has called to check up on you, and your man has not actually helped but you don't want to bother him or feel like a burden on him because you give him excuses because he is taking care of all the bills and that is wrong baby girl. This experience is for the both of you to share, your child is not a burden, but the toll, the mental, and physical stress, you have on yourself it's not for you to carry alone oh no, no, no sweetheart that is why there are two of you. So, you need to talk and communicate and express your feelings you can't let this get you down.

I guess we have to talk about this too while the Elephant is knocking on the door. It has been some time since you and your husband had sex or made love per say. Then he starts coming home late and your insecurities start to run through your mind because you are home alone all day long and there is almost no communication between you and him at all, all day long. The tension begins to build up and then you think of how everything was prior to the baby being in your lives oh and that is when you have to stop. It is not your child's fault and I know that you just think that because the time frame of when things started to change but you must stop. Then you start weighing yourself down with more thoughts, how you have to lose weight because you feel ugly and disgusting, how you think your man, boyfriend, or husband doesn't want to come home to you because you're not taking care of yourself, and baby girl you have to control those thoughts and stop them because if that is how you truly feel then you knew that from the beginning of the relationship and if that is true then why did you even give him a chance. You get into an argument and your husband or whatever says he doesn't feel important because all of the time and attention you give the baby, well sorry to break it to you but your mans a bitch, sorry just had to throw that out there. Anyway, if he makes you feel bad for spending time with your child when in all actuality he is not even helping out, well yea ya gots to drop him sis that man is no good for you.

So, let us open the door to this Elephant in the room. Not a long discussion but I have to admit since I am a man, we are some pieces of shit. So, sex after pregnancy, so after all that you women do, you have the burden to satisfy your man after such a life changing experience. People are going to hate me for this but hey listen what's fucked up is fucked up and we have to discuss it that is what this portion of the book is for. You are hurt, you are healing, and you are taking care of literally everything under the sun and placing everything and everyone ahead of yourself. You are tired, exhausted physically and mentally and on top of not having time to actually take care of yourself, you have to hear how sexually deprived your husband is and how you're not doing your duty as a wife to take care of his needs, yo us men are fucking horrible I have to admit its fucking nuts. The conversations I have had with people are so wild, but this is life. You know what too, many people will just dismiss what I say and ridicule me because I'm a virgin but man ya just don't know how to be adults and communicate, it's insane and I try to do the best I can to repair your relationships because I know how much your women love you but fuck, you all just keep messing shit up and they can't talk to you so they come and talk to me and fuck dude I tried man and you are out there just ruining the woman that loves you to death I hope you all come to your senses before she truly ups and leaves I really do because these are some amazing women you are all emotionally killing. So, listen you just simply have to take care of yourself and your child, us men should be last on the list. If a man starts belittling you about putting weight on after pregnancy or tells you that you aren't spending enough time with him, you ladies have to make a decision. I have been on a rant too long and I am going to have to cut this discussion short but, it is time to grow up and be an adult and put your children and yourself ahead of everything else, no matter how strong your feelings are, no matter how dependent you believe you are on a person you have to make a decision to leave for the betterment of your mental and physical health and well- being of your child. I am not going to get into the discussion of staying with a "significant other" for the kids, simply put just don't do it and that is all I will say about that.

Two final things I will say is one, in a marriage and being Post-Partum, you will feel the weight of doing your best to satisfy your husband. You will feel the weight of taking care of the house, the laundry, you will feel a bit insecure about yourself and you will notice that you are losing a part of yourself trying to regain control of your life. Listen it is ok, you have to express these concerns to your significant other so you can learn to fix these issues when they surface but you, alone cannot, and just because you run away from your problems just because you care for your child all day long then run to clean when the baby finally falls asleep doesn't mean you fixed your issues all you're doing is suppressing them and that is the worst thing you can do so please don't do it.

You need the help of your significant other, you both need to communicate and create a plan to combat these issues and there's a lot more on the list, but just talk to other women going through Post-Partum Depression they will tell you all the things that go on, all I listed were the problems that simply surface easily the rest many people are not willing to discuss because they believe that they are the only ones going through it. Just talk please it is not that difficult and if your significant other simply dismisses your concerns then its time you look for another significant other. Next come the men, so after you guys have a baby there comes a time of abstinence, mmmmmm well I guess that's a poor choice of wording because abstinence is a choice and after birth a woman isn't supposed to have sex for like 6 weeks or something like that but you guys get the drift. Well I guess we could put it like this, sex shouldn't be a priority after your woman gives birth, and it really shouldn't be on your list honestly. What is important is her recovery physically and mentally after giving birth, you really shouldn't be placing any pressure on her to have sex at all. You should be able to control yourself and wait and help her care for your child while she is still recovering. There is no excuse. I understand what it is like to be with someone you love and not be able to be intimate with them, as much as you hate to admit it I understand that it does, it does something to your self-esteem and ego and makes you feel insecure but you know what's not the answer to that? Cheating, so don't do it, and if it is really that important to you guess what? Talk about it, see a trend here, it's called Communication and it works all you have to do is verbalize and express your thoughts and feelings because at times it is not you, and it is not her, at times after pregnancy after your wife has healed and still doesn't want to have sex, it may be that her libido decreased dramatically after the pregnancy because that does happen so she will have to go for a follow up visit with you to check on that. So, what have we learned in this discussion, that Communication helps relationships and if you learn to communicate and verbalize your feelings, we will all be in a better place.

As much as I would like to continue this discussion, I believe it's enough for you all to begin talking about these topics with each other and I hope you do. It is always Love.

The Streets

This will not be a long discussion, but it will be the last, so I hope you all have gained some information from all this, it is all a learning experience, I love you all.

So, this isn't about the streets, this is about the kids that are falling into the street lifestyle, the gangs, the drugs, the dirty money the vices all of it. We have to try and keep the kids away from it. It is not a glorious thing, the path, the loss of life, nothing about it is glorious and when you see someone falling into it you have to intervene. This is difficult because this goes all the way up the chain from the parents, to the friends, to the school system, the teachers, past the police this is such a difficult topic. Ummmmmmmm it is hard because I was asked to intervene for a kid who my friend saw going down a bad path and in trying to help this kid, he ended up in jail it was a bit difficult, but we won't speak about it. What we have to discuss is the intervention. The most important aspect about the intervention is the timing and distance from the pressure and situations. I don't mean afterschool programs even though that is an issue. I need you guys to understand that people want to fit in, they want to feel I guess cool is the word, they want to feel tough they have this mindset of what a man is supposed to be which was a false representation due to whoever told them what a man was but to even get to that part of a person's mind you have to be very close. You have to divide them from their friends you have to isolate them from their peers. Once you do that they turn into a completely different person and when they do that is when you are able to intervene, that is when you are able to break through to them. The issue is the timeframe, there is a certain period of time in a person's life when you are allowed to intervene but, to find that point is very difficult and to make matters worse that point that timeframe it is very small. By small I mean it could be days, weeks, months, even hours honestly it is all situation and individual dependent. It is so hard to intervene with these kids that is why it takes a group of people. It simply can't be a teacher or a coach it has to be a collective group of people constantly talking and intervening and communicating with each other to know what is going on with that child because that child will talk to one person about something and won't discuss it with another so everyone has to come together and find a resolution on how to best intervene and stop this child from roaming the streets and joining a gang and getting into trouble with the law. It takes a group of people who care and who are constantly talking to these children not one person can do it alone because of people's emotional traumas and scars it will kill you slowly if you do it by yourself. The more the better for you and for that kid. The more people ask and talk to that kid the more the kid will believe he is loved and believe he has to live up to these people's expectations and its rough man I know it is, but we can't lose any more kids to this. The streets aren't for everyone and if we could stop a child from running to the streets to find a family and protection then we did something good but it starts from us we have to we have to intervene its important and it kills me inside knowing these kids truly believe no one cares for them but listen I can't do this alone you guys have to start playing your part man enough is enough stop being so selfish and give these kids a chance. I know they are some badass kids, I was one, I was friends with all of them but it has to come a time where we are able to talk to these kids and they listen, it is something we will have to do as a collective, as adults, and as the men in our communities one day it has to happen. These kids need to know that we that we Love them, they deserve more attention and more of our time. It is always Love.

Sex

This is the part where I reiterate that, sex is not the way to a man's heart. Simply because a man becomes emotional and opens up about certain feelings and thoughts during pillow talk doesn't not mean he loves you; I hope we can clarify that. I know and I completely understand that you ladies yearn to feel, yearn to be loved, and yearn for that connection but the only thing you are feeling is pain. I guess it's a bad reference but honestly speaking alcohol makes some people emotional and makes them release feelings and thoughts they wouldn't usually talk about if they were sober but does that mean alcohol is the way to a man's heart, well no so I don't really understand the reference. As well as that relationship is not going to last, I am sorry to say it. You will deny it, reject it, and dismiss it because the feelings you get after sex when a man opens up to you makes you feel important to him, it makes you feel as if you are of a significant value in his life but in reality you are not. I haven't seen any of these relationships last past 5 years and the pain I have seen women feel after the relationship ends because the man cheated its truly disheartening, but I understand why you stay, I understand the need to feel important, wanted, and loved but it's just an illusion honestly. I don't want you to ever fall into this and I definitely will not be a part of that culture and I hope you guys have gained some information, but do with it as you wish but I want no parts of it. I hope you get out of that negative lifestyle I mean the sex may be good but is it worth your mental and physical health that's a decision for you to make but on the other side for the women that enjoy and appreciate this and have no attachments after the pillow talk emotional release you are a different section of women which we won't discuss but there will be a time where you would like to settle and hopefully your decisions haven't polluted and clouded your emotions and thoughts. Best of wishes to all of you. It is always Love.

I think that the worst mistake I have ever made was underestimating the power of sex. There is no reason to get into the details of it. After what happened these past 2 years it broke me but and at the end of the day I will always be the villain I will always be the bad guy, the genuine support the love, placing your needs in front of you self and in front of my own this day and age no one cares. It just sounds good in your head let's just be honest here. You truly know who is there for you and you truly know who loves you and you will never choose them and that is ok I got it I get it I told you before that I acknowledge it and things will never change society has taken its course and will not diverge off it and I understand that it's me that has to adapt to it. I get it you guys won, and since for some insane reason I can't break my integrity and patience I think it is best if we all just stay away from each other, you guys go your way I go mine. I am done helping I am done giving myself up and fighting for you guys every time I do I lose a part of myself and this void gets deeper and I am done thinking about everyone who chose pain over happiness because it's time that you take accountability for it so it stops weighing on my conscious, how I could have changed things for you if you would have accepted me and gave me a place in your life and now you're suffering because of your decisions and I truly feel bad for everyone because I did try my best to help and fight for you all but you made your decisions and you all will forever be in my prayers but it's time for me to let go and move on and start my own family and take care of them and show them how much they are loved and teach them all that I know so they don't fall into this culture you all have created and nursed for many years and turned into a norm, my children won't be a part of that. From a broken man I wish you all the best I truly do.

I Love You All.

Two Final Stories

The Final Stories

These two final stories I am going to share with you, I ask that you use a cautious mind while reading them. These stories are extremely sensitive and I was not going to share them with you due to the fact that there are many situations I could express to you but the only people that know about the situations are me the person involved.

So, with that said there is overly sensitive information here and I ask that you have an adult, sound, and mature mind while reading them. Please do not jump to conclusions which is the usual mechanism the mind does, but I ask that you try to control yourself because one of these situations will upset you very much but please I am being honest with you all, these women involved are very caring and loving individuals and I am only expressing these two situations because there are conversations we need to have and I believe it may help us come together and be better people overall for ourselves, our families, our friends and society as a whole. Please be cautious with this information and please begin having conversations with your friends and families, there is a lot of issues we need to fix. It is always Love, remember that.

Story One

So, a very long time ago, I was spending time with my friend in her house with her husband and kids. While I was in the kitchen talking to her, a little kid came running into the kitchen and she yelled at him. Normal right?

Well, no not at all, when she yelled at him the kid completely stopped in place and the look on his face was one of the saddest look's I have seen on a kid and I was so confused. Like yea we don't want kids running into the kitchen you know we have knives, there is boiling hot water and other foods, sometimes we have mail letter openers and scissors you know we don't want them to get hurt so I am sure he was yelled at before for running in the kitchen but these are things after you yell at a child, then you explain it to them, because they don't know any better you know, we are just protecting them, but that look just wasn't that I couldn't explain that look. He was so still in place looking at my friend and it just didn't make sense, the kid couldn't have been over 4 years old. It was just a cold silent few seconds of just him and my friend staring at each other it didn't make sense to me my mind couldn't figure it out.

So, her son comes into the kitchen looking for this kid. So, me and her son are really close, I didn't know who the kid was I never seen him in the house before and I always hang out there with them. So, her son grabs this kid by the hand and says come on let's go. Before they leave I ask her son, "hey who is that, what is his name?" He replies "that's my brother" and takes him to the living room to go play. Once he said "that's my brother" I already knew what happened and it was the saddest thing in the world. So, I look up to my friend and she is just looking at me and she doesn't want me to ask I can tell by her face but I just had to confirm my thoughts and I don't want to be intrusive but me and her are close and she knows me very well. So, I ask "why did he say that is his brother" she replies, "because it is." Let us just leave it there I will not go into the rest of the conversation.

Now I have to explain what you guys aren't understanding about this situation. This child was not simply a child this child was a symbol of infidelity. It wasn't intentional either. She was so emotionally broken from the infidelity, every time she saw the baby it pained her, and that isn't an excuse for treating him like that because at what point do you take a step back, at what point do you try to heal and say "ok I cannot treat this child like this I have to make peace with the fact my significant other cheated and I have to help raise him, he doesn't deserve this treatment." Honestly I cannot say because a lot of us do not recover from emotional trauma because the people that can help us heal from it are usually not around and I don't know how to say this without sounding harsh and it kills me. So, the kid at his age was already mentally and emotionally broken. He already knows and feels like what it is like to be hated. He knows what it feels like to be alone and unloved and he doesn't know why and he doesn't know that it isn't his fault. Listen we have all heard it takes a village to raise a child, let me tell you it takes more than a village to heal a child from trauma. Me and all my experiences and love alone aren't enough to bring that child back. It would literally take every person that child crosses paths with to show him affection, attention, meaning, purpose, and love to heal him. His soul was already broken, and it was one of the saddest things I have ever experienced in my life.

Standing there just waiting to be punished and yelled at. He knew she was going to lash out at him and the only thing that saved him was my presence. I never heard her yell like that or even get upset to that degree, and even just him running into the kitchen took her to a level I never personally seen her get to was really sad because I understood how hurt she was, and was taking it out on the wrong person you know.

Listen his purpose of being his life isn't a consequence, you cannot hold anger, judgment, and resentment to a child because your spouse cheated on you it is not the child's fault. These are very, very, sensitive subjects to talk about and I don't know how to get through to all of you. You all believe you know what love is and you don't and its ruining everything. We literally just lost a child and not just one, you reading this you know how you treat your child and you know the reason you treat them like that. This isn't an all high and mighty speech because I don't have kids and I am not perfect, but you guys better get your shit together because we are losing kids at a fast fucking rate and its sad.

We could talk about women who despise you for becoming the man they wanted you to become, because you became that man for another woman. So your ex will make your life living hell because they despise the woman you are with because they envy her and wish you were that man for them so they will use the kids to give you hell. Giving you problems when you want to see your own kids, putting child support on you just to make you miserable because they want to see you suffer, as if we aren't people and men don't make mistakes. Now do not take that as a defense for men, no, every fucking body is accountable for their actions, all of us.

We could talk about the men too, how you cheated on the woman you truly loved and cared for and didn't realize what you lost until you saw her raising your child with another man and saw how he was taking care of what should have been your family if you would have stepped up and been a fucking adult. We could talk about anything that has to do with people and relationships but the one thing we don't do as adults, is use our children to spite and inconvenience each other because we hate how you treated us, that is something We Do Not Do! We do not use kids, we are adults we communicate, we co-parent, we grow, we learn, and we raise our kids with love.

I fucking feel exceptionally bad for that kid and there is no one around to save him. I don't know how to fix that it is out of my hands and I have not seen that kid since that day. Listen we just have to do better and that is why I tell you my story because there are good people out there and I am not saying I am a good person, I have made many mistakes but I have tried to be a good person because I genuinely like to see people do well and I do not like to know people are suffering it fucking saddens me. We need to do better, for us, our significant others, our families, and more importantly our children. I will leave this here. It is always Love My People.

Story Two

This story is a bit sad so please bear with me. A very long time ago in a different life I was working in a doctor's office. On this normal day (no day is ever normal with me) or I guess what seemed to be a normal day, in comes this patient. As I called her in, she brought her daughter with her you know in one of those carriers that you can separate from the car seat a cool one. So, as I point her in the direction of the room, I see her husband just sitting down which was weird because couples usually come in together, but I just dismissed it right. So, once I close the door even before introducing myself I close the door and turn around and her baby is just staring at me then looks at her mom and begins crying (cool that's normal I am not the most handsome of men but all good), the lady begins to tell me what is going on as she is carrying her daughter like she is trying to calm her but it didn't make sense to me because the baby stopped crying and so I was just a bit confused, it was like the baby was anxious and she knew that. Just for information the baby was less than 1 year old at that time. So this whole situation going on with all the little details, it is confusing my mind way too much, like I felt an overload of thoughts my mind was trying to break down the details to I guess find something that wasn't there because it just seemed so normal, but as we discussed before the I is aware of the Me and something just wasn't right and I was at the point I was getting annoyed I couldn't control my mind it was just racing with no set finish line.

So, the lady tells me she was having some palpitations and what not. So, ok cool I tell her we are going to do an EKG which is an electrocardiogram it's a non-invasive exam that gives us a lot of info and a base line of how your heart is doing right, even though we adopted EKG because that is how it is spelled in every other country except for America, here its ECG lol useless knowledge. So, at this time I ask her we have two women who are working here that can also do the exam, and if she prefers a woman to do it that's perfectly fine I will go get them, this lady denies and says she is ok with me doing the test. I give her the gown to change in to and she places it on the patient bed, then It happened. Once she placed it on the bed, she was going to put her child in the carrier as I was leaving so she could change, and her daughter let out this scream and cry it was insane. I would never forget it because it wasn't a cry or scream like she needed to be cleaned or was hungry, I am telling you it was like the baby girl was in fear for her life I didn't understand it. Listen I just don't even know how to explain this, the lady literally just grabbed her daughter gently real light to get her off her and maybe moved a few centimeters and the baby just began screaming and crying, I was so confused. So the lady asked me to bring her daughter to her father which I had no problem that's regular we do that all the time its not an issue, but I was not comfortable doing that here with her baby and that child was not letting go of her mother at all, it seemed more of like a protective thing and all this just wasn't making sense at all. I tell you what though that bond that baby and her mother had, I have never experienced something like that, just once before but that specific bond, I would be lying if I told you I did. At this time I went out and got the husband, the baby didn't even want to go with her father but he finally got her and put her in the carrier and apologized and went outside with me while the lady changed. I told him he doesn't need to apologize no one did anything wrong babies cry its ok no one is in a rush here. This guy was an extremely genuine guy and I asked him why he didn't come in with us, and he said because he didn't know he could so I told him yea of course anyone that's family can be in the room as long as she gives the ok because its her medical information, and he said ok then apologized again. I told him to stop apologizing and I was going to go do the test and come and get him, he said ok.

I go back into the room, then the lady apologizes while I am doing the test. I told her that her and her husband needed to stop apologizing. I asked her "is the baby ok" she replied, "yes she is ok, she just doesn't like doctors offices." I say "I get it, it is understandable most babies and children don't like doctors offices but I never heard a child cry like she did," and she says "yes because we just moved here from Central America, I was having the same issues I have now and I went to get checked, my husband was working at the time and I had the baby, I went to the doctors office to get checked and the doctor raped me while my daughter was in the room in the baby seat."

I honestly don't even want to finish this I fucking hate all of you people, and that is an understatement.

Moving forward, this shit pierced my soul, this shit hurts to talk about. I ask her if she went to the cops and pressed charges. She said where she is from they don't do anything about that and they left everything behind family and all and moved here to the states hoping to give themselves a better opportunity at a normal life and give their baby a better life hoping nothing like that ever happens again and hoping nothing like that ever happens to their child. She explained how her husband felt it was his fault for overworking and he has a lot of guilt he placed on himself but she wasn't working and where they lived one income not only doesn't pay bills or food but its like one income is no income. Since then he hasn't missed a doctors office visit and is home more which she expressed it wasn't his fault and things happen and she has moved passed it but she doesn't want them to live that life of paranoia but they do their best.

For a more in-depth explanation for those that didn't understand what just happened. The baby was in the room while her mother was being raped. The baby saw the nurses, the baby saw the doctor, the baby was in the room and heard the horrific screams coming from her defenseless mother. She pretty much remembered and all the details of a doctor's office and attached the trauma she had to those details. So, now every time she sees someone in scrubs, every time she sees someone with a whitecoat, every time she sees a room that resembles a doctor's office, she will let out that scream and cry. I cannot say for sure I am just Mike, but I can assume because I have seen some very intelligent kids but at such a young age with no verbal communication what do babies do when they want something, they cry, and if they cry loud and long enough it becomes an issue that you do not know what is the reason the baby is crying so you remove yourself and the baby from the room not to disturb everyone else so you can figure out the issue with your child. This thought process may be way too advanced for a child but this isn't a normal experience and what I witnessed, the look in that babies eyes when she saw me, the vibes and emotions I was getting that set my mind running, I wouldn't doubt it if that actually was the case for the baby girl. It was a very sad story to hear and I am happy that they left and are doing better than they were in their native country but that is not a situation we never want any of our loved ones to be in, we do have not only an obligation to protect our families but we as a society and as a people in general have an obligation to protect those who cannot protect themselves, these situations shouldn't be happening at all and it is very sad that this is reality and is happening every day, like I keep saying we have to do better for us, for our families, and for our children. We have to begin having serious and deep conversations or things will never change. We have to come to a point where we have to stop being so selfish and thinking about ourselves because we all interact with one another on a daily basis, so start having conversations, begin self-evaluation, begin growing and learning how to communicate to be a better person for not just yourself but everyone around you, it will cause a chain reaction and you will see how things change for the better in everyone's life, not just yours. Just remember it is always Love.

The answer to everything, Will Always Be Love.

Stay Blessed.

www.ingramcontent.com/pod-product-compliance
Lightning Source LLC
Chambersburg PA
CBHW071951290426
44109CB00018B/1985